SOVIET INTERESTS IN THE THIRD WORLD

edited by
Robert Cassen

The Royal Institute of International Affairs · London

SAGE Publications · London · Beverly Hills · New Delhi

SAGE Publications Ltd
28 Banner Street
London EC1Y 8QE

SAGE Publications Inc
275 South Beverly Drive
Beverly Hills, California 90212

SAGE Publications India Pvt Ltd
C-236 Defence Colony
New Delhi 110 024

British Library Cataloguing in Publication Data

Soviet interests in the Third World.
  1. Developing countries—Foreign relations
  —Soviet Union   2. Soviet Union—Foreign
relations—Developing countries   3. Soviet
Union—Foreign relations—1978–
I. Cassen, Robert   II. Royal Institute of
International Affairs
327'.09172'4   DK289

ISBN 0-8039-9720-5
ISBN 0-8039-9721-3 Pbk

Library of Congress catalog card number 85-061574

Printed in Great Britain
by J.W. Arrowsmith Ltd, Bristol
First printing

Contents

Contributors   vii
Abbreviations   viii
Preface   xi

1 Overview
  Robert Cassen   1

I THE REGIONAL CONTEXT

2 Sino–Soviet relations in the Third World
  Gerald Segal   14

3 The Soviet Union and South Asia in the 1980s
  Peter Lyon   32

4 Eastern Europe and the Middle East:
  the forgotten dimension of Soviet policy
  Christopher Coker   46

5 Soviet–African relations: promise and limitations
  Sam C. Nolutshungu   68

6 Soviet arms and African militarization
  Robin Luckham   89

7 The Soviet interest in Latin America:
  an economic perspective
  Nikki Miller and Laurence Whitehead   114

II THE SOVIET ECONOMY AND THE THIRD WORLD

8 Soviet trade relations with the Third World
  Alan H. Smith   140

9 Soviet arms sales to developing countries:
  the economic forces
  Saadet Deger   159

10   The Soviet Union in North–South negotiations:
     revealing preferences
     Colin W. Lawson   177

III COUNTRY CASE STUDIES

11   Economic aspects of the Soviet–Vietnamese relationship
     Adam Fforde   192

12   The political economy of Indo–Soviet relations
     Santosh Mehrotra   220

13   The Soviet Union and South Yemen:
     relations with a 'state of socialist orientation'
     Fred Halliday   241

14   The Soviet Union in the Middle East:
     a case study of Syria
     Kassem M. Ja'far   255

15   Soviet relations with Angola and Mozambique
     Jonathan Steele   284

16   Soviet development policy in Central Asia
     Alastair McAuley   299

Name index   319
General index   324

Contributors

Robert Cassen, Institute of Development Studies, University of Sussex

Christopher Coker, Department of International Relations, London School of Economics and Political Science

Saadet Deger, Department of Economics, Birkbeck College, University of London

Adam Fforde, Department of Economics, Birkbeck College, University of London

Fred Halliday, Department of International Relations, London School of Economics and Political Science

Kassem M. Ja'far, Department of War Studies, King's College, University of London

Colin W. Lawson, School of Humanities and Social Sciences, University of Bath

Robin Luckham, Institute of Development Studies, University of Sussex

Peter Lyon, Institute of Commonwealth Studies, University of London

Alastair McAuley, Department of Economics, University of Essex

Santosh Mehrotra, St John's College, University of Cambridge

Nikki Miller, St Antony's College, University of Oxford

Sam C. Nolutshungu, Faculty of Economic and Social Sciences, University of Manchester

Gerald Segal, Department of Politics, University of Bristol

Alan H. Smith, School of Slavonic and East European Studies, University of London

Jonathan Steele, Chief Foreign Correspondent, *The Guardian*

Laurence Whitehead, Nuffield College, University of Oxford

Abbreviations

ANC	African National Congress
ASEAN	Association of South-East Asian Nations
CIA	Central Intelligence Agency
CMEA	Council for Mutual Economic Assistance
COPWE	Commission for Organizing the Party of the Working People of Ethiopia
CPE	Centrally-Planned Economy
CPI	Communist Party of India
CPSU	Communist Party of the Soviet Union
DAC	Development Assistance Committee
DRV	Democratic Republic of Vietnam
EEC	European Economic Community
FCO	Foreign and Commonwealth Office
FICCI	Federation of Indian Chambers of Commerce
FNLA	Frente Nacional para a Liberatção de Angola
Frelimo	Frente para a Liberatção de Mocambique
FSLN	Frente Sandinista de Liberación Nacional
GATT	General Agreement on Tariffs and Trade
GDP	Gross Domestic Product
GDR	German Democratic Republic
GNP	Gross National Product
HEC	Heavy Engineering Corporation (India)
ICC	Intra-Country Commodity
IBEC	International Bank for Economic Cooperation
IISS	International Institute for Strategic Studies
IMEMO	(Institute of World Economy and International Relations)
IMF	International Monetary Fund
KGB	(Soviet secret police)
LDC	Less-Developed Country
MAMC	Mining and Allied Machinery Corporation (India)
MFN	Most-Favoured Nation
MIT	Massachusetts Institute of Technology
MNR	Movement for National Resistance
MPLA	Movimento para a Liberação de Angola
NATO	North Atlantic Treaty Organization
NCTW	New Communist Third World
NIEO	New International Economic Order

NLF	National Liberation Front (Yemen)
OAU	Organization of African Unity
ODA	Overseas Development Assistance
OECD	Organization for Economic Cooperation and Development
OPEC	Organization of Petroleum-Exporting Countries
PDRY	People's Democratic Republic of Yemen
PLO	Palestinian Liberation Organization
RDF	Rapid Deployment Force
RIIA	Royal Institute of International Affairs
RSFSR	Russian Soviet Federated Socialist Republic
SADR	Saharan Arab Democratic Republic
SAM	Surface-to-Air Missile
SEZ	Special Export Zone (India)
SIPRI	Stockholm International Peace Research Institute
SRV	Socialist Republic of Vietnam
SWAPO	South-West Africa People's Organization
UAE	United Arab Emirates
UNCTAD	UN Conference on Trade and Development
UNECE	UN Economic Commission for Europe
UNITA	Uniao para a Independencia Total de Angola
USACDA	US Arms Control and Disarmament Agency
USSR	Union of Soviet Socialist Republics
YAR	Yemen Arab Republic
YSP	Yemen Socialist Party
ZANU	Zimbabwe African National Union
ZAPU	Zimbabwe African People's Union

Preface

This book is the product of a Study Group which met in the Royal Institute of International Affairs during 1983–4. We set out with the expressed intention of separating, to the extent possible, the Soviet Union's economic interests from its geopolitical and military-strategic concerns. The task of separation has not proved impossible, as the reader may judge. But the papers have ranged quite widely beyond the purely economic.

They fall into three parts: those on broad Soviet interests in the main Third World regions; those on the Soviet economy and its links with the Third World; and case studies of Soviet relations with particular countries.

As convenor of the Study Group and editor of the present volume, I would like to express my gratitude to the whole Chatham House organization, not least its Library, and particularly to Eileen Menzies, Dorothy Carter, Esperanza Durán, William Wallace and Pauline Wickham. I am also greatly indebted to Geoffrey Goodwin, who oversaw the whole enterprise for a considerable period and gave me the benefit of his judgement and watchfulness; and to Adam Fforde, who served as rapporteur of our meetings and my colleague and collaborator in every respect. And of course I have valued the contributions of each and every Study Group member, as well as those of a number of visitors, who made our sessions lively and instructive.

Robert Cassen
January 1985

1
Overview

Robert Cassen

There is an old maxim in diplomatic life that if you want to know what someone is thinking, you should go and ask him. We would be puzzled if we found Soviet scholars trying to divine from studying the behaviour of the West what were our intentions in the Third World, since we are unlikely to regard our own actions as being in any way opaque: our policies may be confused or even contradictory, but to us at least their motives are fairly transparent. Yet in military affairs the Western strategist is commonly adjured not to seek to understand underlying Soviet motivations or intentions, but to make judgements – based on observation of Soviet behaviour – about the probability of various possible actions, and to be prepared for all probable eventualities. In attempting to assess the Soviet role in the Third World, one would be thought lacking in realism if one did not follow the same course.

The definition of 'Soviet interests' must in part be a matter of interpretation. A person has an interest in something if he wants it, or if it leads to something he wants. Similarly for countries, but with a number of caveats: the actions of countries are often the resultant of a combination of conflicting forces; the same forces may combine in different directions on different occasions – thus interests cannot simply be inferred from actions. There may be arguable differences between 'true' and perceived interests. There are differences between long- and short-term interests. And so forth.[1] No country's foreign policy can be reconstructed as the maximization of a unique objective function subject to constraints. The Soviet Union is no exception.

There is some evidence to justify a view of Soviet foreign policy as aggressive and expansionist. One much-read analysis typifies the Soviet leadership as pessimistic about its capacity to solve long-term domestic problems, but increasingly confident militarily, and quite likely to respond with repression at home and attempts at conquest abroad.[2] Use of the phrase 'the Soviet empire' and discussions of the 'cost' of empire tend to characterize this line of thought.[3] It has its appeal in the United States today, where strategists observed that the response to relatively relaxed American policies in the

1

1970s was a massive and continuing military build-up, 'culminating' in the invasion of Afghanistan.[4]

A different view emerges from the studies presented here: the Soviet Union gives much more the impression of a beleaguered major power, beset with difficulties within and hostility without – a country which might look increasingly for relief from defence and international burdens to allow itself greater scope for development at home, if only circumstances permitted. It has succeeded in overcoming the power disparity with the USA, but still sees the world as threatening. It is, after all, encircled by Europe, America China and Japan; its principal physical buffer is the ring of Warsaw Pact countries, hardly any of which feel any great spontaneous sympathy for their major partner. The Soviet Union has few friends of consequence. And its problems are huge: an ailing domestic economy and heavy external commitments, if not overcommitment. In such a view, a more cautious and limited foreign policy would be the expectation; Afghanistan would have to be explained as completely *sui generis*, even an aberration, not presaging further dangerous adventures.[5]

What insights are offered here that might help to understand Soviet behaviour? First of all, there has been a considerable change in perceptions of the Third World since the Khrushchev era. Then the Soviets saw Third World countries theoretically and practically as likely to enter the socialist camp, provided the forces of imperialism could be confronted; active policies were indicated. But a series of reverses in the 1960s and 1970s induced a greater sense of realism. In Algeria, Indonesia, Ghana, Guinea, Somalia, Sudan, Egypt, pro-Soviet leaders either turned against Moscow or were replaced in the seat of power by others with different ideas. And there was the split with China. Some of these experiences had cost the Soviets dear, with billions of roubles poured in and almost nothing in the end to show for them.

Certainly the studies in this book do not bear out the picture of an all-powerful Soviet Union, exerting its influence effectively in every quarter of the globe and making significant gains. On the contrary – and perhaps most clearly in Africa – they point rather to the limitations of Soviet power or of the USSR's willingness to become involved. At the same time, the closer to Soviet borders, the keener the strategic interest; in Asia Soviet power has been used both aggressively – in Afghanistan – and in a subtle, mutually advantageous connection with India; and has also had to cope with fluctuating relations with China, one of many factors leading to a heavy involvement with Vietnam. In the Middle East, important non-economic motives for Soviet behaviour are – as well as cultivating influences with Arab states – to have a presence and be consulted about events, and to frustrate the designs of the Western powers. In Latin America, the Soviet Union sustains the showcase regime in Cuba, for strategic, ideological and economic reasons; and it will take advantage of opportunities presented by events in Central America and US reactions to them. But with most countries the goal is trade, of a fairly unpolitical nature.

The days are past when the Soviets would support every 'progressive' Third World government. Their main efforts are confined to the countries which either belong to the CMEA (Cuba, Vietnam, Mongolia) or which are described as 'socialist' or 'of socialist orientation' (including Afghanistan, Angola, Ethiopia, Kampuchea, Laos, Mozambique, North Korea and South Yemen). The basic principle is that to provide large amounts of Soviet assistance, the Soviet authorities have to have confidence in the stability of the recipient's regime and its dedication to the communist cause. The main requirements are that the country should have a 'vanguard Marxist-Leninist party' and a 'revolutionary' army: that is, the government should have correct ideas and alignments, and be safe from military coups.

Countries which do not satisfy these criteria may get material or political support; and the Soviet Union will trade – especially for hard currency – with countries of a wide spectrum of political hues. But they will not again put major volumes of concessional assistance into countries where their foothold is tenuous.

The papers which look at the Soviet economy and its links with the Third World do indeed find a strong set of economic motives – though little is clear and unequivocal. *Alan Smith* on *trade* examines the extent to which Soviet trade with Third World partners brings genuine economic benefits; in particular, imports which cost less than the same goods from domestic or alternative foreign sources. If the Soviets do not always choose the cheapest source of supply, is this deliberate? And is it economically motivated – e.g. to maintain competition among suppliers over the long term – or political, e.g. to limit dependence on a political adversary? And finally is there some trade with identifiable economic losses, such that the goods exported are of greater value than those obtained in exchange?

While the data do not permit any final answers, trade of all these categories is found, much of it beneficial. Soviet analysts certainly explore the problems and opportunities for trade with various Third World regions considered separately; and trade with the non-CMEA Third World has increased twelvefold between 1964 and 1983, exports consisting mainly of oil, arms and other manufactures, and imports mainly of primary products. The principal examples of imports not bought in the cheapest markets are grain from Argentina and sugar from Cuba. But a large share of Soviet exports are paid for in hard currency – they are sold to oil-exporting or other better-off developing countries.[6]

Both this paper and *Saadet Deger*'s on *arms sales* attempt to assess the profitability of Soviet arms exports, which constitute so large a share of exports to the Third World. This proves difficult to do; the terms of sale are often unknown, and even where they are known – hard currency or other credits and whether concessional or not – we often do not know whether settlement is actually made, and how, if they are not cleared, the consequent debts are handled. The Soviet Union does appear to be accumulating considerable volumes of hard currency and other credit with Third World partners.

Arms sales have a mixture of economic and political motives. But the political motive seems as much a constraint on who *not* to sell arms to as a determining factor in the choice of clients. No arms are sold to political adversaries; but the purchasing countries are by no means all close to the Soviets in outlook. Political and strategic gains are sought. But among the chosen clients, the desire for hard-currency earnings explains much of the volume of arms trade (and of the recent large increases in Soviet arms exports). Deger also shows that the privileged character of defence industries within the Soviet planning system makes them a natural source of exports. The Soviet Union is an effective producer of weapons appropriate for Third World conditions and competitively priced.

The view of the Soviet Union as 'cautious and cost-conscious' in its approach to the Third World is borne out by *Colin Lawson*'s paper on the *Soviet Union in North-South negotiations*. The Soviets have never accepted any general responsibility for the disadvantages suffered by developing countries in the world economy, which they blame on the 'imperialist and neo-colonialist' powers. They therefore claim that the demands made by the Third World in the North-South debate, which arise from these disadvantages, are on the whole just, but do not apply to themselves. They have also sought to ensure that any relevant West-South concessions, such as on trade protection, should also apply to East-West trade. They have not been enthusiastic for new commodity schemes, or for any measures to improve Third World access to markets for manufactures. And so forth. Broadly, they can see the costs of acceding to Third World demands and not many benefits, but seek to justify their negativism on ideological grounds. Developing countries have been critical of Soviet positions on these matters.

Readers may wonder why this volume contains no separate paper on Soviet *aid*. Both Smith and Lawson discuss it, in fact, but it is not a very rewarding subject. The data are unsatisfactory: the Soviets claim that their aid has exceeded one per cent of their GNP in recent years; Western sources put the figure below one-fifth of one percent. Much depends on whether the value of commodity purchases above world market prices (e.g. Cuban sugar) are included. Soviet aid is best regarded as a part of Soviet trade – on a concessional basis, and bringing various benefits to the recipients, but confined for the most part to a few favoured ones. It is modest in quantity apart from them, its terms are uncertain, and it is not easily separable from military assistance'– whose terms are also of varying (and largely unknown) degrees of concessionality.[7]

While the economic motive in Soviet trade seems pre-eminent and of growing importance, the picture of Soviet interests which emerges from the rest of the volume gives the greatest weight to geopolitical factors in overall relations with the Third World. *Gerald Segal*'s paper on *Sino-Soviet relations in the Third World* traces the conflict and competition between China and the Soviet Union in the developing countries from the 1960s, reflecting the state of relations between the two powers. The partial rapprochement between them in recent years is still constrained by the two outstanding regional issues, Afghanistan and South-East Asia. These remain problematic, while the strident denunciations of each other's policies in the rest of the Third World have quietened considerably. Confrontations over Vietnam and Kampuchea are costly to both sides. China wants the Soviet Union to recognize its legitimate concerns in this region; the Soviet Union does not wish to cede the gains it has made there – but the paper suggests a slow meeting of minds as a possible, and certainly the most beneficial, option.

The paper on *Vietnam* by *Adam Fforde* explores various dimensions of the Soviet treatment of a CMEA developing country. It also asks what the Soviet Union stands to gain from a relationship that is quite expensive economically. The answer is, partly, military bases and leverage against China in the region. But equally the Soviets cannot do other than support a country which is ideologically close, and there is also a demonstration effect to the rest of the Third World of the value of such an alliance.

South Asia has been an arena of active concern and involvement for the Soviet Union since the mid-1950s, and this shows no sign of abating, according to *Peter Lyon*, though he stresses that Soviet relations with each and all of the other states of South Asia (which are themselves now beginning to become a reality in tentative organizational terms) are subordinate to Indo-Soviet bilateral ties.

Only India of the South Asian governments has shown marked public 'understanding' of the Soviet position on Afghanistan; other countries – Pakistan most notably – have expressed opposition and criticism.

Oil, arms trade (especially in sophisticated weaponry) and diplomatic support lately have been and still are the three most important ingredients in the Indo-Soviet relationship, though the first may diminish in the next decade, whilst the other two are likely to remain important. Within this theatre of active great-power rivalries (especially of Soviet-American and Sino-Soviet rivalry), in some respects all the countries of South Asia feel the reach and weight of the Soviet Union. Nuclear issues increasingly intrude in the rhetoric and reality of Indo-Pakistan relations and affect Soviet assessments. Developing Soviet naval capabilities heighten its interest in Indian Ocean matters.

Santosh Mehrotra shows the *Indian relationship* to be something of a special case. The Indian economy is at a stage of technological development which makes possible a variety of collaborative arrangements with the Soviet Union of a kind not possible in most poor developing countries. India not only buys Soviet arms but manufactures them under licence; it also exports quite a few of its manufactures to the Soviet Union – in fact the Soviet Union takes one-fifth of all India's exports. The closeness of ties between New Delhi and Moscow may have had its origin in, and be sustained by, the nexus of relationships between the US, the USSR, China and Pakistan. But it is also built on mutual economic interest, and a compatibility of strategic-political interests. Compatibility – but not identity: as the paper points out, there are differences between India and the Soviet Union, and India has consistently tried to maintain good relations with the West at the same time.

Christopher Coker's paper on the *Middle East* is the only one to take full account of the East European dimension of Soviet interests. The CMEA 'Six' – the industrialized CMEA countries other than the USSR – all have significant dependence on oil imported from the Middle East. Their economies are energy-intensive (twice the energy/GNP ratio prevailing in the West), in part because earlier Soviet-subsidized oil encouraged it – oil which is no longer so heavily subsidized or available in adequate amounts. This latter situation is likely to continue, and so therefore will East European imports from the Middle East. But the Six have had little success in concluding long-term agreements with any of the oil-exporting countries, even Libya, which prefer to do such business with Western companies. Eastern Europe will thus have to rely on its own and on Soviet diplomacy to strengthen relationships with important oil-exporting countries.

Soviet policy in the Middle East, as it emerges from *Kassem Ja'far*'s paper, which has special reference to *Soviet-Syrian relations*, has pursued two principal objectives: limiting Western, and particularly US, influence in the region; and cultivating the friendship of Middle Eastern states with military and economic assistance. But the Soviets gave stable relations with the West a higher priority than support for destabilizing and quasi-revolutionary activities in the Middle East. The USSR has not sided with Arab states in denying Israel's right to exist, but has sought a voice for itself and tried to steer a course which takes into account both the dangers of superpower confrontation and the inherent instability of the region.

Relations with Syria until the 1980s followed a pattern not unlike those with other Middle Eastern countries. Arms were supplied with economic and political as well as military goals; but never on a scale to permit an overrunning of Israel. The long history of fairly durable relations with Syria took its first turn towards something more intense after Sadat's visit to Jerusalem and the movement of Egypt closer to the Western camp. The Soviet Union's need for an ally in Syria grew; and under internal and external threats generated by hostilities in the area, Syria found itself needing a closer relation with a major power. A treaty of friendship and cooperation was signed in 1980. Yet the treaty did not mark any significant difference in Soviet actions; that was to come only with the Israeli invasion of Lebanon in 1982. Even then there was no major Soviet move until Israel appeared to be achieving its objectives in Lebanon, when the Soviets finally gave Syria the military means to stand its ground and ensure that any resolution of the conflict would have to be with its consent. The Soviet Union, as so often, had held back and deliberated with great caution until the moment when it and its client's interests were acutely threatened.

South Yemen, about which *Fred Halliday* has written, is a good example of the Soviet treatment of a country 'of socialist orientation', one which aligns itself closely with the USSR on most matters of common interest. It is also a case of a country whose involvement with the Soviets arose mainly from internal political developments with little participation by any foreign influences. Yet the Soviets have sought to curb some of the more radical leanings of successive regimes in domestic and foreign policy; and in terms of practical help the Soviet contribution has been significant but modest.

The USSR and other CMEA countries have provided about $400 million in aid over the fifteen years since independence, but it has been 'controversial' in quality and less than required. At the same time there has been considerable political integration with the Soviet Union, and a gradual expansion in trade, accelerating rapidly in the most recent years. The Soviets have moved with typical caution; but of late the South Yemen authorities appear to have learned how to act so as to consolidate their trust.

The two general papers on *Africa* reflect all the themes so far discussed, with some further emphases. *Sam Nolutshungu* observes that the Soviet Union has established relations not only with left-wing regimes but even with strongly anti-Marxist Morocco – not to speak of supplying arms to Amin's Uganda. Ideological consistency – as in the case of India also – is obtained by stressing the 'anti-imperialist' character of the governments concerned, rather than their socialism. Of course in the 1960s and 1970s there was support for a wide range of anti-colonial liberation movements, as well as for such 'progressive' countries as Ghana under Nkrumah. But most of this cost the Soviet Union little, economically or politically. With Soviet involvement in Somalia, Ethiopia, Angola and Mozambique the stakes and the potential costs and benefits became larger. Soviet economic interests in Africa, apart from the few countries which can afford Soviet exports on hard-currency terms, or supply needed minerals – such as Moroccan potash – are relatively slight. The prizes are strategic and political: military and naval facilities; friendships and alliances. And the Soviets have to be seen supporting their ideological *confrères*.

But the costs have been particularly heavy, perhaps outweighing the benefits. African countries have wanted to turn to the Soviet Union for help most commonly when their political complexion made the West unwilling to provide it. But they have found the Soviet Union lacking in the economic resources to give them the kind of aid and trading possibilities they can expect from the West. And even militarily they may obtain limited and sometimes crucial support; but scepticism about the durability of African regimes makes the Soviets unwilling to go very far in pouring in resources – military or financial. Even where the Soviets (via Cuba if necessary) have made large efforts – Ethiopia, Angola – these may not continue much longer.

The paper concludes that the Soviets are unwilling to see Africa open up as another area of major confrontation between East and West. They believe African countries have to have economic relations with both East and West; the African countries in their turn are forced to relate to the West, whatever their preferences, but are often glad to have the Eastern alternative, for its own sake, or *pour encourager les autres*.

Robin Luckham on *African militarization* asks why, as he shows them to be, Soviet relations with Africa are predominantly military. If Soviet aid, trade and arms sales to Africa are added together, the arms constitute 80 per cent of the total – and for several individual countries, the figure is more than 90 per cent. Soviet interests in Africa are partly maritime – fishing rights as well as naval facilities are keenly sought – and partly, as already described, political and economic. If the Soviets pursue these interests mainly by military sales or assistance, the causes lie both in the nature of the Soviet state, and in the course of African history.

To the categories of developing countries receiving Soviet assistance this paper adds another found in Soviet writings: countries fighting 'wars of nations on the path of socialist development in defence of socialism' – Angola, Ethiopia and, more questionably, Mozambique. To Africans, it must be remembered, both the Soviet Union and the United States are relatively remote, neither of them having a presence, military or other, equal to that of the old colonial powers, notably France. And the great enemy is South Africa. Since so much of the recent African past has been either of liberation movements fighting a colonial power or new governments trying to resist subversion, and since few of these could expect help from the West, they have turned to the East. And as already noted, military assistance is what the Soviet Union is best able to give.

But while Soviet or Cuban assistance have been able to secure the survival of a few African regimes against attack, overthrow or collapse, they have not achieved much more than that. In particular, the military-bureaucratic approach is incapable of assisting a broadly based, participatory movement in consolidating its political support and developmental effectiveness. The fact that Soviet policies 'have been implemented almost exclusively through military relationships with African states has made them self-defeating'.

Jonathan Steele's paper on *Angola and Mozambique* bears out most of these points. There was no Cuban presence in Angola prior to the South African invasion of 1975; it was perhaps more of a Cuban initiative with Soviet consent than a Soviet initiative *per se*. And it was and has remained essentially defensive, protecting the MPLA government from being overturned by force, but not actively engaging with invading South African troops. Trade – especially unrequited trade which may be a form of aid – has been quite substantial; aid other than military relatively modest. But both trade and aid have been on a much larger scale than in Mozambique. It appears that Soviet policy in both cases was to do the minimum necessary to try to keep these potential friends in power, but that both were regarded as too weak to justify any more expensive involvement.

The Soviets studiously avoided any major operation to confront the major threat – destabilization and incursions from South Africa. The Nkomati accords signalled the incapacity, or unwillingness, of the Soviet Union to defend its friends in southern Africa against them. Behind Moscow's policies undoubtedly lay the sense that a true effort to counter South Africa would bring, as well as its enormous cost, conflict with the United States. In the end, events have shown that 'southern Africa remains a region of low priority for Moscow'.

The paper by *Nikki Miller* and *Laurence Whitehead* looks at *Latin America* and *Cuba, Chile, Argentina* and *Nicaragua* in particular. It argues that while political and strategic advantages may be the main motives for Soviet action, economic forces constrain such action powerfully. The decision to supply Cuba with oil in 1960 followed the US refusal to do so, and coincided with a surplus of Soviet oil that sought an outlet. Moscow also undertook to buy any available Cuban sugar, and to give extensive military and financial aid. These decisions coincided very precisely with the cutting off of aid to China. Thus not only did it suit the Soviet Union politically to involve itself with Cuba; the economic complementarity between the two countries made what was to become a costly relationship appear attractive. The authors contrast the case of Cuba with the other three countries in their study. Whilst the Soviets want Argentina's grain, there is little besides arms that Argentina wants from them. Such facts, together with the lack of political sympathy between the two countries, make anything beyond a commercial relationship look most unlikely.

With Allende's Chile one might have thought the USSR could have found a greater proximity appealing; but doubts about the survival prospects of the Allende government soon set in. And even if they had not, economic incompatibility was fairly complete. The Soviets had no need for Chile's main export, copper, in which they are self-sufficient; nor was there much that Chile wanted from them, other than hard-currency loans, which by the early 1970s were not easily forthcoming from a Soviet Union experiencing balance-of-payments stringency, not least because of its grain imports. In the end Chile received negligible assistance from Soviet sources.

The Nicaraguan example does little to contradict the general case. It was many months after the Sandinista victory of July 1979 before any serious contact between Managua and Moscow took place, and it was only after the Reagan administration suspended aid in January 1981 that Managua requested – and received – more significant help. As the US turned from refusal of help to active destabilization, the Sandinista government looked increasingly to Cuba and the Soviet Union for support. But the response has been less than was needed, and other Latin American countries – Mexico, Venezuela – have been crucial in sustaining the Nicaraguan economy. The authors give grounds for doubt that the Soviet Union will commit major resources to the country. Thus far from supporting the case of unconstrained Soviet expansionism found in some (especially US) writings on the Soviet role in Latin America, the countries examined bear out the view that a much more limited involvement is likely, aiming mainly at undermining Latin America's solidarity with the US. As with Africa, Latin America is too far away and presents insufficient strategic gains that can be won at reasonable cost – beyond those already obtained in Cuba – and little economic complementarity to justify much more than arms-length trading arrangements.

This *tour d'horizon* ends where it began, with the Soviet Union itself. Soviet sources have been known to ascribe their limited Third World role not only to their lack of resources to do more, but also to the fact that they have their own 'Third World', namely *Soviet Central Asia*. *Alastair McAuley* considers whether Soviet policy towards the less developed regions of the USSR can be seen as a model for socialist relations with the Third World.

Income levels in Central Asia were, with one or two regional exceptions, little lower than those of the Russian Republic (RSFSR) in the early post-revolutionary years; but the area did lag behind in some general indicators of 'modernization'. By the 1970s the gaps between Central Asia and the 'industrial centre' (RSFSR, Ukraine, Byelorussia) had changed little, perhaps with some tendency to growing disparity. But major development had taken place, with growing economic specialization – based mainly on cotton and agriculture generally – and interdependence with the rest of the Soviet Union. There was also a remarkable increase in the spread of educational and welfare services, as well as of basic infrastructure. The data do not permit any assessment of the extent to which this development was financed by (concessional) transfers from the industrial centre. But the model of development has relied on an increasingly sophisticated division of labour and participation in interregional exchange. It has also brought Central Asia culturally and spiritually closer to the centre. As such, the author judges, 'the Soviet strategy for development ... differs little from approaches advocated in the West'.

This summary does not do justice to the richness of the individual studies in this volume. But it does bring out a few overall themes – particularly that of the limited character, especially in recent times, of Soviet ambitions in the Third World and capacities to pursue them.

One theme little discussed in these papers, but implicit in several of them, is how much Soviet 'success' in the Third World – such as it is – can be ascribed to Western policies rather than Soviet abilities. It is tempting to divide the countries with which the Soviets have close relations into those few which acquired them largely as a result of internal developments – Ethiopia, South Yemen; those far more numerous countries where the Soviet presence arose fairly directly as a reaction sought by the countries themselves because of opposition from the Western powers, which include Cuba, Nicaragua and various countries in South-East Asia and southern Africa; and the unique case, Afghanistan, which has had Soviet power thrust upon it in an abrupt and heavy reassertion of its presence. In such a categorization, India perhaps deserves a place of its own, different from all the rest, owing its somewhat ambivalent connection with the Soviet Union to a combination of Western 'push' and Eastern 'pull', and based on something closer to equality than to a relation of client to patron.

Some of the literature of Soviet relations with developing countries has a regrettable tendency to see them as passive objects of Soviet policy, as if they had few reasons worth discussing for trading with the Soviet Union or seeking its support. The actions of the Western powers which figure among those reasons are often ignored. It may be salutary for those who study these things, and for policymakers who listen to them, to be reminded that most Third World countries value their independence and have no innate desire, once free from domination by the colonial powers, to become beholden to others.

Notes

1. For a lengthier discussion of the nature of national interests, see R. H. Cassen, A. R. Jolly, J. Sewell and R. N. Wood (eds.), *Rich Country Interests and Third World Development* (London: Croom Helm, 1982).

2. E. N. Luttwak, *The Grand Strategy of the Soviet Union* (New York: St Martin's Press, 1983).

3. See, for example, C. Wolf Jr, K. C. Yeh, E. Brunner Jr, A. Gurwitz and M. Lawrence, *The Costs of the Soviet Empire* (Santa Monica, Calif.: Rand Corporation, 1983).

4. P. H. Nitze, 'Strategy in the Decade of the 1980s', *Foreign Affairs*, Vol. 59, No. 1, Fall 1980.

5. For some recent assessments of the issues, see C. Keeble (ed.), *The Soviet*

State: The Domestic Roots of Soviet Foreign Policy (Aldershot: Gower, for the RIIA, 1985), and J. Steele, *World Power: Soviet Policy under Brezhnev and Andropov* (London: Michael Joseph, 1983).

6. Similar conclusions would apply to the trade of the other CMEA (industrial) countries, approximately two-thirds of whose trade with the Third World is concentrated on four OPEC members (Algeria, Iran, Iraq, Libya), four 'technology exporters' (Argentina, Brazil, India, Turkey) and four communist developing countries (Cuba, Mongolia, North Korea, Vietnam). These twelve countries account for four-fifths of the Soviet Union's trade with the Third World. See D. Pineye, 'Le facteur marchand dans les relations économiques Est-Sud', Working Paper No. 84–10, Centre d'Etudes Prospectives et d'Informations Internationales, Paris, September 1984; also M. Lavigne, 'Eastern Europe-LDC Economic Relations in the Eighties', Paper prepared for the Joint Economic Committee, US Congress, January 1984.

7. The interested reader may consult works cited in their chapters by Lawson, Smith and the country-case-study authors. See also S. Schultz and H. Machowski, 'US and Soviet Trade and Aid Relations with the Third World', Berichte des Bundesinstituts für ostwissenschaftliche·und internationale Studien, Paper No. 33, 1983.

I
THE REGIONAL CONTEXT

2
Sino-Soviet relations in the Third World

Gerald Segal

Sino-Soviet conflict is, at least in part, an East-South conflict. Poor, peasant China confronts a rich, (relatively) urban Soviet Union. Yet China is also a military and ideological power, aspiring more to leadership than to simple membership of the Third World. Thus even the basics of Sino-Soviet relations in the Third World are complex, rendering any brief analysis inevitably simplistic. Consequently much is left out and/or glossed over. This is not an analysis of bilateral Sino-Soviet relations, nor does it cover all Third World issues. It is not from the perspective of the Third World states, although they tend to determine the nature of specific conflicts more than do the communist powers. Neither is this analysis concerned with the roots of Sino-Soviet relations, for the emphasis is overwhelmingly on the past decade.

More positively, certain themes are possible to identify. It is clear that Third World conflict is complex and changing. Therefore, not surprisingly Soviet and especially Chinese policy towards the Third World regularly shifts. Yet this has not prevented both powers from taking an active interest in the Third World dimension of their foreign policies, as both sought to validate their claim to great-power status against each other, and against the United States. By 1984, both Moscow and Beijing were gingerly trying to achieve at least a modicum of détente, but on Third World issues they had achieved a curious balance of success and failure.

The 1960s: how deep is the rift?
The importance of the Sino-Soviet rift in the Third World has been far from uniform. It reached different parts of the world before others, and affected certain issues more than others. Therefore, the cracking apart was more a process than a single event. When added to the diversity of political problems in the Third World, neither

China nor the Soviet Union was able to pursue a single uniform policy.

To the extent that generalizations *are* possible, it seems that Sino-Soviet relations were felt first in the realm of ideas, and closer to Asia than in the farther reaches of the Third World. During the early 1960s, and particularly after 1963, China forced the division of the international communist movement into relatively pro-Moscow and pro-Beijing factions.[1] For most Communist Parties this factionalism had little concrete effect, since the Moscow wing tended to predominate. However, in Asia, and especially in North Korea, North Vietnam and Japan, The pro-China sentiments seemed to carry more weight. The Korean and Vietnamese parties, like their comrades in Eastern Europe, were of course ruling parties, and so did not officially split in two. But unlike the East Europeans, as Asians the Koreans and Vietnamese did have extra incentive at least to remain neutral in the split.[2]

In most parts of the Third World China's 'splittist' activities were not greatly appreciated. Many Third World governments and revolutionary parties were most concerned about a united anti-colonial and anti-imperialist front. China may have offered them better advice than the Soviet Union, but on balance China's demands for ideological purity, and the splitting of parties, weakened the revolutionary cause, certainly in the short term. Egypt's President Nasser, a friend of both communist powers, and a giant among Third World leaders, was especially opposed to China carrying its own factionalism to the Third World struggle.[3] The Chinese economic model may well have been better suited to Third World needs, but the price of accepting the model was often a split with Moscow, and distraction from the main anti-imperialist struggle.

Thus the Sino-Soviet rift may have had its first effects in ideological terms, but it soon assumed economic and political implications. However, even if Moscow could feel somewhat satisfied by the mid-1960s that it was picking up more Third World support than China, the problems for Soviet foreign policy were still serious. First, even if it controlled 80 per cent of the international communist movement, it was still 20 per cent less than before. What is worse, the doctrine of the infallibility and inevitability of revolution took a bad knock when China contested the Soviet style of leadership.

Second, there were important economic costs that soon developed for the Soviet Union. Competition in granting aid to the Third World entered a more costly phase, with China bidding up Soviet assistance terms.[4] On the other hand, in the military dimension of the rift, the Soviet Union was less clearly a loser.

Although both China and the Soviet Union gave significant quantities of military assistance, only the Soviet Union could equip the big battalions. After the 1967 Middle East war, Moscow replenished the Arab arsenals while China merely urged the Arabs to wage a people's war on the Maoist model.[5] China's advice may have been best, but it was not what the Arab states wanted to hear. In the Middle East, as in Africa, China found itself supporting revolutionary movements more than established states, for it was only on the smaller scale that China had something useful to offer. Closer to China's home, Beijing could take a more active military role. In the Vietnam war China was a major military ally of Hanoi, but still the most important military assistance came from the Soviet Union.[6]

In the second half of the 1960s Moscow's worry about the China factor in the Third World must have seemed less acute. After China's descent into the Cultural Revolution, Third World states in general saw China as unreliable and extreme. In the Vietnam war, the Soviet Union made significant gains at Beijing's expense. In South Asia, Kosygin scored more points at the Tashkent summit of 1966, where he successfully mediated between India and Pakistan.[7]

Approaching the end of the decade, Moscow could feel relatively confident that China's departure from the bloc was not a complete disaster. Beijing's internal disorder, and its dangerous foreign policy of opposing both superpowers, left the Soviet Union with the more favourable Third World split, but by and large the haemorrhage was under control. In economic terms the Soviet Union refused to get drawn into an open-ended aid competition with China, and in any case it was becoming clear that China had limited economic resources to offer. In military terms, it was seen, even by Vietnam, that only the Soviet Union had the means to play in the superpower league and China's support was of limited value. As the Chinese idiom has it, 'distant waters don't quench fires'.

In sum, the 1960s seemed to be characterized more by a verbal Sino-Soviet split than by an actual competition in military or economic policy in the Third World. Certainly there was no pattern to the rift's effect, varying by place and policy. To be sure, both Moscow and Beijing spoke loudly about each other's dastardly actions in the Third World, but it was only in the 1970s that the Sino-Soviet rift in the Third World assumed more concrete proportions.

The 1970s: from paranoia to pragmatism
The double shock delivered by the Soviet Union to China in the late

1960s – the invasion of Czechoslovakia and the Sino-Soviet border crisis – brought a new level of intensity to Moscow-Beijing relations. In the 1970s, both sides were to reach new peaks of acrimony, with China perceiving a global Soviet strategy of expansion, while the Soviet Union proclaimed the need for Asian collective security to contain new Chinese belligerence.[8]

For the first few years of the 1970s, these exchanges remained largely in the realm of words. But with China's entry into the United Nations in 1971, and its new emphasis on wooing Third World states, it was inevitable that Sino-Soviet relations in the Third World would assume new importance. Neither China nor the Soviet Union initiated this tension, as both found themselves reacting to important 'natural' developments in different parts of the globe.[9] Two events were of primary importance.

First, in the spring of 1975, the North Vietnamese and other South-East Asian communist forces triumphed over their Western-backed foes. While China was pleased to see the Khmer Rouge come to power in Kampuchea, both the Pathet Lao and the North Vietnamese leaned more to Moscow. Vietnam, the most powerful of the three victors, had long-standing reasons to seek great-power support against its massive Chinese neighbour to the north.[10] Who better than China's own northern rival, the Soviet Union, could help contain Chinese pressure? Thus South-East Asian conflicts had passed from a Western phase to a communist phase, and with it came a new quality of Sino-Soviet confrontation in the Third World.

Second, in distant Africa, both communist powers found theselves engaged in their most direct confrontation. In the early 1970s China had outpaced the Soviet Union as an aid donor in central and especially southern Africa, and by 1974 was offering significant military aid to the Angolan independence movement FNLA.[11] As the date for Angolan independence from Portugal approached, the Soviet Union saw its main allies, the MPLA, losing ground, and so provided massive assistance to support its ally. China then retreated from the scene, calling for unity among the revolutionary movements and appearing unable to compete in the aid game.[12]

By 1976 Sino-Soviet competition in the Third World had never been more acute. Yet, although the trend was often ambiguous, it seemed that Moscow rather than Beijing was 'winning' the race. With the death of Zhou Enlai and Mao Zedong in 1976, China's foreign-policy leadership seemed stripped of its best assets just as it faced its most important Third World challenge. Between 1977 and 1980, it became clear that China had failed the test.

The Sino-Soviet conflict in the Third World was largely decided in two theatres. First, in South-East Asia, Soviet-backed Vietnam responded to Kampuchean provocations and Vietnam's own desires for regional power by invading Kampuchea and installing a pro-Hanoi regime by early January 1979. If China was to have any credibility as a Third World power, it would have to defend its Kampuchean allies. Not to act on its own doorstep would be a far worse blow than impotence in Africa. Unfortunately for Beijing, it was deterred by fears of Soviet counter-pressure, and could not act decisively against Vietnam.[13] What is more, China's armed forces lacked the military punch to 'teach Vietnam a lesson'. Although China did attempt to educate Vietnam, its dismal performance was an even greater setback for China's Third World prestige. While Vietnam had been vilified for its use of force, some South-East Asians were now also deeply concerned with a huge China throwing its weight around. Furthermore, Moscow's image as a reliable ally was enhanced when it supported Vietnam with all the material requested.[14]

To make matters worse, in the second major theatre of Sino-Soviet confrontation, Africa, the implications of Angolan events further enhanced Soviet influence in the Third World. A wide array of southern African governments and movements either shifted to a pro-Soviet stance, or became more neutral after having leaned to Beijing.[15] The vivid demonstration of China's military weakness in Africa served the Soviet Union well. In Mozambique, an initially pro-Beijing leadership shifted to closer ties with Moscow when it needed massive aid. In Ethiopia, China refused to contest for allies on the quicksand of east African politics and Moscow again stepped in with aid. Robert Mugabe in the Zimbabwe struggle, SWAPO in Namibia, and such states as Zambia and Tanzania improved relations with the Soviet Union and shifted away from close reliance on China. The débâcle of China's African policy was clear. By 1978, with its intense anti-Sovietism as a shaky underpinning for its African policy, China even found itself siding with reactionary Western policy. In the two Shaba crises in Zaire (1977–8), China joined with the West in propping up a most unpalatable African regime.

Clearly the second half of the 1970s saw serious defeats for China, and important gains for the Soviet Union. However, any calculation of 'gains' and 'losses' must be tempered. Not only did Moscow rarely engineer its gains (it benefited from others' actions), but almost every area of confrontation had a positive and negative dimension. Four such theatres stand out as particularly important.

First, in Africa, China's close alignment with the West against the Soviet Union seriously boxed in Chinese foreign policy. However,

China did manage to retain some independence of action, even during this most extreme phase of anti-Sovietism. For example, in Zimbabwe, Robert Mugabe remained favourably disposed to China, while the Soviet Union continued to bet heavily on Joshua Nkomo.

Second, in the Middle East, although China played only a minor role, the Soviet Union was dealt several important rebuffs by Western action. Following the 1973 Arab-Israeli war, the Kissinger shuttle diplomacy, and the Sadat-inspired offensive leading to the September 1978 Camp David accord, the Soviet Union was squeezed out of centre stage. However the low ebb for Moscow's Middle East policy did not mean there were no strong counter-currents. The Arab world was far from enamoured of Camp David, and Moscow backed the Syrian-led 'rejectionist' front.[16] Also, the fall of the Shah of Iran in 1978–9 was on balance a positive development for the Soviet Union, especially as the United States, and most recently China, were closer allies of the Shah. But certainly in comparison with other theatres of confrontation in the Middle East, Soviet problems had little, if anything, to do with China.

In the third theatre, South-East Asia, the Soviet gains remained clear, although the burdens of victory were now becoming increasingly evident. Moscow reportedly spent more than $1 million a day propping up the Vietnamese economy and maintaining Hanoi's army of occupation in Kampuchea. The Soviet Union gained in such strategic currency as military bases in Vietnam, but the Kremlin could not have been pleased with the continuing conflict. Certainly such instability hampered Soviet attempts to increase its influence with non-communist South-East Asia.

The fourth theatre, South Asia, was most unimportant in Sino-Soviet relations until the end of the decade. China and India began a limited détente and China tied its bonds with Pakistan even tighter in this period.[17] But in 1978 this region began to assume new importance in Sino-Soviet relations as a coup in Afghanistan decisively ended Kabul's careful policy of tilting to the Soviet Union while not antagonizing Beijing.[18] When the Kabul regime tottered, and the Soviet Union invaded Afghanistan in December 1979, Sino-Soviet relations took on board the Afghan issue as second only to South-East Asia in importance.[19]

China's ambivalence about Afghanistan has already been documented,[20] but after the Soviet invasion it was clear that China felt strongly about the need to get Soviet troops out of a second state on China's frontiers. For its part, the Soviet Union claimed to see Chinese machinations in fomenting Afghan instability, but by and large the Afghan problem did not derive from Sino-Soviet conflict. Nevertheless, by the end of the 1970s Afghanistan and South-East Asian confict loomed largest in Sino-Soviet relations in the Third World. However, most change in this state of affairs was to come from China.

The 1970s had left Chinese policy in deep trouble for several reasons. First, its close ties with Western policies (including support for the right-wing regime in Chile) and single-minded anti-Sovietism left the impression that China was no longer a supporter of revolutionary causes. Second, it was equally clear that although China may have the desire for global reach, it lacked the means to play in the superpower league. China had to come to terms with its limits, and this required a fundamental review of how to package its Third World image. By 1980, there were signs that a new Chinese policy was emerging.

For the Soviet Union, its 'victories' in the Third World at China's expense were not without costs. In Africa it could have little confidence that its gains would last. In South-East Asia it saw the need to support Hanoi, but might have wished for an end to conflict in the hope that new opportunities could be developed with non-communist South-East Asia. In South Asia, it found itself tied down in Afghanistan in an unwanted war, but one that 'needed' to be prosecuted.[21] The resulting deterioration in Sino-Soviet relations was equally unwanted.

After more than twenty years of active involvement in the Third World, the Soviet Union had come to accept the limits of its ability to manipulate events. China perhaps had taken longer to learn that lesson, but by 1980 it too had grown more mature. It remained to be seen whether this realism, and especially China's *new* realism, would change the nature of Sino-Soviet relations in the Third World. Just as most of the changes in the first part of the 1970s had come from the Chinese side, so in the early 1980s yet another series of Chinese changes seemed to hold out hope for some Sino-Soviet détente.

The 1980s: normalizing relations

In the 1980s, as in the two previous decades of the Sino-Soviet split in the Third World, the major changes came as a result of alterations in three aspects of Chinese policy.[22] First, in a gradual abandonment of its strident rhetoric of the past few years, China ceased its emphasis on denouncing only the Soviet Union, and took up a more balanced position denouncing both superpowers more equally. The United States was blamed for conflict in the Middle East and Latin America, while Soviet policy in South-East and

South Asia was denounced. It is difficult to pinpoint a specific date
for this change, for it came unevenly. In 1980, China ceased
declaring that a world war between the superpowers was inevitable,
and in 1981 began talking more openly about new ideas on the
nature of world politics other than the Theory of Three Worlds.
China now appreciated 'multipolarity' and the natural 'complexity'
of international relations that rendered any overarching theory too
simplistic. Throughout this period debate raged in Chinese foreign
policy on a wide range of issues, and by 1982 China's statements on
Third World conflict were much more discriminating than its
previous single-minded anti-Sovietism.[23]

Second, as the Theory of the Three Worlds was abandoned, with
its belief that Western Europe would help take on the superpowers,
China turned to a more explicit pro-Third World strategy. Thus in
place of the discredited theory, China produced a hodge-podge of
pronouncements favouring South-South cooperation, Northern aid
to the South, and calls for all states to pursue the Five Principles of
Peaceful Coexistence.[24] China's leaders set off on Third World
tours, offering verbal and the odd bit of material aid.[25] This time,
China was not pretending it could buy its way into the Third World,
but rather was suggesting that as a poor, peasant state, China was
naturally a Third World member. Beijing also championed the
cause of a Third World United Nations Secretary-General, and was
successful in blocking Eastern and Western moves to choose a
European.[26] Finally, China took an active part in the North-South
dialogue, especially at Cancún, in 1981, where it claimed the status
of Third World spokesman at the world's top table.[27]

Third, this new balanced Chinese policy emphasizing its Third
World status was being carried out with more pragmatism. China
seemed to be no longer wedded to assuming a given position just
because the Soviet Union was on the other side.[28] Furthermore, it
was not above simply admitting that problems in the Third World
were not subject to straightforward solutions. In the Middle East it
was at its most pragmatic from 1980, proclaiming its neutrality, and
selling arms to Iraq and Iran when denouncing both superpowers
for similar sins.[29] It also cut back on arms aid to South-East Asian
rebel movements, although it still provided moral support. What is
more, it joined the IMF and the World Bank, drawing loans from
these capitalist bodies, and thereby upsetting some Third World
states who found there was then less money for them to borrow.

All these 1980–2 changes in China's Third World policy were
directly relevant to Sino-Soviet Third World relations. Not only had
China abandoned its excessive anti-Sovietism, but in certain cases it
now even (tacitly) sided with 'pro-Soviet' forces against the United

States. Furthermore, China's new emphasis on the Third World, and its struggle against the rich North, took the Soviet Union out of the limelight of Chinese attention, even if China did see both a North-East/South and North-West/South dimension. Finally, Chinese pragmatism in policy left room for hope in Moscow that compromise was possible with Beijing on more deep-seated Third World conflict. But predictably, in the light of the previous intensity of Sino-Soviet polemics, the Soviet Union was slow to appreciate the importance of these changes in China's Third World policy.[30] To be sure, this Third World dimension of Sino-Soviet relations was one of the last to change in the 1980s, but certainly by 1982 even the Soviet Union could no longer ignore it. Brezhnev's Tashkent overture to China in March 1982 was made in Soviet Asia, perhaps implicitly recognizing the centrality of Third World issues in Sino-Soviet relations. But much as Moscow and Beijing moderated their polemics about Third World conflict in 1982, three decisive aspects of their Third World relationship remained in dispute: South-East Asia, Afghanistan, and to a lesser extent some distant Third World events. Yet in each of the three areas there were some important elements of hope for Sino-Soviet détente.

South-East Asia
The confrontation in Kampuchea between Vietnamese-backed Kampucheans and Chinese-backed rebels is of course far from a simple 'proxy war' between pro-Chinese and pro-Soviet forces. Nevertheless, it does involve the two communist powers, not least because China has declared that Soviet support for Vietnamese aggression is one of the three main obstacles to improving Sino-Soviet relations. Undeniably some Soviet and Chinese interests clash in Kampuchea. China seeks a counterweight to Vietnamese (and Soviet) power, while Moscow wants a counterweight to Chinese influence in South-East Asia. Yet, these objectives can be seen as maximalist, with both powers perhaps willing to settle for minimal principles. Neither Moscow nor Beijing are oblivious to the damage done to their standing in East Asia by their support for continuing conflict. Equally, both powers see risks of an escalation in skirmishes leading to unwanted war. Finally, both powers pay an economic price for supporting their allies, with Moscow clearly bearing the heaviest burden.

These dilemmas of policy – important objectives, sought at high cost – make both Moscow and Beijing receptive to new policy options. Since late 1982, when a general Sino-Soviet détente seemed in gingerly fashion to get under way, South-East Asians looked on warily as both communist powers tinkered with their policy for the area.[31] To date there has been no breakthrough in Sino-Soviet relations concerning South-East Asia, but a number of issues have been clarified.

It seems that South-East Asia is more important to China, and Afghanistan more important to the Soviet Union. Both sides continue to denounce each other's policies in South-East Asia, even though some of their polemics have now become veiled. On general Third World questions from 1983, Moscow often spoke of 'a large Asian country' whose policies serve imperialist interests, but on South-East Asia, Soviet comments retained explicit citation of China.[32] Beijing did not adopt these veiled polemics reminiscent of the early 1960s, and openly rejected Soviet policy towards South-East Asia.[33]

South-East Asia has figured prominently in the preliminary phases of the twice-yearly Sino-Soviet 'talks about talks'. China's insistence on the need to discuss South-East Asia was rejected by the Soviet Union because it involved 'third parties'.[34] China's response was to breach the confidentiality of the talks with the Soviet Union on only one issue, when in March 1983 China made public a five-point plan for Kampuchea presented to the Soviet Union in October 1982. In April, Qian Qichen told a Japanese paper that the South-East Asian issue was of special importance, and Hu Yaobang in May said a Sino-Soviet war in South-East Asia was still not ruled out.[35] In the spring of 1984, as in previous years during this period, Vietnam and China traded (primarily verbal) barrages across their frontier as China tried to halt Hanoi's offensive against Chinese-supported Kampucheans.[36]

Yet there are signs of movement on the issue. First, Chinese officials admit privately that they no longer demand the withdrawal of Soviet bases from Vietnam. These unwanted bases are seen as primarily anti-American and should not prevent normalization of relations, just as the presence of American bases in Asia did not prevent Sino-American normalization. China seems mainly concerned with a withdrawal of Vietnamese troops from Kampuchea. But even here, some form of Vietnamese presence may eventually be tolerated, for China does not require the withdrawal of the thousands of Vietnamese troops from Laos (which, unlike Kampuchea, borders on China) as a precondition for Sino-Soviet normalization. Such variations in Chinese policy may leave some room for compromise.

There has also been some movement from the Soviet side. Moscow seems to understand the Chinese sensitivity about South-East Asia, but is hampered by its desire to maintain the benefits of Soviet-Vietnamese friendship. The Soviet Union shows signs of seeking a cosmetic solution in Kampuchea so that Sino-Soviet relations can concentrate on more important issues. However, at the same time the Kremlin is unwilling to 'bite the bullet' and force Vietnamese concessions (even if it could).

In October 1982, when the first round of Sino-Soviet consultations began, the head of the Vietnamese State Council, Truong Chinh, came to Moscow for high-level talks.[37] From 31 January to 9 February 1983, Soviet deputy Foreign Minister M. Kapitsa, a leading voice in Moscow's China policy, toured South-East Asia (including Thailand), apparently carrying a dual message of support for allies, but hints of flexibility.[38] The Kapitsa tour was not sharply attacked by China, whereas in the past it would have called for a series of derogatory epithets.[39] From 8 to 15 September 1983, Kapitsa visited Beijing, at the invitation of the Chinese, and Xinhua was quick to note that he was the highest-ranking official Soviet visitor to China in over twenty years. But more important than the fact of the Kapitsa visit was that he deliberately twice snubbed the Vietnamese in Beijing, and he also 'opened a new channel of contact, this time on international issues'. The Kapitsa back channel seemed to get around the previous Soviet refusal to discuss 'third parties'.

Although Moscow was at least tacitly willing to discuss 'third parties', it still seemed unwilling to risk change in its support for Vietnam. In October 1983, at the time of the third round of Sino-Soviet consultations, Politburo member and first deputy Premier G. Aliev went to Hanoi, possibly to allay Vietnamese fears of a sell-out. Aliev restated the principles of the November 1978 Soviet-Vietnamese friendship pact in what seemed like an attempt to reassure Vietnam of continuing support. Yet Aliev's speeches in Hanoi were markedly more optimistic about Sino-Soviet ties, and less critical of China, than were those made by his hosts.

Vietnam was of course not unaware of the potential for a Sino-Soviet carve-up. After all, it had a long history of dealing with these two selfish communist powers. Thus the March 1984 Vietnamese concession to ASEAN states, apparently opening the way to a deal on Kampuchea that could squeeze out the Chinese, might well have been an attempt to pre-empt any Sino-Soviet initiative.[40] Although South-East Asian issues remain an important problem for Sino-Soviet relations, both communist powers now have enough complex motives at least to keep open the door to compromise.

Afghanistan

The next most important issue in Sino-Soviet relations concerning the Third World is Afghanistan. Although China felt strongly enough about the December 1979 invasion to suspend Sino-Soviet talks, less than three years later, and with no reduction in Soviet involvement in Afghanistan, China returned to the negotiating table. Chinese policy has been far from uniform on the Afghan question, but it has persistently perceived it as one of the three main obstacles to Sino-Soviet rapprochement, and has insisted that Soviet troops be withdrawn.[41] For Moscow, no withdrawal is possible until some stability is ensured in Afghanistan, and China is seen as in part contributing to instability.[42] While Soviet accusations of Sino-Western collaboration in fomenting Afghan resistance had largely disappeared by 1983, Moscow still acknowledged a Sino-Soviet dimension to the problem. China continued explicitly to condemn Soviet policy in Afghanistan, and the Soviet Union was quick to respond in a critical tone. The level of polemics was less acrimonious than that achieved in the Kampuchean issue, but it was still evident.

In many respects, the importance of the Afghan issue to Moscow is like the importance of South-East Asian issues to China. Given Beijing's abivalent past policy, China is probably more willing to compromise on Afghanistan, although the Soviet Union seems more flexible on South-East Asia. If the new Kapitsa channel on 'international issues' is open for serious discussions, then it is not unreasonable to expect some Soviet concession on South-East Asia, perhaps even tacitly in exchange for a Chinese concession in Afghanistan. But there are several snags with any such expectations. Not only does Moscow have more influence in Vietnam than does China in Afghanistan, but – more important – neither communist power has it within its power to dictate terms in either conflict. The roots of conflict lie deeper, in local issues. If both powers wait long enough they may find that the solution to these two conflicts emerges on its own, thereby offering new hope for Sino-Soviet relations.

Distant Third World conflict
The third dimension to Sino-Soviet Third World conflict is clearly of declining importance. In a 180-degree turn, China and the Soviet Union have sharply cut back their level of recrimination about the sources and conduct of Third World conflict in Africa, the Middle East and Latin America. This is not to suggest that the two powers no longer criticize each other at all on these questions, but, especially on the Soviet side, the vitriolic tone of pre-1982 polemics is gone. Compare China's low-key view of conflict in Chad, and its criticism of 'foreign intervention' in general,[43] with its 1977–8 sharp denunciation of Soviet machinations in central Africa. Compare its

1982–3 comments on the Lebanon conflict, where United States support for Israel was the primary focus of criticism, with its treatment of the honeymoon days of the Camp David process, when United States policy was gently chided and Soviet 'rejectionist tactics' were seen as more serious.[44] Compare its 1982–3 criticisms of Western policies in the Falklands, and pre-eminently Caribbean and central American conflicts,[45] with its late 1970s denunciation of Soviet-backed Cuban intervention in the area. Compare its improved ties with Angola and Libya in 1982–3[46] with its previous attacks on both states as serving Soviet interests.

By 1984 few could doubt the real improvement in Sino-Soviet relations in the Third World. The virtually complete cessation of Soviet attacks on Chinese policy in this respect is fulsome evidence of the change. Some might argue that these distant Third World issues are of less importance for both Moscow and Beijing. But it was precisely these Sino-Soviet conflicts in the Third World that were cited in previous years as evidence of Sino-Soviet discord. On his September 1983 visit to China, Kapitsa spoke of clear Sino-Soviet agreement on many Third World problems.[47] This would not have been possible before 1982, and marks at least a modicum of Sino-Soviet détente.

Yet the Afghan and Kampuchean issues remain more important to both communist powers than all other Third World conflict combined. Although there are signs of some progress on both these Asian issues, as well as a convergence of views on others (India, Korea),[48] rapid progress is unlikely. Especially at a time of leadership uncertainty, neither Beijing nor Moscow are likely to 'bite the bullet' and make concessions. In the end, the Afghan and Kampuchean conflicts, like other Third World events, are unlikely to be resolved by a great-power carve-up. Either China will put aside these two of its three obstacles, or else resolution of local events will remove the conflict from the Sino-Soviet agenda.

Conclusions
Given the complex trends in Sino-Soviet relations in the Third World, the conclusions cannot be simple. On the one hand there has been a marked improvement in Sino-Soviet ties since 1976, and especially since 1981, in Third World issues in the Middle East and beyond. On the other hand, serious problems have emerged since 1976 in the two key areas of South-East Asia and Afghanistan. In part because China had set these two problems as primary issues in current negotiations on Sino-Soviet détente, the general trend must be seen as a deterioration rather than an improvement in Moscow-Beijing ties.

Yet it is also clear that both Moscow and Beijing acknowledge that they have no clear policy options. But where there is uncertainty there is hope for a resolution of the twin Asian problems. Essentially, four options seem open to the communist powers. First, there can be a massive deterioration in relations, leading, for example, to a more direct Sino-Soviet clash either in Vietnam or Afghanistan. While no scenario can be entirely ruled out, it seems more likely that the most dangerous point in both these conflicts has already been passed.

Second, and equally unlikely, is a dramatic improvement in Sino-Soviet relations on these two issues. Scepticism about such change is based on the deep-rooted causes of the conflict and the important interests that both communist powers see in each area. Third, and more likely, is a continuation of the *status quo*. The existence of policy dilemmas is more likely to lead to immobility than to taking a chance on change, certainly under a Chernenko leadership. As both the South-East Asian and Afghan crises are more or less under control, the risks of stoically carrying on for the near future are not high.

The fourth possibility is a degree of improvement on one or both issues.[49] As has already been suggested, the conflict in South-East Asia imposes especially serious costs on both Moscow and Beijing. In Afghanistan, China has less to lose by continuing conflict, but then it also has less motive to hold out for a hard-line policy involving the removal of a pro-Soviet regime in Kabul. A Sino-Soviet deal on Kampuchea is also not to be ruled out, perhaps involving both Moscow and Beijing giving their backing to an ASEAN solution, with a cosmetic broadening of the Phnom Penh regime to include Khmer Rouge forces, which allows large-scale Vietnamese troop withdrawals. At a minimum, this would allow both the Soviet Union and China to cut back their polemical exchanges.

Perhaps the greatest attraction of this fourth course of competitive coexistence is that in the final analysis neither Moscow nor Beijing have complete control over either crisis. Both conflicts will in the final analysis only be resolved when local problems are resolved. If both communist powers acknowledge their limited power, then the limited détente route seems more attractive. They can then turn to the more important, bilateral dimensions of Sino-Soviet relations, and pretend that the bewildering Third World does not exist.

Notes

This paper is drawn in part from the author's *Adelphi Paper* 'Sino-Soviet Relations After Mao' (London: IISS, forthcoming 1985).

1. Early aspects of the rift in Donald Zagoria, *The Sino-Soviet Conflict* (New York: Athenum, 1973); John Gittings, *Survey of the Sino-Soviet Dispute* (London: Oxford University Press, 1968); William Griffith, *Sino-Soviet Relations 1964–65* (Cambridge, Mass.: MIT Press, 1967).

2. Gerald Segal, *The Great Power Triangle* (London: Macmillan, 1982).

3. *Ibid.*, p. 93.

4. Warren Weinstein, 'Chinese Aid and Policy in Central Africa', in Warren Weinstein and Thomas Henriksen (eds.), *Soviet and Chinese Aid to African Nations* (New York: Praeger, 1980); George Yu, 'China's Impact', *Problems of Communism*, Vol. 27, No. 1, Jan.–Feb. 1978; Jan Pryblyla, 'The Sino-Soviet Split and Developing Nations', in Roger Kanet (ed.), *The Soviet Union and the Developing Nations* (London: Johns Hopkins University Press, 1974); Arthur Klinghoffer, *The Angolan War* (Boulder, Colo.: Westview, 1980), pp. 101–3.

5. Yitzhak Shichor, *The Middle East in China's Foreign Policy* (Cambridge: Cambridge University Press, 1979); Alvin Rubinstein, *Soviet and Chinese Influences in the Third World* (New York: Praeger, 1975).

6. Segal, *The Triangle*, Ch. 4.

7. William Barnds, *India, Pakistan and the Great Powers* (London: Pall Mall, 1972).

8. Arnold Horelick, *The Soviet Union's Asian Collective Security Proposal* (Santa Monica, Calif.: Rand Corporation, March 1974); Kenneth Lieberthal, *Sino-Soviet Conflict in the 1970's* (Santa Monica, Calif.: Rand Corporation, July 1978); Gerald Segal, 'The Soviet Union and the Great Power Triangle', in Gerald Segal (ed.), *The China Factor* (London: Croom Helm, 1982); Michael Yahuda, 'China and the Great Power Triangle', in Segal (ed.), *The China Factor*; Raju Thomas, *The Great Power Triangle and Asian Security* (Lexington, Mass.: D.C. Heath, 1983).

9. The thesis of the great powers' reactive policy is the theme of Adeed Dawisha and Karen Dawisha (eds.), *The Soviet Union in the Middle East* (London: Heinemann, for the RIIA, 1982) and Gerald Segal (ed.), *The Soviet Union in East Asia* (London: Heinemann, for the RIIA, 1983).

10. Michael Leifer, 'Conflict and Regional Order in South East Asia', *Adelphi Papers* No. 162, Winter 1980; Takashi Tajima, 'China and Southeast Asia', *Adelphi Papers* No. 172, Winter 1981.

11. Klinghoffer, *Angolan War*.

12. Vice-Premier Li Xianian, interviewed in *The Sunday Times* (London), 27 March 1977, said 'We do not have the resources to afford big quantities (of military aid). If the Russians try to expand anywhere in the world, China will inevitably get involved, but in Africa on the whole all we can do at present is give political support and to expose the Russian sinister motives and crimes. The Russians may take advantage of some African nations, but I must make it clear that we cannot help them much in a big way.'

13. Harlan Jencks, 'China's Punitive War on Vietnam', *Asian Survey*, Vol. 19, No. 8, August 1979; Daniel Tretiak, 'China's Vietnam War and its Consequences', *The China Quarterly*, No. 80, December 1979; Douglas Pike, 'Communist vs Communist in Southeast Asia', *International Security*, Vol. 4, No. 1, Summer 1979;

Harry Gelman, *The Soviet Far East Buildup and Soviet Risk Taking Against China* (Santa Monica, Calif.: Rand Corporation, August 1982), p. 4.

14. Segal, 'The Soviet Union and the Great Power Triangle'.

15. George Yu, 'China's Impact', in *Problems of Communism*, Vol. 27, No. 1, Jan.–Feb. 1978; Colin Legum, 'Sino-Soviet Rivalry in Africa', in Douglas Stuart and William Tow (eds.), *China, the Soviet Union and the West* (Boulder, Colo.: Westview, 1982); RFE/RL No. 105, 1980. Also Weinstein, 'Chinese Aid and Policy'; Klinghoffer, *Angolan War*; Eugene Lawson, 'China's Policy in Ethiopia and Angola', in Weinstein and Henriksen (eds.) *Aid to African Nations*; Vol. 3, No. 4, Winter 1979. See generally Robert Donaldson, *The Soviet Union in the Third World* (Boulder, Colo.: Westview, 1981), Part 2.

16. Yitzhak Shichor, *The Middle East in China's Foreign Policy*. Also Yitzhak Shichor, 'Just Stand and Just Struggle', in *The Australian Journal of Chinese Affairs*, No. 5, 1981; Amnon Sela, *Soviet Political and Military Conduct in the Middle East* (London: Macmillan, 1981); Robert Freedman, *Soviet Policy Toward the Middle East* (New York: Praeger, 1978); Lillian Craig Harris, 'China's Response to Present Soviet Gains in the Middle East', *Asian Survey*, Vol. 20, No. 4, April 1980.

17. William Barnds, 'The Impact of the Sino-Soviet Dispute on South Asia', in Herbert Ellison (ed.), *The Sino-Soviet Conflict* (Seattle: University of Washington Press, 1982); Yaacov Vertzberger, 'The Enduring Entente', *The Washington Papers*, 1983; Robert Horn, *Soviet-Indian Relations* (New York: Praeger, 1982).

18. Rosemary Foot, 'Sino-Soviet Rivalry in Kabul', *The Round Table*, No. 280, October 1980.

19. Yaacov Vertzberger, 'China and Afghanistan', *Problems of Communism*, Vol. 31, No. 3, May–June 1982.

20. Gerald Segal, 'China and Afghanistan', *Asian Survey*, Vol. 21, No. 11, 1981.

21. Henry S. Bradsher, *Afghanistan and the Soviet Union* (Durham, N.C.: Duke University Press, 1983); Alvin Rubinstein, *Soviet Policy Towards Turkey, Iran and Afghanistan* (New York: Praeger, 1982); Fred Halliday, *Threat from the East?* (Harmondsworth: Penguin, 1982).

22. Examples of the rigid anti-Soviet line in Xinhua, 14 February 1980, in BBC, *Summary of World Broadcasts*, Far East (hereafter FE), 6349, A4, 1; *People's Daily*, 25 March 1980, in FE, 6383, A1, 1; Xinhua, 21 April 1980, in FE, 6402, A2, 1.

23. The change is documented in Gerald Segal, 'China's Security Debate', *Survival*, Vol. 24, No. 2, March–April 1982 and Carol Lee Hamrin, 'China Reassesses the Superpowers', *Pacific Affairs*, Vol. 56, No. 2, Summer 1983.

24. *People's Daily*, 5 January 1983, in FE, 7224, A1, 2–3; *People's Daily*, 15 March 1983, in FE, 7283, A1, 3.

25. Vice-Premier Ji Pengfei in Africa, July 1980, visited Kenya and not Tanzania (Kenya had just offered the United States help in basing the RDF). February 1981: Premier Zhao Ziyang in Thailand; June 1981: in Pakistan, Nepal and Bangladesh. Huang Hua in Africa in November 1981. Zhao in Africa in December 1982–January 1983. President Li in the Middle East in 1984.

26. Xinhua, 16 June 1981, in FE, 6883, A1, 1–2.

27. Xinhua, 20 October 1981, in FE, 6860, A2, 1–2. *People's Daily*, 20 October 1981, in FE, 6861, A1, 1. *People's Daily*, 4 March 1982, in Foreign Broadcasts Information Service, *China Report* (hereafter *Chi.*), 82-048-C1.

28. See works cited in note 15 above.

29. Yitzhak Shichor, 'The Middle East', in Gerald Segal and William Tow (eds.), *Chinese Defence Policy* (London: Macmillan, 1984).

30. For examples of Moscow's continuing attacks on China for Third World collusion with the West see Tass, 14 January 1980, in BBC, *Summary of World Broadcasts*, Soviet Union (hereafter SU), 6322, A3, 1; Moscow Home Service, 18 March 1980 in SU, 6386, A3, 2; *Pravda*, 20 April 1980, in SU, 6400, A3, 1; Tass, 10 February 1981, in SU, 6647, A3, 1; O. Borisov in *Kommunist*, 18 April 1981, in SU, 6703, A3, 5–6; V. Ovchinnikov in *Pravda*, 11 February 1982, in SU, 6953, A3, 3. Soviet comments tailed off markedly in 1981 but some articles did continue the hard line and some Soviet academics seemed especially slow to accept the changes. V. Stepanov, 'Peking and the Nonaligned Movement', *Far Eastern Affairs*, No. 3, 1982.

31. *The Times*, 17 June 1982; *Far Eastern Economic Review* (hereafter *FEER*), 3 March 1983. Pao-min Chang, 'The Sino-Vietnamese Conflict over Kampuchea' and Leif Rosenberger, 'The Soviet-Vietnamese Alliance and Kampuchea', in *Survey*, Vol. 27, Nos. 118–9, 1983.

32. *Izvestiya*, 22 July 1982, in SU, 7086, A3, 1; Moscow World Service, 9 August 1983, in SU, 7409, A3, 4; Tass, 27 December 1983, in SU, 7529, A3, 3–4.

33. *People's Daily*, 5 January 1983, in FE, 7224, A1, 2–3; Huan Xiang in *World Knowledge*, 15 August 1983, in FE, 7414, A1, 1; *People's Daily*, 5 February 1984, in reply to *Izvestiya*, in FE, 7559, A2, 2. Also Premier Zhao in San Francisco in FE, 7541, A1, 2.

34. For example, Y. Andropov to *Pravda*, 26 August 1983, in SU, 7424, C, 1–4.

35. *Beijing Review* (*BR*), No. 10, 7 March 1983, and No. 12, 21 March 1983. Also *International Herald Tribune* (*IHT*), 2 March 1983; 5 April 1983 in *Chi*, 83-071-annex, and Hu to Yugoslav journalists on 6 May 1983 cited in FE, 7328, i.

36. *The Economist*, 14 April 1984; *New York Times*, 8 April, 13 May 1984.

37. *The Guardian*, 6 October 1982.

38. *FEER*, 3 March 1983.

39. *People's Daily*, 11 February 1983, in *Chi*, 83-031-C2-3.

40. On Kapitsa see Xinhua, 8 September 1983, in FE, 7434, A2, 1; 15 September 1983 in FE, 7441, A2, 1; *The Guardian*, 17 September 1983; *IHT*, 17 September 1983. On Aliev see FE, 7481, A2, 1–6. On the new Vietnamese proposal see *The Times*, 16 March 1984.

41. *People's Daily*, 27 December 1982, in *BR*, No. 1, 3 January 1983 and No. 3, 17 January 1983. For further evidence of the Chinese debate on the Afghan struggle see the discussion of 'some people's view that the Soviet war effort is slackening', in *People's Daily*, 17 December 1983, in FE, 7520, C, 1–2.

42. *New Times*, 21 July 1983, in SU, 7399, A3, 1; Radio Moscow, 11 August 1983, on 'An Asian Power', in SU, 7413, A3, 2.

43. *People's Daily*, 11 August 1983, in FE, 7410, A5, 1; Zhao on 17 January 1984, in FE, 7543, A1, 3–4.

44. Gerald Segal, 'China and the Middle East', in Colin Legum (ed.), *The Middle East Contemporary Survey*, Vol. 6 (1981–82) and Vol. 7 (1982–83); Yitzhak Shichor, 'In Search of Alternatives: China's Middle East Policy After Sadat', *The Australian Journal of Chinese Affairs*, No. 8, 1982.

45. *World Knowledge*, 1 June 1983, in FE, 7350, A1, 1 and *People's Daily*, 23 July 1983, in FE, 7394, A1, 3. On Grenada see *People's Daily*, 29 October 1983, in FE, 7479, A1, 1. The Soviet view of China in Moscow Radio in Chinese, 28 October 1983, in SU, 7480, A3, 1.

46. Segal, 'China and the Middle East'; *World Knowledge*, 16 July 1983, in FE, 7411, A5, 1–4.

47. See note 40 above.

48. China's mild détente with India since 1982 has brought Beijing's and Moscow's positions closer. In 1984 the slight souring of Sino-Korean relations and the slight mellowing of Soviet-Korean relations also brings the two powers closer. *IHT*, 18 April 1984.

49. For some development of these points see Gerald Segal, 'Towards Sino-Soviet Detente', *The World Today*, May 1984.

3

The Soviet Union and South Asia in the 1980s

Peter Lyon

Because South Asia is a rather protean and unstandardized label, two initial general points need to be made. First, historical experience suggests that South Asia either has provided a platform or springboard for extensive imperial ambitions and activities which fan out much wider than the area of South Asia itself (in this light the British Raj was but one of several historic hegemonies the subcontinent has experienced), or else has itself been overrun in whole or large part from centres of power based in Iran or Afghanistan or from overseas, as successive Arab, Portuguese, Dutch, French and British thalassocracies showed. Second, in the past forty years or so South Asia has been caught up in the cross-currents of great-power rivalries, so that Indo-Soviet relations (or, indeed, those of any South Asian country with the Soviet Union) need to be seen not only binocularly but also through the prism of Soviet-American-Chinese relations as well – even if in this brief chapter this can be done only perfunctorily.

Indo-Soviet relations in the 1980s can be characterized as multidimensional, durable and resilient. Their post-Stalin cordialities began not with Nehru's visit to Moscow in June 1955, nor with the much publicized visit of Bulganin and Khrushchev to India (and also to Afghanistan and Burma) in November and December 1955, but with an Indo-Soviet trade agreement signed in New Delhi on 2 December 1953.[1] Thus, for more than thirty years now, an economic dimension has been present alongside, and interweaving with, the diplomatic, in Indo-Soviet relations. Soviet relations with each and all of the other states of South Asia are subordinate to the Indo-Soviet bilateral ties. Now, as often in the past, Afghanistan obtrudes prominently as a factor in the South Asian correlation of forces, even though this country, currently a Soviet satellite, is not usually included in conventional definitions of which territories constitute the region of South Asia. The Indian Ocean is the maritime theatre (or several sub-theatres) which has relevance and continuing significance for the Soviet Union, both for its intrinsic uses and in relation to matters concerning its littoral and hinterland states, not least those of South Asia.

At the outset some caveats should be registered for the unwary reader. Discussion of this subject has hitherto suffered heavily from one of two kinds of distortion: an excessive Indophilia or a Kremlinology that is often only a diaphanously disguised form of demonology, according to which the Soviet Union is portrayed as a rapaciously expansionist power, seemingly immune from the constraints and inhibitions which usually check and limit the activities of even ideologically self-conscious actors on the world stage. Furthermore, reliable statistics about Soviet dealings with South Asian countries, even with India, are notoriously difficult to come by, and even when officially authorized figures are publicly available they should be treated with caution and scepticism. Neither the Soviet Union nor India is alone in refraining from divulging full and accurate statistics about its oil or arms trade, for instance, but they are practised in the arts of concealment and reticence about such matters.

Steel mills and assistance with India's state planning began in the 1950s; in the 1960s the Soviets began to supply some sophisticated weapons to India on favourable credit terms; in the 1970s much more oil and nuclear fuel was added to their economic transactions, while the earlier elements continued or were enhanced. Like a rope which has been thickened and strengthened with the interweaving of extra strands, the Indo-Soviet relationship thus has in the 1980s considerable length and apparent strength. This chapter does not seek to recapitulate the history of this relationship since the early 1950s (though passing references are made in the notes to some of the best, or best known, secondary sources); rather, it concentrates on its contemporary condition in the 1980s, with a principal stress on the economic dimension and with a short final section which is a speculative sketching of some possible alternative futures.

Changing emphases in Indo-Soviet economic relations

The content as well as the scale of Indo-Soviet trade has changed markedly since the two countries' first intergovernmental trade agreement was signed in December 1953. Soviet imports of machines and equipment from India have grown almost sevenfold, from 23m roubles (about Rs 280m) to 154m roubles (about Rs 1,980m) between 1975 and 1982.[2] Among Indian exports to the USSR in the last few years were not only familiar items such as knitwear, garments, detergents, cosmetics and medicines, but also rolled steel, medical instruments, and large-scale sophisticated equipment. Even in the 1960s up to 60 per cent of Soviet exports were machinery and equipment for Soviet-aided plants in India.

For the Soviet Union aid is organically related to trade and not neatly separable from it. Here again, however, the trend line of continuing Soviet assistance to India is marked. Between 1953 and 1969 India was the principal recipient of Soviet development assistance: it absorbed 18 per cent of total Soviet aid, while only four other countries received more than 4 per cent each. Even so, as Asha L. Datar showed in the posthumously published version of her Oxford D.Phil. thesis,[3] in these years the USSR and Eastern European CMEA countries altogether supplied India with a mere 8 per cent of the total official external finance and by 1969 accounted for only one-fifth of Indian foreign trade. As Joseph Berliner, Asha Datar and others have argued, the very entry of the USSR as a donor influenced some of the OECD powers, and especially the United States, to increase their aid to India. It can be instructive also to recall the terms on which their competitive assistance was made available: United States non-repayable grants were countered by Soviet low-interest loans repayable, as loans became usual, in inconvertible rupees or, in the typical Soviet agreement, in India's traditional exports. Quite a lot of these traditional exports, notably cashew nuts and some textiles and leather goods, were then re-exported by the Soviet Union and East European countries to West European markets, clearly suggesting in the process that India could itself have sold more directly to these hard-currency economies.

For Soviet spokesmen and commentators, if not so much for their Indian counterparts, the Soviet-Indian Treaty of Peace, Friendship and Cooperation signed in New Delhi on 9 August 1971[4] is lauded as an instrument of importance, both for its intrinsically bilateral qualities and as a commendable example of what are to be regarded as good relations for all countries. It is worth quoting at some length an excerpt from an article in a recent Soviet journal, published in October 1983, which expounds this viewpoint clearly and forcibly as follows:

> The provisions of this historic document which stipulate bilateral foreign policy cooperation on a permanent basis are as important today as ever. Specifically, Article V reads that the USSR and India are prepared to maintain regular contacts with each other on important international problems of mutual interest through meetings and exchanges of views between their state leaders, visits of official delegations and special representatives of the two governments and through diplomatic channels. Article IX of the Treaty provides for mutual consultations if any of the parties is attacked or threatened with being attacked with the aim of

removing this threat and taking relevant effective measures to insure peace and security.

These provisions of the 1971 Treaty have materialized in the form of a smoothly functioning ramified mechanism of bilateral foreign policy cooperation which involves and regulates the following activities today: regular consultations between the two countries' foreign ministries and close contacts maintained by Soviet and Indian representatives in the UN and other international organizations; exchanges of personal messages at the top level and, finally, reciprocal visits of Soviet and Indian leaders. In the last decade practically every year witnessed a meeting at the head of state, government or foreign ministers level.[5]

Nowadays Soviet writers stress with some pride that a distinguishing feature of Soviet-Indian relations is their long-term and planned character, which 'enables the partners to make optimal estimates and use of their actual and potential resources and to introduce alterations, if need be, in their national economic programmes and plans of economic cooperation with third countries'[6] – though it should be remembered that this is declaratory policy rather than a sober assessment of the actual record. In recent Soviet writing considerable emphasis is also placed on the importance of the Soviet-Indian accords of November 1973 as signed in New Delhi, and which specifically provided for cooperation between the State Planning Committee of the USSR and India's Planning Commission. These have been represented as a firm base for subsequent major Indo-Soviet economic agreements, such as those of March 1979 or December 1980. Indeed, between November 1973 and September 1983 six joint declarations and several joint statements and communiqués were signed in the course of top-level Indo-Soviet meetings, 'each new declaration being organically related and adding new constructive ideas to the previous similar document', according to Soviet claims.[7]

Since 1960 the volume of Soviet-Indian trade has gone up from approximately Rs 800m to nearly Rs 20,000m (i.e. it has almost tripled) and the Soviet Union has become India's principal foreign trade partner. About eighty major enterprises either have been built or are currently under construction in India with Soviet assistance. Soviet-Indian cooperation is focused on developing the major branches of modern industry in the state, or public, sector. Some indication of the range and character of this Soviet involvement is conveyed in the following passage from a recent Soviet article which conveys factual information for all its overall celebratory tone:

> The Soviet-aided Bhilai and Bokaro steel mills alone account for 40 per cent of India's total steel production. Their products are exported to 40 countries and are a good source of foreign exchange. The Soviet-aided oil extracting and refining enterprises in India account for 60 and 30 per

cent respectively of the extracted and refined oil in the country. All in all, the number of Soviet-aided enterprises in various economic sectors of India – completed, under construction or in the blueprints – totals 80, including the following giant projects: a 5-million-ton-per-annum oil refinery in Mathura; a 3-million-ton steel complex in Visakhapatnam; and a fuel and energy complex in Singanallur consisting of a 3-million-kilowatt thermal power plant and a 900-kilometre-long transmission line. ... Soviet-Indian cooperation in space exploration is also making headway. Three Indian-made earth satellites (Aryabhatta, Bhaskara-I and Bhaskara-II) have been put into orbit in recent years by Soviet rockets.[8]

What these celebratory passages do not say, however, is that the Indian rocket programme suffered several false starts and disappointments. Indeed, the whole question of the quality and performance of Soviet assistance and technology is not touched on in Soviet public utterances and it is difficult for an outsider to get accurate informed judgements about these matters. It is also difficult to assess the significance of what is termed by Soviet writers as 'the mass, truly popular character of the friendship'[9] that binds the two countries and is also eulogized in such language as:

> This cooperation is multifaceted and dynamic; it is manifested in coordinated foreign policy initiatives, in mutually beneficial commercial deals, in joint industrial ventures, and in multifarious and active contacts in the sphere of science, education, culture, sports and arts. 'In both our countries Soviet-Indian friendship,' it was noted at the 26th CPSU Congress, 'has become a deeprooted popular tradition'. The mass character of the Soviet-Indian friendship societies with a membership of many thousand people is added proof of this. ... Soviet-Indian friendship societies hold 'friendship months' in both countries each August to mark the anniversaries of signing the Soviet-Indian Treaty and India's Independence Day.[10]

In fact, however, in recent years India has been reducing imports of capital goods and machinery from the Soviet Union. Not only has India become more self-sufficient in several of the items which used to feature in their trade, but, finding much of the Soviet material old-fashioned or even obsolete from a technological point of view, the government has sought Western suppliers instead. Crude oil and oil products now constitute about 80 per cent of India's imports from the Soviet Union.[11] Current trends do, however, suggest a declining future need for India to import crude or refined oil from the Soviet Union. India's domestic production of crude oil as a percentage of its overall annual consumption has steadily increased from about 40 per cent in the mid-1970s to the current level of about 65 per cent and is expected to increase to about 70 per cent by the end of 1985. Soviet trade with India is on a barter basis; any imbalance is settled by means of 'technical credits'. The Soviet

TABLE 3.1
Indian imports of crude oil

Country of origin	1981–2			1982–3 (provisional)		
	Quantity ('000 tonnes)	Value (Rs crores[a])	Unit rates (Rs/tonne)	Quantity ('000 tonnes)	Value (Rs crores[a])	Unit rates (Rs/tonne)
Iran	5,035	1,246.09	2,475	3,462	798.43	2,306
Iraq	1,623	400.92	2,470	3,110	802.72	2,581
Saudi Arabia	3,680	815.68	2,216	6,524	1,509.13	2,313
UAE	1,605	410.84	2,560	1,196	304.14	2,543
USSR	2,000	493.30	2,466	2,588	610.80	2,360
Algeria	792	225.52	2,847			
Venezuela	563	144.03	2,558	75	19.18	2,557
Total	15,298	3,736.38	2,442	16,955	4,044.40	2,385

[a] 1 crore = 10 million.

Source: *The Economic Times* (New Delhi).

Union did not, however, want these credits in 1983 and accordingly reduced its imports of consumer and other goods from India (see Table 3.1).

Indeed, in mid-1983 there was a publicly perceptible brittleness in the Soviets' commercial relations with India, their most important associate in the non-communist world, and this led to speculation as to whether it portended a substantial change in their thirty-year-old, and generally thickening, economic relationship.[12]

A marked Soviet trade imbalance in its dealings with India began in 1980 as New Delhi reduced its capital goods and machinery imports because of increasing self-sufficiency and its growing dislike of much Soviet technology. Bilateral trade amounting to $3.1b in 1982 produced a Soviet deficit of $668m, and the gap was expected to be substantially higher in 1983 on a higher trade turnover of perhaps $3.6b.*

In the first few months of 1983 Soviet purchases from India abruptly slowed down in a number of respects, causing considerable hardship to sectors of the Indian economy which for years had been dependent on the Soviet market. Rather suddenly the Soviet Union stopped buying Indian cashew and cut back on imports of oilcake, knitwear and other consumer goods. Critics of the Indo-Soviet rupee trade arrangement were therefore encouraged to point out that heavy dependence on a single market is imprudent. Just

---

* In this chapter the term 'billion' refers to the US thousand million (10^9).

because more than 80 per cent of Soviet exports to India consist of crude oil and refined products, both rather in glut at present in world markets, it is quite probable that Soviet leaders are uneasily aware that the economic links could be snapped from the Indian side without disastrous consequences ensuing for the Indian economy. Present signs are, however, that this is most unlikely to happen; indeed, it is more likely in the immediate future that Indo-Soviet economic, and other, links will be reaffirmed and redefined.

Two aspects of the current and continuing Indo-Soviet connection which hardly get mentioned in Soviet media at all are Soviet supplies of sophisticated weaponry and of assistance in the nuclear field, yet both are of considerable importance to India.

Weapons[13]

From the early 1960s until the mid-1970s India was heavily dependent on Soviet arms for its first-line supplies.[14] Then during the Janata government, 1977–9, and as the service chiefs began to press hard for a new generation of up-to-date weapons, Jaguar bombers and Sea Harriers were bought from Britain and orders were placed for submarines from West Germany and for the Mirage-2000 aircraft from France. During 1983, however, India seems to have been tempted to place a substantial new arms order with Russia as a result of being offered low prices and easy credit. No less important, as we have seen, India amassed a trade surplus of $680m with Russia in 1982–3, partly because of the fall in the price of Soviet petroleum products. India's defence minister said, during a visit to Moscow in June 1983, that Russia had agreed to sell India aircraft, missiles, tanks and warships. One aircraft believed to be on the shopping list is the MiG-29, a two-engined fighter-bomber not yet fully operational even with the Soviet air force but thought to be at least a match for Pakistan's American F-16s. Recently Russian leaders apparently have been urging India to buy more machinery and arms with its surplus bank balance.[15] India is not now so keen on much of the Russian machinery, but the arms on offer seem to be a bargain.

The nuclear dimension

Although Indo-Soviet discussions and dealings about nuclear matters are pre-eminently conducted behind closed doors, there are a number of studies from the Western world which shed some light on this subject.[16] Certainly, India's atomic energy establishments are widely scattered around the subcontinent. There is recent evidence of the continuing importance to India of Indo-Soviet collaboration in this field.

The Chairman of India's Atomic Energy Commission, Dr Raja Ramanna, led a five-member delegation to Moscow in December 1983 to discuss the Soviet offer to set up a giant nuclear power plant in India. He had been sent to Moscow to look into the political, economic and technological aspects of the Soviet offer in the light of India's capacity to absorb and develop two parallel systems, even assuming that the safeguards applicable in both cases would be acceptable to it.

The Tarapur plant (in Maharashtra), built by the United States, uses enriched uranium and natural water for its two reactors, with a total output of 420 MW, while the Rajasthan plant near Kota, based on Canadian designs, is fuelled by natural uranium, which is moderated by heavy water in its two units, with a combined capacity of 440 MW. The Kalpakkam and Narora plants have two standardized reactors, each of 235 MW, fabricated in India, with a capacity of 470 MW in both cases, using the natural uranium and heavy water system.

According to press reports, the Indian atomic delegation led by Dr Ramanna returned much impressed with the technological excellence of the Soviet designs and the operational efficiency of its nuclear power plants. Although the Russians are building giant reactors of 1,000 MW each for some of their own giant power plants, the great majority of the new ones under construction in the Soviet Union and in countries of Eastern Europe will have 440-MW reactors, which currently are being mass-produced at the Tommash complex in the Ukraine at the rate of eight big plants a year.

The original Soviet offer was first made by Mr Kosygin in 1979 to Mr Morarji Desai and repeated by Mr Brezhnev to Mrs Gandhi in 1982, and was for a giant single-reactor power station of 1,000 MW, which would have required an altogether new grid, since the existing one in the country could not cope with it. So the Soviet leaders suggested that India should go in for 440-MW reactors instead of one 1,000-MW unit.

The Indian government has yet to reach a decision as to whether it would be desirable to accept a Soviet offer to help develop a second fuel system, with all the inherent advantages and disadvantages of opting for another fuel-cycle system. The Soviet-built reactors will have to be run with imported enriched uranium which could provoke political complications, as has happened in the case of the Tarapur plant. One view within the atomic establishment is that India should concentrate on standardizing its nuclear-power-plant designs based on natural uranium and light water systems, while another school of thought believes that the Soviet offer should be accepted if Moscow is prepared to assist India in setting up a uranium enrichment facility using the new laser technology that is considerably superior to and cheaper than the centrifuge method developed in the West.

It is essentially a matter for political decision at the highest level whether India should go in for an enrichment plant to become totally self-reliant in fuel supply for the new Soviet-designed nuclear power stations. If such a decision were taken, it would be bound to lead to the charge being made, or heightened, that India is indirectly acquiring the capability to exercise the nuclear option, although it could do the same by using the reprocessing facilities already in existence.

All these aspects will have to be carefully considered, both at the political and at the technical levels, to assess the plus and minus factors of developing simultaneously two different fuel systems, while the long-term goal is to base the country's nuclear power programme on fast-breeder technology, using plutonium fuel instead of enriched uranium. The Indian government will also have to study the implications of the new safeguard obligations, if India purchases enriched uranium and returns spent fuel to the Soviet Union, or establishes its own enrichment facility with Soviet help, leaving the country free to reprocess the spent fuel under agreed conditions.

Apparently it is expected to take at least a year to arrive at a final conclusion as to what terms India should accept from the Soviet Union, after carefully examining its political, economic and technical implications. Apparently, also, the Indian government is in no hurry to arrive at a decision.

The Soviets and South Asia generally

While the Soviet Union has a presence in each of the countries of South Asia (usually with, by local standards, a very sizeable embassy) the very fact of the closeness and durability of Indo-Soviet relations has inhibited and constrained Soviet relations with each of these other countries.[17] Whilst even with Pakistan Soviet policy has not been uniformly hostile and has even been compatible with some economic ties, there can be no doubt that Soviet relations with each of these countries – except India – cooled rapidly and markedly as a result of the Soviet invasion of Afghanistan in December 1979. Sri Lanka and the Maldives are certainly conscious of the USSR as a naval and fishing power. Pakistan mostly, but also Nepal, Bhutan and Bangladesh, are conscious of Soviet military strength and diplomatic reach. The government of Bangladesh has moved recently to lessen the Soviet presence in their country.

Since the mid-1970s the governments of Bangladesh have repeatedly and publicly expressed misgivings about the large Soviet representation in Dhaka. The issue became sharper in June 1981 when two customs officials were seized at Dhaka airport for trying to stop Soviet diplomats removing truckloads of sophisticated electronic equipment brought in by the Soviet airline Aeroflot. Apparently they were trying to take out the cargo without customs clearance. The diplomats were sent home and the equipment returned quietly.

Further evidence of the Bangladeshi government's misgivings about the scale of Soviet representation was provided in November and December 1983, when it formally requested the Russians to close their cultural centre in Dhaka and to reduce their embassy staff 'substantially'. No specific reasons were publicly divulged, and the request was rejected. Within a month the government of Bangladesh ordered the expulsion of between nine and twelve Soviet diplomats and the closure of the Soviet Cultural Centre, with the instruction to comply immediately. The Soviet Embassy was then reported to be the largest in the country, with thirty diplomatic and more than 100 non-diplomatic staff.[18]

Afghanistan[19]

Despite the political costs of its invasion and subsequent occupation of Afghanistan since December 1979 (to be assessed in terms of deteriorating relations with the United States and with the Western world, with China and fairly widely in the Third World), it may well be that overall the Soviet Union will be seen to have made both strategic and economic gains as a consequence of its intervention and occupation. The strategic arguments (which can be made in terms of advancing and improving Soviet air power and access to the Gulf and the Indian Ocean,[20] the relatively low number of Soviet troops now engaged in active combat as distinct from guard and patrol duties and the comparatively low number of mortalities suffered) are by now well known and certainly do not suggest that this is the Soviet Union's 'Vietnam'. The economic aspects are less discussed and are thus worth sketching here.

It should be borne in mind that for all Soviet analysts a decisive change in the history of Afghanistan came not at the end of 1979 but earlier, in April 1978, with the inauguration of the so-called Saur revolution which Western analysts tend to discuss, much too emphatically, as a mere *coup d'état*.

Since the Soviet invasion in December 1979 there has been

mounting evidence that Afghanistan has become more dependent than ever on the USSR. From a value of $34m in 1979 Soviet aid increased to an average of over $250m in the three subsequent years: a substantial proportion was commodity assistance such as petroleum, foodstuffs and textiles. The Russians tend to concentrate their aid either on sectors closely related to their military occupation, such as the plan to link the two countries by rail, or on other projects of direct benefit to the Soviet economy, such as prospecting for energy and minerals, which are then almost entirely exported to the USSR. By early 1983 publicly made promises of Soviet aid to Afghanistan stood at nearly $3,000m, of which more than half had been disbursed by the end of 1982.

Afghanistan does not benefit from any preferential pricing arrangements made by its Soviet 'friend'. The Soviet Union imports 95 per cent of Afghanistan's natural gas at low world market prices. Afghanistan's net earnings from gas exports are in any case notional, as their value is offset against that of her imports and loans from the Soviet Union. The USSR also benefits by reselling Afghan produce (olives, nuts, raisins and honey) at a profit in Eastern Europe.

Deliveries of Soviet arms to the Afghan armed forces (according to IISS and SIPRI sources) were estimated to be worth about £100m in 1980, and direct military aid in 1981 has been assessed at more than £200m, exclusive of the cost of maintaining about 110,000 to 120,000 Soviet troops in the country at any one time. Unlike Cuba or Vietnam, Afghanistan does not receive free Soviet military equipment and the quality tends to be lower. The Afghan army apparently is not trusted with the most modern equipment, not least because of the risk that some of it would pass by theft, sale or gift into the hands of the resistance fighters.

Whatever the future holds for Afghanistan (whether to be 'Mongolia-ized' or 'Finlandized', partitioned, neutralized, maintained in protracted guerrilla warfare or involved in a wider war which engulfs either Pakistan and/or Iran as well) it is clear that this future will be consequential for South Asia, for the Soviet Union, and perhaps for the international system as a whole.

Conclusion

Only two major changes seem likely to be capable of substantially altering the pattern of relationships in Soviet Asia which has been sketched in this chapter. One would stem from the publicly avowed (or at least widely believed) decision of either Pakistan or India to 'go nuclear' in military terms: that is to detonate a nuclear bomb and to go over to regular manufacture and production of nuclear weapons. If this occurred it would no doubt be a factor for considerable perturbation throughout South Asia and the wider world. But it by no means follows that it would severely disturb, still less entirely disrupt, the Indo-Soviet connection which has endured for many years already, despite the fact that formally speaking the Soviet Union is a progenitor and custodian of the Non-Nuclear-Proliferation Treaty (NPT) system and India is a foremost critic and non-signatory. Even so, it is undeniable that the nuclear dimension now hovers over Indo-Pakistani relations as a further complication and threat. Whether this will result in new nuclear arms control measures or a nuclear arms race in South Asia remains to be seen.

Second, and finally, to a considerable extent Indo-Pakistani relations and the foreign and security policies of each of the states of South Asia have been influenced and conditioned by the character of great-power rivalries (their disbursement of arms being but one obtrusive factor), particularly since the early 1960s. For South Asia the Soviet Union, the United States and China have been the principals, and much more obvious as rivals in this region than as collaborators. If there were to be a substantial change in relations between the United States and the Soviet Union or between China and the Soviet Union – which on present indications does not seem probable – then this might lead to some rapid Indian disillusionment with its Soviet connection. Continuities rather than major change have characterized the Soviet involvement in South Asia in recent years, and this situation seems likely to continue.

Notes

1. For a text of this treaty, initially valid for five years, see R.K. Jain (ed.), *Soviet-South Asian Relations 1947–1978* (London: Martin Robertson, 1979), Vol. 1, pp. 206–9, and for a judicious and well-informed review of this extensive selection of documents, see Charles Heimsath, *Journal of Asian Studies*, Vol. 40, No. 2, February 1981, pp. 407–8. I am aware that some people invest Indo-Soviet relations with a much longer pedigree: back to the formal establishment of diplomatic relations and exchange of ambassadors in 1947, or to Nehru's visit in 1927, or to the October Revolution. Bulganin in his address to the Indian Parliament on 21 November 1955 recalled that the Russian traveller, Afanasy Nikitin, visited India and wrote a book that was an outstanding work for the time about the wonderful country in which he had lived for several years and for which he had conceived a warm affection (Jain, *op. cit.*, p. 226). See also the historical introduction (pp. 1–53) to Bimal Prasad, *Indo-Soviet Relations 1947–1972. A Documentary Study* (New Delhi: Allied Publishers, 1973).

2. See *The Times of India*, 25 November 1983, p. 8, based on an APN report from Moscow.

3. Asha L. Datar, *India's Economic Relations with the USSR and Eastern Europe 1953–1969* (Cambridge University Press, 1972).

4. For text see R.K. Jain, *Soviet-South Asian Relations*, pp. 113–16, where the treaty appears under the sub-heading of documents about the 'Bangladesh Crisis and

Indo-Pakistan War of 1971', which indicates some of the differences between the Soviet and Indian readings of the treaty.

5. A. Ladozhsky, 'India: a Path of Peace and Cooperation', *International Affairs* (Moscow), 10 October 1983, p. 28.

6. *Ibid.*, p. 30.

7. See A. Ladozhsky, *op. cit.*, p. 30, and also B. Chekhonin, 'Soviet-Indian Friendship and Co-operation', *International Affairs* (Moscow), 5 May 1982.

8. A. Ladozhsky, *op. cit.*, p. 30.

9. *Ibid.*, p. 31.

10. *Ibid.*, p. 31. Earlier the same author had elaborated on this theme. See A. Ladozhsky, 'USSR-India: To Strengthen Peace', *International Affairs* (Moscow), 12 December 1982, p. 77, which reported that a House of Soviet Science and Culture was opened in Delhi in early 1982 and is intended to help expand scientific and cultural ties between the two countries and acquaint the Indian public better with the Soviet way of life. Regular exhibitions, meetings with Soviet scientists, concerts of Soviet artists and many other events are to be held in this new state cultural temple. According to this Soviet academician, the Soviet Union has already made a noteworthy contribution to the training of India's national personnel; by the end of 1982 it had trained nearly 100,000 specialists.

11. For a perspective view see Biplab Dasgupta, *The Oil Industry in India. Some Economic Aspects* (London: Frank Cass & Co., 1971) and P.D. Henderson, *India. The Energy Sector* (Oxford: Oxford University Press, for the World Bank, 1975).

12. See, e.g., *The Financial Times* (London), 11 May 1983, p. 4.

13. For general discussion see Peter Lyon, 'Strategy and South Asia: twenty-five years on', *International Journal* (CIIA Toronto), Vol. 27, No. 3, Summer 1972, and Peter Lyon, *South Asia in Contemporary Geostrategics* (London: IISS, forthcoming) and SIPRI, *Arms Trade with the Third World* (Stockholm: Almqvist and Wiksell, 1971). See also M. Rajan Menon, 'The Military and Security Dimensions of Soviet-Indian Relations', pp. 232–50 in Robert H. Donaldson (ed.), *The Soviet Union in the Third World: Successes and Failures* (Boulder, Colo.: Westview, 1981).

14. Raju G.C. Thomas, *The Defence of India: A Budgetary Perspective of Strategy and Politics* (Columbia, Missouri: South Asia Books, 1978) and Raju G.C. Thomas, 'The Armed Services and the Indian Defense Budget', *Asian Survey*, Vol. 20, No. 3, March 1980, pp. 280–97. See also IISS and SIPRI data.

15. See various world press reports in June and August 1983. See especially Salamat Ali in *The Far Eastern Economic Review*, 11 August 1983, p. 30.

16. Most notably see Wayne Wilcox, *Nuclear Weapons Options and the Strategic Environment in South Asia* (Southern California Arms Control and Foreign Policy Seminar, June 1971); and K. Subrahmanyam (ed.), *Nuclear Myths and Realities. India's Dilemma* (New Delhi: ABC Publishing House, 1981). See also Ashok Kapur, *India's Nuclear Option: Atomic Diplomacy and Decision-Making* (New York: Praeger, 1976) and Ashok Kapur, *International Nuclear Proliferation. Multilateral Diplomacy and Regional Aspects* (New York: Praeger, 1979), especially Ch. 8, 'South Asia: Nuclear Chains or Intraelite Politics and Creeping Dependences'.

17. There is, so far as I know, still no good study of this subject at all, though aspects of it are treated in the works cited in note 13. See also G.S. Bhargava, *South Asian Security After Afghanistan* (Toronto: Lexington Books, 1983). Analysts of this subject nowadays have to come to terms with incipient South Asian regionalism as well as a variegated and rather volatile set of Soviet presences and capabilities. On the first theme see Peter Robinson, 'Pattern of Economic Cooperation in South Asia', *The Round Table*, No. 287, July 1983, pp. 292–305.

18. See *The Times of India*, 25 December 1983, p. 9.

19. The literature on this subject is voluminous. In my view the best introductory guide is Louis Dupree, *Afghanistan* (Princeton: Oxford University Press, 1980). See also K. Subrahmanyam, 'The Afghan Situation and India's National Interest', *Foreign Affairs Reports*, Vol. 29, No. 8, August 1980 (the author is Director of the Institute of Defence Studies and Analyses, New Delhi); Zalmay Khalilzad, 'Soviet-Occupied Afghanistan', *Problems of Communism*, November–December 1980, pp. 23–40 (the author is an Afghan-born scholar who was educated in the USA and is domiciled there); Henry S. Bradsher, *Afghanistan and the Soviet Union* (Durham, N.C.: Duke University Press, 1983) (the author is an experienced American journalist who has long specialized in Soviet affairs); *The International Herald Tribune* for 6 November 1983, which summarizes the assessments of Yossef Bodansky, an Israeli expert on the Soviet military, regarding Russia in Afghanistan; and Fred Halliday, *Afghanistan. The Threat from the East* (Harmondsworth: Penguin, 1981).

20. In the past ten years the literature on this subject has become extensive, whereas before about 1970 very little indeed of note had been written about the Indian Ocean. The most recent general work of note known to me is by Dieter Braun, *The Indian Ocean. Region of Conflict or 'Peace Zone'?* (London: C. Hurst & Co., 1983). See especially pp. 47–67 on the Soviet Union, which include a useful but not comprehensive bibliography. Larry W. Bowman and Ian Clark (eds.), *The Indian Ocean in Global Politics* (Boulder, Colo.: Westview, 1981) has some useful essays, especially Ian Clark's 'Soviet Arms Supplies and Indian Ocean Diplomacy' pp. 147–71. The CIA's *Indian Ocean Atlas* (Washington, DC, 1976) has sections on resources, oil and trade up to the mid-1970s.

Two recent Soviet essays are A. Chicharov, *Indian Ocean: Some Changes of the Structure of International Relations (at the end of the Seventies and beginning of the Eighties)* (paper presented at the 12th World Congress of the International Political Science Association, Rio de Janeiro, August 1982) (Moscow: Nauka Publishing House, Central Department of Oriental Literature, 1982) and D. Nikolayev, 'For Peace and Security in the Indian Ocean', *International Affairs* (Moscow), 9 September 1982, pp. 57–64.

Two recent, and contrasting, Indian analyses are K.P. Misra, *Quest for an International Order in the Indian Ocean* (New Delhi: Allied Publishers, 1977) and S.N. Kohli, *Sea Power and the Indian Ocean, with special reference to India* (Bombay: Tata McGraw-Hill, 1978). The latter author is a retired Indian Admiral, who commanded the Indian fleet from 1967 to 1969 and was in overall command of the western fleet during the Indo-Pakistan conflict of 1971. He was India's Chief of Naval Staff from 1973 to 1976.

4

Eastern Europe and the Middle East: the forgotten dimension of Soviet policy

Christopher Coker

Since 1973 the East Europeans have voiced their misgivings about Western political initiatives in the Middle East more often and more openly. They have become more sensitive to Western policies, more alert to Arab opinion. The patently unilateralist policies which the United States has pursued since the Geneva Conference (1973–4) and in which Western Europe has tacitly though not always enthusiastically concurred have added to Eastern Europe's concern about the future of the Middle East. That concern has been expressed in a political language which is authentically East European. And yet when it comes to interpreting these overtly political statements we are often reluctant to admit that the East Europeans are independent agents, or that their economic interests in the region are real.

East European comments about recent developments reflect fears and aspirations similar in many respects to those expressed in the West. Take, for example, Bulgaria's condemnation of the Camp David settlement which prompted it to break off diplomatic relations with Anwar el Sadat in December 1978. In a speech a few years later Todor Zhivkov, its head of state, assured Libya, one of Sadat's most critical Arab neighbours, that Eastern Europe would continue to support the struggle of the Rejection Front against 'the plots of imperialism, Zionism and reaction', the last three terms being thinly disguised euphemisms for American, Israeli and Egyptian policies.

Echoing these sentiments Radio Prague accused the Camp David accords of being no more than an 'anti-Soviet alliance and an American military pact in the Middle East'.[1] The Slovak Communist Party newspaper *Pravda* claimed that Washington was obsessed with the idea of 'establishing a bastion' in the strategically important oil-rich Middle East.[2] The following month Radio Prague warned that following the treaty between Israel and Egypt the Eisenhower doctrine had, to all intents and purposes, been revived.[3]

These claims should not be dismissed as mere propaganda. They have been voiced by many Arab countries as well. More importantly, they reflect very real concern that the situation in the Middle East, certainly in the Fertile Crescent, has been shaped by a country whose interests conflict with those of Eastern Europe. The Middle-East, like southern Africa, reflects a peculiar looking-glass world in which both the Soviet and the Western alliance systems have come to see each other as a threat, each threat being a reflection of the other.[4]

In recent years the threat has extended beyond the Arab-Israeli conflict to the Straits of Hormuz. During a visit to Kuwait in October 1982, Hungary's head of state, defending the right of the Gulf states 'to maintain their own security to the exclusion of foreign powers', condemned imperialist attempts to place the region and its oilfields under foreign hegemony, a veiled reference to the ever-increasing American military presence.[5]

In the past it used to be true that Romania expressed much less concern than its allies about American intervention in the Middle East. Those differences were real, as was made clear in 1979 during talks between the Romanian Foreign Minister Stefan Andrei and his East German counterpart Oskar Fischer.[6] But one should not make too much of them. Romania is more interested than ever in maintaining good relations with Arab countries, especially the oil producers, so as not to lose its *main* source of oil imports. It has good cause to be; the Middle East is its *primary* market.

Romania is not alone in suffering from the cancellation of oil contracts with Iran after the revolution (1979–81), and the shortfall in Iraqi sales following Iraq's war with Iran. The Iranian revolution occasioned a crisis in its oil-refining industry which drastically reduced the differential between what it paid for its oil and what it received from the sale of its oil products. By 1982, 35 per cent of its oil-refining capacity lay idle.[7]

Although Romania continues to be the Warsaw Pact's odd man out, accepting the Camp David accords (March 1979) and the Reagan Plan as steps in a process leading to 'a global, just and durable Middle East settlement', it has always insisted that such a settlement must include the Soviet Union. It would not be to Romania's advantage for the regional order in the Middle East to be determined by the NATO powers, whose priorities, in the event of another crisis in which oil supplies were to be embargoed, might differ considerably from its own.

Indeed, it is interesting that the actual terms advocated by

Bucharest for a comprehensive political settlement have in recent years grown gradually closer to those advocated by Moscow: that Israel should withdraw from the occupied territories; that it should accept the creation of an independent Palestinian state, with the PLO as the sole representative of the Palestinian people; and that such a settlement should be reached within the framework of an international conference, possibly under UN auspices, with the participation of all interested parties including the Soviet Union.

The last time these terms were discussed by the Soviet Union and Egypt was during the Fahmi-Gromyko talks of 1977. Since then the Soviet Union, to all intents and purposes, has been excluded from the Middle East to its own discomfort and that of its closest allies. The East Europeans cannot be happy that, at a time when their own oil purchases from the Middle East have grown so substantially, their principal patron has had little, if any, role to play in shaping the security of the region. Many Americans themselves were doubtful of the wisdom of the Camp David agreement precisely because it took little account of the fact that the Soviet Union and its allies had very real interests in the regional order, interests which were in no way served by the unilateral diplomacy of the past ten years.[8]

It would, in short, be foolish to ignore that Eastern Europe has become increasingly preoccupied with the security of supplies in the Middle East since 1974, a fact which must be an ingredient in Soviet policy if only because its own failure to supply its allies with all their oil needs has compelled them to look outside the socialist world. (See Tables 4.1–4.4, pp. 63–4, for some statistics on the energy economy.) The competition between Eastern Europe and the West has become more direct recently and potentially more disruptive both in terms of its impact on regional stability and its implications for superpower relations.[9]

The impact of two crises (1973–9)

The first round of OPEC oil price rises in 1973–4 elicited very little in the way of an immediate response from the East Europeans. Czechoslovakia made some half-hearted attempts to respond to soaring oil prices in the West by exploring the possibility of oil purchases from the Arab world, and by raising the price of petrol in March 1974. But underlying the government's economic philosophy was a deep-seated belief that an energy problem, let alone an energy crisis, could not happen in Czechoslovakia.

In January 1974 its permanent representative to the CMEA said that no shortage of oil or natural gas threatened his country, and that the oil crisis in the West would have very little overall impact in

Eastern Europe. Michael Sabolcik, the Minister in charge of the Federal Price Office, stated: 'Crisis phenomena of this nature, which could lead to a similar critical situation in our country as they have done in the capitalist world, find no reflection in the socialist community.'[10] Even after the Soviet Union raised the price of its own oil deliveries in 1975 in response to the OPEC increase and warned that deliveries would have to be fixed at a ceiling quite soon, thus necessitating oil purchases from the Middle East, the general mood remained one of optimism. The Czech Five-Year Plan (1976–80) envisaged high growth in the economy with commensurately high energy consumption.

When the second round of oil price increases hit the world six years later (1979–80), the East Europeans were much less sanguine. In Ceausescu's report on the Seventh Five-Year Plan (1981–5) the world energy crisis figured prominently.[11] Romania's Long-Term Energy Programme looked forward to coal replacing oil as the country's principal energy constituent (40 per cent of total production),[12] and Ceausescu himself stressed the need to restructure industry more radically to ensure that coal would account for no less than 60 per cent of energy production.

Poland, already in the grip of an economic crisis that was soon to threaten the survival of the Communist Party itself, criticized OPEC for dishonesty in its price-setting procedures, a note very different from that struck in 1974: 'They say that the main reason for it is the shortage of oil. This is not so. In fact there is now a demand-supply balance ... [OPEC] has become a cartel of dependence on which hangs to a greater or lesser degree, the prosperity of the whole world.'[13] By 1979, not only Poland, but most East European countries, had become increasingly dependent on the world oil market at a time of rapidly rising world market prices. Eastern Europe was still importing 100,000 barrels a day from Iraq and Iran in 1981. It was hardly surprising, therefore, that its interest in the Middle East should have grown accordingly.

The energy crisis in Eastern Europe
The decline in the growth of Soviet energy supplies to Eastern Europe began in the mid-1970s and has accelerated ever since. In the case of oil the rate of growth of Soviet supplies decreased from 9.5 per cent between 1971 and 1975, to 4.5 per cent in the period 1976–80.[14]

Like many forecasts of Soviet production, the worst-case predictions of institutions such as the CIA were not realized in the 1970s. The CIA's forecast that Soviet oil production would peak in 1978 and that the fall-off would be sharp did not come true.[15] The Soviet

Union, nevertheless, was forced to reduce quite substantially its subsidized oil exports to CMEA's European members. The production goals set for the end of the Tenth Five-Year Plan (1976–81) were later revised as costs escalated and produced ever diminishing returns. Expenditure per rouble of the marketed output of oil rose by 14 per cent between 1969 and 1975. Outlays for fuel in general rose by another 7 per cent between 1976 and 1979, a much greater increase than the cost increases in the economy as a whole. By 1975, it was already clear that diminishing returns in resource extraction would become more, not less, pronounced and that none of the ways most discussed for halting the increase in costs would work for very long.[16]

Falling rates in the growth of production forced the Soviet Union to increase the intra-CMEA price of oil and to revise the terms of its implicit subsidies. Given the fourfold increase in the world market price of crude oil, as well as large increases in the world market prices of other key raw materials, it is not surprising that the Soviet Union pressed the CMEA into accepting a new price-setting formula in 1975. Prior to that year the price of oil had been held constant during five-year periods and had been based on the average of world market prices during the preceding five years. In 1975 the Russians more than doubled the price of their oil exports to Eastern Europe much to the dismay of their allies.

The OPEC price rises, of course, provided the ideal occasion for the Soviet Union to implement policies it had long wished to pursue. The cost to Moscow of supplying oil well below the market price had been rising steeply for some years. The Soviet Union had paid for grossly overpriced East European goods with grossly underpriced raw materials. Even though the East Europeans resented the 1975 price increases, they still saved foreign exchange by buying within the bloc rather than on the open market. What they continued to save, the Russians continued to lose. These implicit subsidies cost the latter $5.8bn* per annum between 1975 and 1978; even after the price was revised upwards again in 1979 the Soviet Union found itself subsidizing its CMEA partners to the tune of $15.1bn (at 1982 figures) a year.[17]

The extent to which the Soviet Union continued to subsidize sales to Eastern Europe met with little thanks within the CMEA. After 1975 the East Europeans repeatedly argued in favour of a formula for the 'world market price' that would have been much lower than the market for OPEC prices on which the Bucharest formula was based (1975). Their concern reflected, of course, the extent to which the Soviet subsidy had begun to fall. The implicit discount

---

* In this chapter the term 'billion' refers to the US thousand million (10^9).

given by the Soviet Union amounted to 60 per cent of the OPEC price in 1975 but to only 25 per cent three years later. After a brief recovery it dropped to 20 per cent in 1983.[18]

As the intra-CMEA price-setting formula gradually began to reflect the near tripling of world oil prices in the years 1979–81, the situation grew progressively more serious. But, forewarned of the shortfall in oil deliveries by the Soviet Union, the CMEA had already begun to look to the Middle East shortly before the 1973 Arab-Israeli war.

Eastern Europe and the Middle East

Since the early 1970s economic planners and policy makers in Eastern Europe have been attempting to formulate energy policies which would facilitate the adjustment of their economies to increasingly evident energy-supply constraints and to rapidly rising world market prices. The policies which ultimately emerged included increased purchases from the Middle East – principally, though not exclusively, from Iraq and Iran. Most East European governments were strongly influenced at the time by the assumption that following the 1973–4 price rises world energy prices would remain stable at the new higher level, and that energy production in the Gulf would continue at present levels, or beyond. Neither the second round of price increases, in 1979–80, nor the political developments that unseated the Shah and precipitated a war between Eastern Europe's two principal suppliers could have been, or were, foreseen.

Poland

Poland was not typical of most East European countries because of its severe economic crisis and the political crisis it precipitated at the end of the 1970s. Even the trend of falling Soviet oil imports affected it much less than its neighbours. Throughout the 1970s it purchased 80 per cent of its crude oil from the Soviet Union (16.6m tons*) at prices 25 per cent lower than those on the free market. Nevertheless, between 1975 and 1978 oil imports rose by only 22.3 per cent, compared with their cost, which went up by 69.2 per cent.

Faced with this rise in prices, most economic forecasts in 1978 predicted that if the economy continued to grow at the same rate Poland would need 20m tons of crude oil a year by 1980, and possibly as much as 35m ten years after that.[19] Although the economic crisis had clearly set in when these forecasts were devised, a fact patently obvious to all but the forecasters themselves, the need for Arab oil did not diminish in relative terms, even if its

---

*Long and metric tons (tonnes) are referred to as 'ton'; US short ton is not used.

absolute value may have declined. The investment downturn which began in 1976 and the resulting slowdown in economic activity, with its concomitant lower energy inputs, combined with the near doubling of open market oil prices in 1979–81, may have made the forecasted targets unrealistic, but they did not lead to a substantial lessening of the country's need for imports from outside the socialist bloc. In 1980, as the political and economic crisis came to a head, Poland faced the prospect of importing from the Middle East up to 13m tons of crude oil per year at a cost of at least $1.5m per annum, and possibly a good deal more.[20] As the Polish economist Henryk Chadzynski admitted, 'In view of the limited possibilities of increasing oil exports from the Soviet Union any additional crude oil to cover the CMEA's total growth in demand will have to be purchased with hard currency outside the bloc.'[21]

The crisis in the Polish economy coincided unhappily with the Iraqi–Iranian war in the Gulf. Since 1977, in preparation for increased Middle East imports, the government had pursued an active policy towards the Shah. His fall from power eighteen months later forced Warsaw to look elsewhere, notably to Libya. Libya made up for the loss of Iranian oil in 1979–80, though its own need for foreign exchange made Colonel Qaddafi less than eager to sign a long-term oil delivery contract with Poland for the delivery of as much as 4.5m tons within the next ten years.[22] Indeed, in 1979 Libya delivered less oil than Poland actually requested. So far Poland has not found a full-time supplier. During Qaddafi's visit to Poland in September 1982 General Jaruzelski offered to make available Poland's substantial spare industrial capacity in exchange for oil. Even this offer does not appear to have been sufficiently enticing to have changed Qaddafi's mind.

Hungary

By 1980 Hungary was buying 8m tons of crude oil per annum from the Soviet Union. It needed, however, a further 8m tons, only 2m of which it could find from its own domestic sources. For some years the country's *per capita* energy consumption had exceeded the world average. In the past five years its energy consumption has been growing at an annual rate of 4 per cent.

Hungary began importing oil from the Middle East in 1971 to meet the difference between its own needs and Soviet imports. In that year Iraq represented its seventh largest trading partner in Asia. Some 300,000 tons of oil were delivered in 1973–5; this had risen to 1m tons at the end of the 1970s.[23]

Like Poland, Hungary has met with difficulties in recent years, which are due only in part to the Iraqi-Iranian war. Since the second price rise, oil has become, in the official vernacular, a 'scarce material' with a 'prohibitive price'. Hungary has also been forced to contend with a quota for Soviet oil (7.5m tons) which was fixed at the CMEA price in 1981. The Soviet Union is prepared to sell more but only at the OPEC price. The excess must be paid for either in hard currency or in 'convertible' goods (mostly wheat). The worsening of the terms of trade in both the rouble and the non-rouble areas has been a nightmare for the economic planners. According to Hungary's deputy Prime Minister, Gyorgy Aczel, it has inflicted greater damage on the economy than did World War II.[24]

Czechoslovakia

In view of Czechoslovakia's sanguine response to the first OPEC price rise, it is somewhat ironic to find that the country has suffered more than any other in recent years from high energy costs. Since 1979 the price of Soviet oil has risen by almost 50 per cent, a heavy burden for a country whose payments for oil deliveries already represent over 30 per cent of the total value of Soviet imports and 31 per cent of the total value of Czech exports to the Soviet Union. The Czech economy had to pay five times more for its oil in 1980 than it had ten years previously.[25] The imported volume may have doubled, but the cost has grown nearly tenfold. That the cost would have been higher still if the oil had come from non-socialist suppliers is an indisputable fact, but no consolation to its economic planners.[26]

The Czechs began importing oil from Iran before the 1973 crisis. Czechoslovakia's hopes that Iran would supply a third of its oil needs by the end of the 1980s – a much larger percentage than would have been the case for any other CMEA member – were dashed by the fall of the Shah.[27]

Before the Iranian revolution Czechoslovakia was preparing to import a substantial percentage of fuel from outside the socialist bloc, putting itself at risk in the highly volatile situation that the Middle East had become in the early 1970s. After the revolution the loss of supplies forced a major revision in its fuel consumption for the 1970s – the first case where this was true for an East European country. Its Sixth Five-Year Plan (1976–80) had reckoned on oil imports of 26m tons by 1980, the difference between Czech demands and Soviet supplies being covered by purchases abroad. The price increases of 1979, however, coupled with the grave uncertainty of Iranian production, reconciled the Czech government to substantially lower fuel imports and a marginally lower rate of growth.[28]

German Democratic Republic (GDR)
The GDR has benefited from being the Soviet Union's closest ally in Eastern Europe, with a privileged agreement to import oil above and beyond its annual quota. As late as 1978 as much as 93 per cent of its oil was imported from the Soviet Union. What supplies the GDR imported from the Middle East in the 1970s were purchased very largely from Iraq and Iran. Trade with Iraq increased by more than 600 per cent between 1973 and 1979, making Iraq its largest trading partner in the Third World. Two-thirds of that trade consisted of oil deliveries which were interrupted in the first year of the 1981–5 Five-Year Plan, the first to take specific account of the fact that Soviet supplies had permanently levelled off at 19m tons.

Even the GDR has been forced to look to outside suppliers. In February 1980 it expressed an interest in importing Angolan oil to make up for the exported Soviet supply shortfall over the next five years (projected for 5m tons by 1985). Its interest in a country which, though Marxist by conviction, has hitherto sold almost all its oil to the West (primarily, though not exclusively, to the United States), provides an interesting comment on the impact of the Iranian revolution and the Gulf war.

Bulgaria
As for most other CMEA members, oil imports have become a markedly more important constituent of Bulgaria's import bill in recent years. By 1974 the greatest share of imported commodities from the Middle East was already accounted for by crude oil (55 per cent compared with only 18 per cent in 1960). Trade with the Middle East accounted for as much as 45 per cent of Bulgaria's exchange of goods with the developing world.[29] By 1973 its interest in the Middle East was already substantial.

The first known deliveries of Iraqi crude oil were made in 1972; in 1977 they were 50 per cent up on 1976,[30] a development that would have been confirmed following an agreement signed between the two countries in April 1980 but for the interruption of the Gulf war.

Imports from Bulgaria's other major source, Libya, are less easy to verify. Non-Bulgarian authorities claim that the country imported up to 1m tons between 1972 and 1975; Sofia itself claims only 200,000 tons per annum.[31] The country's keen interest in Libya is less in doubt. Through geological surveys it has discovered reserves which have been developed with Japanese assistance.[32] Libya remains, of course, an unpredictable and unreliable trading partner that seems quite prepared to disappoint East European expectations. Poland was one such disappointed party in 1981; but shipments to the GDR were also interrupted in 1978, and then resumed for no apparent reason.

Romania
Until recently Middle East oil formed the major part of Romania's oil imports. In 1977, the last year of uninterrupted supply, Iran supplied Romania with 5m tons out of a total import bill of 8.8m tons.

Like many other East European countries, Romania looked to Libya and Iraq as its principal overseas suppliers of oil. It began to discuss oil deliveries from Libya back in 1972, but it was only in 1976 that it agreed to buy 1.5m tons of oil per year subject to annual review. This trade was paid for in convertible currencies, a practice codified in an agreement signed in 1979.

In recent years oil imports have been increasingly responsible for the deficits in Romania's foreign account. As its domestic oil industry has gone into decline, imports from the Middle East have been supplemented, for the first time, by imports from the Soviet Union (1979). In 1981 the production of crude oil reached 11.6m tons, only 100,000 tons more than the previous year, and actually 1m tons less than was anticipated in the 1981–5 Plan. July 1982 saw massive increases in Romania's energy bill – of between 7 per cent and 10 per cent liquid fuels. The restructuring of prices was one of the main conditions of the extension of IMF credits. In the negotiations Romania was forced to acknowledge that its trade deficit was largely due to its increasing dependence on imported energy. Only a fraction of Romania's trade with the Third World is represented by oil imports, but the trade imbalance in oil deliveries is large. The difference between imports of oil and exports of manufactured goods to its oil suppliers (including those that were not developing countries) is now as high as 53 per cent.[33]

When Romania first began buying Soviet oil in the early 1980s it had to pay the OPEC price. Since then it has complained that Soviet oil purchases are actually *more* expensive then those on the open market. Romania is not the only country to have discovered that in certain years Soviet prices are actually higher than those on the open market. The Soviet Union had increased its prices for oil well above what the Bucharest formula allowed by the early 1980s, even when taking into account changes over the year in rouble and dollar exchange rates.[34] The difference between the world and the CMEA price for oil had shrunk so much by 1979 that some CMEA countries found themselves paying more than the current world price for Soviet oil until the renewed OPEC increases once again widened the gap.[35]

More recently, a former Romanian ambassador to Moscow, Gheorghe Badrus, blamed some of the CMEA's difficulties on its own pricing system, which had failed to take account of the *drop* in OPEC prices in 1982.[36] Romania officially raised the question at a

CMEA Executive Committee meeting in January 1983 and then at a meeting in Kiev of the Council's Committee for Cooperation in Technical and Material Supply. On both occasions the Romanian delegation warned that if the system were not revised soon, other East European countries might be forced to increase their purchases from the Middle East, despite their chronic indebtedness and shortage of hard currency reserves.[37]

Future developments

At the moment there seems no likelihood that Eastern Europe will be able to reduce its purchases from the Middle East; indeed these are likely to increase substantially over the next ten years. One reason for this is that energy consumption grew rapidly in the 1970s – at a faster rate than domestic energy production. Poland is the only country in the region which remains a net energy exporter (coal), Romania having lost this status in 1975.

In the 1970s, the consumption of liquid fuels increased at a considerably faster rate than the consumption of solid fuels. Technological imperatives played an important role in this development. A major element of economic policy in these years was the purchase of Western technology which, for the most part, required the direct consumption of energy, as opposed to its indirect use in the form of electricity. Much of the technology was designed to consume liquid rather than solid fuels.

In addition, the decision to import Western technology was taken at a time when capital investment declined quite substantially in Western Europe largely as a result of the OPEC price increases. As Cam Hudson writes: 'It is not unreasonable to suppose that East European purchases of Western technology consisted largely of machinery, equipment, and know-how which was difficult to sell in the West either because of its energy-intensive character or because it required the use of an energy resource (i.e. oil) which had suddenly increased in price.[38] It is also not unreasonable to assume that the CMEA economies will continue to be 'locked' into an energy mix which has a high proportion of liquid fuels. As these are the energy resources which are both increasingly expensive on world markets and relatively scarce in Eastern Europe, this is likely to magnify the dimensions of the energy crisis which now faces the Soviet bloc.

Attempts to reduce national consumption are also unlikely to succeed. The Czechs have been worried for some time about the ratio of annual energy consumption to the growth rate of their national income. In order to reduce energy consumption to 0.5 (or 0.65):1.0 the Czechoslovak economy would need to consume 12.5m tons less fuel than it did in 1980.[39] Such a huge saving in energy costs can be achieved only by shifting the emphasis from huge investment projects demanding high energy inputs to greater productivity.

The problem is that high rates of material consumption – 30-40 per cent above those in the West – have squeezed down productivity increases. Moreover, it is the energy-saving branches of the economy which require major investments, mainly by way of imports of Western technology (an irony which has not escaped some East European economists,)[40] at a time when foreign exchange reserves are low, and future prospects of trade surpluses in hard-currency markets remain bleak, to say the least.

The high rates of energy consumption raise another question. By providing cheap fuel imports, the Soviet Union has encouraged wastefulness on the part of its East European partners. Eastern Europe consumes at least twice as much energy per unit of GNP than does the West. A comparison on an industry-by-industry basis reveals that energy consumption per unit of output typically runs 50–150 per cent higher.[41]

This lack of competitiveness is unlikely to be redressed in the short term. It is true that the economical use of crude oil and oil derivatives has been given absolute priority in an effort to reduce foreign trade deficits. The saving on hydrocarbons and their substitution by alternative energy sources (mainly coal) is currently the centrepiece of economic planning.

But energy consumption per unit of *per capita* GDP in Eastern Europe shows no signs of coming down to the Western level. The main explanation for the high disparity is an excessive energy intensity in industrial production. By contrast, the consumption of energy for non-productive purposes, including private use, is much lower than it is in Western Europe. Experience in the West, unfortunately, suggests that private consumption is far easier to bring down than is industrial consumption, a fact which in Eastern Europe's case will almost certainly be compounded by the inflexibilities of central planning.[42]

The problem Eastern Europe faces is that its energy conservation measures are designed to restructure the *composition* of energy consumption, not to reduce overall levels. Policies designed to change the dependence of the Eastern European economies on expensive energy resources to dependence on relatively less expensive resources are bound to have only limited impact in the short term because of technological constraints. Even in the long run the distorted price system within the CMEA will make it difficult for enterprise management and economic planners to determine the relative prices of various energy resources and thus difficult to determine which technology is most appropriate from the specific viewpoint of energy rationalization.[43]

There is one further factor that needs to be considered. The Soviet Union may be willing to increase its oil exports at world market prices, or in exchange for joint investments, or even to forgo sales of oil on the open market in order to maintain its implicit subsidies at their current level. But the little evidence we have suggests that the Soviet domestic oil industry will not be as favourably placed as it was in the 1970s to reverse the present trend. At the CMEA's 34th sessional meeting in 1980, the East Europeans were told that supplies until 1985 would remain at the 1980 level. This would have represented a mean increase of 20 per cent by comparison with the period 1976–80. Even this level, however, was not maintained. At the end of 1981 the Russians warned their partners that oil supplies would fall by at least 10 per cent in the coming year.[44] The CMEA's most recent experience provides no grounds for optimism.

The exchange of energy between the Soviet Union and its allies may – in the words of one member of the Hungarian Central Committee – be 'a natural geographic phenomenon'; and its further reduction an 'unnatural process',[45] but it will be maintained at a level sufficient to *reduce* oil imports from outside the socialist bloc only if the Soviet Union is prepared to provide low-cost rouble trade credits, if not outright rouble grants: in short, to recycle petro-roubles in the same way that the OPEC countries recycled their petrodollars in the 1970s. In order to prevent its European partners from falling into massive indebtedness the Soviet Union would have to write off most of its subsidies. And this must raise the question whether it would really be prepared to provide genuine financial aid.[46]

What all this suggests is that Eastern Europe is likely to remain dependent on oil imports from the Middle East for many years yet, possibly indefinitely, and certainly to a much larger extent than was previously thought. It suggests also that the East Europeans are likely to become increasingly interested in the future of the Middle East, having suffered particularly badly from events which they had little role in shaping.

In recognising that like the West it is dependent on the purchase of oil from the Middle East, though to be sure its own dependence is far less significant, Eastern Europe, and by extension the Soviet Union, are likely to be far less tolerant of their exclusion from the region than they have been hitherto. Indeed, one Hungarian economist has drawn attention to three factors that the East

Europeans have already had to take into account when looking at non-CMEA sources of supply.[47]

1. They have found themselves in *increasing* competition with the multinational companies, which already command strong positions in key branches of the oil industry. They have become increasingly concerned at the declining trend in the proportion of intercompany trade and especially of free-market sales. It has not escaped their notice that 75 per cent of international trade in fuels is currently transacted in closed markets (within the framework of intracompany turnover and long-term supply contracts). Such closed markets obviously represent a threat to CMEA access, and may well encourage some countries, notably the GDR, to embark on political initiatives in an attempt to circumvent what they may see as a very real economic threat.

2. The East Europeans are also concerned at the number of long-term contracts with Middle East countries that are being drawn up by Western companies, sometimes twenty years in duration, with the prospect of twenty-five-year contracts in the near future. Libya's patent unwillingness to commit itself to *any* long-term contracts with CMEA members, and Romania's patent failure to persuade the UAE to enter into a binding agreement despite ten years of negotiations, contrast rather worryingly with the recent success of many large Western oil companies.

3. The most worrying factor of all is that Western Europe's concern for the security of oil supplies, which dates from 1973, actually mirrors similar concerns in Eastern Europe. The East Europeans, too, need stable, long-term contracts with major Arab oil producers. The consequences of instability for a country like the GDR were shown all too clearly in the winter of 1979, when after the cancellation of its barter agreement with the Shah it experienced serious oil shortages which forced it to purchase oil on the very expensive Rotterdam spot market.[48] Unfortunately, their needs are precisely parallel to the requirements of all other oil-consuming nations, whose ability to pay in hard currency puts them at a clear comparative advantage even with states such as East Germany with a relatively high level of technology.

Conclusion

Eastern Europe's problems in the Middle East should not be seen in isolation. Oil has not been the only commodity within the CMEA trading system which has begun to fail. Despite the existence of vast raw material reserves in the Soviet Union their commercial viability began to look doubtful by the end of the 1960s, when the Soviet economy began to encounter problems in meeting both domestic demand and the CMEA quotas. This development prompted its East European partners to look to southern Africa for the first time.

Although investment in the Soviet mineral industry has been consistently higher than investment in the developing world, this concentration of capital has fuelled a substantial rise in real costs as the frontiers of expansion have shifted at an accelerating pace to marginal fields. The CMEA is now faced with the real possibility, not of short-term shortages of the type which confront the Western economies as a result of cyclical factors (such as unexpected international crises or protracted strikes), but of long-term supply shortages which are the result of a *structural* deficit, a problem which is much more difficult to live with. In the past there have been shortages of a number of important commodities in the CMEA, most notably aluminium and coking coal, of which there has been an oversupply on the world market. The increasing difficulty of obtaining supplies from the Soviet Union, coupled with limited hard-currency purchasing power in world markets, looks set to create a sustained regional disequilibrium between demand and supply.[49]

Even the existing supply of minerals is beginning to prove, if not prohibitively expensive, more expensive than ever. The Soviet Union continues to sell its trading partners natural resources at a much higher price than its manufactured goods. Between 1975 and 1977 the export prices of raw materials rose at a much faster rate than the export prices of machinery and consumer goods.[50]

The first factor in common, then, between Eastern Europe's interest in southern Africa and the Middle East was a similar need to look outside the socialist community to supplement existing and future demand for fuel and non-fuel resources. The second was the critical period 1973–4. For what changed in southern Africa at this time was the political order in the region following the collapse of the Portuguese empire and the emergence of what appeared to be 'authentic' Marxist-Leninist regimes in Mozambique and Angola. This development was particularly welcomed by countries such as East Germany which had invested much money and effort in supporting national liberation movements in the 1960s in the hope of gaining preferential access to the raw material resources of southern Africa.[51]

After 1974 every East European country, with the single exception of Czechoslovakia, concluded interparty agreements with

Frelimo in Mozambique and the MPLA in Angola. The GDR was in the forefront of these developments, in part because the cost of developing its own coal reserves had risen by at least 50 per cent between 1973 and 1978.[52] East Germany played a central role in the nationalization of Mozambique's largest coalfields in Moatize. Four years later (1982) it joined the Soviet Union in a tripartite agreement on coal and tantalite exploration.

Unfortunately, the East Europeans have found that political developments in Africa are as unpredictable as those in the Middle East, and that the Soviet Union has played an even more marginal role in shaping them. Back in 1977 attempts to pump out the Chipanga 7 coal-mine in Moatize following an instance of severe flooding were hampered by persistent Rhodesian raids on the railway line, which in turn stopped the import of diesel fuel for the pumps.[53] Five years later the East Germans stood by helplessly as attacks by anti-Frelimo guerrillas brought to a halt the renovation of the Condo-Derunde railway, causing a bottleneck on the line to the Moatize fields where more than a year's production was already stockpiled.[54]

But, perhaps most important of all, the similarities between the two regions is that the East Europeans face similar threats from Western business. Indeed the competition for finite resources may even be more real. There is, in fact, a remarkable similarity in the composition of Africa's trade with both the CMEA and the European Community (EEC). Raw materials are exchanged for manufactured goods. Trade is largely concentrated on a few 'sub-imperial' states. African-CMEA relations are no closer to those of the New International Economic Order than are those between Africa and the EEC. Both are compatible with the traditional picture of economic exploitation.[55]

The situation for the East Europeans is particularly worrying because the high oligopolistic pattern of the past – the high level of company concentration on the supply side – is actually increasing, not diminishing. In the 1960s fewer than ten companies were responsible for producing 60 per cent of the non-socialist world's output of all minerals. Nationalization and state control may have reversed that trend, but it has done very little to reverse the trend of vertical integration. The quest for greater security of supply has produced two notable changes in the marketing of minerals: an increase in long-term supply contracts and a declining share of free-market sales in the trading of some major commodities. The proportion of free-market sales in the trade in non-ferrous metals, for example, is now only 10–15 per cent.

In short, in southern Africa as in the Middle East, Eastern

Europe has found itself more disadvantaged than in the past by multinational corporations commanding strong positions in key branches of the extractive industry. Closed markets obviously represent a threat to those countries outside the Western economic orbit, notably the GDR and Czechoslovakia, who have already embarked on political initiatives to circumvent economic constraints imposed by the Western powers.

Most serious of all, however, is the fact that even if the East Europeans were able to negotiate *secure access* to Arab or African producers by paying higher prices in hard currency, like the West they would risk suffering the *same* economic dislocations, with all their political implications.

It is precisely for this reason that they may have to rely on Soviet diplomacy to challenge the West's predominant position. In the Soviet Union they have an ally that has first-hand experience of the vagaries of Middle East politics. In this respect, the Middle East is unique. At the beginning of the 1980s the Soviet Union suffered more severly than any other country from the abrupt termination of natural gas supplies from Iran. Unlike the OPEC embargo of 1973, the cut-off was permanent.

TABLE 4.1
A projected development of Soviet oil production, consumption and
exports (million tons)

	1973	1980	1990[a]
Production	432	602	645
Consumption	328	443	513
Exports	117	160	132
to Eastern Europe[b]	55(47%)	70(44%)	80(61%)
to Western Europe[b]	48(41%)	66(41%)	25(19%)

[a] Estimate of the Secretariat of the Economic Commission for Europe.
[b] Figures in parentheses represent the shares in total exports.
Source: United Nations Economic Commission for Europe (UNECE), 'The Energy
Economy of Europe and North America: Prospects for 1990', in *Economic Bulletin
for Europe*, June 1981, p. 233.

TABLE 4.2
Estimated price of Soviet oil in Eastern Europe

Year	1 Estimated world market price[a]		2 Estimated price of Soviet crude oil in Eastern Europe	Column 2 as a percentage of Column 1
	$ per barrel	$ per metric ton	$ per metric ton	
1975	10.72	78 26	27.96	35.7
1976	11.60	84.68	41.13	48.6
1977	12.92	94.32	55.10	58.4
1978	12.98	94.75	70.70	74.6
1979	18.67	136.29	85.18	62.5
1980	31.00	226.30	97.66	43.2
1981	34.60	252.60	127.27	50.4
1982	33.30[b]	243.10[b]	160.85	66.2
1983	?	?	190.61	—

[a] Average OPEC price as reported by Wharton Econometric Forecasting Associates.
[b] Estimate.
Source: As in Table 4.1.

TABLE 4.3
Possible developments in the price of Soviet oil in Eastern Europe

Year	1 Postulated world market price[a]		2 Estimated price of Soviet crude oil in Eastern Europe	Column 2 as a percentage of Column 1
	$ per barrel	$ per metric ton	$ per metric ton	
1983	29.00	212.57	214.17	100.7
1984	29.00	212.57	229.42	107.9
1985	29.00	212.57	226.68	106.6
1986	29.00	212.57	218.67	102.9
1987	29.00	212.57	212.57	100.0

Source: As in Table 4.1.

TABLE 4.4
Tonnage and value forecast for 1990 for imports of petroleum/natural gas by the European CMEA countries from the developing countries

	Quantity (million tons)		Price ($/ton)		Volume ($ million)			
	Variant 1	Variant 2	Current dollars	1977 dollars	Variant 1[a]		Variant 2[b]	
					Current dollars	1977 dollars	Current dollars	1977 dollars
Petroleum	80–100	65–70	500	265	40,000 –50,000	21,200 –26,500	35,500 –35,000	17,200 18,500
Natural gas	30–40	25–30	—	—	—	—	—	—

[a] Variant 1: Unsuccessful demand limitation policy.
[b] Variant 2: Successful demand limitation policy.
Source: *Economic Relations between the European CMEA Countries and the Developing Countries,* UNITAR Research Project, directed by Jozsef Bognar, Institute for World Economics, Budapest, 1980, p. 91.

Notes

1. Radio Prague, 30 August 1978.
2. *Pravda*, 21 February 1979.
3. Radio Prague, 27 March 1979.
4. I have put forward the same argument with respect to the increasing reliance of Eastern Europe on raw materials of southern Africa in 'Adventurism and Pragmatism: the Soviet Union, COMECON and Relations with African States', *International Affairs*, Autumn 1981. For a critique of these views, see Colin Lawson, 'The Soviet Union and Eastern Europe in Southern Africa: is there a Conflict of Interests?', *International Affairs*, Winter 1982/3, and for a rejoinder my 'The Soviet Union and Eastern Europe: Problems of Competition and Collaboration in Southern Africa', in Craig Nation (ed.), *The Soviet Union and Africa* (Lexington, Mass.: Lexington University Press, 1984). These views are further developed in my book, *NATO, the Warsaw Pact and Africa 1949–83* (London: Macmillan, 1985).
5. *Radio Free Europe Report*, 3 December 1982, p. 10.
6. *The Financial Times*, 17 February 1982.
7. *Neues Deutschland*, 2 July 1979.
8. See David Astor and Valerie Yorke, *Peace in the Middle East: Super Powers and Security Guarantees* (London: Corgi, 1978) for a useful summary of these views which were held at one time by two of the later architects of the Camp David accords, Zbigniew Brzezinski and Jimmy Carter (pp. 64–7).
9. The only study of East European interests in the Middle East concentrates almost exclusively on East German military operations. See Edwina Moreton, 'The East Europeans and the Cubans in the Middle East: Surrogates or Allies?', in Adeed Dawisha and Karen Dawisha (eds.), *The Soviet Union in the Middle East: Policies and Perspectives* (London: Heinemann, for the RIIA, 1982).
10. *Pravda*, 30 March 1974.
11. *Scienteia*, 6/12 July 1979.
12. 'The Programme Directive on Research and Development in Energy in the 1981–90 period and the main orientations until the year 2000', *Scienteia*, 24 July 1979.
13. *Zycie Warszawy*, 8 November 1979.
14. *The Financial Times*, 17 December 1981.
15. *The Soviet Situation*, Select Committee on Intelligence, US Senate, Washington, D.C., May 1978.
16. Abram Bergson, 'Soviet Economic Slowdown and the 1981–5 Plan', *Problems of Communism*, No. 30, May–June 1981, p. 27.
17. These subsidies largely explain why it has been quite impossible for the Soviet Union to meet the demands of Third World clients other than Vietnam and Cuba, both members of the CMEA. Ethiopia, although an official 'observer' at CMEA meetings, has so far failed to persuade Moscow to supply oil at the preferential prices enjoyed by Cuba. See David Albright, 'The USSR and Africa: a Disinclination to Assume new Responsibilities', in *Africa Contemporary Record 1981–2* (London: Rex Collings, 1982), p. A174.
18. Cam Hudson, 'What do the OPEC Price Changes Mean for Eastern Europe?', *Radio Free Europe Background Report/59*, 17 March 1983. All such calculations are fraught with difficulties. Dollar prices are a problematic guide. Since the East Europeans do not pay dollars for their Soviet imports the official exchange rates between the dollar and the rouble and between the rouble and the transferable rouble do not reflect the purchasing power parity of the respective currencies. To sell their machinery to the West and purchase oil on the open market the East Europeans

would have to accept such large discounts that they would not be able to buy as much oil.

19.   *Trybuna Ludu*, 8 September 1978.

20.   See Research Paper, 'The Scope of Poland's Economic Dilemma' (Washington, D.C.: National Foreign Assessment Center, July 1978).

21.   *Zycie Warszawy*, 8 October 1979.

22.   *Zycie Gospodarcze*, 22 August 1982.

23.   See I. Horvath Psule, 'Development of Hungarian Economic Relations with Countries of the Arab Gulf', in *Economic Relations of Africa with the Socialist Countries*, Vol. 1: *Hungarian Contributions* (Budapest: Institute for World Economics, Hungarian Academy of Sciences, 1978), pp. 73–81.

24.   *Nepszabadsag*, 24 December 1981.

25.   For the same amount of money Czechoslovakia is getting considerably less Soviet oil than in 1982, possibly of the order of 10 per cent. *Zivot Stranyi*, No. 1, 1983, p. 16.

26.   'The Inducement of Economic Depression in Czechoslovakia', *Radio Free Europe Background Report*, 26 March 1982, p. 7.

27.   *Rude Pravo*, 12 November 1976. In 1978, the year the Iranian crisis began, Czechoslovakia imported one seventh of its oil from the Middle East.

28.   *Rude Pravo*, 19 March 1979.

29.   A. Cvet Kova, 'Economic Relations between Bulgaria and the Arab Countries', in *Economic Relations of Africa with the Socialist Countries*, Vol. 3, p. 51.

30.   *Petroleum Times*, No. 5, 19 August 1977.

31.   *Vanshna Torgovia*, issue 2, February 1978, p. 9.

32.   *The Times*, 1 August 1979.

33.   *Scienteia*, 7 July 1981.

34.   A. Tiraspolsky, 'Les prix du pétrole livré par l'URSS au CAEM', *Le Courrier des Pays de l'Est*, No. 229, May 1979.

35.   Marie Lavigne, 'The Soviet Union inside COMECON', *Soviet Studies*, Vol. 35, No. 2, April 1983, p. 138. This does not take into account, of course, grants at the pre-1975 price to Czechoslovakia and the GDR. Similar special prices for non-fuel commodities such as iron ore have been negotiated with Bulgaria and Poland.

36.   Gheorghe Badrus, 'Full Viability of the Basic Principles of Co-operation within the CMEA', *Era Socialista*, No. 4, February 1983.

37.   Even some Soviet economists have no doubt that market imports will become cheaper in the future. 'The improvement of the existing forms of cooperation between CMEA countries and the developing world, and the introduction of new forms of cooperation, may well lead to a situation where, *even under the different price patterns of the world market*, imports of fuel and minerals from the developing countries might well prove cheaper than imports from the Soviet Union', A.I. Zubkov (ed.), *Toplivno Sirevaya v Vsloviyakh Sotsialisticheukoy ekonomocheskoy integratsii* (Moscow, 1979), p. 126.

38.   Cam Hudson, 'Eastern Europe and the Energy Crisis: an Overview', *Radio Free Europe Background Report/136*, 10 June 1980, p. 7.

39.   *Czechoslovak Foreign Trade*, No. 1, 1982, pp. 18–19.

40.   See Laszlo Csaba, 'The Place of the CMEA in the World Economy of the 1980's', *Valosag*, July 1982, p. 9.

41.   *Consequences of Soviet Subsidisation of East European Economies*, Wharton Centrally Planned Economies Current Analysis (Washington, D.C.: 1982).

42.   John R. Haberstroh, 'Eastern Europe – Growing Energy Problems', in *East*

European Economies Post-Helsinki, US Congress, Washington, D.C., 1977.

43. Hudson, 'Eastern Europe and the Energy Crisis', p. 11.

44. *The Financial Times*, 17 December 1981.

45. Rezso Nyers, 'Tradition and Innovation in CMEA Co-operation', *Kozgazda-sagi Szemle*, April 1982.

46. Jan Vanous, 'East European Economic Slowdown', *Problems of Communism*, Vol. 31, July–August 1982, p. 10.

47. E. Dobozi, 'Projected Trends of Raw Material Supply', in *Economic Relations of Africa with the Socialist Countries*, Vol. 1, p. 34.

48. *The Times*, 17 October 1979.

49. Dobozi, 'Projected Trends of Raw Material Supply', p. 20.

50. R. Dietz, *Price Changes in Soviet Trade with CMEA and the Rest of the World since 1975* (Joint Economic Committee of US Congress, Washington, D.C., 1979). See also S. Rosfielde, 'Comparative Advantage and the Evolving Pattern of Soviet Commodity Specialisation', in S. Rosfielde (ed.), *Economic Welfare and the Economics of Soviet Socialism* (Cambridge: Cambridge University Press, 1981).

51. Hans Siegfried Lamm and Siegfried Kupper, *DDR und die Welt* (Munich, 1976).

52. Jochen Bethkenhagen, 'Energy Sector of the German Economy Faces Difficult Tasks', *Deutschland Archiv*, No. 5, May 1981, pp. 505–6.

53. *African Economic Digest*, Vol. 1, No. 24, October 1980.

54. *African Economic Digest*, Vol. 3, No. 36, September 1982.

55. Peter Mandi, 'Trade Perspectives between European CMEA Countries and Africa and the Middle East', in *Economic Relations of Africa with the Socialist Countries*, pp. 35–41.

5
Soviet-African relations: promise and limitations

Sam C. Nolutshungu

The political context

The Soviet Union's role in Africa has always been more important for its potential than for its actual effect on the day-to-day politics of Africa or, indeed, the world. To Western governments – and interest groups – the Soviet threat in Africa has been a useful rallying cry to often diffident domestic publics. At times, Soviet diplomatic and military success – though never unambiguous or secure – has been taken as a measure of the West's declining influence and resolve, justifying corrective means and more active policies in Africa. For African governments, beginning with Nasser's the Soviet Union has been a potential alternative source of economic, technical and military support, becoming actually so largely through the action of its rivals. Some have supped with it with a long spoon – cooperating on important economic projects but resisting its ideological and political influence, like Guinea under Sekou Touré. It has also been a bogeyman that right-wing regimes have invoked to chastise Western patrons when they have seemed too slow to aid a favoured project, or overanxious about human rights in Africa. It has been a vague, but evidently real, source of anxiety even to such an aberrant regime as Bokassa's, which clearly faced greater dangers nearer home, and, as it turned out, from France rather than the Soviet Union.

The Soviet Union itself has both emphasized the socialist revolutionary potential of African conflicts with the West and presented itself as a practical partner tolerant of quite diverse African social systems and widely differing degrees of progressiveness. Where there have been revolutions backed by Soviet military supplies, their attainment of socialism has never been taken for granted. Despite the optimism of the early days of African decolonization, socialism proper has always seemed to lie in a distant future. There is no 'actually existing socialism' – it is something more tentative, more precarious and, by necessary implication, demanding prudent support policies on the part of fully socialist states. Soviet action has shown recognition both of the pre-eminent position of the West and the weakness so far of the

68

socialist movement in Africa. Yet with the future potentialities in mind, Soviet policy does not concede any unchallengeable Western sphere of influence in Africa, or even a general *droit de regard*, except in its prudent avoidance of direct confrontation (or entanglements that could produce it).

There is nevertheless, a real basis for Soviet-African cooperation over a wide range of issues even within the evident limitations imposed by the balance of power, differences of interest and circumstance, and ideological diversity. It is a relationship that derives both its strengths and its weaknesses, real and potential, from its inherent ambiguities.

At the most general level, Soviet policy towards Africa has reflected the belief that there is a conflict of interest between the former colonial states and the Western capitalist powers; this will feed an anti-imperialism linked to the internal social struggles that are a necessary part of the development of the new states. Such anti-imperialism is complementary and helpful to the Soviet Union's own resistance to the dominant capitalist powers. At the same time there is, in specific countries and movements, a particular potential for radical development which would ally those countries closely to the Soviet Union and to the socialist bloc as a whole. Thus, while anti-imperialism creates a basis for some cooperation with all African states, there are nevertheless specific revolutionary causes to be supported as such. The Soviet Union has never had to choose between the broad support of all African states (or even of all progressive African states) and specific collaboration with distinctly Marxist causes, largely because revolutionary socialist movements independent of the governments with which it has good relations either do not exist or are weak – as in the Sudan, where Moscow maintained good relations with the anti-Marxist Numeiry government in spite of the repression of local communists. Furthermore, African states have not become ideologically polarized, despite their evident ideological cleavages, except on specific crises, as in the Congo in 1960, Angola in 1975, and Western Sahara at present; and even here neither have the cleavages been consistent nor do they yield an unambiguous Marxist or pro-Soviet grouping on one side. States that have adopted a strong and consistent anti-Soviet stance have generally not been very influential or very active in continental politics; while those collaborating with the Soviet Union have nonetheless been concerned to remain credibly non-aligned. Certainly they have not decided their African relations on the basis of their external alignment, as cooperation between Mozambique and Zimbabwe (with an anti-Soviet bias) amply demonstrates.

Even within the liberation movements which have been heavily dependent on Soviet arms, there has been a tension, a balance perhaps, between the promotion of revolutionary socialism and the encouragement of radical nationalism which does not, except in some distant future, carry the promise of a Marxist development of either the movement or the country concerned. On the liberation of territories still under colonial or racist rule there has, of course, been a considerable measure of agreement between the Soviet Union and African states.[1]

The Soviet Union has developed an approach to Africa which can be described as 'plural' involving cooperation with states with different social systems and ideological aspirations, and often cooperation and conflict with the same state at the same time. It is an attitude that has made possible gainful economic cooperation and the initiation of patterns of economic assistance that could be even more important in the future, as well as political collaboration on various international issues, especially those which have a bearing on colonial and neo-colonial issues and South African racism. However, the emphasis placed on anti-imperialism rather than internal political and ideological features of African states has often meant Soviet support for regimes that have otherwise no socialist potential in Marxist terms – the worst example being Idi Amin's Uganda, which was able to obtain Soviet arms. In other cases there has been a reluctance on the part of the Soviet Union to interfere too directly in the internal political and ideological debates.

This was evident in the decade of cooperation with Somalia, when Barré's regime maintained a rather idiosyncratic institutional character and ideology while professing scientific socialism, and in the continuing cooperation with a Libya which not only is non-Marxist but has supported causes and individuals in Africa and the Middle East with which Moscow could not sympathize, a recent instance being the divergence of Libyan and Soviet attitudes towards the Palestine Liberation Organization in 1983 in Lebanon (although Libya was more or less in accord with Syria, another Soviet-backed regime). Libya's support for Amin against the Tanzanian forces after the Ugandan dictator's ouster, in 1979, was not in accord with Soviet policy as it then stood. The ups and downs of Libyan involvement in Chad and its provocations against its Arab neighbours in Africa could not possibly serve any Soviet purpose. At the other extreme, Soviet economic cooperation continues apace with actively anti-socialist Morocco that has been implicated in subversion against Marxist Benin, and which actually sent troops to the aid of the American-backed Zairean dictator during the Shaba crisis in 1978.

In many ways, pluralism and ambiguity are the very stuff of international politics, the Soviet approach differing little from that of other states. However, there is the difference that Soviet policy is informed by an underlying revolutionary optimism about the possibilities of structural change both within African states and in the international system generally – a belief often mistaken for a conspiratorial Soviet strategy for Africa, particularly when Moscow makes dramatic moves, as during the Angolan and Ethiopian crises of the middle and later 1970s.[2] However, a general optimism about progressive development is just as likely to encourage a patient and flexible attitude to day-to-day problems and developments as it is to encourage attempts to 'give history a push'. In either case much depends on what is happening on the ground, the internal dynamics of African development and the demands made by African states on external helpers. While the Soviet Union has supported revolutions in Africa, no African revolution and no African dispute with a Western power has been in any sense the result of Soviet instigation or conspiracy. Nor has Soviet support for such struggles, once initiated, been overzealous.[3]

Until the Angolan operation in 1975–6, the demands made upon the Soviet Union by the states and movements it supported in Africa were modest. States required it to supplement rather than replace, or even equal, Western trade and aid. Only in Somalia did the Soviet Union become the principal economic as well as military backer. While states bought Soviet arms, received instructors and sent their men for training in Warsaw Pact countries, the Soviet military presence was insignificant everywhere except in Egypt – and Egypt was more important in an Asian, Middle Eastern context than in an African one. In no case, including Somalia, was the Soviet Union expected to assume any military commitment, nor did it. The weapons supplied to sub-Saharan Africa were without exception very basic and generally supplied from existing stock. To the various liberation movements the Soviet Union gave arms, training and financial support but took no part in the planning and execution of their actual struggles. Contrary to some Western views, the Soviet Union showed absolutely no sense of urgency either about the development of socialism or about changing the East-West balance of influence in Africa. For most of the period the Soviet Union neither was in a position to exercise direct military influence in Africa nor possessed the global strategic posture that would have enabled it to benefit significantly from military allies in

Africa other than in North Africa. In backing progressive states and organizations the costs were low and the risks negligible.

Africa as a whole was of very limited economic importance to the Soviet Union, of negligible military significance, and with only a remote prospect of revolutionary transformation. Above all, the USSR's military capabilities – measured always against more pressing commitments elsewhere – and its economic resources (relative to those of the West, and absolutely) simply did not encourage costly entanglements in a region which was, and remains, peripheral to Soviet security – with the exception of the Mediterranean and Red Sea countries which are important to key potential theatres of East-West confrontation in Asia and Europe.[4]

Since the mid-1970s some significant changes have occurred both in Africa and in Soviet capabilities. If the Soviet Union's capacities have increased, the demands made upon it are becoming more onerous and more entangling. By contrast with the early 1960s when the world economy was buoyant and African states seemed to have good prospects of fairly rapid development, the outlook in the 1980s is bleak and revolutionary governments inherit ruined economies. For the socialist economies, also, times are lean. Although Soviet policy retains a remarkable continuity in its capacity to support revolutionary causes, at the same time maintaining good relations with anti-revolutionary African governments (such as the government of Morocco), and although it continues to insist on the validity of the common ground of anti-imperialism, it is entering into a testing time which will require clearer definitions of the limits of its support for friends, and of the relative weights of, on the one hand, the theme of anti-imperialism directed at global issues and, on the other, the theme of class struggle focused on the internal development of states. By the same token, African states of differing ideological hue face a changing, generally worsening domestic and international economic situation which in some cases draws them to a closer collaboration with the socialist countries, and in others leads to an even more abject dependence on Western patrons.

With the emergence of revolutionary regimes in Ethiopia, Angola and Mozambique, the Soviet Union assumed a more onerous burden of supporting states that were fragile, internally divided and subject to severe military pressure. The international conjuncture in which its relations with these states were established was radically different from the present – in several respects. Neither the crisis in Afghanistan nor the social conflict in Poland had yet erupted, with their considerable demands on the Soviet exchequer. Vietnam's relations with China had not yet resulted in war. America had withdrawn from Vietnam amid deep internal division and a constitutional crisis which for a time restrained American military assertion abroad. The East-West relationship itself was on a somewhat less dangerous footing than at present and may have seemed less likely to be disrupted by peripheral involvements in Africa. All this has changed and, much more importantly, the pressure on Angola and Mozambique from South Africa or South-African-backed anti-revolutionary forces, with tacit Western support, has impeded the consolidation of socialism. In retrospect Soviet military action in these countries appears to have made little difference either to the role of Africa in Soviet military strategy or to the respective strengths of East and West, although it did upset Soviet-American relations and gave added impetus to the development of the American Rapid Deployment Force, involving the use of the territory of some African states.

Angola and Mozambique are physically remote and situated in a region which the West regards as the most important in Africa because of South Africa's economic and defence resources. A substantial direct involvement by the Soviet Union against the rebel movements comparable to that in Afghanistan would be costly and hazardous. The possibility of confrontations with South Africa could not be ruled out and the aspiring socialist states would not be able to secure themselves without a continuous Soviet – or Soviet-guaranteed Cuban – military presence. Given Western interests in South Africa, the dangers of widening and escalating regional conflict would be considerable. Not only would the Soviet Union have severe logistical disadvantages but its host states would be exceedingly weak ones in terms both of their capacity to absorb Soviet military aid and of their ability to contribute to the common effort. When Mozambique was constrained to sign a non-aggression pact with South Africa in 1984, committing itself to evict from its territory militants of the exiled African National Congress, questions were raised about the level and efficacy of Soviet aid that had apparently failed to prevent such a submission.

It is difficult to determine what kinds of assistance would have been appropriate in the case of Mozambique, what was asked for and what refused and for what reason. Economic and financial aid could have been increased substantially, but it is not at all clear that this would have provided the answer to Mozambique's security problems. Similar observations might be made with regard to Angola. Short of a substantial increase of men and sophisticated equipment, from Cuba or another allied country, but backed increasingly directly by Moscow, it seems impossible to drive out the rebel UNITA and its South African backers. With South Africa still strong internally and the United States holding to its present policies in southern Africa,[5] the moment would seem inopportune for vigorous Soviet action in the area. Yet it also seems unlikely that the Soviet Union could stand idly by if the MPLA and the Cubans faced defeat in the limited areas they have decided jointly to hold.

In Ethiopia the Soviet Union is involved in a war against secession which seems impossible to bring to a conclusive end by military means. The ruling military committee, the Derg, has so far proved none too eager to find a negotiated solution, yet its independent capacity to win the war appears to be getting no greater. Armed revolt in other provinces of Ethiopia, notably Tigre, has created a condition of permanent conflict to which no credible political solution has yet emerged. On the other hand, the Derg has been very slow in developing popular political institutions and has made slow progress on a project considered crucial by the Soviet Union, namely the creation of a vanguard party.[6] To be added to all this are Ethiopia's enduring economic problems and the drought. Ethiopia continues to rely on Western aid, particularly food aid, encouraging a belief in the West, and among the Ethiopian middle classes as well, that the pro-Soviet orientation of the country is not irreversible. With this possibility of 'regression' and the very limited advances towards the institutionalization of socialism, it would be surprising indeed if Moscow considered its own commitment absolute and irrevocable.[7]

The problem that has emerged in the Soviet Union's relationship with revolutionary states is the familiar one of each state's having to define what it can and cannot do with Soviet aid within a realistic appreciation of the limitations of the power of both the African revolutionaries and the Soviet Union and within some broad sense of mutual advantage.

Soviet relations with revolutionary African states do to some extent depend on the view taken by the Soviet leadership about the possibility of socialist development in Africa. In this regard there has been an inconclusive debate, as old as African independence,[8] which nevertheless seems to have produced some clear views: that 'socialist orientation' is a distinct developmental alternative which Moscow ought to support; it is distinct from and less than socialism but can lead in that direction provided certain conditions are met. Above all there should be no backsliding; a strong vanguard party should be developed, and the leadership must pursue the 'correct' policies. In a speech to the plenary meeting of the Central Committee of the CPSU in 1983, Yuri Andropov seemed to indicate a certain reserve about the countries of socialist orientation:

> We and they are brought together not only by peaceful anti-imperialist, peaceful goals in foreign policy but by common ideals of social justice

and progress. We do of course see both the complexity of their situation and the difficulties of their revolutionary development. For it is one thing to proclaim socialism as one's goal, and it is quite another thing to build it. *This requires a defined level of productive forces, and of culture, and of social consciousness.* The socialist countries solidarize with these progressive states, give them aid in the sphere of politics and culture, and promote the strengthening of their defence. *We also assist their economic development to the extent of our possibilities. But, fundamentally, that – as the whole social progress of these countries – can of course only be the result of work by their own people, and of a correct policy on the part of their leadership* [italics added].[9]

On a previous occasion Andropov had conceded that there were different roads to socialism but insisted that the principles which lay at the 'foundation of a socialist structure for society, its class nature, are one and the same for all countries and all peoples'.[10]

Quite clearly Soviet commitments to African revolutionary states, if they were to be based on shared socialist ideals, would have to pass quite rigorous tests. Needless to say, the African partners have yet to work out their own principles and are in a weak position to lay down conditions. However, it is evident that they do at the very least insist on their autonomy in international affairs, and above all in domestic policy, as the examples of Mozambique's dealings with South Africa and Ethiopia's internal political policy illustrate only too clearly.

The existence of states of socialist orientation in Africa, heavily dependent on Soviet military support, would seem to make very little difference to Soviet strategic options and to the central balance of military power between East and West. Port facilities offered by pro-Soviet states are undeniably useful to the Soviet navy, and so are airport facilities and overflying rights of assistance to naval surveillance. In the event of crises in Africa, access to affected territories is made easier, as was the delivery of arms to the MPLA via, among others, Tanzania, Burundi and Congo in 1974–5.[11] Yet it is important to emphasize that there are no Soviet naval bases and no forward bases with men and arms ready for deployment. Soviet and Warsaw Pact advisers simply do not have the independent operational capability enjoyed by, for example, the French advisers in several African countries. Soviet allies in Africa are either not sufficiently secure or securable, or have deliberately circumscribed the extent of military cooperation.

To intervene militarily in any country in the interior or to the south of the continent, the Soviet Union would face very long lines and might need to fly through the air space of several countries. While neither fact need always be a decisive obstacle, it is quite clear that each provides a powerful counsel for caution, given that the West is unlikely to react passively.

Despite the advances made by the Soviet Union in the past two decades with respect to the global reach of its power, its capacity to project force in Africa, as demonstrated in the Horn and Angola, and its diplomatic achievements, its position in Africa is weak. History and tradition, as well as the interests of the leadership classes in Africa, favour continued dependence on the West, just as the structure of the world economy greatly reduces the scope for the significant reordering of African external economic relations. It is only in exceptionally difficult conditions, when Western countries have been unwilling to provide adequate assistance, and especially when the security of the African state has been in peril, that African governments have made particular efforts to increase their cooperation with the Soviet Union. Such choices often carry heavy penalties in terms of Western retaliation which may range from the withholding of what little assistance was previously available to subversion and destabilization.

The West's hegemony in Africa is sustained by a substantial superiority in air and sea power in the continent and the surrounding oceans as well as by the firm Western orientation of the more powerful African states – South Africa, Egypt, Nigeria, Senegal and, in an economic sense, Ivory Coast and Kenya. The willingness of some Western countries to intervene militarily to defend their protégés is a part of that strength.

The dilemma of African states in their relations with the Soviet Union lies precisely here. In military terms they can contribute so very little to Soviet needs that the relationship tends to be one of dependence. While Western leaders have emphasized the danger of Soviet dominance, there is, from the point of view of those who need Soviet aid, a far greater danger – that of non-reciprocity, leading to a Soviet reluctance to commit significant resources to their aid. Equally, there is a danger that such states may predicate their policies on a level of Soviet support that is, by any realistic standard, unfeasible.

The fate of the states of socialist orientation, recognized and aided as such by the Soviet Union, cannot fail to have an important effect on the ideological development of other states in Africa, particularly those that are led by radicals, sometimes Marxist by their own lights – states like Zimbabwe and, with a very different history and leadership, Benin; other states like Rawlings' Ghana and Bourkina Fasso under Sankara, have no familiar name for their revolutionism. In these two instances social radicalism, led by military men, has grown out of desperate local circumstances, and is populist and fiercely patriotic – and empirical, an attitude well expressed by Sankara: 'We do not want the dogmatism and servility that would lead us to proclaim ideologies which the people of Bourkina Fasso have not internalised.'[12] There is, indeed, considerable diversity within the African left, which reflects the differing histories of African countries, such that there seem to be not only different roads to socialism (or 'socialist orientation') but substantively different *meanings* to the concept. Whether Soviet conceptions of socialism will prevail, or whether socialism of any kind, even, will remain a credible alternative to the present condition of African states, will depend largely on the fate of those who have associated themselves closely with the socialist bloc.

Soviet relations with non-socialist African states focus increasingly on economics rather than politics. Nevertheless for many such countries the Soviet Union represents a country upon which they know they may one day have to call for arms or aid when Western states fail them, and most of the time it is an ally in international negotiations for a reform of the currently Western-dominated international economic order. In most of these countries the Soviet Union does not actively support the incipient left oppositions, nor have the states it does support threatened their neighbours in ways that implicate Soviet policy. As a result, conservative African governments, though anti-Marxist, do not much concern themselves with Soviet activities. Even when there was agitation against the Soviet-Cuban action in Angola in 1975–6, this was largely a response to Western anxieties and preoccupations. Similarly, although African governments have condemned the Soviet Union's invasion of Afghanistan and have criticized its economic aid policy, Soviet opposition to neo-colonialism, and particularly to Western policies towards South Africa, is still generally seen in a favourable light.

The Soviet Union and its CMEA partners value their economic links with the more important trading countries in Africa independently of political and ideological differences. Curiously, Soviet-African relations can be much easier in these cases than in those where there is an ideological affinity, based as they are on the narrowly defined mutual advantage of states within a conservative framework of mutual toleration and non-interference.[13] Furthermore, the Soviet Union does not seem to feel that there is, in these cases, a presumption of a Soviet obligation to give economic aid. Whatever may be the long-term political and ideological outlook of these countries, and indeed of all African countries, it is quite evident that economics provides, in the immediate future, the one area in which there is scope for an expansion of Soviet relations with African countries in all their diversity.

The economic context

In economics, as in politics, Africa has significance for the Soviet Union as part of a Third World which seeks large-scale adjustment of the existing international order, a matter on which the Soviet Union and its CMEA partners believe they have a common interest with the Third World despite their reservations on some of the demands of the less developed countries. The CMEA countries have consistently stressed their belief that a new international economic order of the kind demanded by the Third World could not be achieved without the removal of the disabilities suffered by the socialist countries in East-West trade due to protectionism and discrimination, and in North-South trade due to the monopolistic activities of multinational companies.[14] Increasingly, the Soviet Union has stressed the unity between increased international economic cooperation and détente, disarmament and world peace.

The significance of Soviet-African economic cooperation lies not only in the volume of transactions with individual partners but also in the essentially long-term hope – though, in some ways, a pressing immediate need – for a restructuring of the international system as a whole. In pursuit of this aim the Soviet attitude is reformist rather than disruptive. There is but one international or world economy: economic secession and autarky are neither feasible nor desirable. This militates against the idea of detaching African allies from their links with the capitalist economies; rather these links must be made more advantageous, with the curtailment of restrictive imperialist practices and through structural change in the developing countries themselves.[15] Indeed, in the early stages of the development of cooperation between the European socialist countries and the less developed countries, the traditional specializations of the less developed countries are assigned an important part.[16]

In the long term, advantageous economic cooperation and trade can be developed by conscious effort between countries, between economies that were previously not complementary, or, at least, were isolated from each other – something the Soviet Union believes to have been proved by the expansion of trade in the CMEA. Thus although African partners may contribute very little – in some cases, next to nothing – to the Soviet economy, that is no reason for not laying the foundations for a future in which significant exchange, on a basis of mutual advantage, can be achieved.

Long-term projects of trade creation and cooperation are vulnerable to changing political circumstances, which may explain a certain caution and deliberation in the negotiation and signing and, above all, execution of agreements as well as in the disbursement of financial grants. But they also require a certain patience and willingness to tolerate the swings of government policy, and even changes of personnel and direction, in African states. Guinea provides a classic example of cooperation being sustained despite a difficult political relationship.[17] Uganda is perhaps the most dramatic instance. This country, having been one of the earlier recipients of Soviet aid under the first Obote government, was still able to tap Soviet assistance under Amin. Similarly, Soviet economic cooperation with Ethiopia (which did not begin with the revolution) had been growing, in small ways, even under Emperor Haile Selassie despite the tension between Ethiopia and Somalia, then an ally of the Soviet Union's. Although Soviet cooperation with Sudan and Egypt has suffered greatly from the breach under Sadat, economic relations between these two countries and the European CMEA remain important.

Virtually all the countries with significant trade links with the Soviet Union, with the exception of the Ivory Coast, have a history either of radicalism in their early days (Tunisia, Morocco, Algeria, Ghana, Guinea and Mali – some of which are still to the left in African politics) or of having had, at some point, to turn to the Soviet Union for arms (Nigeria, Sudan and Zambia). Political circumstances created the opportunity for trade, largely by alerting African governments to the possibilities of such cooperation, and once started, such collaboration is quite resilient in the face of subsequent ideological estrangement and quarrels. Where the Soviet Union becomes economically involved, the other European socialist countries also tend to become active, partly as a result of a conscious specialization policy on their part. Typically, the Soviet Union and the CMEA countries seek broad intergovernmental cooperation agreements extending beyond just the exchange of commodities, and this does to some extent reflect the limited significance of trade as such and stresses the development perspective – the long-term view – that underlies the Soviet approach to such relations.

Trade with Africa represents only a very small proportion of Soviet external trade: a little more than 5 per cent of its trade with all less developed countries, barely 2.5 per cent of the CMEA's world exports and under 2 per cent of its imports. In recent years Soviet exports have increased substantially while imports have fallen. The trading partners are of varying political inclination: of the half-dozen or so countries to which Soviet exports exceeded $10m, four were under right-wing governments: Morocco ($167m), Egypt ($160m), Nigeria ($43m) and Tunisia ($16m). Ethiopia was the only Marxist trading partner of any size ($116m). Soviet imports came principally from Egypt ($136m), Ivory Coast ($84m), Morocco ($62m), Ghana ($59m), Tanzania ($33m) and Algeria ($427m).[18]

Figures for 1979 reveal the commodity structure of the trade. Some 60 per cent of CMEA exports by value were of manufactured goods, mostly machinery, and nearly 20 per cent were agricultural raw materials and food items. About 47 per cent of imports were divided equally between food items and agricultural raw materials, and manufactured goods amounted to 10 per cent.[19]

The size and character of trade with Africa reflects the character of the African economies, their respective abilities to trade and to diversify, and the level of their industrial development. However, it is nowhere great, and most of the trading partners are among the least developed countries, with *per capita* GDP of less than $500 – Algeria, Ivory Coast and Libya being the only ones with *per capita* GDP higher than $1,000. The most radical countries are among the very poorest. The trade of the sub-Saharan countries that were previously colonies is heavily oriented to the West, often to the former colonizing power, trade with other regions, including Latin America and Asia (excluding Japan), being very small. It is probably with this non-Western trade that Soviet and East European trade ought to be compared. For African countries, it is in the context of the expansion of their non-Western trade, generally considered desirable, that the East European trade is important.

Soviet trade expansion in Africa requires the cooperation of African governments to facilitate the medium- and long-term agreements favoured by the Soviet Union, covering quantities and prices and the means and terms of payment. The state sector provides the focus of development cooperation and assistance, although direct enterprise-to-enterprise agreements exist and may become an increasingly important factor, involving not only private African businesses but Western companies as well.

Trading with private businessmen does raise difficulties. It requires considerable local knowledge and risk-taking, and often a willingness to bend rules or get round them, in some cases through plain corruption, which socialist enterprises are not well placed to do. Private traders have a preference for easily negotiable means of payment that may be less easily subject to official control. Generally, they have little awareness of business opportunities outside the traditional trading partners, although this is changing at least with regard to African imports.

Although Soviet trade with the stronger economies is increasingly concluded in hard currency, bilateral clearing arrangements are still an important means of payment for the poorer countries.[20] Despite considerable encouragement from the UNCTAD secretariat of multilateralization of payments through the International Bank for

Economic Cooperation (IBEC) of the CMEA (i.e. such that African partners can use positive balances with one state to offset deficits with another CMEA country), this has not been an issue in Africa-CMEA trade. Means of payment are not considered a decisive factor in the expansion of trade, although flexibility of payment arrangements and credit seems to have some advantages for the developing countries.[21]

Much has been made of the inferior quality of Soviet goods as an obstacle to the expansion of trade. However, African markets show a considerable tolerance for a great variation of standards, and indeed the higher-quality, or higher-technology, goods are often beyond what Africans can afford as well as being difficult to maintain and service. With regard to plant and machinery supplied for specific development projects, the objection is often academic, since the project would, very often, not have been undertaken without Soviet participation and aid.[22] Even the advanced industrial countries do manage quite well in many areas of their economic life on less than the newest technology or the best quality. The real problems probably lie elsewhere: in the comparative pricing, availability and delivery, marketing and distribution of CMEA goods and services.

Two areas of cooperation seem likely to prove very significant for the expansion of trade. One is the establishment of joint ventures in industrial production, finance and banking, and agriculture. The other is tripartite cooperation between the CMEA countries, their African trading partners and the Western industrial countries.

Joint-venture companies have existed since the 1960s with Nigeria, Ethiopia and Guinea, but this form of cooperation has advanced furthest with the North African countries, Algeria, Morocco and Libya. It can be the basis of tripartite cooperation defined by UNCTAD as 'cooperation at the enterprise/organization level between the industrial sectors of developing countries, socialist countries and developed market economies'.[23] It links the expansion of East-West trade directly with the growth of North-South cooperation. Several such agreements exist, as in the cooperation between the Soviet Union and the United Kingdom for the construction of oil pipelines in Nigeria, between West and East Germany in cotton-spinning in Ethiopia, and between Poland and West Germany in metallurgy in Algeria. Some arrangements specifically envisage the supply of productive equipment and technical assistance by the Soviet Union to an African country, which then produces for export to a third, Western industrial, country. Examples include phosphate exports from Morocco to the United States and bauxite exports from Guinea to France. The scope is greatest in extractive industries but could in principle be extended to other areas with other markets, including those in other less developed countries. Much will depend on the willingness of the CMEA countries to take risks assertively and on the extent to which African trading partners, particularly the stronger ones, are able or willing to exploit these essentially complex arrangements which presuppose a dynamic state sector. Equally decisive will be the evolving attitudes of the advanced industrial countries both to East-West trade and to the inflow of manufactures and semi-processed goods from the African countries.[24]

It is a paradox of the Soviet situation that economic cooperation and planned trading is in principle easier with the countries of socialist orientation, which are also the least able to trade or industrialize. Numerous cooperation agreements have been concluded with these countries, including some potentially very important ones with Mozambique in 1982 relating to agriculture and the development and exploitation of bridges and dams in Angola. There has been agreement on the partial coordination of plans.[25] However, data on performance, and, indeed, on the way the agreements were made, are hard to come by so that it is difficult to evaluate the practical efficacy of the agreements and the seemingly interminable ministerial and bureaucratic visits and consultations which surround them. It is also exceedingly difficult to gain any reliable indication of the views of the governments involved on what has been and what could be achieved.

If the long term is what matters in Soviet-African economies, the cooperation with Mozambique, Ethiopia and Congo cannot yield much advantage to the Soviet Union except in a very distant future. The uncertainty of that distant future may make the Soviet Union and its European allies unwilling to assume the role of economic patron unreservedly. It is in this light that the rejection of Mozambique's application to join the CMEA in 1978 may be viewed. Nor are the European socialist countries ready to create a system of associated states by analogy with the EEC's Lomé Convention. For one thing, the volume of trade simply would not justify the trouble, and, for another, it would go directly against the present emphasis of Soviet economic cooperation policy, which is bilateral and based on specific agreement with a partner government rather than on general concessions and rules.

In one respect, however, Soviet economic policy has attracted criticism from African states and seems likely to continue to do so if conditions in Africa go on worsening, especially for the countries of socialist orientation. The level of grant aid, and especially in the area of disaster and humanitarian relief, has provoked dissatisfaction. Soviet commentators may argue that Western responsibility for the plight of these countries imposes an obligation on the West to make reparations, and that much financial aid disbursed by Western governments to regimes pursuing futile economic policies is ineffective: nevertheless, the credibility of the socialist states is dinted when regimes they regard as being progressive or of socialist orientation, and therefore particularly close to themselves, succumb to the pressure of their enemies – as Mozambique appeared to be doing in 1984 when it added the Nkomati accords, a non-aggression pact with South Africa, to its Treaty of Friendship with the Soviet Union. The reasons were, in part, economic.

While the extent of Soviet financial assistance to its African trading partners is not fully reported – data on loans to Mozambique and Angola have not been published in the usual sources, for example – it is clear that concessional lending has been increasing, although it is still far from Western levels. The beneficiaries are the countries with trading links with the Soviet Union (and the CMEA generally) and the loans are mostly intended to finance purchases of East European goods and services under agreed projects. (See Table 5.1.)

Although doubts have been expressed about whether CMEA lending is on more generous terms than that provided by the West, it is evident that it has represented a very substantial proportion of the foreign borrowing for some of the poorer countries at least (Mali, Ethiopia and Guinea), and for all states it is in addition to, rather than in place of, what can be obtained from Western

TABLE 5.1
African indebtedness to the CMEA: selected countries (US $ million)

Country	1975	1982	Debt to all countries 1982
Algeria	347	438	16,794
Egypt	636	532	16,625
Ethiopia	13	104	898
Ghana	75	47	1,233
Guinea	354	401	1,284
Mali	105	214	829
Morocco	27	17	9,643
Sudan	127	157	5,473
Tunisia	12	103	3,768

Source: OECD, *Survey of Third World Indebtedness, 1983* (Paris, 1983).

sources.[26] Trade debts, though hard to estimate, clearly also constitute a form of borrowing.

Within the long-term perspective that characterizes the Soviet approach to cooperation, educational and scientific assistance to African partners has an obvious importance. Many states have benefited from Soviet training of technical and professional personnel as well as from the provision of general higher education for their students in the Soviet Union and Eastern Europe. In this regard, Cuba's role has also been of signal importance, especially for southern African countries.

Given the high importance attached to education by Africans, there is no doubt that the Soviet contribution in this area is valued. From an economic point of view its significance may lie in breaking down the cultural barriers between Africans and Eastern Europeans and in making future decision-makers more aware of the possibilities of Soviet-African cooperation. At the very least the emergence of high administrative cadres with proficiency in the Russian language should be helpful whatever may be the ideological inclination of their country.

In this regard, the growing number of technical and economic advisers from the socialist counties working in Africa may also be of importance, though their impact may be more deeply felt in the sending countries, where knowledge of African conditions may increase. At the African end such personnel have very little contact with the ordinary population – with the notable exception of Cubans – while the attitude of the middle strata in bureaucratic positions tends to be ambivalent towards advisers regardless of where they come from.

Though still limited, the Soviet economic presence in Africa is varied and important. Clearly there are states with whom cooperation can occur on a basis of mutual economic advantage, either as suppliers of increasingly needed raw materials or as customers paying in equally needed hard currency. There are also states whose economic promise lies in the future but whose economic advance is important to Soviet prestige – even in an economic sense – in that it demonstrates to better-placed countries Soviet willingness to contribute to African development and to the new international economic order which both African and socialist countries desire. In that broader struggle goodwill is important, albeit unquantifiable in terms of its economic worth.

If African states have benefited from Soviet cooperation, probably more than the Soviet Union and its allies have benefited from cooperation with them, the number of states among the non-radicals that have devoted any effort to exploring and exploiting the possibilities of economic collaboration with the CMEA countries is still low. With the bleak economic outlook now facing most African countries this attitude may change. The image of the Soviet Union as a benign economic force, rather than an austere political and military presence, may come to acquire greater significance, a development which, on ideological grounds at least, should not displease Moscow.

Conclusion
Contrary to a view – still very prevalent in the West – that African states, like other Third World states, may join either the East or the West, the reality which emerges from a review of Soviet-African relations is the absence of such a choice – at least in the economic field. Soviet policy recognizes, and the experience of the African states demonstrates clearly, that there is only one world economy and that the European socialist states and the Africans are ultimately of use to each other economically only in so far as they can help each other improve their respective positions in their economic relations, above all with the West. The socialist bloc may insist that structural change is necessary in Africa itself if its position is to improve, while Africans may demand more financial aid from the socialist bloc, but neither side pretends that there is relief outside a general expansion of world trade and cooperation with all countries.

Similar counsels seem to be indicated in politics. Neither the Soviet Union, nor its African allies, nor yet the countries of capitalist orientation, question the rightness of the attitude of non-alignment, imperfect though it is – a position that has been traditional since African independence. At the very least, the Soviet Union could derive no benefit from the continent's being opened up as a further theatre of confrontation with the Western powers; Africans would have little to gain from such a development. The best hope for African non-alignment, as well as economic development, lies in East-West détente, and that is clearly the view of African governments of different ideological persuasions.

The fundamental dilemma for Africans lies in the fact that their own internal development produces crises that in their turn produce their own radical solutions. In general, however, they are too weak to extricate themselves from such crises without assistance, including military aid. In Western eyes, such military assistance, where it involves Soviet or Cuban soldiers, is incompatible with détente. The last détente, according to Zbigniew Brzezinski, was buried in the sands of the Ogaden.

For African states in revolution, there is therefore a built-in limitation in the international system, an externally imposed restraint, on the means and aids they can use to consummate their revolutions. In certain areas, such as southern Africa, the Soviet Union faces in this regard a powerful constraint on the extent of military aid it can provide.

For African states aspiring to be socialist, there is, in addition to the delicate balances that must be maintained (as between socialist internationalism and dependence, anti-imperialism and gainful cooperation with the West), the problem of reconciling their specific conditions, and the concepts and possibilities of socialism to which they give rise, with those of the Soviet Union, which derive from a vastly different experience. In the absence of working classes of any size and organization, and of appropriate levels of material and cultural 'development', the advances towards radical reform and revolution in Africa will for a long time fall short of Soviet expectations and criteria. African states may then find that Soviet aid dries up, although this would be a dereliction – on the part of the USSR – of one of the avowed duties of socialist internationalism. Military leaders and middle-class intellectuals turn to the Soviet bloc for aid in circumstances which often suggest that there is no comfort to be had from anywhere else. Whether they can find ways out of such dilemmas and their infinite ramifications clearly does not depend on Africans alone. An overbearing, interfering Soviet presence is not the prospect that faces most African states; rather they are left to resolve alone a deepening continent-wide crisis affecting all aspects of social and economic life. For Africa can call on neither the Soviet Union nor the West for help in the resolution of this crisis: the former because it is constrained by both the perceived and absolute limits of its power; the latter because it is often deeply implicated in this crisis both by history and by its present partisanship within African conflicts. Yet, even so, increased cooperation with the socialist states has the same potential that it always had: it offers both a supplement to Africa's troubled relations with the West and, one hopes, a means to agitate for an improvement in its position within that association. In different ways, and with perhaps less urgency, Africa, ultimately, has the same significance for Moscow.

Notes

1. See, among others, D.E. Albright, 'Moscow's African Policy of the 1970s', in D.E. Albright (ed.), *African and International Communism* (London: Macmillan, 1980).

2. Cf. M. Rothenberg, *The USSR and Africa: New Dimensions of Soviet Global Power* (Advanced International Studies Institute, Washington, D.C., 1980); I. Greig, *The Communist Challenge to Africa: an Analysis of Contemporary Soviet,*

Chinese and Cuban policies (London: Foreign Affairs Publishing Co. Ltd., 1977).

3. See also S.C. Nolutshungu, 'African Interests and Soviet Power: the Local Context of Soviet Policy', *Soviet Studies*, Vol. 34, No. 3, 1982.

4. Cf. R.B. Remnek, 'Soviet Military Interests in Africa', *Orbis*, Spring 1984.

5. For example, the policy of 'linkage', demanding eviction of Cubans from Angola in exchange for a negotiated end to the South African occupation of Namibia.

6. See F. Halliday and M. Molyneux, *The Ethiopian Revolution* (London: Verso Editions, 1981); see also Colette Braeckman, 'La Corne de l'Afrique dans la tourmente', *Le Monde Diplomatique*, October 1982, pp. 18–21. The Constitutent Congress of the Ethiopian Workers Party was held in September 1984 but no indication was given of when or how power would be transferred from the Derg to the party.

7. It is, for example, highly unlikely that Soviet combat troops, as distinct from advisers, would be sent to Ethiopia (as they have been sent to Afghanistan) other than in the event of an external attack on Ethiopia. On famine aid see, among others, Colette Braeckman, *Le Monde Diplomatique*, February 1985, and for Soviet views on Western aid see *Current Digest of the Soviet Press*, 5 December 1984, 12 December 1984 and 19 December 1984.

8. Cf. T.J. Zamostny, 'Moscow and the Third World: Recent Trends in Soviet Thinking', *Soviet Studies*, April 1984.

9. *Pravda*, 12 July 1983 (reported in *USSR and the World*).

10. *Current Digest of the Soviet Press*, 7 November 1982–6 March 1983.

11. Burundi had been the scene of Sino-Soviet rivalry, while Tanzania had previously been much closer to China than to the Soviet Union on international questions.

12. *Afrique Asie*, No. 327, 30 July–12 August 1984, p. 31.

13. Contrast, for example, the evolution of Indo-Soviet with that of Sino-Soviet relations. However, ideological and general foreign policy questions cannot be pushed aside at will. These depend on social conflicts within cooperating states and on the attitudes of other states.

14. 'Evaluation of the World Trade and Economic Situation ...' *Proceedings of the United Nations Conference on Trade and Development*, Fifth Session, 7 May–3 June 1979, Document TD/249 (New York: United Nations, 1983), Vol. 1.

15. *Ibid.* See also M. Lavigne, 'Ni riches ni pauvres: la réponse des pays du Comecon', *Le Monde Diplomatique*, June 1983.

16. *Innovations in the Practice of Trade and Cooperation between the Socialist Countries of Eastern Europe and the Developing Countries* (New York: United Nations, 1970), pp. 13ff.

17. It is almost certain, though, that Sekou Touré's policies inhibited the full development of cooperative ventures not only with the Soviet Union but with Western countries as well, notably France and the US – something he tried to change in the later years of his rule.

18. Sources: United Nations, *International Trade Yearbook 1983* (New York, 1984) and UNCTAD, *Handbook of International Trade and Development Statistics: Supplement, 1981* (New York, 1982).

19. *Ibid.*

20. UNCTAD, *Multilateralization of Payments in Trade between Socialist Countries of Eastern Europe and Developing Countries: Selected Documents* (New York, 1978), *passim*.

21. *Ibid.*, pp. 23ff.

22. This was true, for example, of the Nigerian steel project, although there was considerable competitive Western interest in it as it neared fruition.

23. *Proceedings of the United Nations Conference on Trade and Development*, Fifth Session, Supplement 5.

24. Cf. M. Radu, 'Romania and the Third World: the Dilemmas of a Free Rider', in M. Radu (ed.), *Eastern Europe and the Third World: East vs South* (New York: Praeger, 1981), pp. 253ff.

25. *Current Digest of the Soviet Press*, various issues.

26. Cf. R. Kanet, 'Patterns of Eastern European Economic Involvement in the Third World', in Radu, *Eastern Europe and the Third World*, p. 315.

6
Soviet arms and African militarization

Robin Luckham

Development assistance to Africa has been offset to a considerable extent by spending on arms. African arms imports rose faster in the 1970s than those of any other world region, though tailing off sharply in the early 1980s. By this time weapons represented at least 6 per cent of Africa's total imports and two-thirds of the value of total net official development assistance. Moreover such figures almost certainly underestimate the real value of the trade, which could well be twice as large (though we simply do not know what proportion is actually paid for in hard currency).[1]

This arms flow has arisen from and helped sustain more or less permanent armed conflict. A series of anti-colonial wars were fought on African territory and have been followed by conflicts over the unfinished agenda of independence. These wars have disrupted economic life in vast areas of the continent. They have created a huge refugee population, estimated by the UN's High Commissioner for Refugees at about 2.7 million in 1983,[2] not to speak of even larger numbers of people who have been displaced in their own countries. In some parts of the continent, most especially southern Africa, conditions of insecurity can be said to be the single most important obstacle to development. At the same time the use of force has become institutionalized in African politics, not just in military regimes (about half the continent's governments are of military origin) but also in non-representative civilian governments.

The historical roots of this situation are in colonial rule and the far from peaceful process of decolonization. Since then conflict has been 'internalized' in the sense that the protagonists are now mainly African. Nevertheless foreign powers remain deeply involved. Their transfers of arms to African countries have increased. They still have major roles in the training of African armed forces. Foreign troops remain (though in diminished numbers) on African soil and still fight in African wars.

Yet the character of the foreign military presence has changed in two important respects. First, the former colonial powers now share their role as the continent's military patrons with the superpowers, especially the Soviet Union. And, second, during the past decade the continent has become incorporated in the strategic terrain of the new cold war.

So the accumulation of arms and conflict cannot be considered without analysing the role played in them by the Soviet Union and the other socialist countries. I do not share the view of those who see in this an expansion of communism, or the replacement of colonial empires by Soviet social imperialism. On the contrary, I would regard the role that the Soviet Union has played as in some broad sense compatible with African interests. The USSR, with other socialist countries, has supported (however hesitantly) the liberation movements in southern Africa. It has enabled even relatively conservative African states such as Nigeria to diversify their sources of arms and diplomatic support. It has helped to underwrite non-capitalist development options in countries such as Tanzania and Mozambique.

Nevertheless some awkward questions must be faced. Why has the Soviet Union given so much emphasis to military assistance and so little to economic assistance? How far have its policies been shaped by considerations of national interest and the imperatives of 'actually existing socialism' in the Soviet Union? To what extent has the military presence of the Soviet Union and of its allies in Africa (like that of other powers) prolonged conflict, sustained unrepresentative governments in power and diverted energies and resources from development?

The socialist military connection

In spite of the euphoria of independence and non-alignment in the 1960s, the Soviet Union had little reason at that time to expect a major readjustment of forces on the continent.[3] Most African states remained firmly under the neo-colonial security umbrella of the former colonial powers. One of the USSR's first attempts to offer an alternative, in the former Belgian Congo, suffered major diplomatic defeat at the hands of the Western powers and the UN bureaucracy, when a request by the government of Patrice Lumumba for a limited quantity of Soviet arms to deal with the Katanga insurrection was blocked and Lumumba himself was overthrown.

In Ghana the Soviet Union and East Germany were asked by President Nkrumah to assist in the training of military officers and security advisers, but this assistance was abruptly terminated after the 1966 coup. In Nigeria the Soviet Union made diplomatic gains by selling combat aircraft and other equipment that Western powers had been unwilling to supply during the 1967–70 civil war, even though it was under no illusions about the conservative nature of the military regime.

In Guinea and Mali the Soviet Union maintained the long-term military relationships established at independence – being until recently the exclusive supplier of arms and military assistance. However, it got precious little in return. Guinea did not allow the USSR to use Conakry airport to airlift supplies during the Cuban missile crisis, although it had been expanded by the Russians for this very purpose. For a short period it allowed Soviet maritime patrol aircraft to patrol the Atlantic from its airfields but terminated these rights in 1977. President Sekou Touré was already re-establishing economic and military ties with the Western powers (especially France) before his death in 1984; the the process was accelerated by the military coup which followed his demise.

In Somalia the Soviet Union's gains were initially more tangible. In 1963 it agreed to train and equip a larger force than the Western powers had been prepared to provide support for. Following the 1969 coup which brought General Siad Barré to power, it consolidated the relationship. It brought forward arms deliveries, increased the size of its military assistance team (which was the largest in Africa in 1974, numbering 2,000, compared with Somalia's own armed forces of 13,500), extended the port and airfield facilities at Berbera and began to use them for its naval and air surveillance in the Indian Ocean. Nevertheless Somalia abruptly terminated these facilities in 1977 after the USSR and Cuba had attempted to restrain it from invading the Ogaden.

The 1970s brought a dramatic increase in the communist countries' military activities in and around Africa. Regular Soviet visits to the Indian Ocean began in 1968 (the USSR had established a naval presence in the Mediterranean since 1963) and came to a peak during the Iranian hostage crisis. In 1975 the Soviet Union and Cuba organized 'Operation Carlotta', a major air- and sealift of Cuban soldiers and Russian military equipment to Angola, enabling the MPLA government to defeat the invasion organized jointly by the FNLA, UNITA, the American CIA and South Africa. It was soon followed by an apparently still more decisive demonstration of the communist countries' ability to 'project their power', the airlift of equipment and Russian and Cuban military advisers to Ethiopia during the 1977–8 Ogaden war and the subsequent offensives in Eritrea – these being the largest operations of their kind that the Soviet Union had undertaken outside its own borders since World War II.

This chain of events also seemed to establish the basis for a longer-term Soviet and Cuban presence in the region. According to US figures, there were approximately 10,000 Soviet and 37,000 Cuban troops and military 'technicians' in Africa in 1981.[4] The great majority were based in Ethiopia and Angola, their numbers having

TABLE 6.1A
Main suppliers of arms to Africa — USACDA estimates
(percentage shares)

Period	USSR	Other socialist[a]	USA	France	Other NATO[b]	All others	Total	Total value of arms transferred ($ million, current prices)
1964–73	27	6	17	26	14	10	100	2,259
1973–77	47	5	6	15	12	15	100	7,738
1978–82	51	5(7)	3	11	14	16	100	27,300

TABLE 6.1B
Main suppliers of arms to African sub-regions, 1978–82
(percentage shares)

Sub-Region	USSR	Other socialist[a]	USA	France	Other NATO[b]	All others	Total	Total value of arms transferred ($ million, current prices)
North Africa	52	6(8)	3	12	10	17	100	17,560
Horn and East Africa	54	4(4)	5	3	20	14	100	4,750
Southern Africa	64	6(6)	0	1	11	29	100	2,225
West and Central Africa	23	3(3)	3	34	25	12	100	2,735

[a] Includes the three other largest socialist suppliers: China, Czechoslovakia and Poland. Figures in brackets (1978–82 only) also include Romania.
[b] Includes the three other largest NATO suppliers in each period: UK, West Germany and Canada in 1964–73, UK, West Germany and Italy in 1973–7 and 1978–82.
Source: USACDA, *World Expenditures and Arms Transfers, 1963–73, 1968–77 and 1972–82.*

slightly increased since the crises which had initially brought them there. Meanwhile some 23,000 African officers and men had been trained in the USSR and Eastern Europe, roughly a third of them since 1976.

The increases in Soviet and East European arms transfers to Africa were equally impressive. According to the US Arms Control and Disarmament Agency the total value of Soviet arms supplied to Africa in the ten-year period 1973–82 was $17.6b,* almost thirty times their value in the preceding decade. Moreover, they had increased markedly, both as a proportion of Soviet supplies to the Third World (from 6 per cent to 29 per cent of the Soviet total) and in comparison with other major suppliers. Between 1978 and 1982 the Soviet Union provided more than half (51 per cent) of Africa's arms, compared with only 3 per cent by the USA, 11 per cent by France and 28 per cent by all the major Western suppliers combined (Table 6.1A). The Soviet Union's domination of the market was most pronounced in Southern Africa, the Horn and North Africa. By contrast in West and Central Africa (Table 6.1B) it controlled less than a quarter of the market.

Major problems surround the use of data produced by the US defence and intelligence communities, whose data and calculations are not accessible to outside researchers.[5] Broadly speaking, however, their statistics for arms transfers are consistent with those of the independent Stockholm International Peace Research Institute (Table 6.1C). It seems unlikely that if more adequate estimates were available they would alter the conclusion that major increases in Soviet arms transfers took place, and that these established the USSR as the continent's largest supplier of weapons.

Such figures as are available for the physical qualities of military hardware supplied to African governments (Table 6.2) tell the same story (though they cover only the major weapons systems). During the five-year period 1978–82 the Soviet Union and Eastern Europe supplied to African governments no less than 4,915 armoured vehicles, 4,630 artillery pieces, 685 supersonic aircraft and 3,760 surface-to-air missiles, more than all the Western countries combined (whose supplies matched the USSR's in only two categories: naval craft and transport aircraft). At the same time the USSR's own specialization in military transactions has increased. By 1976–80 its arms exports represented no less than 79 per cent of all its transactions with Africa including its commercial exports and its gross aid disbursements (Table 6.3). It is notable that the only major African recipients to which it has supplied more exports and development assistance than arms are Morocco, Tunisia and Nigeria, all strongly linked to the West.[6] (Morocco indeed is its largest non-military trade partner in Africa and the second largest recipient of its development assistance).

---

* In this chapter the term 'billion' refers to the US thousand million (10^9).

TABLE 6.1C

Main suppliers of arms to Africa — SIPRI estimates
(percentage shares)

Period	USSR	Other socialist	USA	France	Other NATO	All others	Total	Total value of arms transferred ($ million, 1975 prices)
1960–69	24	3	14	23	34	2	100	1,950
1970–9	52	2	7	23	11	5	100	11,575
1980–3	48	1	14	12	22	4	100	6,424

Note: Percentages for 1980–3 do not add up, due to rounding.
Source: SIPRI, *Yearbooks* and worksheets.

TABLE 6.2

Major weapons supplied to Africa, by weapon type (numbers)

	1978–82			
Weapon type	USSR	Other Warsaw Pact	China	NATO[d]
Land Armaments				
Armoured vehicles[a]	4,410	505	155	2,110
Artillery[b]	4,000	630	415	745
Naval craft				
Major combatants[c]	17	3	—	21
Missile attack boats	20	—	—	7
Other	45	—	2	110
Aircraft				
Supersonic combat	685	—	65	100
Subsonic combat	75	15	—	70
Helicopters	255	70	5	200
Others	110	150	10	310
Surface-to-air missiles	3,660	100	—	205

[a] Tanks, armoured cars, self-propelled guns and armoured personnel carriers.
[b] Includes both field and anti-aircraft artillery.
[c] Includes major surface ships and submarines.
[d] France was much the largest NATO supplier, transferring 1,245 armoured vehicles, 240 artillery pieces, 7 major surface combatants, 7 missile attack boats, 26 other naval craft, 2 supersonic aircraft, 35 subsonic combat aircraft, 80 helicopters and 20 other aircraft.
Source: USACDA, *World Military Expenditures and Arms Transfers, 1972–82.*

But has this flow of military resources to Africa actually shifted the overall correlation of forces in favour of the USSR in the manner that the cold warriors of both sides allege? The evidence is less conclusive than it might seem at first sight. Socialist arms and military personnel have been concentrated in relatively few countries. The only African states in which significant numbers of Soviet, Cuban and East European military advisers have been present are

TABLE 6.3
Soviet arms deliveries to Africa compared with gross aid and exports,
1978–82 ($ million)

	1 Arms deliveries	2 Commercial exports	3 Gross aid disbursed	Arms as percentage of all flows to Africa (columns 1, 2 and 3)
Libya	6,000	444	—	93
Algeria	3,200	132	129	92
Ethiopia	2,200	517	30	80
Angola	950	(72)[e]	21	(91)
Tanzania	260	13	3	94
Mozambique	250	(213)[e]	24	(51)
Zambia	220	4	1	98
Congo	120	7	—	94
Nigeria	90	94	0.2	49
Madagascar	90	24	13	71
Morocco	—	718	49	0
Tunisia	—	141	21	0
Total Africa	14,000	3,389	298	79
Group 2 LDCs[a]	37,420	52,961	1,937	41
Group 1 LDCs[b]	7,080	n.a.	10,358 (25,099)[c]	22[d]

[a] Group 2 includes all LDCs except Group 1.
[b] Group 1 LDCs are those most closely integrated with the CMEA: Cuba, Vietnam, Afghanistan, Kampuchea, Laos, North Korea.
[c] The figure in brackets is the FCO estimate of gross concessional disbursements to Group 1, including not only official aid but also all other payments and subsidies.
[d] Percentage based on gross concessional disbursements (note c) and is perhaps an overestimate, because exports (but not trade subsidies) are excluded.
[e] Figures for Angola's and Mozambique's trade with the USSR are not available. The estimates provided in the brackets are derived from their residual trade with 'country or area not specified' in *IMF Direction of Trade Statistics Yearbook*.
Sources: USACDA, *World Military Expenditures and Arms Transfers, 1972–82*, Foreign and Commonwealth Office, *Soviet, East European and Western Development Aid 1976–1982*, Foreign Policy Document No. 85 (London, 1983); *IMF Direction of Trade Statistics Yearbook 1984*. Trade figures are based on imports of African countries from USSR rather than on Soviet recorded exports.

Angola and Ethiopia (although there are small training teams in a handful of the other countries). Three states – Libya, Algeria and Ethiopia – have imported more than four-fifths of all the Soviet weapons exported to the continent. The first two are members of OPEC, have acquired their arms mainly on arm's-length commercial terms, and have also diversified by purchasing from other suppliers in Europe and the Third World. Only Ethiopia is dependent on the Soviet Union in the sense that it cannot easily obtain its arms from anywhere else. Moreover, the diversity of African recipients is difficult to reconcile with the stereotype of a Soviet grand design. At least six categories can be distinguished.

1. The original but much depleted group of states passing through 'national democratic revolutions' to which the socialist countries gave economic and military assistance in the immediate post-war independence period: Ghana under Kwame Nkrumah, Guinea under Sekou Touré, Mali, Tanzania, Zambia, etc.
2. The national liberation movements in southern Africa – Frelimo, the MPLA, ZAPU, SWAPO, etc. – which the USSR and Eastern Europe and Cuba support or have supported in the past. This support was nevertheless always modest. Moreover, it has been complicated by Sino-Soviet rivalry and has not always been given to the most effective movements (notably in Zimbabwe, where the USSR supported ZAPU in preference to ZANU).
3. Countries to which the Soviet Union has sold arms or provided military aid in order to win specific economic or strategic advantages, regardless of ideological concerns. These are surprisingly few, including Somalia before 1969, Uganda under Idi Amin, and Nigeria, which the USSR has cultivated because it is the richest and most powerful black African state.
4. State socialist regimes with substantial foreign-exchange earnings available for arms expenditure, notably Libya and Algeria, this being as critical a characteristic of their relationship with the USSR as their classification as 'states of socialist orientation'.
5. 'States of socialist orientation' qualifying for assistance because they possess the required structural characteristics (a vanguard party, a revolutionary army, adherence to scientific socialism, etc.) and relationships with the Soviet bloc (dependence on Soviet arms, presence of Soviet, Cuban or East European military and police advisers, and in some cases Treaties of Friendship and Cooperation) although not otherwise central to the socialist countries' strategic concerns. This

TABLE 6.4

Foreign military presence in Africa (numbers of foreign troops, *ca.* 1981)

	USSR and Eastern Europe	Cuba	Western powers	South Africa
Southern Africa	2,200 (Angola 1,600)	24,000 (Angola 23,000)	400	70,000+ (in Namibia and Angola)
West and Central Africa	(1,200)	(910)	4,800	—
Horn and East Africa	2,000 (Ethiopia 1,900)	12,000 (Ethiopia 12,000)	3,800	—
North Africa	4,600	50	3,200	—

Sources: US Department of State, *Soviet and East European Aid to the Third World, 1981* (Washington, D.C., February 1983); Robin Luckham, 'French Militarism in Tropical Africa', *Review of African Political Economy*, No. 24, December 1982; International Defence and Aid Fund, *Apartheid's Army in Namibia*, Fact Paper on Southern Africa No. 10 (London 1982).

group includes countries such as Congo, Benin, Madagascar and Guinea Bissau. Their ideological credentials have sometimes been superficial, and in practice they are not easy to distinguish from the former category of states passing through 'national democratic revolutions'.

6. Countries still fighting 'wars of nations on the path of socialist development in defence of socialism', notably Angola and Ethiopia and more questionably Mozambique, which still require direct and large-scale military aid from 'fraternal socialist countries'.

TABLE 6.5

Main suppliers of weapons to the northern tier of Africa and the Middle East (percentages)

Recipients	Suppliers						Total value of arms transferred ($ million)
	USSR	Other socialist[a]	USA	Other NATO[b]	Others	Total	
1964–73							
Northern tier of Africa[c]	74	4	7	12	3	100	3,872
Middle East and northern tier	49	3	33	12	3	100	10,812
1973–7							
Northern tier of Africa[c]	60	1	3	22	14	100	6,818
Middle East and northern tier	36	1	38	17	8	100	28,637
1978–82							
Northern tier of Africa[c]	45	6	13	26	10	100	25,485
Middle East and northern tier	37	4(6)	19	24	16	100	77,585

[a] Includes Czechoslovakia, China and Poland. Figures in brackets (1978–82 only) also include Romania.

[b] Comprises the four largest NATO suppliers in each period: France, UK, West Germany, and Canada in 1964–73; France, UK, West Germany and Italy in 1973–7 and 1978–82.

[c] Northern tier comprises all countries on northern coast line of Africa, from Morocco in the west to Somalia in the east, including Egypt.

Source: USACDA, *World Military Expenditures and Arms Transfers, 1963–73, 1968–77 and 1972–82.*

Characterizations of the Soviet Union's 'expansionism' in Africa are often based on comparisons with the activities of the United States. But Africa is unique in the extent to which the former colonial powers, especially France, have continued to maintain a military presence after independence. They, rather than the USA, have been the USSR's main rivals in the African arms market. France maintains a network of bases, military agreements and training teams in Africa that at the very least compares with that of the socialist countries and links it to a larger number of countries.[7] It has fewer forces on the ground (Table 6.4) but the capacity of its recently reorganized Forces d'Action Rapide in the metropolis to 'project power' has been amply demonstrated in Chad, the Central African Republic ('Operation Barracuda', which overthrew Bokassa in 1979) and Zaire (the 1977–8 Shaba operations).

Another critical component of the African correlation of forces often left out of cold-war analysis is South Africa, with one of the largest, best equipped and certainly most effective military machines on the continent. As far as its black African neighbours are concerned, it is, though physically present on African territory, a foreign power. It maintains (in Angola and Namibia) a large permanent military force outside its own boundaries and has intervened more often and with greater force than any external power. Moreover, there has been at the very minimum a convergence of strategic interest between South Africa and the Western powers, if not an undeclared alliance. This is not the place for a discussion of Western transfers of military technology to South Africa, nor of the complex politics of 'constructive engagement'. The basic point is that South Africa's military and economic destabilization of its neighbours has blocked revolution and contained the Soviet Union, at minimum political and military cost to the West.

Another reason why assessments of the Soviet, Cuban and East European presence tend to mislead is that they do not situate Africa within the broader strategic picture. The USSR's establishment of military ties with sub-Saharan Africa has approximately coincided with the decline of its influence in the Middle East.[8] Nowhere is this more clearly illustrated than in the northern tier of Africa, stretching from Morocco in the west across to Somalia and Kenya in the east, and including Egypt (which is customarily excluded from African figures, including those presented in the remainder of this chapter). This is a region in which the USSR has been the largest supplier of arms since the 1960s. Yet the United States has also made large strategic investments, including the facilities negotiated in the early 1980s with Morocco, Egypt, Somalia and Kenya for the US Central Command's Rapid Deployment Force. Thus the USSR's share of the northern tier's arms market declined from almost three-quarters in the period 1964–73 to well under a half in 1978–82, mainly reflecting Eygpt's and the Sudan's transfer of their military business to the USA. Moreover, the major powers' military activities are also shaped by their relations with the Middle East and the Persian Gulf. If the arms transfer figures for the northern tier are put together with those for the Middle East, the NATO powers control at least 59 per cent of the arms market, compared with the Warsaw Pact countries' 41–43 per cent.

The wider point is that it does not make much sense to add up the military numbers and infer from them a major Soviet 'threat', 'thrust towards globalism' or 'presence' in Africa. The plain fact is that the Soviet Union and Cuba exercise much less economic and political leverage than do the Western powers. Moreover, they are now less able to influence the course of events than they were in the mid-1970s. Soviet and Cuban arms and military advisers have become immobilized in a classic counter-insurgency in Eritrea. The revolutionary governments of Angola and Mozambique have been seriously undermined by South Africa's military interventions and its support for the rebellions mounted by UNITA (Angola) and MNR (Movement for National Resistance – Mozambique). The shift in the correlation of forces is nowhere more dramatically illustrated than in the Nkomati agreement signed in 1984, under which Mozambique agreed to curtail the activities of the ANC and open up relations with South Africa in exchange for undertakings by the latter to cease supplying the MNR and to normalize economic relations with Mozambique. The Soviet Union and Cuba themselves are evidently well aware of their vulnerability. Since bringing the South African-CIA invasion of Angola to a halt in 1975–6, they have avoided direct combat between their own teams of military advisers and the South African forces, even when the latter have been deployed in Angola itself. Their arms deliveries to Angola and Mozambique since then, though not negligible, have totalled only about half those supplied to Ethiopia in the same period.

In sum, the central structural feature of Soviet, Cuban and East European relations with African states has been their reliance on military ties, and the central paradox is that this has done little to shift the correlation of forces in their favour.

Strategic and economic interests in Africa

Has the USSR acted like any other major power, in defence of its global economic and strategic interests, as defined by those who control the Soviet state? Access to maritime routes around the African continent is important for the USSR's commercial shipping fleets, and it has acquired fishing rights around the coasts of a number of its African partners. In addition, its partners in the CMEA have a commercial stake in the continent at least as large as that of the Soviet Union itself. Economic interests thus certainly exist. But they have probably not been the major factor in Soviet calculations, Soviet commercial trade with and aid to Africa being small compared with its military transfers.

On the other hand there is no shortage of strategic explanations for Soviet interest in Africa. Some observers regard the development of Soviet naval power as the crucial influence, following from the decision to build up a 'blue water' navy capable of preventing the kind of humiliation suffered during the Cuban missile crisis (this might be termed the 'Gorshkov factor', after the admiral who played such a crucial role in reorganizing the USSR's fleet and its naval doctrines during the two decades following this crisis). Others assert that more specific strategic interests have been at stake, in particular the need to monitor the West's naval presence in the Indian Ocean, the Diego Garcia base and the possible deployment of US nuclear-armed submarines.[9] Some have argued that the USSR has wished to protect its vulnerable sea lines of communication to Asia, which became more vital when the Sino-Soviet conflict cut off the alternative direct land routes.[10] Others situate the Soviet Union's African policy in terms of the broader international correlation of forces in the Middle East and Gulf – regarding the shift into sub-Saharan Africa as compensation for the collapse of the USSR's strategic alliances in Egypt and the Sudan.[11] Others again place it in the context of the emergence of the USSR as a truly global power, with an ability to project a 'peacetime' military presence in the Third World – demonstrated by its naval visits to the Indian Ocean and its ability to airlift troops and equipment to Angola and Ethiopia.[12] Few serious strategic analysts on the other hand have maintained that the USSR has developed or even intends to develop an offensive capability in Africa, such that it could interdict Western energy supplies and military installations.

The individual merits of such arguments cannot be discussed within the limits of this chapter. Tog ther or in combination they may suffice to explain the USSR's development of an Indian Ocean strategy, centred on the facilities obtained in exchange for arms and military support in the Horn of Africa and the Arabian peninsula. However, it should be stressed that these facilities are limited in comparison with those possessed by the Western powers in the region. Since being ejected from Berbera the Soviet Union has been careful not to become too dependent upon local bases, for example preferring to install movable equipment on the Red Sea island of Dahlak rather than to build up the mainland ports of Assab and Massawa. At best such facilities reduce the cost of Soviet peacetime deployment in the Indian Ocean. They are not vital strategic assets to be held on to at any price.

Strategic interests do not, moreover, explain the momentous Soviet decisions taken in 1977–8, to arm Ethiopia and participate in the Ogaden and Eritrean wars. The military facilities obtained in Ethiopia are (to say the least) no improvement on those lost in Somalia. Ethiopia is the larger country and a more influential ally in Africa. The Soviet Union's decision to assist it in preserving its territorial integrity could be defended at the OAU and may even have won some diplomatic credit. It is possible that the Soviet Union took a calculated risk that it could establish an alliance with Ethiopia hoping that it would not provoke Somalia into an open breach, believing that an acceptable formula for compromise could be found in the proposed socialist confederal alliance between Ethiopia, Somalia, the Yemen and Eritrea which Fidel Castro promoted during his visit to the region in 1977.

But if these were indeed the Soviet Union's calculations, they were inaccurate, not just about Somalia's reactions and the Ethiopian Derg's willingness to negotiate with the Eritrean rebel movements but also about the prospect of bringing the war in Eritrea to a conclusion by pumping in weapons and carrying through a conventional military campaign of the kind that drove Somalia's army out of the Ogaden. The 1977–8 air- and sealift demonstrated that the Soviet Union and Cuba were capable of using force in the Third World to protect their allies. But before long they had become trapped in a war that could not be won, in Eritrea. At the same time the US was given the pretext it needed to break off the Indian Ocean naval arms limitation talks and to acquire facilities for its own Rapid Deployment Force. Thus although it established a much more *visible* presence in the Horn, the Soviet Union may well have ended up in a weaker strategic position.

The military facilities the Soviet Union has been able to acquire elsewhere in Africa have been less extensive. It has the use of airfield and port facilities in Angola for maritime surveillance activities off the west coast, having enjoyed similar facilities in Guinea up to 1977. More crucial perhaps has been its ability to make use of transit and refuelling facilities for African military operations. Facilities in Guinea and the Congo were vital in the 1975–76 airlift to Angola. The latter in turn was a transit point for the 1977–8 airlift to Ethiopia, to which Cuban troops serving in Angola were directly reassigned. Important as such facilities may have been for the socialist countries' deployments in Africa, however, they do not by themselves explain why these deployments were undertaken in the first place.

The Soviet arms economy

To what extent have Soviet strategy and its arms transfers stemmed from the interests of its own immense military bureaucracy and arms industries? We know that a substantial (and increased) proportion of the USSR's production of conventional armaments – a third to a half of its output of tanks, armoured vehicles and artillery pieces, slightly less than a half of its combat aircraft, around a quarter of its helicopters and around half it surface naval craft – are exported.[13] And in addition to these there are the weapons absorbed by its own naval and military deployments in the Third World.

It is doubtful whether the military threat from the Western powers (though real) is sufficient to explain this accumulation and export of weapons by the USSR and its corresponding exercise of global military power. Some observers have therefore argued that the Soviet Union has a military-industrial or military-bureaucratic complex; or even that it *is* one.[14] But the military sector is not sufficiently separate from the party and state to justify the former description; nor does it sufficiently dominate the accumulation process to justify the latter.

It may be argued instead that the Soviet state and social formation are nationally and internationally reproduced through the control of organized force. This control is located in the commandist structure of the Communist Party although it is exercised through the interlocking hierarchies of the party, military and state security bureaucracies. It is also built into the collectivist mode of production. Central planning tends to privilege the military sector and to sustain an arms economy, competing with its Western counterparts yet operating through different mechanisms.

The process of armament has thus become internalized within the structure of state socialism. Once built into the planning mechanism, the priority of the military sector has become self-reinforcing. The Soviet economy as a whole functions under conditions of aggregate excess demand. In consequence there is constant pressure to increase imports, especially of food and technology. The need for technology has become all the more urgent because of the shift from extensive growth based on large-scale investment to intensive growth based on technical change and more efficient use of resources. But at the same time the supply bottlenecks and excess demand which persist in most sectors mean that there is little incentive to export.

The military industries are the only ones in which such supply constraints do not seem to operate. Indeed, the reverse is true, for it is likely that excess capacity is deliberately maintained in order that increases in output at times of international crisis may be guaranteed. Furthermore, the resources devoted to military R & D are enormous. As a result, the performance of the USSR's weapons compares favourably with that of Western products, ensuring that they are relatively easy to market. To be sure, the military sector remains a major burden on the Soviet economy. But this does not alter the fact that the arms industries are able to thrive and remain internationally competitive in a command economy in which the *state* has given overall priority to military production.

Meanwhile the USSR and its partners in the CMEA have been gradually restructuring their relations with the global economy.[15] In the process they have all but abandoned the theory of 'two world economies' under which capitalist exploitation of the Third World would be replaced by planned long-term exchange between the latter and the socialist countries. Foreign trade has been rationalized as a dynamic 'artery in the blood circulation' of the Soviet Union's (and other socialist countries') 'economic organism', rather than on the previous basis of the barter of residuals.[16] And the socialist countries have moved away from long-term barter agreements with their Third World partners towards a variety of more flexible arrangements, in which open-ended 'framework agreements', joint enterprises and settlement in hard currencies at world prices have been introduced. The application of such principles in an economy which possesses a comparative advantage in the military sector has, however, had one major unanticipated consequence: reinforcement of the USSR's tendency to organize its relations with the Third World around transfers of military technology.

Yet although one can presume powerful commercial incentives to sell arms in the Third World, in order to pay for imports of grain and technology, estimates of Soviet arms transfers and, even more so, of hard-currency earnings from them are extremely difficult to arrive at.[17] It is generally accepted that the export of arms has increased greatly, this being almost the only sector of international trade in which Soviet exports have matched those of the United States. Moreover, it is believed that more of these weapons are being sold on commercial terms than previously. Nevertheless it is unlikely that the proceeds exceed 10–15 per cent (at most) of the USSR's foreign earnings.[18] Such earnings may be one reason for the Soviet Union's interest in selling weapons. But they are certainly not enough to explain why arms should have become *the* major instrument of Soviet relations with the Third World.

Nor are such commercial considerations relevant to all recipients of the socialist countries' military aid. Ethiopia, the largest recipient in black Africa, imported arms to the value of 140 per cent of its total export earnings in the critical years between 1976 and 1980. Some of these were outright gifts. The remainder were supplied on generous credit terms (to be paid back over ten years at 2 per cent interest, with repayments deferred to 1982 or 1983). Nevertheless the Ethiopian government will almost certainly not be able to repay more than a small fraction of these credits. Their function may well be as much political as economic: to remind the Derg of the political debt it owes to the communist bloc.

On the other hand the USSR and its partners have earned substantial quantities of hard currency from arms sales to Libya, Algeria and Nigeria (and perhaps even Angola in spite of its dire economic situation, although we simply do not know what proportion of the cost of Soviet and East European arms and Cuban personnel is paid from its oil and diamond revenues). Commercial gains from these sales – two-thirds of Soviet arms transfers to Africa – may thus offset subsidies and write-offs in respect of other African countries. Nevertheless they are probably not sufficient to be the prime consideration in Soviet calculations.

The comparative advantage the Soviet economy enjoys in the military sector is important for a different reason: that it increases the attractiveness of arms as an instrument of Soviet policy. The (politically determined) opportunity costs of weapons are less than those of other forms of trade, assistance and influence. Moreover, the Soviet Union's weapons – unlike its aid and its commercial exports – are competitive in performance, price and speed of delivery. In much the same manner as the USSR's nuclear arsenal has been used to establish parity with the USA in the arms race, its conventional armoury has been used to consolidate its superpower position in the Third World: not only through its arms transfers but also through its naval strategy and its Third World intervention forces, whose capabilities were tested in Angola and Ethiopia.

However, there remains a sharp contrast between the USSR's treatment of the small number of developing countries whose economies belong to (or are integrated with) the CMEA – Cuba, Vietnam, Afghanistan, Kampuchea, Laos, North Korea – and those that do not. The huge cost of subsidizing the former – along with the relative scarcity of non-military goods and services – reinforces the tendency to be generous with arms and parsimonious with economic assistance to all other developing countries, including the African states of socialist orientation.

Military force and the defence of socialism

Public pronouncements by Soviet leaders mirror those of their Western counterparts in stressing that their activities in the Third World are a response to the activities of their cold-war opponents. Nevertheless they differ in being formulated in terms of a far more explicit theory of history: not a Soviet blueprint *for* the Third World, the Brezhnev, Andropov or Chernenko doctrine described by some Western commentators, so much as a view of how the laws of historical development work out *in* the Third World itself. These laws intensify the contradictions of capitalism, hasten national liberation and establish conditions under which (to quote a statement made by the Foreign Minister, Andrei Gromyko, in 1975) 'the present marked preponderance of the forces of peace and progress gives them the opportunity of laying down the direction of international politics'.[19] The bottom line, however, is Leonid Brezhnev's statement at the 26th CPSU Congress that: 'We are against the export of revolution, and we cannot agree to any export of counter-revolution either.'[20] Thus, under the rubric of 'proletarian internationalism', the Soviet Union has a responsibility to protect the gains achieved by progressive forces from attempts by the imperialist camp to undermine them. And the Soviet armed forces have come to play a crucial role in the 'reliable defence of the entire socialist camp'.[21] Soviet military thinkers have introduced a new category into their classification of Third World conflict, namely wars of nations on the path of socialist development in defence of socialism, such as in Angola, Ethiopia, Kampuchea and Afghanistan.[22]

In so far as the goals of Soviet and Cuban policy are ever publicly discussed, it is in the ideological discourse of official Marxism-Leninism. Of course we will never know the real reason that one course of action rather than another was followed. But this discourse has situated policies in reference to a changing view of the transition to socialism in the Third World. Over the period from the mid-1960s to the early 1980s there took place a gradual retreat from the optimistic assumptions of the Khrushchev era: that the national bourgeoisie could play a progressive role; that as the contradictions of colonial capitalism worked themselves out, a broad-based alliance of progressive forces would emerge in support of a national-democratic revolution and a policy of non-capitalist development; and that this could in the right circumstances open up the way towards a transition to socialism.

Following some of the early failures of Soviet policy in the Third World – for instance, in Ghana, Indonesia and Egypt – this was replaced by a more sceptical analysis both of the difficulties of implementing socialism and of the vulnerability of progressive regimes to cooptation or destabilization by the Western powers. Attention was concentrated instead on a limited number of 'states of socialist orientation' where there was some prospect of implementing a more orthodox Marxist-Leninist model of transformation. The difference between the two views may have been overstated – both, for example, assume that the stage of capitalist development can be bypassed – and their terminology is often inconsistent. For our purposes the crucial difference is the insistence in the more recent discussions on a strong organizational base for the revolutionary state in a vanguard party and revolutionary armed forces, and on closer ties with fraternal socialist countries.

Equally interesting (but less often discussed) has been the development of sophisticated analyses of Third World military establishments in which their revolutionary potential is recognized. This emerges in the writings of the Soviet military establishment's own strategic thinkers (usefully summarized by Katz)[23] and is reflected in the more recent output of the USSR Academy of Sciences' regional institutes. A recent study of *Society and State in Tropical Africa* by a team from the African Institute distinguishes between three situations in which the military establishment can play a progressive role.[24] First, it can be the auxiliary of a 'revolutionary-democratic' post-independence party, as in Tanzania, Guinea and Ghana. Second, military establishments may emerge from guerrilla armies created in the course of protracted armed struggle, as in Mozambique and Angola, the foundations thereby being laid for a relationship between army and society that resembles 'that which usually exists in socialist countries'. Third, the military may play a leading role as a consequence of 'the advent to power of a progressive military group as a result of revolutionary violence', as for example in Ethiopia, Benin and the Congo. In the last case the situation is complex because

> the national armed forces constitute not a revolutionary 'party' army, but one created under the previous overthrown regime... Studies are yet to appear that shed light on how revolutionary ideology arises in the officers' ranks, a professional corporative milieu well removed, in formal terms, from the popular needs...
> Whereas the 'national revolutionary' nature of the military in most

liberated countries is logical and law-governed, their devotion to social revolution is selective and conditioned. Nevertheless people have emerged (sometimes even those who lead armies) who managed to step over the traditional threshold of purely nationalist, petty-bourgeois army-corporative convictions and have become convinced of the need to reform society on socialist principles.

But even if radical soldiers can make the leap from national to social revolution, the latter can succeed only if it is based upon

> a well organised efficient vanguard party in the activities of which the lowest strata of society are involved and which is guided by the principles of scientific socialism. Controlled and educated by a vanguard party, popular armed forces with socialist orientation will then inevitably become an important instrument in the struggle for a new society and in the defence of revolutionary gains.

Thus the Soviet Union and Cuba have actively promoted the creation of vanguard parties in the military-controlled states of socialist orientation. In the Congo and Benin such parties have been formally established since 1969 and 1975, respectively. In Somalia the Somalia Revolutionary Socialist Party (SRSP) was established amid great fanfare in 1976, only months before the break with the Soviet Union. In reality, however, the vanguard parties of all three countries have operated much like the patronage parties of the 1960s.

In Ethiopia, the theory that a vanguard army could in some circumstances stand in for a vanguard party was taken seriously, at least by the Cubans, although it was not regarded as a satisfactory foundation for socialism over the longer run.[25] In 1979 the Commission for Organizing the Party of the Working People of Ethiopia (COPWE) was put in charge of preparations for the establishment of a new single-party constitution, a task which received rather less priority than the war in Eritrea. But the senior cadres of the Workers Party of Ethiopia which was finally created in 1984 are almost exclusively drawn from the Derg, the military establishment and the state bureaucracy.

It is not too difficult, in sum, to characterize the socialist countries' goals in Africa in terms of the principles of official Marxism: namely, support for states of socialist orientation; aid to vanguard parties and revolutionary armies; and, more questionably, the application of Marxist-Leninist nationality doctrines to the complex relations between states and nations. But it is difficult to say how far their policies would have been any different if they had not been formulated in terms of such principles. The theory of states of socialist orientation and the recognition of the revolutionary potential of armies were perhaps as much a recognition of developments already taking place in the Third World and Africa as a blueprint superimposed upon them.

Military aid and socialist transformation?
The socialist countries have inserted themselves in a historical situation with its own dynamic. Broadly speaking, moreover, the development of their relations with African states has fitted into a wider process of radicalization, initiated by the process of decolonization but renewed in the mid-1970s by the Ethiopian revolution and the intensification of the liberation struggle in southern Africa. This struggle brought into being revolutionary regimes in Angola, Mozambique and Zimbabwe (the last being revolutionary in origin only), which almost immediately became the permanent targets of South African destabilization. Elsewhere in the continent the process of radicalization has been sustained, though far more unevenly, by the failures of the post-independence regimes either to cope with the crises of underdevelopment or to establish loyalty to the fragile framework of the nation-state.

It is arguable, therefore, that it was not the policies of the Soviet Union and its allies that were decisive in shaping military relations with African states, so much as the spread of armed conflict in Africa itself. African states requested arms to defend themselves; and received them from the socialist countries. A major proportion of these weapons were acquired by revolutionary or progressive governments whose very survival was at stake. For only if such governments were secure could they continue socialist transformation. But not all recipients of Soviet arms faced such threats, least of all Libya, which was the largest single customer (although it has played a major role in resupplying with socialist weapons a wide spectrum of 'anti-imperialist' governments and movements).

Nor is it yet clear whether socialist military assistance has actually protected a process of transformation – or whether it has merely entrenched conflict and perpetuated underdevelopment. As we have already seen, the flow of socialist weapons to Africa has not been followed up by a corresponding rise in economic assistance. Far from it: arms have constituted a substantially larger proportion of the USSR's transactions with Africa than of its transactions with other developing regions (Table 6.3). Soviet arms transfers (like those of other suppliers) have diverted resources from development: directly to the extent that some Soviet and East European arms are paid for in foreign exchange; indirectly to the extent that the acquisition of arms, even when subsidized by the USSR, generates other military expenditures.

Nevertheless it can be argued that socialist arms may have helped mobilize resources for development through their political functions in sustaining revolutionary armies and vanguard parties. The reality, however, is more dubious. Not all the arms have gone to governments that could, by any stretch of the imagination, be regarded as left wing. Socialist countries have supplied arms to some of the continent's most repressive regimes, such as those of Idi Amin in Uganda and Macias Nguema in Equatorial Guinea. In addition they have sold weapons to earn hard currency and to extract political advantage from states such as Nigeria with which they have little ideological affinity (although in these respects their record is no worse than that of other suppliers). But the major part of their arms and military assistance have still gone to governments that can in some broad sense be regarded as progressive. Yet the value of even this assistance remains open to question. For there is no African state in which socialist transformation has yet been successfully undertaken – whether of the non-revolutionary variety (as in Tanzania) or of a more orthodox Marxist-Leninist kind (as in Ethiopia, Angola or Mozambique).

The reasons for this state of affairs are complex[26] and would have to be evaluated relative to the parallel failures of capitalist development in other African countries. What is crucial for our purposes is that socialist assistance may have actually made matters worse. The model of transformation from above – whether by Leninist parties or by vanguard armies – is in itself problematic. The combination of central planning and proliferating state, military and party bureaucracies has tended to bring atrophy even to those revolutions which arose from the mobilization of the mass of the peasantry in support of people's war, as in Mozambique, Angola and Guinea Bissau. And the retraining of former guerrillas as professional soldiers by military advisers from the socialist countries has tended to cut revolutionary armies off from their popular base.[27]

Furthermore, the socialist countries have failed almost totally to provide the economic assistance that would be required for these African revolutions to achieve economic transformation. Without such assistance they have come under increasing political pressure, fast losing the popular support they enjoyed at independence. Even Angola and Mozambique have been treated stingily, in spite of their revolutionary records and the overwhelming economic difficulties that they faced due to drought and insurrection. If one may judge the Soviet Union's own evaluation of the prospects for socialism by where it places its economic bets in Africa, those prospects are bleak indeed.

Nevertheless, socialist military aid has at least assured the bare survival of most of the states of socialist orientation. Without it the Ethiopian Derg would not have come through the events of 1977 and the revolution would arguably have disintegrated. If Cuba and the Soviet Union had not come to the aid of the MPLA in 1975–6, Angola could well have collapsed into the kind of chaos which disrupted the former Belgian Congo in the early 1960s; and SWAPO's war of liberation in Namibia would have been severely hampered. Furthermore, the Soviet Union cannot very well be held responsible for the build-up of conflict in southern Africa, which arose from the struggle for liberation, and from South Africa's military intervention across its own boundaries against the liberation movements and the front-line states.

Even so, major questions hang over the effectiveness of the socialist countries' protection, as well as the limited scale of their assistance to the liberation movements. In southern Africa they have been manifestly unable to protect the crumbling revolutions in Angola and Mozambique from destabilization by South Africa. In the Horn it is a matter for dispute how far the Soviet Union's fluctuating military alignments were a contributory factor in the outbreak of the 1977–8 Ogaden war. There is little doubt that since 1977 Soviet and Cuban military aid has reinforced the centralization of the Ethiopian revolution in the hands of the military Derg. The latter has frustrated even Soviet and Cuban attempts to persuade it to broaden its power base; and it has mobilized the country's meagre resources for a war it cannot win, against liberation movements in Eritrea whose revolutionary credentials are as valid as its own.

Thus, to conclude, even if Soviet policies in Africa can be accepted at face value, the fact that they have been implemented almost exclusively through military relationships with African states has made them self-defeating. This is a classic case of social relations, those of the production and control of force, prevailing over ideology.

Notes

1. The figures used for arms transfers are those of the US Arms Control and Disarmament Agency (USACDA); those for aid are the OECD's estimates of total official development assistance. On the tendency of most existing statistical series, including those of USACDA and the Stockholm International Peace Research Institute (SIPRI), to underestimate the value of arms transfers, see E.A. Kolodziej, 'Measuring French Arms Transfers', *Journal of Conflict Resolution*, Vol. 23, No. 2, June 1979, and Moshe Efrat, 'The Economics of Soviet Arms Transfers to the Third World – A Case-Study: Egypt', *Soviet Studies*, Vol. 35, No. 4, October 1983. The

reader is also referred to the discussion of the problems of estimating Soviet hard-currency earnings from arms sales in Chapter 9 below.

2. *Refugees Magazine*, No. 5, December 1983, p. 53.

3. A useful factual account of Soviet relations with Africa up to the early 1970s is Christopher Stevens, *The Soviet Union and Black Africa* (London: Macmillan, 1976).

4. Central Intelligence Agency, National Foreign Assessment Center, *Communist Aid Activities in Non-communist Less Developed Countries, 1979 and 1954–79*, ER80-10318U, Washington, D.C., October 1980 and Department of State, *Soviet and East European Aid*, Washington, D.C., February 1983.

5. A comprehensive assessment of the coverage and reliability of the sources of arms transfer data is provided in Michael Brzoska, 'Arms Transfer Data Sources', *Journal of Conflict Resolution*, Vol. 26, No. 1, March 1982.

6. Morocco is not shown in Table 6.3, because it has not been a major Soviet arms purchaser. However since the 1970s it has been the beneficiary of the USSR's single largest economic assistance programme in Africa, earmarked for the development of its phosphates and linked to the requirements of the Soviet fertilizer industry.

7. Robin Luckham, 'French Militarism in Africa', *Review of African Political Economy*, No. 24, May–August 1982.

8. Some observers indeed have argued that it was the *consequence* of this decline; see Hélène Carrère d'Encausse, 'L'URSS et l'Afrique: de la détente à la "guerre fraîche"?', *Politique Internationale*, No. 1, Autumn 1978.

9. There is a good summary of the debate among the proponents of the above two views in Ken Booth and Lee Dowdy, 'Soviet Security Interests in the Indian Ocean Region', in David R. Jones (ed.), *Soviet Armed Forces Review Annual 6, 1982* (Gulf Breeze, Fla.: Academic International Press, 1982). See also Keith A. Dunn, 'Power Projection or Influence: Soviet Capabilities of the 1980s', *Naval College War Review*, September–October 1980, which stresses the limitations of the USSR's naval deployments and of its 'global power projection' capability.

10. Gary D. Payton, 'The Somali Coup of 1969: The Case for Soviet Complicity', *Horn of Africa*, Vol. 4, No. 2, 1981.

11. Carrère d'Encausse, 'L'URSS et l'Afrique'.

12. See particularly Stephen S. Kaplan, *Diplomacy of Power: Soviet Armed Forces as a Political Instrument* (Washington, D.C.: Brookings Institution, 1981) and David D. Finley, 'Conventional Arms in Soviet Foreign Policy', *World Politics*, Vol. 33, No. 1, October 1980. A rather hawkish overall assessment which gives some prominence to Soviet 'intervention' in Angola and the Horn is Stephen T. Hosmer and Thomas W. Wolfe, *Soviet Policy and Practice toward Third World Conflicts* (Lexington, Mass.: Lexington Books, for Rand Corporation, 1983).

13. David Holloway, *The Soviet Union and the Arms Race* (New Haven, Conn.: Yale University Press, 1983) pp. 123–6, and Ultrich Albrecht, 'Soviet Arms Exports', *SIPRI Yearbook 1983* (London: Taylor and Francis, for SIPRI, 1983), Ch. 12.

14. On the concept of a Soviet military industrial complex, see Vernon A. Aspaturian, 'The Soviet Military-Industrial Complex: Does it Exist?', in Steven Rosen, *Testing the Theory of the Military Industrial Complex* (Lexington, Mass.: Lexington Books, 1973); Egbert Jahn, 'The Role of the Armaments Complex in Soviet Society (Is There a Soviet Military-Industrial Complex?)', *Journal of Peace Research*, Vol. 12, No. 3, 1975; Mikhail Agursky and Hannes Adomeit, 'The Soviet Military-Industrial Complex', *Survey*, Vol. 24, No. 2, 1979; and David Holloway,

'War, Militarism and the Soviet State', in E.P. Thompson and Dan Smith, *Protest and Survive* (Harmondsworth: Penguin, 1980). Holloway raises the question whether the USSR *is* a military-industrial complex (p. 158). Nevertheless he is somewhat more circumspect in his more detailed treatment of the politics and economics of Soviet military power in D. Holloway, *The Soviet Union and the Arms Race*, Chs. 6 and 8.

15. See particularly Elizabeth Valkenier, 'The USSR, the Third World and the Global Economy', *Problems of Communism*, July–August 1979. Her arguments are developed at greater length in her *The Soviet Union and the Third World. An Economic Bind*, (New York: Praeger, 1983).

16. N. Patolichev, 'Lenin's Decree is Still Effective', *Foreign Trade*, Moscow, No. 6, 1978, p. 13, quoted in Valkenier, 'The USSR, the Third World and the Global Economy', p. 23.

17. See the discussions in this volume by Smith (Ch. 8) and Deger (Ch. 9).

18. According to USACDA, *World Military Expenditures and Arms Transfers, 1971–1980* (Washington, D.C., 1983), arms sales fluctuated between 11 and 25 per cent of total Soviet exports during the 1971–80 period. The value of these arms transfers may well be underestimated by USACDA (see Efrat, 'The Economics of Soviet Arms Transfers to the Third World'). On the other hand, the hard-currency proceeds from them are unlikely to exceed half the value of the weapons transferred.

19. Quoted in R. Judson Mitchell, 'A New Brezhnev Doctrine: The Restructuring of International Relations', *World Politics*, Vol. 30, No. 3, April 1978, p. 381.

20. Quoted in an article by the Director of the African Institute of the USSR Academy of Sciences, Anatoly Gromyko, 'Soviet Foreign Policy and Africa', *International Affairs*, Moscow, February 1982.

21. As Marshal Grechko put it in 1974: quoted in Mitchell, 'A New Brezhnev Doctrine', p. 380.

22. Mark N. Katz, *The Third World in Soviet Military Thought* (London: Croom Helm, 1982), pp. 126–32.

23. Katz, *op. cit.*

24. Anatoly A. Gromyko et al., *Society and State in Tropical Africa* (Moscow: Nauka Publishing House, 1980). Summarized in English in *Africa in Soviet Studies, 1982*, (Moscow: Nauka Publishing House, 1982), pp. 233–7, from which the extracts below are taken.

25. Raúl Valdes Vivo, *Ethiopia, The Unknown Revolution* (Havana: Editorial de Ciencias Sociales, 1977), pp. 23–33 and 113–15. For reasons of space I have not dealt in any detail with Cuba's role in Africa. The most thorough discussions of this subject are to be found in Carmelo Mesa-Lago and June S. Belkin (eds.), *Cuba in Africa* (Pittsburgh: Center for Latin American Studies and University Center for International Studies, University of Pittsburgh, 1982).

26. Richard Sandbrook, 'Is Socialism Possible in Africa?', *Journal of Commonwealth and Comparative Politics*, Vol. 19, No. 2, July 1981.

27. Horace Campbell, 'War, Reconstructions and Dependence in Mozambique', *Third World Quarterly*, Vol. 6, No. 4, October 1984, pp. 839–67.

7

The Soviet interest in Latin America:
an economic perspective

Nikki Miller and Laurence Whitehead

Introduction

Viewed from Moscow, Latin America is the most distant part of the Third World; the continent with the most exposed and vulnerable lines of communication; an area where the military, economic and socio-political ascendancy of the United States is especially well entrenched; a region, in short, in which the USSR faces a large array of serious handicaps that would tend to limit its capacity to project its power or to consolidate a strong economic presence. Indeed, the Soviet interest in Latin America (excluding Cuba) is so weak that over the period 1954–78 the CIA estimates that the subcontinent received only 5.6 per cent of the aid supplied by Moscow to all non-communist developing countries, and took under 2.5 per cent of Soviet military deliveries to the Third World. In terms of conventional trade the links were even weaker. Between 1975 and 1978 Latin America (other than Cuba) supplied barely one per cent of Soviet imports and absorbed less than one-quarter of one per cent of Soviet exports. Even at this low level of exchange the imbalance in trade was over four to one against Moscow, obliging the USSR to pay in hard currency for most of its Latin American purchases.[1]

Prior to the 1960s, Soviet economic relations with Latin America were highly sporadic, unstable and confined to only a few countries. This can be attributed to three main factors. First, until the 1950s foreign trade played only a subsidiary role in the inward-looking Soviet economy (as analysed in Chapter 8). Within that schema, trade with the geographically remote and politically unpredictable countries of Latin America naturally occupied a low priority. Second, political considerations obstructed the development of commercial relations. It was not until the early 1970s, with the onset of détente and the emergence of nationalist governments in several Latin American republics, that Moscow succeeded in establishing a widespread diplomatic presence in Latin America.

The third reason is more basic, and provides the major theme of this chapter. The structure of production in the two regions shows markedly little complementarity, so that the opportunities for economically advantageous exchange between the Soviet Union and Latin America always have been, and still are, quite restricted. This is not to exclude the possibility of 'planned' or 'forced' convergence over the longer term, when the political conditions are ripe, but such processes must overcome severe resistance given the physical obstacles to trade and the high opportunity cost of reorienting it from more natural markets.

Much has been written on the ideological and strategic objectives thought to motivate Soviet initiatives in the region, and on the destabilizing political consequences these might have. Insufficient attention has been paid to the economic constraints that have so far limited the Soviet presence in Latin America and that, in our view, will present a most formidable impediment to the growth of Soviet power in the subcontinent for the foreseeable future. In this chapter we attempt to rectify the balance by dwelling on the economic dimension of Soviet-Latin American ties. As such it cannot provide a total explanation of Soviet behaviour. Undoubtedly strategic and ideological factors must play their part, but only within the quite limiting constraints that are emphasized here. It is also intended as a challenge to those who view Soviet expansionism as essentially unconstrained to explain why they feel they can overlook these material obstacles.[2]

Historically, Latin America and the Soviet Union both underwent a period of export-led expansion as suppliers of primary products to the expanding industrial economies of Western Europe. During the period of greatest outward orientation, these economies were rivals not partners. After the revolution, the USSR of course turned drastically inwards, and after 1929 the Latin American economies also shifted towards import-substituting industrialization; but whereas the USSR emphasized heavy industry and energy self-sufficiency, Latin America remained largely dependent on the advanced capitalist economies for its capital goods, and attempted self-sufficiency in consumer goods rather than raw materials or intermediate inputs.

There was a brief episode before the Great Depression in which the USSR explored the possibilities of commercial exchange with Latin America (mainly Argentina), as part of its attempt to break out of what was seen as an economic blockade by the major capitalist powers. Between 1926 and 1936 the trade organization Yuzhamtorg was responsible for state trading with South America.[3] Shipping costs were initially extremely high; the trade balance was already a cause for concern, running eight to one in Latin America's favour; and the quality and packaging of Soviet goods proved a problem. Already petroleum products were listed as the best export prospect. Initial Soviet purchases were of hides, quebracho extract, wool, live sheep, iodine and nitrate, and there were plans to buy Brazilian coffee direct, thus cutting out the European intermediaries. However, the depression promptly destroyed creditworthiness on all sides, and in the 1930s anti-communist governments in Buenos Aires and Montevideo denounced Yuzhamtorg as a conduit for subversion.

First in the early 1930s (and then more successfully in the early 1960s) the USSR looked to the oil-importing nations of the Southern Cone as a possible vent for surplus for Soviet crude. In both periods Moscow saw the monopoly power exercised by the major multinationals as the main obstacle to their entry into these markets, and viewed local state-owned oil enterprises as potential allies. In 1931 the USSR offered Santiago a barter agreement whereby Soviet crude would be supplied for Chilean nitrates (the market for which had just collapsed). But Shell and Esso, as owners of the only existing refineries in the country, refused to handle Soviet supplies. In this context Chilean politicians briefly toyed with the idea of creating a national oil company and building a state-owned refinery, before the emergence of a right-wing government strong enough to turn down the Soviet offer. Moscow made a similar offer to Uruguay, where a state enterprise was already in existence. In 1932 this company took 39 per cent of the Uruguayan market, distributing Soviet petroleum products, In 1937 the Uruguayans broke this trade link, just as Moscow was beginning to obtain some return on its investment.[4]

Once again in the late 1950s, after big new discoveries in the Urals, Moscow found itself with a surplus of crude, and began to probe for weak links in the worldwide marketing network controlled by the major capitalist producing companies. In 1959 the Mexican state-owned oil company PEMEX rebuffed a Soviet offer, but its Italian counterpart, ENI, accepted, and Soviet oil soon made substantial inroads into the Italian market. By 1960 some Soviet oil was also flowing to Argentina, Brazil and Uruguay.

This was the economic backdrop to the Soviet-Cuban alliance of 1960, a development which is usually interpreted in purely political terms. In fact there was an unusual convergence of economic interests which greatly facilitated and perhaps accelerated the pact established between Castro and Khrushchev in the summer of 1960. Indeed a purely political explanation of this realignment must overcome an unusually neat and plausible counterfactual objection. How would Moscow have reacted to a Castroite revolution if it had taken place – as it might well have done – not in oil-importing Cuba, but in adjacent Venezuela, another crude surplus economy and one whose voracious import requirements were totally out of line with what Moscow had to offer?

Moscow and the Cuban economy

The events of 1960 must be briefly reconstructed in order to demonstrate the significance of oil as a factor contributing to the completeness and abruptness of Cuba's reversal of alliances. Imported oil accounts for an exceptionally high proportion of the island's total energy consumption (approaching two-thirds). Between 1954 and 1957 Cuba's refining capacity (operated by Esso, Shell and Texaco) increased sevenfold. Thus at the time of the revolution Cuba had the modern refining capacity to match the Soviet Union's surplus of crude. After 1960 the private companies sought to integrate themselves with the new regime by paying taxes in advance and allowing the government to run up dollar debts with them.

However, in February 1960 Anastas Mikoyan visited Havana and negotiated a trade agreement. The USSR would buy one million tons* of sugar per year for five years, paying 20 per cent in dollars and the rest in Soviet goods. It very soon became clear that Soviet crude was much the most attractive item on offer under this heading. Moscow, still trying to place surplus oil, agreed to supply about half Cuba's normal requirements of crude, at a price well below what the American refiners were paying for their Venezuelan product. The US companies refused, alleging that in the absence of expensive alterations their refineries would be seriously damaged. In June 1960 the US Treasury advised the companies not to refine Soviet crude. The startled US ambassador, Philip Bonsal, cabled Washington that if Havana and Moscow could force the US to back down over this issue it would give the Cuban revolution a 'shot in the arm' comparable to Nasser's experience with the Suez Canal, and so it proved.[5]

In July 1960 the refineries, now Cuban-operated, switched to complete reliance on Soviet oil, a situation that persists to the present day. This was a famous victory for the USSR, though not entirely painless. According to Khrushchev's testimony, 'The Americans had cut off the Cubans' supply of oil, their main source of power, and the Cubans were obliged to turn to us for help. Life on the island was in danger of coming to a standstill ... But ... we didn't have enough oceangoing vessels in our own tanker fleet. Our

---

* Both long and metric tons (tonnes) are referred to as 'ton' in this chapter; the US short ton is never used.

efforts ... put a heavy burden on our own shipping system and forced us to order extra tankers from Italy.'[6]

Prior to the oil price rises of the 1970s Soviet oil accounted for about 10 per cent of Cuban imports. The CIA has estimated cumulative Soviet economic assistance to Cuba from 1961 to 1979 at $16.7bn,* of which $11bn took the form of implicit grants, including $1.9bn in underpriced oil. However, this refers only to the oil price subsidy received since 1974, and makes no allowance for the opportunity cost of supplying the island with between 1 and 2 per cent of Soviet crude production over vast distances and at below Western prices between 1960 and 1973.[7]

In July 1960 Havana not only reoriented its entire oil supply from Maracaibo to Baku; it also (as a result of the nationalization, without compensation, of the American refineries) forfeited the United States market for its sugar, a market that had provided the principal impulse to the entire Cuban economy for the preceding half-century. That month Khrushchev decided that the USSR should purchase whatever Cuban sugar the USA had turned away. This Soviet decision to give Cuba virtually unlimited economic aid was announced on 9 July. A full explanation of this Central Committee decision would have to determine how it related to another momentous step taken by the Central Committee at the same time. All economic aid to China was abruptly halted, under a resolution apparently adopted, but not announced, on 11 July.[8]

In Bonsal's words, 'Khrushchev was now confronted with far more than he had bargained for in February when he allowed Mikoyan to make trouble for the Americans in Cuba. The Soviet sugar economy would have to be profoundly readjusted.'[9] Already before the revolution the USSR had begun importing Cuban sugar (half a million tons, or about a tenth of the harvest, in the peak year of 1955), but this rose to 1.5m tons in 1960 and a peak of 3.3m tons in 1961 (almost half that year's harvest). This compares with a total Soviet sugar consumption of about 10m tons p.a. However, according to Bonsal, the sudden availability of plentiful imported sugar was quite welcome to Soviet leaders, who were at that moment seeking to improve supplies to the consumer. After some initial dislocation 'through increased consumption per capita, through the development of markets for refined sugar among Russia's clients in third world countries, and with assistance from other communist countries Russia not only solved the problem of absorbing the portion of the Cuban crop formerly taken by the United States, but did so in the context both of a resumption after 1964 of the upward movement of its home production and of a

---

* In this chapter the term 'billion' refers to the US thousand million (10^9).

contractual willingness to buy far more Cuban sugar than Castro has so far produced for the Russian market.'[10]

In January 1964 Khrushchev signed a six-year agreement to purchase 24m tons of Cuban sugar (2m tons in 1965, 3m tons in 1966, 4m tons in 1967, and 5m tons p.a. thereafter). This was the basis on which Castro commited his revolution to the famous (and failed) '10-million-ton harvest' of 1970. In the event, Cuba managed to supply only 54 per cent of the 24m ton total that Moscow was willing to purchase. Even so, Cuban sugar was supplying 17 per cent of both Soviet and CMEA consumption requirements by the early 1970s.[11] Over the past twenty years sugar has normally accounted for over three-quarters of Cuban export revenue, and trade with the socialist bloc has continued to represent above two-thirds of Cuba's total trade. This high degree of trade integration culminated in July 1972 when Cuba became a full member of the CMEA, and undertook to coordinate its economic plan for 1976–80 with those to be drawn up by the other members. In practice, however, the 1970s witnessed an even more exclusive Cuban economic involvement with the USSR, while links with other socialist countries slackened somewhat.

A recent study of Soviet efforts to assist the mechanization of the Cuban cane harvest provides some significant insights into what this economic integration has meant at the sectoral level. Charles Edquist suggests that the 'inherent deficiencies' of the Soviet-supplied cane-cutting machines was a significant factor in the failure of the 1970 '10-million-ton' harvest. This resulted in the need to deploy large numbers of 'voluntary' labourers, causing severe dislocation among all other sectors of the Cuban economy. Edquist also concludes that even now these problems remain unsolved, despite the introduction in the 1970s of a more advanced model, and that 'there is still a technology gap between Cuba and producers of combine harvesters in other countries'. Moreover, he adds that although this gap 'decreased considerably during the first fifteen years of efforts in harvester design and production ... recently it has increased, and will continue to do so unless Cuba manages to design and manufacture more efficient machines in the near future'.[12] Even in this key area of Cuban-Soviet economic cooperation, after twenty years of effort, the USSR seems unable to provide Cuba with a product that matches the capitalist alternatives.

In the light of this record it is possible to return for a moment to our counterfactual hypothesis. How would the Soviet Union have reacted to a Castroite revolution in Venezuela in 1959? The new Venezuelan regime would be seeking outlets for its crude oil, in competition with Moscow. Neither side would have possessed adequate tanker or refinery capacity. A major concern of the Caracas revolutionaries would probably have been to maintain or increase popular food supplies, meaning essentially increased food imports. Hence it seems improbable that Moscow could either have absorbed Venezuela's export surplus or have supplied virtually any of its sophisticated import requirements. However strong the political incentives for a 'reversal of alliances' to save the hypothetical Venezuelan revolution, it seems extremely doubtful whether the minimum material conditions would have existed to make such an experiment viable.

It is beyond the scope of this chapter to assess the entire Cuban-Soviet economic relationship that has developed since 1960, let alone to appraise its political, strategic and ideological ramifications. However, it is clear that in response to US pressure and Cuban domestic failings the association has become far more intimate, comprehensive and lopsided than Moscow can initially have envisaged. On Cole Blasier's most recent figures, Cuba takes up to 5 per cent of Soviet trade, and in 1979 Soviet aid was allegedly equivalent to about 25 per cent of Cuban GNP.[13] (It is appropriate to compare this with the financial assistance from Washington received by the Commonwealth of Puerto Rico. The net transfer of Federal funds accounted for 15 per cent of that island's gross product in 1970, rising to 22 per cent in 1975, and to 31 per cent in 1980. Recent cuts by the Reagan administration may have brought this back below 25 per cent by 1984.) On the CIA's figures, cumulative Soviet economic aid to Cuba up to 1979 exceeded total Soviet aid to all non-communist Third World countries over the same period, and even greatly exceeded official US aid to Israel.

Information about the most recent trends in the Cuban-Soviet relationship is very fragmentary and impressionistic. However, there are signs of quite considerable jockeying for position, perhaps occasioned by the crisis in the Caribbean, or the setbacks to Cuban-Soviet influence in southern Africa, or simply by the absence of a clear leadership in Moscow. On the economic front critical negotiations are in progress, as the USSR increases the price charged for supplying oil, and as Cuba works out its next five-year plan, due to be synchronized with the CMEA, and approved in 1985. In January 1986 Cuba is scheduled to begin repaying the accumulated debt to Moscow that was postponed in 1972. Although it can be virtually taken for granted that Moscow will agree to a further postponement, this may provide the occasion for the first comprehensive Cuban-Soviet economic negotiations since 1972.

However incomplete this evidence may be, it seems safe to assume that the Soviet leadership will be wary of the long-term economic burden that could accompany the establishment of any more Cuban-type client regimes in Latin America. Indeed the original alliance with Cuba might not have taken on such a binding character in the first place had it not been for the combination of the following three highly exceptional circumstances: the existence of a rare economic complementarity (oil for sugar) that created a favourable momentum in the early stages (when the political links were very tentative); Khrushchev's probable need to 'compensate' for his break with China (a 'hare-brained' scheme, as his successors would say); and a United States blockade intended to destroy the revolution, but pursued only up to the point of a 'self-fulfilling prophecy'.

No such conditions were in operation a decade later, when Moscow had to decide on the scale of economic assistance it was willing to provide to the Popular Unity government in Chile. On the contrary, just as Allende's need for Soviet aid reached its peak, in mid-December 1972, the CPSU found itself required to redouble the scale of its assistance to the floundering Cuban economy.

The Chilean experiment

After the Cuban revolution no other country in Latin America presented itself as a candidate for large-scale Soviet support until the Marxist Salvador Allende led Popular Unity to victory in the Chilean presidential elections of 3 September 1970. For the first time in Latin America, where the Soviet Union had spent the past decade competing for ideological influence with Castroism and Maoism, the popular front tactics advocated by Moscow since 1935 had proved successful. In ideological terms, Allende's Chile was a far more obvious candidate for Soviet aid than Castro's Cuba had been in 1960. However, whereas in the case of Cuba an initially cautious reaction had subsequently given way to a long-term commitment, Soviet policy towards Chile was restrained throughout the three years of Allende's presidency. The USSR consistently sought to avoid being identified with Chile. Moscow sent only a low-level delegation to Allende's inauguration, and in the Soviet media commentators habitually cited Marxist Chile along with the 'progressive' military governments of Peru and Bolivia as testimony of 'the multiplicity of forms within the framework of which Latin America is paving its way to true independence'.[14]

Political caution was reflected in the level of economic assistance granted to Allende. Total credits offered by the Soviet Union amounted to approximately $350m, of which perhaps $260m consisted of long-term credits and the remainder of short-term loans. This figure may be compared both with the volume of

concessionary credits extended by Moscow to Havana to finance
Cuban trade deficits,[15] and with the $600m loan extended to
Argentina's Perón in 1974. Nor was the lack of aid to Popular Unity
compensated for by any substantial bolstering of trade. According
to Popular Unity figures, Chile's exports to the entire socialist bloc
represented only 7 per cent and 6.3 per cent of total exports in 1972
and 1973 respectively. Total imports from socialist countries (of
which the Soviet Union's share was 20 per cent) accounted for 2.5
per cent of all Chilean imports in 1971, 2.7 per cent the following
year and rose to 7.7 per cent during 1973.[16]

The USSR's failure to substantiate its rhetorical expressions of
solidarity with the Chilean revolution can be explained by a
combination of three main factors. First, Allende's years in power
coincided with the height of détente between the two superpowers:
Nixon went to Moscow in May 1972 and Brezhnev returned his visit
the following year, shortly before the Chilean coup of 11 September. From the Soviet point of view, the prestige to be gained among
the world's left-wing forces by supporting Allende simply did not
compare with the potential economic and political benefits of
peaceful coexistence with the United States, and Moscow was
concerned not to overplay its hand in a country which Washington
regarded as being within its 'sphere of influence'. This was
particularly so during 1972, when the Soviet Union's massive grain
imports from the West made it doubly unwilling to jeopardize
superpower cooperation.

The second and third major obstacles to large-scale Soviet
economic assistance for Allende were connected with strictly
Chilean conditions. The second – a fundamental difficulty – was that
the material basis for economic cooperation was largely absent: the
Soviet and Chilean economies were simply not very compatible.
The USSR was at least self-sufficient in Chile's major export,
copper[17] (indeed there were some intermittent Soviet copper
exports to the West), and, like Chile, had long since relinquished its
role as a grain exporter. In the early 1970s both countries were
significantly dependent on grain imports for their urban food
supplies. Allende clearly hoped that the USSR would buy Chilean
copper for re-export to other CMEA countries, particularly
Romania. From the Soviet point of view, however, such a
commitment made neither political nor economic sense, and
Moscow refused to undertake it, despite the fact that Santiago was
having severe difficulties in marketing its copper in the face of
attempts by expropriated US multinationals to block Chilean sales.
In addition, development assistance, particularly within the copper
industry, was rendered problematic by the difficulty and expense

involved in adapting the US-designed and US-built copper mines to accommodate incompatible and perhaps technologically inferior Soviet equipment. Thus very few of the credits granted by the USSR for the purchase of copper-mining machinery were taken up by the Chileans.

Third and last, the reluctance of the USSR to enter into an unequal trading relationship with Chile was compounded by the instability of the Allende government. During the course of 1972 two reappraisals were under way simultaneously. The Chileans seem to have drastically increased their expectations of aid from the Soviet Union (perhaps encouraged by Castro's visit, perhaps spurred on by desperation). At the same time Soviet evaluations of the viability of the Popular Unity experiment were being scaled down as strikes and opposition mounted.

By the beginning of 1972 Popular Unity found itself increasingly unable to supply the consumer demand that its initial policies had stimulated. Faced with an economic blockade by the Nixon administration, depletion of foreign exchange reserves and a growing balance-of-payments crisis, Chilean requests for short-term Soviet credits to finance imports became increasingly urgent throughout 1972, particularly after May, when the economic situation reached a crisis point and inflation slipped out of control. But, as Chilean needs became more acute, Moscow must have seen all its original grounds for caution amply confirmed. Allende had failed to consolidate his power (unlike Castro and the Nicaraguan revolutionaries, he lacked control over the armed forces) and he faced mounting economic harassment by a Nixon administration that seemed set fair for another four-year term.

When Allende went to Moscow in December 1972, he was apparently asking for $500m in short-term loans. But the Soviet Union was itself short of hard currency that year, in part because of its huge grain import bill. Moreover, after the disappointing results of the 1970 sugar harvest in Cuba, Moscow faced the need for a massive increase in economic assistance to maintain the viability of the Castro regime. Although Castro and Allende naturally felt solidarity for one another as leaders of the only two Marxist governments in the Western hemisphere, they were in effect competing for Soviet aid. It was probably the same meeting of the Politburo on 18 December 1972 that both decided against giving a favourable hearing to Allende's request for massive economic aid to Chile and authorized the 1972–6 economic package rewarding Cuba for its full membership of the CMEA. At first it seemed possible that Allende would leave Moscow completely empty-handed. In the event he returned to Chile with only token aid.

The Soviet authorities preferred to allocate all the resources that they had available for Latin America to the integration of Cuba into the socialist system, rather than to risk any part of them in an attempted rescue operation for Chile's politically and economically unstable Popular Unity government. In retrospect it seems fairly clear that, however Moscow had responded in December 1972, the Allende administration would probably have fallen in any case within a year or two. If the Soviet Union had supplied more aid it would have sustained heavier economic losses when the coup finally came. As it was, the Pinochet regime broke all economic links with Moscow and Russia sustained some hard-currency losses. In the long run, however, it seems unlikely that either of the two economies have forgone valuable opportunities for commerce because of their political estrangement. From a strategic viewpoint Chile would have been a doubtful asset to the Soviet Union; and in ideological terms the 'negative example' of Pinochet might be considered almost as useful as the 'positive example' offered by Allende. The thesis of unconstrained Soviet expansionism in Latin America seems hard to reconcile with the Chilean experience.

Argentina and the grain embargo

In sharp contrast to the Chilean case, Moscow has a strong economic incentive to consolidate good relations with Buenos Aires. However, it was not until 1973, with the onset of Juan Perón's second presidency, that this trading relationship acquired a sound basis. Earlier initiatives taken by Perón (who had established relations with the Soviet Union in 1946 and who signed a series of trade agreements between 1952 and 1954) were stymied by a sharp imbalance in bilateral trade, attributable to Argentine reluctance to replace US or European imports with inferior Soviet goods. Subsequently, in the 1960s, economic relations were disrupted by the frequent political intervention of an Argentine military deeply imbued with anti-communism. The 1966 coup, in particular, frustrated a direct oil-for-grain swap of considerable interest to the Soviet trading authorities.

By contrast, in 1973, there were strong incentives – both political and economic – for the two countries to overcome their past differences. As in the 1950s, the Peronists (drawing on their own particular variant of Argentine nationalism – the so–called 'Third Position') were driven by the desire to use trade as a tool of sovereignty,[18] in order to seek a counterweight to US preponderance in South America. The only difference, twenty years on, was that the consolidation of the Cuban revolution and its challenge to US hegemony now made the strategy more realistic. From

Moscow's point of view Peronist nationalism, regarded in the aftermath of World War II as a 'fascist' phenomenon, now fitted in very well with its broad policy towards Latin America of undermining US influence whilst seeking to cultivate its own ties with independent and 'popular' governments. In this context it was highly significant that Perón's election came only a fortnight after the military had intervened to crush the Popular Unity experiment in Chile. Clearly Perón's Argentina was in no sense a substitute for Allende's Chile from the ideological standpoint. It offered no model for the construction of socialism, but it did give Moscow an opportunity to counterbalance the setback in its relations with Latin America caused by the Chilean coup.

The political factors pointing to the opening up of relations between the two countries were underscored by crucial economic motivations. To an Argentine industry that could produce relatively sophisticated consumer goods, the hitherto closed markets of the Soviet Union and Eastern Europe must have looked very promising, and there was also the possibility of securing Soviet technology and equipment for the various hydroelectric schemes intended to solve Argentina's energy problems. For the USSR, the primary incentive was the prospect of an additional source of grain, of which Argentina is one of the world's major exporters. In 1972 it became clear that the Soviet leadership had taken a decision to compensate for the disastrous shortfall in its own harvest with massive imports, rather than further weakening the country's long-term capacity to feed its population by a premature slaughter of livestock. Practically all of the USSR's purchases on the international market in what became known as the 'Great Grain Robbery' of 1972 had come from the United States, and by 1973 Soviet leaders were anxious to diversify the sources of such a politically sensitive commodity.

All these factors help to explain the highly successful visit of Economy Minister José Gelbard to the Soviet Union and Eastern Europe in May 1974. The eastern bloc signed fourteen long-term trade and economic cooperation agreements and offered $950m in CMEA credits ($600m of which was granted by the USSR). The Soviet offer was well over twice the most commonly accepted estimates for Soviet long-term credits to Allende mentioned above. These agreements, together with a Peronist commitment to state control of foreign trading, facilitated a three-fold increase in the volume of trade from 1973–6. However, this expansion was very lopsided: in 1976 Argentina exported about twenty times as much to the USSR as it imported from the USSR. Even so the Soviet market absorbed only about 10 per cent of Argentine exports in that year.

At first it seemed that this newfound trading relationship might be threatened by the March 1976 coup led by the strongly anti-communist General Jorge Videla. The Soviet Union, however, made haste to indicate that commercial logic would take precedence over ideological distaste. The Soviet media did not carry any condemnation of the coup, and the USSR subsequently used its veto in the UN to thwart US attempts to secure international condemnation of Argentina's appalling human rights record. For his part, Videla decided not to repeat the mistake of his predecessor General Onganía, whose 1966 coup had abruptly halted a promising upsurge in trade with the Soviet Union. By 1978 Argentina had overtaken Brazil as the USSR's foremost non-communist trading partner in Latin America.

Both parties saw their policies vindicated in 1980. On 4 January President Carter announced a US embargo on shipments of grain, meat and dairy produce to the USSR, as sanctions against Moscow for the invasion of Afghanistan. This presented Argentina with the opportunity to become for well over a year the Soviet Union's principal source of grain supplies. (President Reagan lifted the US embargo in April 1981.) Argentina's refusal to support the embargo can be explained by the fact that there were no political considerations sufficient to outweigh the overwhelming commercial incentives. Carter, by making Argentina a prime target of his human rights campaign, had minimized his leverage over the highly nationalistic Argentine military, who dismissed American moralism as hypocritical. In 1980 Argentina sold 80 per cent of its grain exports to the USSR, thereby tripling the volume of trade between the two countries, A long-term supply agreement was signed in July of that year.

At this stage Soviet officials may well have considered that their early hopes of mutually beneficial and stable trading agreements with Argentina, first raised by the 1974 agreements, had come to fruition. However, speculation throughout 1981 and 1982 that Argentina would permanently replace the United States as the Soviet Union's principal grain supplier was brought to an end by the announcement in July 1983 that the two superpowers had signed a major long-term grain agreement. The US embargo had proved more economically damaging to US farmers than to the Soviet authorities, and, moreover, Soviet import requirements had begun to diminish because of somewhat improved grain harvests. In the light of Yuri Andropov's remark that at this time relations with the United States were 'tense in virtually every field', the 1983 agreement shows that the United States must enjoy a significant commercial advantage over Argentina as a grain supplier to Moscow. Soviet grain imports from Argentina have shown a steady decline – from 13.4m tons sold in the peak year 1981–2 to 11.0m tons in 1982–3 and 6.9m tons in 1983–4.[19] Although the Soviet harvest is expected to show yet another serious shortfall in 1984–5 (pushing import needs to a possible 45m tons compared with 31.5m tons in 1983–4), early indications are that Soviet grain buyers are turning to the EEC and the United States for their extra supplies. (In September 1984 the Reagan administration, presumably with an eye to appeasing the powerful US farm lobby in the light of the forthcoming presidential elections, gave the Soviet Union the option of buying 10m tons of grain over and above the 12m tons available under the 1983 agreement.) 1984–5 Soviet imports from Argentina are expected to remain static at around 7.0m tons.[20] It appears that, even with so much at stake for both sides, the Soviet Union and Argentina have been unable to consolidate the close trading relationship temporarily brought about by the US embargo.

Soviet concerns about Argentina as a grain exporter derive from two factors: (1) the unreliability of supplies; and (2) the costs of the operation.

The clearest instance of disrupted exports occurred during the Falklands–Malvinas war of May–June 1982 as a result of the extension of a British naval blockade to only twelve miles off the Argentine coast. The ports of Bahía Blanca and Quequén, which together account for 20 per cent of total grain exports, were particularly badly hit by the blockade. More generally Argentine supplies have never been very reliable. There are two main reasons. First, Argentina's port and storage system is constantly operating at full capacity and is therefore endemically prone to breakdown and delay. Second, the agricultural sector itself is not geared to steady production. Some of the difficulties are caused by nature – droughts and floods – but then some have been compounded by the erratic, short-term economic measures of the 1976–83 military government, which could not decide whether it preferred to stimulate production with subsidies or to cream off much of the revenue generated by the agricultural sector by the imposition of high export taxes.

Four factors contribute to the high costs of purchasing grain from Argentina. First, throughout the embargo Argentine grain was selling at well over 10 per cent above US price levels. Moreover, Soviet officials have indicated serious concern about the poor quality of Argentina's 1983 wheat shipments. Second, transportation costs are high. Since mid-1980 freight rates on the Argentina–Black Sea route have always been at least $10 per long ton higher than on the corresponding United States run, and the differential has often been far greater. The third problem lies in Argentina's inability to provide credit facilities. This factor may be particularly significant at a time when gold and/or oil prices are declining and when the Soviet Union experiences cash-flow difficulties, as happened at the beginning of 1982.

Last, and perhaps most important from the Soviet point of view, there is the problem of the trade imbalance, an issue persistently raised by Soviet officials as early as May 1981. The complaint is hardly surprising, for in 1981 Soviet imports from Argentina exceeded exports to Buenos Aires by a ratio of eighty to one. In May 1983 Soviet negotiators proposed setting a target of $300m for Argentine imports from the USSR during that year, to consist primarily of railway and oil production equipment, and hydroelectric turbines (all to be supplied to Argentine public enterprises). However, Argentine state companies appear almost as resistant as private businessmen to the acquisition of Soviet equipment, and although there may have been a political motive for this resistance under the 1976–83 military government (which appointed conservative officers to run the public sector), the prospects for Soviet exports hardly seem much better under the current democratically elected administration. In the context of Argentina's current profound economic crisis, infrastructural investment projects and those with high capital intensity and long gestation periods are most likely to be cut back. Buenos Aires prefers to sell as much of its grain as possible for hard currency, rather than for Soviet equipment of doubtful quality and low compatibility with existing plant.

Overall there may well be a stronger material basis for convergence between the Soviet Union and Argentina than is true of any other country in Latin America, including pre-Castro (but not post-CMEA) Cuba. Even so this has not produced any deep or lasting economic realignment. The most frequently cited obstacle is the deep strain of anti-communism that has long existed within the powerful Argentine armed forces. Yet such ideological obstacles to economic cooperation have not proved insurmountable over the long run. The more fundamental problem is that since Argentina does not need Soviet oil, and has not been willing (to date) to become dependent on Moscow for more than a fraction of its military equipment, the economic complementarity is hopelessly one-sided. Argentine abundance is not matched by any desirable Soviet export lines. In a particularly tense international conjuncture it might nevertheless be worth Moscow's while to commit the hard currency required to cement the relationship. However, when it comes to allocating scarce foreign-exchange resources, Soviet planners seem properly parsimonious – they will not pay over the odds for their supplies from a non-client state except in temporary emergencies. Argentina would have to restructure its economy and its politics to a very far-reaching and improbable extent in order to achieve lasting complementarity with the Soviet Union. Since there is no prospect of Argentina's becoming a Soviet client, and since Argentine nationalism would always limit the positive content of any strategic cooperation, the only basis for Soviet-Argentine convergence is that of hard-headed economic calculation. Even in the Argentine case the material basis for such a convergence is distinctly limited.

Before leaving the topic of Argentina a second counterfactual speculation seems worthy of mention. How would Moscow have reacted if Allende had achieved his electoral victory not in Chile, but in Argentina, and not at the height of détente, but in the midst of the grain embargo? Would the combination of the economic incentives that Argentina could offer, and the ideological appeal of the Popular Unity model, have induced Moscow to take the risks and to make the commitments that would validate the charge of Soviet expansionism? Even if Latin America had presented the USSR with this exceptionally favourable combination of inducements, it seems to us far from certain whether the Soviet leadership would really take the plunge a second time. On a sober calculation of risks and advantages it would surely be a question of fine judgement. Our case studies suggest that, with the possible exception of Khrushchev's personal impulsiveness in the summer of 1960, sober calculation normally governs Soviet behaviour at least in the most distant area of the globe, with a substantial bias against costly forms of risk-taking.

The Sandinista revolution
Does Soviet behaviour towards Nicaragua since the 1979 revolution contradict this overall judgement? Apart from Castro, the Sandinistas are the Latin American leaders most willing – for reasons of ideological conviction, and also perhaps of political necessity – to carry through domestic restructuring in order to 'lock-in' Soviet economic assistance.

The July 1979 victory of the Nicaraguan FSLN (Frente Sandinista de Liberación Nacional) apparently came as a great surprise to Soviet Latin Americanists,[21] for whom Central America had long been an area of low priority. Neither the Soviet Union nor its local supporters had played an active role in the FSLN struggle. Moscow gave no direct material aid. Of course Castro's Cuba played a more active role in promoting the Sandinista cause, but we doubt whether the direct support provided even by Havana was by any means decisive. Indeed it seems likely that other Latin American countries, notably Panama and Venezuela, made a more active contribution in terms of matériel. Even after the triumph of the revolution the Soviets took care to contain their enthusiasm.

However, as the Sandinistas began to consolidate their power, Soviet commentaries took on a more positive tone. Academic specialists began to argue that the Sandinistas had been able to avoid many of the mistakes made by Allende in Chile, primarily because they had understood that the issue at stake in revolutionary Nicaragua was 'not ... the broadness of the economic reforms but ... the reliable securing of all (or the maximum possible) fullness of power'.[22] The successes of the Sandinista government in securing control of the armed forces, promoting a mixed economy in order to avoid antagonizing the middle classes, and developing organizations of mass participation were all noted approvingly.

Despite the enthusiasm shown in academic circles for the Sandinista revolution, at an official level Moscow has proved no keener to grant Nicaragua the 'socialist' status that would command a major Soviet commitment than it was with Chile. For a long time Sandinista statements of adherence to Marxism-Leninism were conspicuously ignored in Soviet commentaries. It was not until 1982 that Nicaragua was granted the status of a 'people's democracy' which was 'socialist-oriented'[23]. However, during 1983 this designation was largely dropped in favour of the more neutral term 'progressive' in the light of heightened tension throughout Central America. In summary, Soviet officials have been wary of conceding the Sandinistas a political status that would entitle them to unlimited protection. Although US commentators frequently express alarm at the scale of Soviet military assistance to Nicaragua, American-backed forces seem to have enjoyed an immunity both in Nicaragua's air space and in its territorial waters (at least until mid-1984) that could occur only if the Russians were exercising considerable restraint.

Moscow's reluctance to become overcommitted to Nicaragua was reflected in the slowness with which economic relations were developed with the Sandinista government. Initially the Sandinistas themselves (like the Chilean Popular Unity) were not sorry if the Soviet Union kept its distance. There was a fierce controversy in the United States over whether or not aid should be sent to Nicaragua, and Castro impressed upon the Nicaraguans the need for workable relations with Washington. The Nicaraguan revolution had attracted much support within Latin America and from more progressive European governments, and the Nicaraguans had some success in their attempts to diversify away from the United States without tying themselves to the Eastern bloc. Emergency aid donated by the USSR in the immediate aftermath of the revolution was of negligible value and far overshadowed by contributions from Western sources. No significant contacts were made between the two governments until March 1980, when a delegation of Sandinista leaders travelled to Moscow. They returned with a reciprocal most-favoured-nation trading agreement and various other accords providing for Soviet assistance in fishing, water power resources, mining and geological surveys. An agreement was signed to foster the development of ties between the CPSU and the FSLN, and the Nicaraguans endorsed Soviet policy on such contentious issues as Afghanistan and Kampuchea.

However, in 1981, when the incoming Reagan administration adopted a manifestly tougher approach, symbolized by the suspension on 17 January of a $75m aid package (on the grounds that Nicaragua was supplying arms to the guerrillas in El Salvador), the Sandinistas started appealing for greater assistance from the Soviet Union. The first tangible response came in April 1981, when the USA's refusal to deliver a wheat shipment to Nicaragua enabled the USSR to win an easy propaganda victory, and demonstrate its disdain for Washington's grain embargo, by donating 20,000 tons of grain and other supplies. Nevertheless no official credits were offered until September 1981, when a visit to Moscow by Interior Minister Tomás Borge yielded the opening of a $50m credit line for the purchase of Soviet machinery and equipment (at an annual interest rate of 4 per cent rather than the 2.5–3 per cent more usually granted to 'revolutionary' Third World governments).[24] US intelligence estimates quoted by the *Los Angeles Times* (*International Herald Tribune*, 13 January 1984) put Soviet and East European aid to Nicaragua in 1982 at a total of $81m, of which $25m was for economic aid and $56m for military aid (cumulative military aid 1979–82 was put at $125m). This source states that Cuba provided Nicaragua with almost no economic or military aid that was not supplied or paid for by Moscow and its allies. (By comparison the US supplied Nicaragua with $60m in economic aid in fiscal year 1981, falling to only $6m in fiscal year 1982, and US economic aid to El Salvador nearly doubled from $105m to $186m between fiscal years 1981 and 1982.)[25]

Around mid-1982 the Sandinistas stepped up their search for Soviet support. This can be traced directly to the destabilization policies adopted by the Reagan administration. These activities, and their consequences within Nicaragua, vindicated the position of those members of the FSLN who argued for integration with the socialist bloc as the best defence against Washington. 'Coordinator' Daniel Ortega's May 1982 visit to Moscow followed the declaration of a state of emergency in Nicaragua and tougher economic measures indicating a move away from a mixed economy towards a more centralized model with emphasis on the public sector. Ortega negotiated a $100m Soviet credit for deliveries of industrial machinery and equipment, a $50m credit for a feasibility study of a proposed hydroelectric station and secured a promise of Soviet assistance in the expansion of facilities for ship repair at the Pacific port of San Juan del Sur.[26] In June, the USSR sent $31m of emergency aid to help repair damage caused by widespread flooding. A succession of visits by Sandinista leaders to Moscow since mid-1982, including ones by Tomás Borge in September 1982 (apparently at the invitation of Yuri Andropov, although not publicized by Moscow) and by Daniel Ortega in March 1983 and again in June 1984, seem to have produced fairly little in the way of concrete economic assistance. However, one agreement was apparently signed in January 1984 for the construction of a $20m yarn mill to enable Nicaragua to substitute imported yarn. Military aid has probably been increased substantially as the CIA's covert war has become more serious.[27] We have no reliable figures on these recent developments, but it seems likely that Nicaragua's needs – both for military equipment and for balance-of-payments support – continue to outstrip Soviet bloc support by a large margin.

As was the case with Chile in 1970 the USSR's reluctance to make a substantial economic commitment is unsurprising given Nicaragua's very exposed strategic location, and the many competing claims on Soviet resources. Moreover, the material basis for economic cooperation is quite tenuous. Even in good years Nicaragua has little to offer the Soviet Union, for its exports consist primarily of sugar, coffee and cotton, which are already supplied, for example by Cuba. In any case in present conditions the surplus available for export is very limited and what the Nicaraguans need most is hard currency rather then the bilateral arrangements that Moscow prefers. The 1980 trade agreement, by the Soviet Union's own admission, did not come into operation until July 1981.[28] Although the Soviet Union increased its exports to Nicaragua in 1982, there has been no corresponding growth in its purchases of Nicaraguan goods. According to Nicaraguan Ministry of Foreign Trade data, 12 per cent of Nicaragua's $775m imports in 1983 came from the socialist countries (about the same as in 1982) as compared with 15 per cent from Central American countries, 27 per cent from other Latin American countries and 19 per cent from the United States.[29]

Nicaragua is acutely dependent on imported oil, but under the San José agreement of 1979 it received all its supplies until late 1983 (at below market prices) from Mexico and Venezuela – as do ten Caribbean countries of varied political complexions. Although Venezuela suspended shipments in mid-1983 because of Nicaragua's inability to pay its oil debts, Mexico undertook to supply the Venezuelan quota. The first Soviet oil delivery reportedly took place at the port of Corinto in January 1984, following counter-revolutionary attacks on Nicaragua's only three oil-unloading ports, and at a time when Mexico started to delay shipments, apparently also because of Nicaragua's payment arrears.[30] On 20 March 1984 the Soviet vessel Lugants, carrying 250,000 barrels of crude oil, was damaged at Puerto Sandino by a mine planted with the active involvement of the CIA. Although no definite information is available about the extent to which the Sandinistas have turned to Moscow as a source of oil, in August 1984 an unconfirmed report stated that Nicaragua received one million barrels of crude oil and petroleum products from the Soviet Union in the first half of 1984, compared with 484,000 from Mexico, and forecast that the Soviet Union could account for 65 per cent of Managua's 1984 oil imports.[31]

Following Castro's advice rather than his example, the Sandinistas have left much of their export economy in private hands, and still aim wherever possible to sell in Western markets. Thus five years after the revolution there has been no reorientation of the Soviet and Nicaraguan economies remotely comparable to the Soviet-Cuban embrace of 1960–1. Moscow planners can no doubt foresee that in the short-term the Nicaraguan economy is (like Allende's Chile) moving rapidly towards a desperate shortage of hard-currency reserves, not a deficiency the USSR would be eager to make up from its own limited resources. The Sandinistas came to power after a lengthy period of civil war which proved highly destructive to both the manufacturing and the agricultural sectors. In order to implement their reforms and sustain the revolutionary momentum, the Sandinistas were forced to import massive quantities of basic goods in 1980–1. The results of these policies began to emerge in 1982 in the form of a severe balance-of-payments crisis, a desperate shortage of foreign exchange, and the need to curb imports or borrow heavily on the international markets. The economic situation has been exacerbated since mid-1982, when attacks by US-inspired counter-revolutionary forces have obliged the government to divert a substantial part of its local resources to defence spending. By early 1983, Nicaragua had joined most Latin American countries in failing to service its external debt, which reached the level of $3bn in September 1983.[32] In present circumstances how much the Soviet Union supports Nicaragua economically comes down to the question of to what extent it is prepared to subsidize an extremely weak economy.

For the present the verdict must remain open on how far Moscow is willing to go in order to aid the beleaguered Sandinista regime. Some observers suggest that there has been a large increase in Soviet backing for Nicaragua since early 1983 and point, for example, to the fact that Managua obtained 'observer' status in the CMEA in September 1983. The Nicaraguans have perhaps done better than, for instance, Mozambique (see chapter 15), but not necessarily well enough to protect their revolution. Despite the appeal of Sandinista ideology and Moscow's undoubted satisfaction at seeing the United States entangled with the radical nationalists of Central America, there is no conclusive evidence on the fifth anniversary of the Nicaraguan revolution that the Soviet leadership had decided on a high-risk expansionist course in the area. Probably the best way for the USSR to maximize Washington's difficulties is to provide only moderate levels of direct support and to rely on the Contadora* states and the US Congress to exert restraint. The material obstacles to a 'forward' Soviet policy on the isthmus should powerfully reinforce Moscow's traditional reluctance to become overcommitted in Latin America.

Conclusion

The Monroe Doctrine, made public in November 1823, was first formulated as a secret communication to *Moscow* as well as to London. 'It is impossible', according to the Doctrine, for either of these European powers 'to extend their political system to any portion of [the American] continent without endangering our peace and happiness; nor can anyone believe that our southern brethren, if left to themselves, would adopt it of their own accord.' Since 1979 the US has sought to shelter the Americas from Soviet revolution by invoking a doctrine originally inspired by fear of European monarchism and reaction as exemplified by the Tsar and his holy alliance.

Between 1917 and 1958 Moscow was intermittently portrayed as posing a serious revolutionary threat in various parts of the Americas (including the United States). Soviet ideology and Comintern control over the local communist parties of the region both lent credence to this fear. Yet for forty years the reality was far less formidable than the propagandists on either side have maintained. As late as 1959, although a fully-fledged world power, the

---

* The Contadora states are Mexico, Venezuela, Colombia and Panama, which agreed on 9 January 1983 to work together to promote a peaceful solution to the Central American crises.

Soviet Union had less presence in Latin America, and probably less interest in the subcontinent, than in any other area of the globe, with the exception of black Africa. Moscow's information was poor, Soviet economic links were minimal, and political and military links were virtually absent.

From the Soviet standpoint the 1960 Cuban reversal of alliances can be regarded as essentially a lucky accident. However that may be, the consequences were momentous. Thenceforth one vulnerable island in Latin America become a vital strategic asset, a crucial source of information and guidance, and a potential platform for further Soviet gains in the western hemisphere. On the other hand, Cuba was also for the first decade or more a wayward, and over the long haul a very costly and potentially embarrassing, economic dependency. The Cuban revolution cannot be allowed to falter, nor can the Cuban economy be seen to fail. Thus Moscow has found it far from easy to limit the costs of its western hemisphere exposure, or to consolidate the gains that initially seemed on offer. Even in the freak year 1981, Soviet trade with Cuba exceeded trade with all the rest of Latin America (Argentine grain included). In more normal years, perhaps four-fifths of all Soviet transactions with the subcontinent have been focused on one physically isolated Caribbean island. For a quarter-century Cuba has overshadowed all other potential Soviet interests in the Americas, and has provoked a degree of polarization throughout the region that has always overshadowed Moscow's opportunities for normal ties with the other republics.

One consequence of this abnormal history is that much of the literature on Soviet policy towards Latin America has neglected the economic factors that are in general found to motivate and constrain relations between nations during times of peace. This chapter has sought to rectify the balance by emphasizing such traditional considerations, and by stressing how powerfully they may affect the political, military and ideological factors so heavily emphasized elsewhere. Some otherwise neglected themes are thrown into high relief by this approach, namely:

1. the formidable physical and communications problems that must be overcome if the USSR is to project its presence into this region;
2. the significance of Moscow's intermittent surpluses of crude oil as a factor in shaping Soviet economic (and therefore political) links with the Latin American republics. Several other (highly politicized) primary product markets could be analysed in similar terms. Soviet ties with Bolivia, for example, have been substantially affected by the peculiar conditions of the

international tin market. Similarly, special conditions apply to grain, sugar and copper;

3. the almost total lack of complementarity between the Soviet economy and non-communist Latin America across virtually the entire range of industrial products and financial services. It seems that apart from armaments, Soviet industry has almost nothing to offer that any Latin American purchaser would wish to buy, even at artificial prices.

Why so? Latin American industrialization concentrated on substituting imported consumer goods, not a high priority for the USSR. Consequently Soviet industry compares unfavourably with much of Latin America in this sector. Soviet industrialization emphasized capital goods, and here the USSR may well be stronger than Latin America in various sectors. However, since Latin America still imports much of its sophisticated capital equipment from the OECD nations, here too Soviet products are mostly inferior to present sources of supply.

In the other direction, Latin American industry could probably supply various items of interest to Moscow if it were not for acute difficulties over the means of payment. Gold, oil and bilateral barter deals seem to provide the only viable means of finance that either side can activate. On this basis Moscow must exercise extreme parsimony, and in practice regards the region mainly as an occasional source of offset to the chronic deficiencies of Soviet agriculture; and, finally,

4. in theory, given a strong enough political commitment and sufficient time, any two countries can overcome their initial lack of economic complementarity by making sufficiently drastic efforts to restructure their productive arrangements. The integration of the Cuban economy into the CMEA would at first sight appear a striking confirmation of this theory. However, we argue that there was in fact an exceptional (and largely unnoticed) potential for economic complementarity between Cuba and the Soviet Union before the decisive political commitments were made. Even so, the subsequent restructuring has proved economically costly to both sides, and the structural integration which may finally be achieved must be far from optimal for either country in conventional economic terms. This experience does not provide real confirmation of the theory indicated above. Indeed, in the light of its Cuban experience, Moscow has been quite reluctant to undertake further such commitments in Latin America. Since Chile and even Nicaragua have both encountered major

obstacles in the path of 'forced integration', the larger and stronger economies of Latin America are unlikely to entertain many illusions.

Since the 1950s the Soviet bloc has certainly expanded its influence in Latin America, but it is still not great either in absolute or in relative terms. What are Soviet objectives in Latin America, and how high a priority do they receive in Moscow? A Soviet-dominated Latin America is surely a highly improbable scenario and one which is likely to receive a negligible degree of priority in Moscow. On the other hand, Russian policy makers *are* likely to welcome any low-cost opportunity to drive a wedge between Latin America and the USA, just as Washington seeks to prise Moscow and its Third World friends apart. But the USSR might be expected to proceed with greater caution than the USA, given that it has less to offer in economic terms, and given the degree of suspicion and distrust that the Russians must overcome if they are to build goodwill in Latin America.

Hard evidence is always difficult to come by on Soviet policy formation, but our conclusion is that Soviet medium-term goals in Latin America are likely to be quite sober and realistic. Contrary to the 'unconstrained expansionism' school, we expect them to be mainly negative (i.e. undermining Latin America's solidarity with the US – a policy that Washington can best counter by attending to Latin America's real problems). Like all great powers, the USSR may sometimes be tempted or provoked into distant and costly commitments, but on the record outlined above it would be surprising if it were willing to pay a very heavy price in other areas in order to secure its objectives in Latin America.

Notes

1. Calculated from CIA estimates summarized in Robert H. Donaldson (ed.), *The Soviet Union in the Third World: Successes and Failures* (London: Croom Helm, 1981), pp. 339–49.

2. For a recent, and well-constructed, example of the dominant view, see Robert S. Leiken, *Soviet Strategy in Latin America*, The Washington Papers 93 (Washington, D.C.: Praeger, 1982).

3. Stephen Clissold (ed.), *Soviet Relations with Latin America 1918–68* (London: Oxford University Press, for the RIIA, 1970), pp. 74–6 and 79–81.

4. These episodes are described in George Philip, *Oil and Politics in Latin America* (Cambridge: Cambridge University Press, 1982), pp. 183–6 and 190–2.

5. Philip W. Bonsal, *Cuba, Castro and the United States* (Pittsburgh, Pa: Pittsburgh University Press, 1971), p. 150.

6. *Khrushchev Remembers* (London: Sphere, 1971) p. 451. It seems that Eisenhower's calculation was that the United States could put enough pressure on the owners of independent tanker fleets to prevent their being chartered to the Russians. Moscow would fail to meet Havana's minimum requirements, the Cuban

economy would collapse, and the revolution would fail. However this ignored the fact that not all America's allies viewed Castro's revolution with equal abhorrence, a divergence of view exacerbated by the over supply of tankers at this time, and by resentment of many independents at the overbearing conduct of the 'Seven Sisters'.

7. Cole Blasier, *The Giant's Rival: The USSR and Latin America* (Pittsburgh, Pa: Pittsburgh University Press, 1983), p. 124, gives the CIA estimate in detail.

8. Indeed, K.S. Karol, *Guerrillas in Power* (London: Jonathan Cape, 1971), argues, perhaps provocatively, that 'the Cuban affair gave him [Khrushchev] an unexpected internationalist alibi' for harsh measures against the Chinese economy (pp. 203–4).

9. Bonsal, *Cuba*, p. 156.

10. *Ibid.*, p. 208.

11. See Maurice Halperin, *The Taming of Fidel Castro* (Berkeley, Calif: California University Press, 1981), pp. 13–15, for the 1964 agreement, and Cole Blasier, 'Comecon in Cuban Development', in C. Blasier and Carmelo Mesa-Lago (eds.), *Cuba in the World* (Pittsburgh, 1979), p. 243, for CMEA sugar imports 1969–73. Cuba accounted for 59 per cent of the GDR's sugar supply at that time.

12. Charles Edquist, 'Mechanisation of Sugarcane Harvesting in Cuba', in *Cuban Studies* (Pittsburgh), Summer 1983, pp. 47, 50, 56, 61–3.

13. *The Giant's Rival*, pp. 117–26.

14. *Pravda*, 26 January 1971, p. 1, in *Current Digest of the Soviet Press*, Vol. 23, No. 4, p. 12.

15. Cuba may have been loaned about five times as much over the same period (see section on Cuba, above).

16. See Alexis Guardia, 'Structural Transformations in Chile's Economy and in its System of External Economic Relations', in S. Sideri (ed.), *Chile 1970–73: Economic Development and its International Setting* (The Hague: Martinus Nijhoff, 1979), pp. 45–101, 96.

17. *Mining Annual Review* (London), 1979, p. 568, estimates the Soviet surplus of copper available for export in 1978 at 31 per cent of domestic requirements. On the same basis many other traditional Latin America commodity exports must compete against Soviet supplies – gold (145 per cent), aluminium (44 per cent), petroleum (35 per cent), iron ore (20 per cent), lead (17 per cent), silver (10 per cent), nickel (9 per cent), zinc (6 per cent). The only significant Latin American mineral export for which the USSR is in deficit would seem to be tin (21 per cent deficit). Bolivia is currently the only Latin American country with communists in the government – a tin-exporting country, it has a communist Minister of Mines.

18. Economy Minister José Gelbard, cited in the *Buenos Aires Herald*, 8 May 1974, and Tass, 4 and 7 May 1974, in E. Milenky, *Argentina's Foreign Policies* (Colorado: Westview, 1978), p. 156.

19. *Latin America Commodities Report* (London), CR–84–08, 20 April 1984, p. 2.

20. International Wheat Council, *Market Research*. 20 September 1984.

21. Richard Feinberg, who visited Moscow in 1981, states that the Nicaraguan revolution took by surprise both experts at the Institute of Latin American Studies and government officials. Richard E. Feinberg, 'Centroamérica: el punto de vista de Moscú', in *Estados Unidos: perspectiva latinoamericana. Cuadernos semestrales* (Centro de Investigación y Docencia Económicas, Mexico, 1983) pp. 375–85, 376.

Abe Lowenthal, who travelled in the same group as Feinberg, also reports that S. Mikoyan, editor of the Soviet monthly publication *Latinskaia Amerika*, told him that 'few could see the possibility of a Sandinista triumph even in 1979'. Abe Lowenthal,

A Latin Americanist Encounters the USSR: Informal Notes (unpublished, 1981), p. 10.

22. S. Mikoyan, 'On the Peculiarities of the Revolution in Nicaragua', *Latinskaia Amerika*, July 1982, p. 41, cited in Morris Rothenberg, 'Latin America in Soviet Eyes', *Problems of Communism*, September–October 1983, Vol. 32, No. 5, pp. 1–18, 8.

23. These terms were used in *New Times*, 19 March 1982, and in N. Yu. Smirnova, 'Nicaragua: The Revolution is Developing', *Latinskaia Amerika*, March 1982, pp. 36–42, cited in M. Rothenberg, 'Latin America', p. 8.

24. *Barricada Internacional* (Managua), 16 October 1981, p. 5.

25. The $56m estimate of Soviet bloc military aid to Nicaragua three years after the Sandinista victory can be compared with $115m of military aid supplied by the US to other Central American countries in fiscal year 1982. In addition the US government reportedly spent somewhere between $20m and $55m on covert operations against Nicaragua in fiscal year 1982. Thus Soviet military aid to the internationally recognized government in Managua was only of the same order of magnitude as the CIA's military aid to the counter-revolutionary forces engaged in destabilizing that government.

26. In May 1983 it was reported that this assistance would in fact take a slightly different form. The USSR was to build a 7,000-ton drydock and a 60-foot floating pier to adapt the port for tuna fishing. For the use of this facility, the Russians were to pay Nicaragua an annual rent of $200,000.

27. According to Robert Leiken, 'The USSR now coordinates the economic, political, operational, and intelligence aspects of military assistance in one tightly managed Bureau. The State Committee for Economic and Foreign Relations reports to the military council of the Politbureau, bypassing the normal bureaucratic lines and directly linking political and economic objectives to arms sales programs and to the KGB.' (*Soviet Strategy*, p. 83). But the scale and purposes of Soviet military assistance to Nicaragua remain a matter for speculation.

28. An article in the Soviet monthly *Foreign Trade*, reporting a sale of Nicaraguan coffee to the Soviet Union, states that this was the first commercial transaction between the foreign trade organizations of the two countries: *Foreign Trade* (Moscow), Vol. 7, 1981, pp. 30–3.

29. Anatoli Kuzmin, 'Nicaragua Defends its Liberty and Independence', *Mezhdunarodnye zhizn*, in *Panorama Latinoamericano*, Novosti Press Agency (Moscow), No. 69, February 1984.

30. *Petroleum Economist*, May 1984, p. 190.

31. *The Washington Post*, 30 August 1984.

32. *Latin American Regional Report: Central America and the Caribbean*, (London) RM-83-08, 23 September 1983, p. 6. In 1983 Nicaragua failed to pay for imports received from other Central American countries or for Mexican oil even at the concessionary rate.

II
THE SOVIET ECONOMY AND THE THIRD WORLD

8
Soviet trade relations with the Third World

Alan H. Smith

The object of this chapter is to examine why the USSR trades with the Third World, and in particular to ask whether this trade is conducted for political or for economic motives (or both), and to examine how Soviet attitudes vary in relation to different countries and/or how they have altered through time. It is therefore necessary to examine the partner and commodity structure of Soviet trade with the Third World to see what the USSR acquires from this trade and at what cost, and with whom it trades.

The definition of economic interest

An initial problem concerns the definition of 'economic interests'. At first glance it would appear that there are clear economic interests that the USSR might seek to pursue through its trade relations with the Third World. The inflexibility of the Soviet price system frequently prevents planners from identifying emerging bottlenecks, and they often seek to balance domestic supply and demand for inputs by importing deficit items. In addition, the Soviet development model has tended to increase the demand for many of the traditional exports of Third World countries, such as fuel and energy, raw materials, foodstuffs and labour (and thus labour-intensive commodities), faster than domestic sources of supply, while the inability to generate a large volume of hard-currency earnings is a further limitation on the ability to alleviate bottlenecks through imports involving the expenditure of hard currency.

Securing a supply of these inputs could be considered an economic motivation for trade with the Third World. The Western economist would also want to consider the opportunity cost of the resources used in the acquisition of such inputs, and in particular whether trade with Third World countries enables the USSR to

140

satisfy domestic demand at a lower resource cost than would be involved in meeting demand either from domestic sources or from alternative world suppliers. Only if the answers to both parts of this question are positive can a clearly economic motive be established. In practice such unambiguous answers are difficult to obtain, and it is also highly unlikely that the Soviet leadership will interpret the economic benefits of trade relations with the Third World in the same way as would the Western microeconomist.

Many *a priori* possibilities could arise, but I will attempt to identify just four major economic categories into which, from the Soviet viewpoint, trade could fall.

Category 1: Clear economic benefits as described above. Domestic demands are satisfied by trade with Third World partners at a lower cost than they would be from either domestic or alternative foreign suppliers.

Category 2: Resources are obtained from trade with Third World partners at a lower cost than from domestic sources of supply, but at a higher cost than from alternative foreign suppliers. This situation could arise by accident or by design, and could result from unfavourable terms of trade, additional transport costs, the granting of credits and subsidies, etc. A specific version, however, could be:

Category 3: The diversion of imports to more costly suppliers in order to limit trade dependence on a single supplier or group of suppliers. This may have a primarily long-term economic motive – the desire to maintain competition among suppliers in order to keep prices lower in the long term (e.g. EEC negotiations with natural gas suppliers) – or a primarily political motive – to limit dependence on a political opponent.

Category 4: Clearly identifiable economic losses. The goods exported to Third World countries are clearly of greater domestic value than the imports obtained in exchange.

The evaluation of such resource flows is complicated by the lack of detailed information on the prices and quantities involved in Soviet-South trade, and in particular the paucity of data concerning time-flows in cooperative ventures. Consequently machinery and equipment delivered to Third World countries to be repaid at a later date by deliveries of raw materials may appear initially to be a clear example of trade falling into category 4, but could result in the longer term in a situation falling into any of the other three categories. In addition, trade agreements that may have appeared to be economically rational at the time of signature may appear uneconomic when evaluated with hindsight. The largest 'information gap' may well be the lack of detailed data on the methods of payment, and in particular on settlements made in hard currency.

Partner structure

The Third World as a whole is a non-homogeneous group of countries and to evaluate trade at this level involves an excessive degree of aggregation. Moreover, to aggregate countries into groups involves an initial decision on whether to group them by essentially economic or political categories. N.A. Tikhonov, who as Chairman of the Council of Ministers bears the responsibility for the execution of trade policy, normally prefers a political denomination in which a distinction is made between the countries that have adopted the socialist path and joined the CMEA (Mongolia, Cuba and Vietnam); other socialist countries such as China, North Korea, Albania and Yugoslavia; countries with a 'socialist orientation', including Angola, Afghanistan, Mozambique, Ethiopia, Laos, Kampuchea and the PDR Yemen (all of which, except Kampuchea, were observers at the October 1983 CMEA session); and the remaining developing countries, although some of these may also be considered to be members or potential members of the preceding group.

Elizabeth Valkenier, by contrast, has demonstrated that Soviet economists in institutes such as IMEMO (the Institute of World Economy and International Relations) have recognized the need for a purely economic categorization and have started to analyse separately the trading problems (and opportunities) for the USSR of such diverse groups as the oil-rich Middle Eastern states, North Africa, North Asia, South-East Asia, Latin and Central America, and the poorer sub-Saharan states.[1] Table 8.1 disaggregates Soviet trade statistics relating to trade with 'developing countries' by means of a principally geographical categorization – after netting off one major political grouping, 'the New Communist Third World', defined here as the countries listed above as being 'of socialist orientation', but excluding Laos, which is officially designated as 'socialist' in Soviet trade statistics.

The 'continentality' of much Soviet trade with the Third World is immediately apparent. This can be explained partly, but not entirely, by partners' factor endowments. Soviet imports from the American continent are almost entirely composed of foodstuffs, notably grain. This applies equally to imports from North America, where a higher volume of imports of capital goods might be expected, and to imports from Central and South America. Energy predominates in the USSR's imports from the Middle East, and traditional local produce in its imports from other regions.

Soviet exports are highly concentrated on countries that are contiguous or proximate to Soviet borders and in particular to European Russia and to Black Sea ports. (This also applies to the

TABLE 8.1
Soviet trade with the Third World: partner structure
(excluding full CMEA members) (million transferable roubles)

	1955	1960	1964	1972	1979	1981	1982	1983
Exports								
Total	128	302	868	2,008	6,292	8,669	10,180	10,524
NCTW	10	33	49	47	363	771	820	1,020
Middle East	33	117	216	586	1,646	2,123	2,367	1,800
North Africa	1	10	24	91	161	253	275	289
Sub-Sahara								
(n.e.s.)	–	10	47	76	132	212	317	355
India	7	42	211	139	525	1,064	1,040	1,272
Turkey	7	7	9	111	290	318	153	130
Asia (n.e.s.)	1	25	89	52	249	270	265	236
Americas	22	29	26	26	74	108	287	192
Identified	82	273	671	1,128	3,440	5,119	5,524	5,294
Unidentified	81	29	197	880	2,852	3,550	4,656	5,230
Imports								
Total	144	481	564	1,350	3,189	7,777	6,703	7,175
NCTW	10	17	24	33	175	353	307	301
Middle East	32	146	158	536	1,039	1,400	1,951	2,630
North Africa	2	5	11	89	96	220	110	46
Sub-Sahara								
(n.e.s.)	8	51	31	79	301	272	191	235
India	4	62	140	319	510	1,334	1,474	1,051
Turkey	–	5	8	34	89	130	95	83
Asia (n.e.s.)	43	151	130	120	430	908	649	613
Americas	38	32	52	127	511	3,030	1,799	2,003
Identified	137	469	554	1,337	3,151	7,647	6,576	6,962

Notes: NCTW = Angola, Mozambique, Afghanistan, Ethiopia, PDR Yemen, Kampuchea; Middle East = Iraq, Iran, Lebanon, Jordan, Kuwait, Saudi Arabia, Syria, North Yemen, Egypt, Libya; North Africa = Algeria, Tunisia, Morocco; n.e.s. = not elsewhere specified.
Source: Vneshnyaya Torgovlya, various years.

Soviet arms trade.) Although Soviet export penetration in the American continent is negligible, the exception which probes the economic rule is Cuba, which as a member of the CMEA received nearly twice as much Soviet machinery and equipment as the entire non-socialist Third World.

Changes in Soviet policy towards the non-socialist Third World
In 1951 Stalin formulated the theory that Marx's 'universal world market' had been irrevocably divided into two separate and independent economic systems, socialist and capitalist. Developing countries were of course exploited by the industrialized capitalist countries, therefore remaining part of the capitalist system (and were designated as such in Soviet statistics), and were not considered to be either the responsibility of the USSR or eligible for Soviet assistance while they remained in the capitalist camp. It was, however, hoped that developing countries would divorce themselves from colonialism, follow the example of socialist construction and join the socialist bloc. Valkenier demonstrates that even at this time some senior Soviet officials were aware of the possibilities of mutually advantageous trade links betweeen the USSR and South-East Asia and the Middle East, involving Soviet exports of excess production of machinery and equipment (presumably including arms when the Korean war ended) in exchange for imports of cotton, jute, leather, foodstuffs, rubber and non-ferrous metals.[2]

Valkenier argues that following Stalin's death, Khrushchev retained the doctrine of two separate world markets, but gave it an overtly political interpetation by emphasizing the need to win over non-aligned states to the socialist camp. It is possible to detect a shift in this policy after 1959, following the growth of Khrushchev's ascendancy over rival factions, which is reflected in Soviet trade statistics and is partially illustrated in Table 8.1. From 1953 to 1959, priority was given to establishing relations with Asian and Middle Eastern non-aligned states, notably India, Egypt and Indonesia, while bordering Afghanistan became the first recipient of Soviet aid. During this period trade was largely undertaken on the basis of bilateral repayments arrangements, and the USSR actually incurred trade deficits with Third World partners, importing cotton from Egypt and rubber from Malaysia. A more costly and adventurous policy was pursued from 1959 to 1964, as the USSR extended its trade links with North Africa, and, more crucially, with sub-Saharan Africa, becoming particularly involved with Guinea, following President de Gaulle's trading ultimatum to French colonial Africa. Arms were supplied to the Congo, and trade links were developed with Ghana and with other countries whose leaders were described as 'revolutionary democrats'.[3] Valkenier argues that as these countries were not richly endowed with the industrial minerals the USSR needed, trade effectively became aid, with repayments in the form of local produce and/or local currencies delayed over long periods. Simultaneously the USSR placed greater emphasis on grandiose construction projects in its bilateral dealings with existing partners, again resulting in an inability to secure a return flow of imports to pay for machinery exports.[4] This is shown in Table 8.1 by an excess of Soviet exports over imports from the Third World in the period 1960–4, the surplus being largest in trade with the Middle East (not just Egypt) and India. The remainder of the Soviet trade surplus can be attributed to 'unidentified' exports to developing countries (for an explanation, see below), which probably reflected the growing volume of arms exports to India, an item that was not recorded in civilian trade statistics. It appears, therefore, that at the end of the Khrushchev era Soviet trade relations with the non-aligned states fell into category 4 (possibly inadvertently) and involved the USSR in an economic loss.

Parrott shows that the downfall of Khrushchev led to a more realistic appraisal by the Soviet leadership of the relative strengths and weaknesses of the Soviet economic system and consequently to a more sombre assessment of the economic benefits of Soviet policies to both the USSR and its trade partners.[5] Valkenier also argues that at this time the concept of two separate world markets was gradually modified, being eventually replaced by a more global approach to trade, in which greater emphasis was laid on economic rather than political factors, and in particular on the distinctive economic circumstances of individual countries, while greater priority was given to the pursuit of 'mutually beneficial trade'.[6] Similarly, in the 1970s, greater emphasis began to be placed on multilateral trade involving payments in hard currency.

The post-Khrushchev implementation of Soviet policy
If the objective of Soviet policy has become more commercial since the fall of Khrushchev, how successfully has this been implemented? Table 8.1 shows that the money value of Soviet trade turnover with the Third World outside the CMEA increased twelvefold between 1964 and 1983. Unfortunately, the evaluation of this trade is complicated by the fact that nearly 50% per cent of exports cannot be identified by country of destination, and nearly 60 per cent cannot be identified by commodity. The conventional explanation of these gaps in the statistics is that while aggregated Soviet statistics may be an accurate measure of total Soviet exports (although this is questioned by some analysts),[7] the USSR attempts to conceal its trade in some strategic items and precious metals by omitting them from the more detailed breakdowns of trade. Table 8.1 also shows that, when trade that can be identified by country of origin and destination only is considered, instead of being in surplus in its trade with the Third World the USSR is, most years, in deficit.

TABLE 8.2
Soviet exports to the Third World: commodity structure
(excluding full CMEA members) (million transferable roubles)

	1974	1978	1980	1981	1982	1983
Total	3,389	5,715	6,870	8,669	10,180	10,524
Machinery and equipment	682	1,202	1,404	1,572	1,832	1,996
Fuel, energy, minerals	294	388	1,072	1,437	1,494	1,624
Other identified	645	362	522	717	555	535
Unidentified	1,768	3,763	3,872	4,943	6,299	6,369

Source: Vneshnyaya Torgovlya, various years.

TABLE 8.3
Soviet imports from the Third World: commodity structure
(excluding full CMEA members) (million transferable roubles)

	1972	1980	1981	1982	1983
Total	1,350	5,092	7,777	6,703	7,175
Fuel, energy, minerals	233	788	1,206	1,667	2,382
Foodstuffs, agricultural raw materials	814	3,001	5,083	3,486	3,282
Manufactures	172	400	675	789	663
Other identified	68	256	265	197	221
Unidentified	63	646	548	565	627

Source: Vneshnyaya Torgovlya, various years.

Clearly we need greater information on the composition of these unreported exports, and on how (if at all) they are paid for, before we can estimate the profitability of Soviet trade with the Third World. Some analysis of the residuals is therefore unavoidable.

Soviet statistics on trade with developing countries provide the following information: an aggregate figure for exports (imports) to developing countries, and a set of country statistics detailing the commodity composition of exports (imports) (Tables 8.2 and 8.3). The most important residuals in this context are therefore:

(a) The LDC residual – the difference between the figure given from exports to developing countries and those specified by

country of destination. A comparison of the unid
component of exports and imports under this heading sh
Table 8.1 indicates that this does not result purely fro
non-inclusion of certain countries in the country statistics.
(b) The intra-country commodity residual – the volume of exp
to individual countries that are not identified by commodity.

The categorization of trade partners

The USSR's largest trade partner in the non-CMEA Third World,
according to statistics of identified trade, is India. Although trade
with India is conducted on the basis of a bilateral clearing
agreement whereby deficits are to be cleared by payments in local
products, not in hard currency, it is noticeable from both Indian and
Soviet data that the USSR incurred consistent deficits in its visible
trade with India during 1969–78 and again in 1981 and 1982. These
deficits had accumulated to 1.1bn roubles by the end of 1978
(approximately $1.4bn), and to 1.7bn roubles by the end of 1982.*
The most probable explanation of these deficits in the period up to
1978 is that Soviet import data include repayments made in civilian
products for arms deliveries which have been included in the LDC
export residual. The US Arms Control and Disarmament Agency
estimates that Soviet arms deliveries to India totalled $1.4bn
between 1967 and 1976, while other sources have estimated Soviet
military deliveries to India between 1973 and 1982 at $1.5bn. A new
agreement signed in 1980 allowed for Soviet deliveries to the value
of 1.6bn to be repaid, commencing in 1983, over 17 years.

Over 80 per cent of Soviet identified exports to India since 1979
have been composed of crude oil, which has been delivered at world
market prices. In exchange, the USSR imports traditional foodstuffs and clothing, at prices similar to those paid to other exporters
for comparable items.[8] It is unlikely, however, given its shortage of
hard currency, that it would attach a high priority to these imports
that it exchanges for its principal hard-currency earner. Without
further data on the profitability of Soviet arms exports it is
impossible to make definitive statements on the value of this aspect
of Soviet-Indian trade. There does appear to be some *prima facie*
evidence to suggest that Soviet trade with India falls into category 2:
i.e., that the USSR obtains from India useful imports of goods

---

* In this chapter the term 'billion' refers to the US thousand million (10^9).

which could be produced domestically only at a high cost, but that it could receive greater gains by exporting its oil elsewhere.

Tropical foodstuffs also predominate in Soviet imports from North Africa and sub-Saharan Africa but are relatively small in volume, although they may make a far more significant contribution to Soviet consumption when measured at the price at which they are sold in state retail stores. The principal components of imports from Asian states are rubber from Malaysia, and sugar from Thailand and the Philippines. The prices paid for all these commodities are broadly comparable with world market prices. It is, however, noticeable that items for which Soviet demand is high (e.g. rubber from Malaysia, and cocoa from the Ivory Coast and Ghana) have not been covered by exports, and that the USSR has presumably paid in hard currency. Logically, trade in these items should be considered to fall into category 1, but there is little sign that the USSR is penetrating these markets on any large scale with exports of machinery and engineering goods as a means of saving on hard-currency expenditure. The major recipients of Soviet machinery and equipment in Africa and Asia (other than the Middle East and India) have been the countries of the New Communist Third World.

This factor is most noticeable in Soviet trade with South America. Soviet imports from South America are almost entirely composed of foodstuffs, particularly grain, which increased dramatically following the partial grain embargo imposed by the USA in response to the Soviet invasion of Afghanistan. Approximately one-half of Soviet maize consumption (for use as animal feedstocks) is imported, the major supplier until 1980 being the USA. Argentina is the other principal world exporter of maize and the USSR sought to diversify its sources of supply of animal feedstocks by increasing imports of maize and sorgo (as well as of wheat) from Argentina in the early 1980s. This policy may have contributed to the increase in world maize prices in the early 1980s and, as Miller and Whitehead show in chapter 7, the cost of purchasing and transporting Argentine grain to the USSR in 1981–2 may have been as much as $30–$40 per ton* higher than that for US grain. (Soviet statistics provide no quantity data for grain imports from Argentina on the basis of which a price comparison can be made.) In 1981 Soviet imports from South America reached 3bn roubles ($4.6bn), of which Argentina accounted for 2.4bn roubles. After President

---

* All data is taken from Soviet sources and is in metric tons (tonnes).

Reagan lifted the grain embargo in April 1981, the USSR continued to import grain from Argentina, but at a greatly reduced rate (Soviet imports from Argentina fell back to 1.2bn roubles in 1982 and 1983), although imports from the USA have not been resumed at their 1979 levels. The major factor hindering the growth of Soviet-Argentine trade, according to Soviet sources, is the low level of Argentine purchases of Soviet manaufactures so that the USSR has to pay for its grain with hard currency.

Grain imports from Argentina, together with other feedstock purchases from South America, clearly fall into category 3: it is more economic for the USSR to import grain than to seek total self-sufficiency (although attempts are being made to improve CMEA cooperation in increasing the output of animal feedstocks), but by importing from South America the USSR incurs higher costs, and possibly greater supply uncertainty, in order to limit its dependence on the USA. There appear to be limits to the cost the USSR is willing (or able) to bear in order to maintain this independence, and an agreement with the USA for the continuation of long-term supplies was signed in August 1983.

The Middle East accounts for over a third of the USSR's identified trade with the Third World. Soviet exports to the Middle East that are identified by country of destination increased from 0.6bn to 2.4bn roubles between 1972 and 1982, but the greater part of this increase (1.4bn roubles) was unidentified by commodity, while exports of machinery and equipment increased from 0.3bn roubles to 0.8bn roubles. The Middle East was also the largest recipient of Soviet armaments that have not been included in the data for trade with individual countries during this period. Soviet imports from the Middle East grew from 0.5bn roubles in 1972 to 2.6bn roubles in 1983, the principal component being crude oil, which is lifted from Libya, Iraq and, in 1983, Saudi Arabia, and re-exported, principally to Western Europe, for hard currency. The value of this trade is included in Soviet export and import data, but no quantity data are available which would allow an estimate of its profitability. Western oil specialists believe that the price paid to Libya is slightly higher than that obtained by the USSR in Western markets, but Libyan oil is of course not paid for in hard currency. Thus, about 90 per cent of the value of Soviet imports from Libya results in hard-currency earnings for the USSR when re-exported. Imports from Libya were running at about 400 million roubles a quarter, from the first quarter of 1982 to the first quarter of 1983 (equivalent to an annual rate of about 8 million tons), but have subsequently declined to about 200 million roubles a quarter, although this has been offset by increased imports from Saudi Arabia and Iraq. Although this trade clearly contributes to Soviet hard-currency earnings, its profitability cannot be properly assessed without more information on the composition of Soviet exports (see below).

The USSR also imports natural gas from Afghanistan and Iran, which it uses to meet the needs of the southern Soviet republics, thereby releasing West Siberian gas for export to Western Europe. As the price of natural gas in Western Europe is substantially higher than that prevailing at the borders of exporting countries, this trade is clearly profitable to the USSR, which hardly incurs any additional transport costs in the overall process. The events in Iran and Afghanistan throughout 1979 resulted in cutbacks in supplies, and the USSR had difficulties in meeting its Western contracts. Imports from Afghanistan are currently running above 1979 levels, but supplies from Iran have oscillated substantially in recent years. Difficulties in maintaining secure levels of supplies from Libya, Iran and Afghanistan give an indication of the political constraints the USSR faces in securing stable trade links with the region.

The profitability of Soviet arms sales
There is general agreement among Western specialists that Soviet arms sales are a major source of Soviet hard-currency earnings, which increased significantly during the 1970s and are continuing to grow. Holloway, for example, argues that arms sales yielded the Soviet Union $21bn in hard currency between 1971 and 1980.[9] There is, however, good reason to question whether Soviet arms sales have in fact realized hard-currency earnings quite as large as this.

Estimating the profitability of Soviet arms exports involves a number of procedures that are subject to considerable error. First, the volume of actual arms deliveries must be estimated; second, the prices paid must be estimated and allowances made for grants, discounts, credits, etc.; third, the means of payment (hard currency, local produce) must be estimated; and, finally, an estimate must be made of domestic production costs to facilitate a calculation of profitability. In view of the complexities of the task and the informational uncertainty, it is perhaps not surprising that it is chiefly intelligence agencies that attempt to estimate all stages of this process, and that many writers in the field are compelled to use figures that originate from unclassified intelligence sources.

TABLE 8.4
CIA estimates of Soviet arms deliveries and hard-currency earnings
(US $million)

	1974	1975	1976	1977	1978	1979	1980	1981
Zoeter's estimates (1983)								
Arms deliveries	1,980	1,860	2,270	3,810	4,130	4,270	4,670	4,960
Hard-currency receipts for arms sales	1,500	1,500	1,850	3,220	3,965	3,855	4,200	4,200
Current-account balance plus gold sales	2,666	−3,882	−1,847	2,080	2,944	3,668	3,484	2,600
Capital account balance	488	5,797	2,519	1,212	−788	−1,152	48	3,240
'Net errors and ommisions'	−3,154	−1,915	−672	−3,292	−2,156	−2,516	−3,532	−5,840
Ericson and Miller's estimates (1979)								
Hard-currency receipts for arms sales	1,000	793	1,108	1,500	1,644			
'Net errors and omissions	−2,400	−980	21	−1,919	−640			
Trade residuals								
LDC residual	2,015	1,899	2,318	3,890	4,207	4,344	4,794	4,899
LDC plus ICC[a]	2,349	2,301	2,745	4,631	5,505	5,800	5,990	6,821

[a]ICC, Intra-Country Commodity.
Sources: Joan Parpart Zoeter; 'USSR: Hard Currency Trade and Payments'; P.G. Ericson and R.S. Miller, 'Soviet Economic Behavior in a Balance of Payments Perspective'.

The CIA, for example, attempts to calculate both Soviet arms deliveries to the Third World and Soviet hard-currency earnings from these sales. The latter is part of a continuous attempt to calculate the Soviet hard-currency balance of payments, the results of which are published periodically in the form of papers presented to the Joint Economic Committee of the US Congress. These figures are widely quoted, although there have in the past been substantial differences between studies prepared by the same agency. The most recent studies have been presented by Ericson and Miller (1979)[10] and Zoeter (1983)[11] and data from these studies, together with dollar conversions – for purposes of comparison – of the export residuals shown in Tables 8.1 and 8.2, are shown in Table 8.4. The principal method used to estimate Soviet hard-currency surpluses (deficits) on current account is to assume that all trade surpluses and deficits in trade with non-socialist countries with which the USSR has settlement arrangements specified in hard currencies are *actually* cleared in hard currency, and to add estimated Soviet hard-currency earnings from arms sales to this figure.

Ericson and Miller have applied a ratio of 43 per cent to intelligence-based CIA estimates of Soviet arms deliveries to arrive at an estimate of the value of Soviet hard-currency earnings from arms sale for years after 1973. This ratio was derived from CIA intelligence estimates of the proportion of Soviet arms deliveries that were paid for (or credited in) hard currency in 1977. Zoeter's estimates indicate a substantially higher value of arms sales for hard currency, which are described as 'Additional military deliveries to LDCs, f.o.b.', with a further footnote: 'This item excludes the value of arms related commercial exports included in Soviet reporting on exports to individual LDCs.' No other information on the source of these estimates is provided, but it is apparent from this wording, and by comparing rows 1 and 8 in Table 8.4, that Zoeter has taken the LDC residual as an estimate of Soviet arms sales and also considers that additional quantities of arms are contained in the trade statistics for individual countries, presumably in the intra-country commodity residual and possibly in deliveries of machinery and equipment.

The high proportion of arms deliveries that have been considered to be sold for hard currency in Zoeter's estimates are surprising. The proportion for 1973–4 has been increased to over 75 per cent, and for 1975–81 it varies between 81 per cent and 96 per cent. As a result, Zoeter's estimates indicate that Soviet hard-currency earnings from arms sales totalled $22.7bn from 1971 to 1980 or $25.8bn from 1973 to 1981.

Zoeter, and Ericson and Miller also estimate the Soviet balance of payments on capital account from Western banking and government sources. The major capital inflows are new borrowings from Western banks and governments, minus repayments of outstanding loans, plus/minus changes in financial assets held by the USSR in the West. Gold sales provide an additional source of hard currency which has not been included in capital or current account. Thus any surplus (deficit) in hard-currency trade on current account, plus receipts from gold sales, should be exactly offset by a deficit (surplus) on capital account. Following accountancy practice, the difference between deficits (surpluses) on current account plus gold sales and surpluses (deficits) on capital account have been designated 'net errors and omissions' by Zoeter, and by Ericson and Miller, a negative sign in this item indicating that estimated hard-currency earnings have not been accounted for in the capital account.

These estimates have been summarized in Table 8.4, It can be seen that where Ericson and Miller have a far lower estimate of Soviet hard-currency earnings from arms sales, their item under 'net errors and omissions' is correspondingly lower. Zoeter's estimates appear to indicate that although the USSR made a surplus on its trade in hard currency plus gold sales equivalent to $14bn in the period 1972–81, it also increased its indebtedness to Western banks and governments by $11.9bn during this period, as a result of which 'net errors and omissions' totalled $25.9bn for these years.

Since these estimates were prepared without the cooperation of the Soviet authorities the most probable explanation of such a high and consistently negative balancing item is that Soviet hard-currency earnings have been consistently overestimated, or outgoings underestimated, or that the USSR has offered extended credit terms which are not reflected in the balance sheets of the principal Western banks. Zoeter admits that estimating errors may be substantial, but also argues that hard-currency assistance and payments to other communist countries, plus net credits to LDCs and oil credits granted to the West, may account for the discrepancy. Estimates of Soviet hard-currency trade with other communist states are also liable to considerable error, but it is possible that such payments, combined with subventions to East European states with hard-currency problems, accounted for $2–3bn in 1981 and 1982, but would not have been so large in the 1970s. Furthermore, Soviet civilian aid disbursements outside the CMEA have been insignificant, and have probably been offset by repayments in the late 1970s. Repayments in products (e.g. Libyan oil) would have been netted off in the trade surpluses as hard-currency imports and would not therefore contribute to 'net errors and omissions'.

The most probable explanation of the high 'net errors and omissions' is that actual hard-currency earnings from exports have been overestimated, and that this overvaluation arises from trade with Third World partners, a significant proportion of which results from arms exports. Thus, if the LDC residuals do indeed reflect arms trade with the Third World, a significant proportion of these do not appear to have been paid for in either currency or produce, and appear to have been delivered on extended credit terms.

A recent article by N. Shmelyev, albeit propagandist in tone, casts some light on Soviet and East European credit relations with the Third World.[12] He argues that Third World debts to the CMEA region as a whole, designated in hard-currency, would be sufficient to offset nearly a half of the region's hard-currency debt to the West (and would therefore be approximately \$30bn), and that the USSR is a net hard-currency creditor, not a debtor, when Third World hard-currency debts to the USSR are taken into account.

There is as yet, therefore, insufficient evidence to indicate that the USSR actually received payment in hard currency for much of its arms deliveries made in the 1970s. The USSR appears to be accumulating credits in its relations with the Third World which should be repaid in the future in hard currency (or commodities that can be exported for hard currency) and which should, *if realized*, make a significant contribution to the Soviet hard-currency balance in the late 1980s when Soviet oil revenues start to decline.

But how successful will the USSR be in securing the repayment of these credits? Although repayments of civilian aid and credits given to non-socialist Third World nations in the past may now outweigh new development loans and assistance, military credits carry a far higher risk of repudiation following changes in government or policy. In the past, Indonesia and Egypt have failed to repay arms credits granted by the USSR, while relations with the principal hard-currency recipients of Soviet arms – Libya, Iraq and Algeria – are all subject to economic and political risk.

The policy of exporting oil to the USSR as repayment for arms may have encountered domestic opposition in Libya as the resale of Libyan crude on world markets has tended to push the price down. Similarly, the USSR is one of Algeria's major competitors for sales of natural gas to Western Europe, and Soviet price policy has already forced down the price offered to Algeria. Relations with Iraq are of course complicated by the Iran-Iraq war.

The low level of hard-currency earnings of the states of sub-Saharan Africa makes a substantial repayment of arms credits by these countries unlikely, while their staple exports, although useful to the USSR, would not be given high priority by a Soviet leadership faced with hard-currency shortages, and re-exporting on any reasonable scale would again drive down prices.

There is clearly insufficient evidence to place Soviet arms trade with non-socialist countries in any of the four categories mentioned above. Although some individual deals may involve a clear economic gain to the USSR one should certainly caution against an over-hasty placement of the arms trade in category 1.

Soviet trade relations with the socialist Third World
Soviet civilian aid is primarily concentrated on the socialist countries inside the CMEA and on Third World countries with a 'socialist orientation', the majority of which possess observer status

at the CMEA. The British Foreign and Commonwealth Office has estimated that Soviet net aid disbursements (i.e. gross aid payments minus repayments of earlier development loans) to developing countries within the CMEA (Cuba, Mongolia and Vietnam) plus Laos, Kampuchea and Afghanistan doubled between 1976 and 1982, and that this increase took place (absolutely and relatively) at the expense of aid to Third World countries of a non-socialist orientation.[13] This conclusion would have been further strengthened if Angola, Mozambique, Ethiopia, PDR Yemen and Nicaragua had been included in the socialist group, since these countries' share of the remaining Soviet gross aid disbursements increased from 2.5 per cent in 1976 to 29 per cent in 1982. Net aid disbursements were still quite small, however, and were estimated to be only $2.4bn in 1982.

Aid deliveries partly account for Soviet visible trade surpluses with CMEA developing countries and the communist Third World, which reached 3bn roubles in 1983 compared with an average of around 0.5bn roubles in the mid-1970s. The value of gross aid disbursements was far larger for the full members of the CMEA. Gross aid disbursements were estimated by the FCO to be approximately $0.5bn for both Cuba and Mongolia and nearly $1bn for Vietnam in 1982. In the case of a relatively small economy, such as that of Mongolia, this volume of aid can have a significant impact. My own estimates (based on a slightly higher aid estimate than that of the FCO) indicate that Soviet technical and financial assistance accounted for 70 per cent of Mongolian investment in the 1976–80 five-year plan and was probably as high as 35 per cent of GNP.[14]

The major component of Soviet assistance to developing countries within the CMEA is the use of concessional prices paid for by these countries' exports, which exceed world market prices according to a predetermined formula which is guaranteed over a long period of time. Similarly, Soviet exports (notably oil) may be delivered at concessional prices which are lower than world market prices.

Cuba is the largest recipient of this form of assistance, making it the largest recipient of Soviet concessions. The Soviet guaranteed price for Cuban sugar has frequently been three times higher than the price paid to alternative suppliers, and a further increase in 1983 resulted in Cuba receiving prices that were six times higher than those paid to Thailand and the Philippines. Sugar accounts for 95 per cent of the value of Cuban exports to the USSR, making this concession worth nearly 2bn roubles in 1983.

In comparison with these figures, Soviet assistance to socialist-oriented countries is relatively small and the additional costs that are involved in the CMEA's 'levelling up' commitments form a considerable barrier to any further enlargement of the CMEA in the immediate future, particularly since the decision to admit Vietnam in 1978 encountered some East European opposition.

But what lessons, if any, can be drawn from this experience? Soviet trade with the developing members of CMEA clearly falls into category 4 in the short run, involving the USSR in a net resource cost. This results chiefly from the low volume of Soviet imports from these countries rather than from the nature of the commodities received, and it is important in this case not to overestimate the costs. The principal component of Soviet exports to these countries is machinery and equipment. The USSR has been singularly unsuccessful in selling civilian machinery and equipment in non-socialist countries, and a significant proportion of this machinery has been concentrated on the production of commodities for re-export to the USSR. Soviet machinery exports to Mongolia have been concentrated on the development of infrastructure and the extraction and processing of non-ferrous metals. As a result, minerals and metals accounted for 40 per cent of Mongolia's exports in 1982 compared with 7 per cent in 1978.

Development assistance to Cuba has been concentrated on the sugar industry and recently on the development of nickel. Despite the high price paid for Cuban sugar, it is noticeable that in 1975 the USSR actually paid Brazil and Australia prices that were nearly double those paid to Cuba. A major cost to the USSR of intra-CMEA assistance is the lost hard-currency earnings arising from deliveries of crude oil. This amount is of course larger than the nominal value of oil exports as a result of concessional pricing.

The economic commitments to Mongolia and Cuba were initially entered into during Khrushchev's more expansionary phase in the early 1960s (Miller and Whitehead suggest he may even have anticipated economic benefits arising from the export of oil in exchange for sugar) but have subsequently imposed higher costs on the USSR than were perhaps initially envisaged. The majority of the principles involved in Soviet trade with the developing CMEA members apply to trade with countries with a socialist orientation, but the scale of operation is far smaller. Sounder economic councils than those offered to Khrushchev seem to have prevailed in the late 1970s, and the USSR appears to have avoided making large-scale commitments to Angola and Mozambique.

Trade relations between the USSR and socialist developing countries inside the CMEA, and to a far lesser extent with countries of a socialist orientation, help to strengthen the sectoral links between the Soviet economy and those of its Third World partners. These may even be considered to constitute 'joint planning' in the sense that a joint plan is really a long-term bilateral contract involving the USSR in exports of machinery and equipment for the development of infrastructure and basic staple industries in exchange for some of the outputs of those industries in the longer run.

In the short run this assistance involves the USSR in costs, but provides benefits to the recipient. The Soviet leadership may therefore see this assistance as 'strengthening socialism'. The concentration of civilian aid flows on developing countries within the CMEA and, to a far lesser degree, on countries with a socialist orientation at the expense of other Third World countries, particularly since 1976, appears to indicate that the Soviet leadership is still influenced by the concept of two world markets. It also provides confirmation of Valkenier's argument that Soviet development strategies distinguish between members of the socialist (CMEA) bloc which are irreversibly committed to socialism, and therefore receive the greatest proportion of Soviet aid, and those countries of 'socialist orientation' to which the Soviet commitment in both financial and political terms is less strong and may prove to be less enduring.

Notes

I am grateful to members of the study group, and in particular to authors of other papers in this volume, for the knowledge and information they have provided which has helped in the preparation of this paper.

1. Elizabeth Kridl Valkenier, *The Soviet Union and the Third World* (New York: Praeger, 1983), p. 82.

2. *Ibid.*, p. 1.

3. The development of these ties is discussed in Christopher Stevens, *The Soviet Union and Black Africa* (London: Macmillan, 1976).

4. Valkenier, *The Soviet Union and the Third World*, Ch. 1.

5. Bruce Parrott, *Politics and Technology in the Soviet Union* (Cambridge, Mass: MIT Press, 1983), Ch. 5.

6. Valkenier, *The Soviet Union and the Third World*, Ch. 2.

7. T. Wolf and E. Hewett in *The Soviet Economy in the 1980s* (US Congress, Joint Economic Committee, Washington, D.C., 1983).

8. For more details on the composition of Soviet-Indian trade, see Chs. 3 and 12 of this volume.

9. David Holloway, *The Soviet Union and the Arms Race* (New Haven, Conn.: Yale University Press, 1983), p. 125.

10. P.G. Ericson and R.S. Miller, 'Soviet Foreign Economic Behavior in a Balance of Payments Perspective', in *The Soviet Economy in a Time of Change* (US Congress, Joint Economic Committee, Washington, D.C., 1979).

11. Joan Parpart Zoeter, 'USSR: Hard Currency Trade and Payments', in *The Soviet Economy in the 1980s* (US Congress, Joint Economic Committee).

12. Reprinted in English as N. Shmelyov, 'Credits and Politics', *International Affairs* (Moscow, April 1984).

13. *Soviet, East European and Western Development Aid 1976–82*, Foreign Policy Document No.85 (London, 1983).

14. Alan Smith and Adi Schnytzer, 'The Mongolian People's Republic', in Peter Wiles (ed.), *The New Communist Third World* (London: Croom Helm, 1982).

9

Soviet arms sales to developing countries: the economic forces*

Saadet Deger

Introduction

The Soviet Union has long been a major exporter of armaments. Its international supply of arms during the 1960s matched that of the United States, and the two superpowers effectively dominated the world trade in arms. However, a large part of this trade was directed to the USSR's Warsaw Pact allies. Both in volume and in value terms, Soviet exports to LDCs, though significant, were not abnormally high. The value of exports to LDCs expressed at *constant* (1975) prices was US $429m in 1963, rising to $836m in 1969.[1] Though the rate of growth of exports was relatively high, the absolute amounts were small if they are compared with those of the 1970s.

The past decade has seen a rather remarkable increase in Soviet armaments exports to the Third World. The USSR was the world's largest supplier of major weapons systems to developing countries during the period 1978–82,[2] outstripping the United States. Set against the background of the debate on Soviet growth performance, balance-of-trade prospects and convertible-currency problems, as well as of economic and political relations with the North and the South, the very high levels of arms sales take on an added significance.

Before we proceed to analyse the causes and effects of this trade, it will be useful to give some data in order to put the trends into perspective. From $1,136m dollars in 1970, the value of major weapons exports to LDCs rose to $3,774m dollars in 1980 (all measured in *constant* 1975 prices). Estimates for 1981 show that arms exports were sufficient to finance all investment machinery imports to the Soviet Union.[3] During 1978–82, the annual volume

* This work has been financed by the Economic and Social Research Council under a Post-doctoral Fellowship. I am also grateful to the Ford Foundation Fellowship Program in Combined Soviet/East European and International Security Studies, administered by Columbia University.

of Soviet armaments exported to LDCs was 16 per cent more than the corresponding figure for the US. Table 9.1 gives an indication of the figures involved. There is little doubt that arms exports and related convertible-currency earnings provide a crucial source of foreign exchange for the Soviet economy.

TABLE 9.1
Soviet arms exports (US $million)

	1970	1971	1972	1973	1974	1975[d]	1976	1977	1978	1979	1980	1981[e]
Arms exports[a]	904	789	1,166	2,346	2,217	2,248	2,693	4,532	5,398	5,626	5,677	6,950
Arms exports[b]		1,136	1,515	1,225	1,537	1,930	2,160	1,554	2,156	3,682	3,631	3,774	–
Imports of investment machinery[c]		1,105	1,035	1,361	1,947	2,556	4,999	5,826	6,192	7,091	6,935	7,142	6,032

[a] Current prices, taken from Portes, 'Deficits and Détente', Table A–25.
[b] Constant 1975 prices, from SIPRI, *World Armaments and Disarmament Yearbook 1982*.
[c] Current prices, from Portes, 'Deficits and Détente'.
[d] Rows 1 and 2 may not match owing to differing sources and methods of estimating data.
[e] Provisional data.

It must of course be noted that there is a high degree of uncertainty involved in evaluating data for the arms trade, particularly Soviet data. Since the Soviet Union does not publish any information on this subject, estimates have to be made of the quantity of various types of armaments sold, their prices and financing: hard currency, credit, barter or grants and aid. Much discussion and controversy has arisen from estimating arms-trade data; a succinct summary can be found in Albrecht[4] and a more general analysis of the problems related to military expenditure data in Deger.[5] However, most analysts agree that even if the exact numbers and figures may not be totally accurate, there can be little doubt about the *trends* involved.

In addition to the quantitative increase, it is now generally agreed that there has been a qualitative transformation in the nature of the arms trade of the Soviet Union with the developing countries in the last few years.[6] Specifically, straightforward sales of arms, often in convertible hard currencies, are becoming increasingly more important. The arms now tend to be sold rather than given as bilateral aid, economic prices are often charged, credit terms have become more stringent, interest rates on loans are higher, and deposits or cash payments in hard currency are unusual. In general, economic forces are much more evident than the political or strategic forces so common in the past. It is not surprising that oil-producing states such as Iraq, Libya and Algeria have to pay for arms in petrodollars. But there definitely seems to have been a fundamental change in attitude when countries like Ethiopia and Zambia have also to pay for their military equipment from the USSR in hard currency.[7] Kanet reports evidence that between 1973 and 1978 hard-currency arms exports amounted to 43 per cent of all military transfers abroad.[8] Given this trend, soon over half of Soviet arms transfers could be paid for in dollars. As Kanet observes, 'What is clear from the available evidence is that arms exports to Third World states have become an important source of hard currency, and that they now play a major role in covering the large deficits in Soviet trade with the world market'.

The purpose of this chapter is to study the USSR's armaments exports to LDCs within the broader perspective of Soviet growth and balance-of-trade problems as well as within the general context of East-South economic relations. There are studies which deal with these issues separately; the emphasis here is on the interrelationships between them. As will be seen, given the current problems of the Soviet economy and the constrained macroeconomic regime in which it operates (i.e. aggregate excess demand), imports play an increasingly important role in growth, whereas there is generally little incentive for export promotion. However, accumulated deficits in commodity trade will force the USSR to increase exports of some goods. It will be shown that it is easiest for the Soviet industrial structure to export armaments, since the constraints are least binding here, and defence industries may actually be in an excess supply position – unlike other sectors. Thus the internal logic of the Soviet economic system pushes it towards arms exports.

This chapter stresses the economic rationale of arms trade. It is undeniable that political and strategic factors have been important determinants of Soviet weapons exports abroad, and there is substantial literature on this.[9] However, the focus has definitely changed in the recent past, and economic motivations are now crucial to arms transfers. The literature admits the trends, but is grudging on the analysis. I shall try to redress the balance.

In the next section the supply side of the arms trade is analysed, with exports being related to the growth and external trade gap of the Soviet Union. I then discuss the impact of the trade on LDC recipients, as well as the characteristics of the market where the

Soviet Union is one of a few oligopolistic sellers. The political and security-related issues of the arms trade are considered in brief in the following section, and my arguments are drawn together in the conclusion.

The supply side
The rapid rise and high volume of Soviet arms exports in recent years can be explained by factors emanating from both the supply and the demand sides. In this section I try to analyse how the domestic problems of the Soviet Union and concomitant structural characteristics motivate the growing arms trade.

The first factor is declining growth rates. US sources show that the USSR's average annual growth rates in GNP fell from 5.2 per cent during 1966–70 to 3.7 per cent in 1971–5 and finally to 2.7 per cent in 1976–80. Soviet sources put the growth rate of Net Material Product at about 8.2 per cent during 1965–70 but again this falls rapidly to 5.8 per cent in 1970–5 and 4.0 per cent during 1975–80.[10] Various reasons have been cited for this reduction in growth, which is striking when compared to the startlingly high growth rates of the past. Of course a maturing economy, with less access to abundant labour and an increasing capital/output ratio, would inevitably see its growth rate decline. Centralization and rigid planning work well at the early stages of development but become increasingly inefficient as the economy grows more complex. Agriculture remains a lagging sector, and recent massive imports testify to its unreliability (five harvest failures in the past decade). But, even in industry, the slowdown in productivity and efficiency must be a cause for concern.[11]

One way of increasing productivity (and growth) is to use more imported intermediate investment goods in the production of domestic output. This was done in the early planning years of the 1930s as well as during post-war reconstruction. A major advantage of the method would be the avoidance of bottlenecks within the economy, without the need for major reforms which may be otherwise unacceptable or difficult, As Table 9.1 shows, imports of investment goods have increased quite rapidly during the 1970s, even if account is taken of an inflationary bias in the data. Imports of capital stock, technology, know-how, and even grain to increase the quality of livestock are all crucial in the sense that modest amounts of these inputs, applied strategically, could potentially lead to considerable increases in output.

More generally, imports play a very important role in CPEs, both by providing intermediate input in the production of gross output and by increasing aggregate supply for final use. Thus Holzman writes, 'foreign trade is conducted to obtain essential imports, with exports viewed as a necessary evil, to pay for the imports'.[12] This attitude is understandable since the Soviet Union lies in a general excess demand regime (in the sense of Malinvaud),[13] and is thus supply-constrained; desired demand for goods is not satisfied and some form of rationing takes place. There is also full employment of resources and the economy operates on its aggregate supply schedule. The rationing scheme allows for an equilibrium character-ized by realized or actual demand being constrained by total production.

This macroeconomic rationing implies that no export multiplier is induced by an autonomous change in export demand.[14] Thus there is little incentive for export promotion. But if imports of sophisti-cated machinery, technology or intermediate goods tend to increase production of national output directly and to ease supply constraints indirectly, then they will play a crucial part in determining a rationed equilibrium. This is the rationale behind the bottleneck multiplier discussed by Portes.[15] For CPEs, structural characteris-tics such as full employment, aggregate excess demand, supply bottlenecks and overall rationing explain why exports *per se* are not generally desirable. Overall, therefore, it may be preferable for CPEs to increase their imports, thus easing their supply constraints and increasing domestic production. Furthermore, it may not be desirable to increase exports much, since this worsens domestic rationing and does not have the advantage of an export multiplier.[16] Thus, instead of the usual export-led growth that one would expect from an underemployed economy, the Soviet Union and other CPEs tend to rely on import-fed growth which assists in alleviating their structural bottlenecks and reduces rationing in the demand system. The developed capitalist countries of the West are the major source of intermediate imports that contribute significantly to import-fed growth.[17] Soviet trade with the West is crucial for investment, productivity and growth. The technological 'stage' of economic development makes an autarkic economy unfeasible. Given the inability of the USSR to increase exports substantially (again because of its macroeconomic constraints), balance-of-trade deficits with industrial countries are endemic to the system. Current-account deficits in convertible currency and the cumulative debt burden are major problems for the USSR's economy, which are resolved by earning hard currency through the sale of certain products which are not subject to specific sectoral supply con-straints: and it is here that arms exports become relevant.

It is necessary at this stage to review briefly the nature of the Soviet defence industry in order to understand why supply constraints are not crucial in this sector. As Holloway states, 'The defence sector is both an integral part of the Soviet economy and the highest priority sector in Soviet industry with ... special features of its own'.[18] In addition to having higher pay and incentives for workers, better day-to-day management, more sophisticated R&D facilities (its own research and design centres, for example), 'defence plants have the power to commandeer what they need from civilian industry, and this must be an advantage in an economy where *supply problems* are chronic'.[19]

Though the Soviet defence industry operates within the general framework of the state plan, the top priority attached to it ensures that it is not hampered generally by overall shortages, particularly of intermediate goods. It is shielded from the rationing prevalent in other sectors and thus finds it easier to expand production if necessary. The defence sector also has its *own* supply industries which produce intermediate products required for final output. Stricter quality requirements and technological innovations are maintained by the defence sector's own interindustrial linkages. Furthermore, as Holloway, drawing on Leonid Brezhnev's 1971 speech to the 24th Party Congress points out, a sizeable proportion of defence industry output is for non-defence purposes.[20] CIA estimates show that over one-third of shipbuilding and aircraft production by defence sectors in the 1970s were for civilian uses.[21] It is also worth noting that Defence Ministry representatives are present in many design and production centres, which enables them to see that their own requirements and specifications are met properly and bottlenecks do not appear. Thus the armed forces have a 'degree of consumer power unusual in the Soviet Union'.[22]

To turn now to sales of armaments abroad, Pierre puts it succinctly: 'The Soviet Union's ability, and perhaps willingness, to send arms to the Third World is also affected by the large quantity of surplus equipment available. It stocks reserve arms in large quantities, more than the West does, and these provide a cushion, obviating the need to ship operational stocks. *The Soviet defence industry routinely overproduces with potential exports in mind.* Large production runs are established which manufacture extra new weapons'.[23] It is not surprising that in these circumstances the Soviets are able and willing to ship arms very quickly and that the lag between sale and delivery is very small. The CIA gives figures which show that the USSR takes half the time taken by the United States to deliver arms after supply contracts are agreed upon.[24] Overall, therefore, the very size of the arms-producing sector allows it to take advantage of extended production runs and gives it the capability to increase output for export markets relatively efficiently.

As the Pentagon states, 'The Soviet Union alone produces more weapons systems in greater quantities than any other country'.[25]

All this suggests that defence production and arms industries in the Soviet Union are not subject to the form of rationing common to other areas of industrial production and consumer demand. Defence is characterized by excess supply within an overall economy characterized by generalized excess demand. It is not surprising that it is possible to expand exports of arms in preference to those of other goods.

However, international trade based on some form of implicit comparative advantage does not depend on supply factors alone; demand considerations also come into play. We shall examine the financial aspect of arms transfers later, but in terms of technical quality, delivery times, help with personnel, adaptation to local factors and degree of sophistication relative to the needs of recipient countries, Soviet arms are considered competitive with the West. As Portes claims, military equipment is 'the only type of machinery on which the East can claim a rough technical parity with the West, and even superior quality or performance for cost in some areas'.[26] Thus from the LDCs' point of view, Soviet arms are as desirable as any other – provided, of course, the price is right.

Data suggest that exports are qualitatively quite important in total military output and not simply a 'vent for surplus'. For example, 58.2 per cent of the production of major naval combatants and 70 per cent of minor naval combatants are for export, while the corresponding figure for combat aircraft is about 40 per cent. A quarter of the helicopters produced and about 10 per cent of submarines manufactured were exported during 1976–81.[27] Exports of tanks and self-propelled assault guns amounted to 42.2 per cent of production during the same period. In recent years some of the most sophisticated weapons systems were sold to Third World countries before the Warsaw Pact allies were issued with them. Not only is export dependence high but export promotion is being carried out in a systematic and planned way, and there seems to be a 'need' within the Soviet economy for the sale of weapons abroad.

Table 9.2 gives details of the Soviet balance of trade in relation to arms exports and sales revenue during the past decade. Row (3) shows the rise in the non-defence trade deficit (imports minus exports), from its very low levels in the early 1970s to its peak in the mid-1970s and its still high value by 1981. Rows (7) and (8) clearly demonstrate the importance of arms sales in the total value of exports. The ratio of military to non-military exports rises from 3.6 per cent in 1970 to 15.5 per cent in 1981. Row (8) shows the crucial importance of hard-currency earnings from weapons in financing

TABLE 9.2
USSR hard-currency balance-of-trade accounts (US $ million, except rows (6) – (8))

	1970	1971	1972	1973	1974	1975	1976	1977	1978	1979	1980	1981[a]
(1) Exports (without arms) f.o.b.	2,201	2,630	2,801	4,790	7,470	7,838	9,721	11,345	13,157	19,549	23,498	23,800
(2) Imports	2,701	2,943	4,157	6,547	8,448	14,257	15,316	14,645	16,951	21,585	26,017	27,800
(3) Non-defence trade deficit	500	313	1,356	1,757	978	6,419	5,595	3,300	3,794	2,036	2,519	4,000
(4) Arms sales	80	70	100	550	1,000	1,000	1,250	2,300	2,500	2,750	3,500	3,700
(5) Exports (with arms)	2,281	2,700	2,901	5,340	8,470	8,838	10,971	13,645	15,657	22,299	26,998	27,500
(6) Arms/total exports ratio	0.035	0.026	0.034	0.103	0.118	0.113	0.114	0.168	0.16	0.123	0.129	0.134
(7) Arms/non-military exports ratio	0.036	0.026	0.035	0.1148	0.133	0.127	0.128	0.202	0.190	0.140	0.149	0.155
(8) Arms/non-defence trade deficits ratio	0.16	0.223	0.073	0.313	1.022	0.155	0.223	0.696	0.658	1.350	1.389	0.925
(9) Petroleum	430	608	600	1,304	2,741	3,391	4,748	5,583	5,710	9,585	11,995	12,287
(10) Natural gas	14	21	24	32	95	220	358	566	1,072	1,404	2,704	3,956

[a] Data for 1981 are provisional.
Source: Portes, 'Deficits and Détente', Tables A-8 and A-19, and author's calculation.

the overall commodity trade deficits. The ratio of convertible-currency arms sales to the non-defence trade balance (deficit) rises from 16 per cent in 1970 to 92 per cent in 1981 while in some years (1974, 1979, 1980) it is over 100 per cent. Thus on average for 1973–81 the data show that about 63 per cent of the trade deficit in non-defence goods and services was financed by hard-currency earnings from international sales of armaments. This is quite a remarkable figure.

This does not mean that hard-currency trade in other sectors is unimportant. Exports emanating from the energy sector – principally petroleum and natural gas – were the major hard-currency earners for the Soviet Union during the 1970s. However, doubts have been expressed recently regarding the viability of continued growth in energy products – particularly oil. There is of course a great deal of controversy surrounding the evidence, and the forecasts have tended to conflict with each other.[28] Nevertheless, it is reasonably clear that energy (and oil) may no longer be the 'booming sectors' that they were over the past decade, and some decline in their capacity to generate a surplus for world markets is inevitable. The dependence of the Soviet Union's allies in Eastern Europe, Cuba and elsewhere on energy supplies from the USSR also limits size of the export surplus available to earn hard currency.

Natural gas exports have done extremely well during the 1970s in terms of volume sold, even though in value terms they have lagged behind oil, since the price rise in oil has been considerably higher than that in gas. Table 9.2 gives the value of petroleum and natural gas exports in current dollars, showing the importance of the former in terms of convertible-currency revenue earned. However, in *real* terms, petroleum exports rose from $430m to $574m between 1970 and 1981 (measured in 1970 US dollars, i.e. in constant prices), while gas exports increased from $14m to $322m – a truly phenomenal rise in quantity. Current opinion and estimates suggest that this trend might continue in the future. However, even here exploitation and transportation will depend very much on imports of Western equipment and technology, so the costs could be high in terms of hard-currency expenditures.

One must remember two basic points in any discussion of exports of natural resources. First, these are exhaustible resources and their depletion rates depend on a whole host of technological and economic factors, which may make it unwise to extract and sell when independent considerations, such as balance-of-trade problems, might require such sales. Second, these resources now lie in relatively more inhospitable territory, and exploitation costs will be significantly higher than in the past. Siberia may be awash with resources, but the incremental capital/output ratio to extract them is reputedly twice that obtaining elsewhere in the Soviet Union; if so, some difficult cost/benefit calculations will be necessary.

The overall conclusion seems to be that the Soviet arms industry can easily be geared to export promotion, and, even though other sectors are important, arms exports should continue to play as significant a role in the future as they have done in the past, earning much-needed hard currency. However this, the supply side, is only half the story: equally important are demand and the market.

LDC recipients

The rapid increase in Soviet arms exports to LDCs during the 1970s and the concomitant rise in commercial transactions have not been isolated phenomena. The overall market for arms has expanded fast, as also have direct sale and credit transfers as opposed to grant and aid. The value of *major* weapons exported to Third World countries was $2,939m in 1970, at constant (1975) prices. By 1980, this had risen to $9,841m.

Both the United States and West European countries increased their arms sales considerably during the past decade, vying with each other and the Soviet Union for markets in the developing world. Though military aid remained significant, its importance diminished, and more commercial transactions became the rule rather than the exception. During 1955–69 the distribution of US military exports, among grants, cash sales and military credits, was of the order of 78 per cent, 19 per cent and 3 per cent respectively. In 1975, these figures had changed dramatically to 14 per cent, 89 per cent and 6 per cent. The overwhelming importance of cash sales after the first oil shock subsequently declined somewhat, and, by 1979, grants, cash and credits were of the order of 5 per cent, 61 per cent and 34 per cent of total US arms sales.[29] Other European countries have followed suit. France and, recently, Italy have increased the real value of their exports many times since the 1970s and are currently the third and fourth largest exporters after the two superpowers.

The Soviet Union was thus not operating in a vacuum, nor did it have a unique position among international arms sellers. It is possible to argue that this was a case of demand creating its own supply. The unprecedented oil price rise and surfeit of petrodollars, together with rising tension in the LDCs, must have been important causes for the expansion of the trade. But, as our previous analysis suggests, the domestic economic problems of the Soviet Union and its rising hard-currency deficit in the non-arms sector must have prompted it to take advantage of the favourable situation.

Two major features of LDC recipients of Soviet armaments are noteworthy. The number of countries to which the Soviet Union supplies major defence equipment is still much lower than the number of those supplied by the US. The SIPRI arms register for 1981 and 1982 lists 31 countries for the USSR[30] as compared to 67 for the US; but the number seems to be rising. Furthermore, the past decade has seen a significant extension of the regional distribution of countries which buy weapons from the USSR. For example, African countries have become important recipients of arms and the USSR has recently replaced France as the continent's major supplier. Thus the scope of Soviet arms exports and concomitant influence seems to be on the increase.

Secondly, the commercialization of Soviet arms transfers has meant the LDCs overall have to pay more than they did in the past for these systems. It is no doubt true that the opportunity cost may be even higher; so also may be the cost from alternative sources of supply. But the basic point still remains. Import costs, particularly payment in hard currencies, are becoming a sizeable burden on LDCs and the trend is likely to continue. Nowadays 'new transfers (of arms) on generous terms appear to be the exception rather than the rule'.[31] Even in emergencies, such as the Arab–Israel war in 1973, Egypt had to make immediate cash payments for the Soviet arms airlift.

The Soviets have also been interested in barter-oriented trade relations with LDCs. However, hard-currency arms sales go against the spirit of barter transactions and thus create a different type of problem. With the expected increase in direct sales and convertible-currency payments, the qualitative character of East–South trade relations may change. Nevertheless, relatively large amounts of arms are still transferred on a commodity exchange basis. This occurs particularly if, for individual countries, the USSR runs up a sizeable trade deficit and puts pressure on the other nation to buy arms and set the trade imbalance right. Recent large sales of arms to India may have been prompted partly by large Soviet deficits on bilateral transactions. We should not be surprised if, after the post-Falklands-Malvinas liaison between Argentina and the USSR and given the large grain imports from the former, some sales of arms by the Soviets take place.

Arms transfers may induce or allow belligerent behaviour by the recipient, against the supplier's interest. The issues of 'moral hazard' and 'adverse selection' involved are discussed by Sen and Smith,[32] and the 'arms-race' consequences by Deger and Sen.[33] One way of minimizing such adverse consequences is through the interlinking of markets. Thus arms transfer is followed up or coupled with other types of trade for economic goods and services. If economic interrelationships are well established and the arms trade goes hand-in-hand with trade in other goods, then it is easier to influence the recipient LDC if it falls out of line. Under these circumstances, if the arms receiver uses arms for purposes which are disapproved of (such as going to war with a neighbour with whom the Soviet Union is also trying to build economic relationships), then either or both types of sanctions – economic and strategic – can be imposed. As the LDC becomes trade-dependent on the Soviet Union, it will find it increasingly difficult to use the weapons for 'wrong' purposes. In addition, the LDC concerned may find it difficult to go to a different supplier of arms or to renege on payment, because it is inextricably bound by many trade ties with the USSR.

Several arms buyers from among the LDCs have elaborate trading arrangements with the Soviet Union, demonstrating the relevance of this factor. India, Syria, Iraq and others are relatively dependent on the USSR, not only for sophisticated arms but also for export markets and some investment goods. The genuine dangers involved for the USSR are exemplified by the case of Egypt. The cancellation of repayment for arms by Egypt could have cost the USSR something of the order of $5,000m. The similar figure for Indonesia is around $3,000m. To prevent such losses, as well as to preclude the use of arms for belligerent activities which are not thought desirable, the Soviet Union should in principle trade in a wider range of products with arms recipients and have more leverage in controlling the end use of weapons. This is not to claim that interlinking of markets will necessarily solve the problem. Indonesia (post-Sukarno), Egypt and Somalia are examples of Soviet failures, where, in spite of strategic, trade and aid relationships, the Soviet Union was unceremoniously dumped, and the weapons were used for whatever actions the recipient government thought necessary. However, it is preferable to have diversified economic relations so that both civilian and defence goods are traded – especially the more the links, the greater the control over the recipient.

Political and strategic factors

Strategic and security-related factors have of course played a role in the Soviet Union's willingness and ability to supply arms to LDCs. Weapons transfers have sometimes gone hand-in-hand with rights to acquire bases – particularly naval facilities. As the Soviet Union has blossomed into a full-fledged superpower, it has tried to gain overseas bases, especially for its rapidly expanding 'blue-water' navy, and armaments sales have often helped it in its objective. Mali and the Congo have received arms in exchange for aircraft landing rights, as have Guinea and Somalia (before 1977–8) for naval facilities. In the latter case, of course, the Soviets lost their excellent naval bases at Berbera when they were thrown out in 1977 because of Somalia's conflict with Ethiopia. But the Soviets continued to use the facilities at Aden in South Yemen (the People's Democratic Republic of Yemen), again in exchange for large arms transfers. Access to strategic facilities in Iraq, Libya and South Yemen facilitated the transfer of equipment and (Cuban) troops to Ethiopia after the dramatic expulsion from Somalia. The Soviet Union is reputedly interested in the Red Sea Ethiopian ports of Assab and Massawa (a replacement for the Somali bases), and arms exports to Ethiopia must have helped its strategic interests.[34]

Egypt must have seemed a classic success story in the early 1970s from the point of view of Soviet arms exports. The Egyptian armed forces were completely dependent on Soviet military equipment, training and aid. In exchange there were at one time about 20,000 Russian military personnel in the country, with access to port and air facilities and sometimes even the actual manning and operational use of bases. Egypt was a prime example of what Harkavy claims for the USSR, that it 'has accelerated the use of arms transfers for acquiring strategic access, expanding a once limited network to near global dimensions'.[35]

Yet it was Egypt that turned out to be the Soviet's most important failure from the point of view of overseas defence and arms transfers policies. From 1972 onwards, the Soviet presence declined swiftly. Initially advisers were thrown out, then base facilities were reduced and, finally, denied; eventually Anwar El Sadat abrogated the Soviet-Egyptian Treaty of Friendship and Cooperation. A similar fate befell the USSR in Somalia with the loss of its Red Sea port facilities and the reduction in its security-related influence. India is another, though different, case in point. In spite of being a large recipient of Soviet arms, it has allowed only very limited servicing facilities for the Soviet navy, and these are similar to those provided to other countries. One should therefore be very careful in expecting too close a relationship between arms transfers and the achievement of strategic interests. The links are definitely present, but, given the volatile nature of international strategic relations, they are difficult to predict.

Care must be taken in analysing the political motives of the Soviet Union in recent years. Some analysts have generally considered this to be the most important reason for Soviet arms exports. It is possible, with respect to the transfer of arms, that 'military assistance and arms transfers have been an integral part of Soviet policy towards developing countries since the shift in Soviet policy towards the non-aligned states in the mid-1950s.[36] Arms exports in search of political ends – such as weakening Western support (India after the 1965 war), out-manoeuvring Chinese influence (North Korea, Tanzania), gaining a political foothold (Ethiopia), providing help for 'progressive' states based on 'scientific socialism' (Mozambique, Angola), and so on – have played a contributory role in the rapid expansion of the Soviet arms trade with the LDCs. Yet the failure of political control and the rather tenuous links on which some of the political relations have been constructed gives rise to doubts about their alleged overriding importance. Although political relations play an important role, economic motives are a major 'engine' of the recent burgeoning arms trade.

Conclusion

This chapter looks at Soviet arms exports to LDCs in the economic context of domestic investment, growth and balance-of-trade problems. Given the necessity of import-fed growth and the desire to avoid bottlenecks within the economy, intermediate imports (particularly technology, capital goods and know-how) from the West become important for development.[37] As its convertible-currency deficit increases, its growing international debt burden forces the USSR to search for 'ideal' exportables.

I have argued that the internal logic of a system where the civilian economy exhibits excess demand, and where the military sector is not supply-constrained, pushes the Soviet Union towards increasing arms exports. Since the weapons are competitive with those produced by the West and embody 'appropriate technology', there is also demand for these exports from the LDCs. Civilian trade and political links tend to grow hand-in-hand with arms transfers. But even though the overall framework of trade may be political in nature, the basic motivation is economic, particularly the domestic constraints faced by the open economy. As this motivation becomes stronger, arms may be sold to countries which demand them, without undue regard to political affiliation. There is an interesting equivalence to be observed here: both the arms trade and other liaisons are seen to occur together, whether a country receives arms as a result of an initial friendliness towards the Soviet Union, or whether the cooperation arises from the sale of weapons. It is difficult in principle to distinguish between cause and effect.

Analysing the arms trade policy of the USSR, Albrecht clearly shows the weakness of the hypothesis that Soviet weapons are used to serve world revolution or are distributed according to a well-defined political plan for the Third World. Quoting Schmiederer, he states: 'Soviet politics in the Third World have been and are opportunistic: they take what they can get.'[38] A classic recent example of this is Kuwait's apparent intention to buy Soviet arms worth $327m.[39] It was reported that the US Congress refused the sale of the American Stinger missile to Kuwait, which the latter wanted as a defensive measure against Iranian aeroplanes in the event of a spill-over of the Gulf war. In retaliation, Kuwait decided to purchase surface-to-air missiles from the USSR and it was even expected that Foreign Minister Gromyko would visit Kuwait to sign the deal, a remarkable event in itself considering the hostility of the conservative sheikhdoms towards the Soviet Union. Nowadays political distinctions often get blurred where arms sales are concerned. It is possibly desirable to emphasize the basic economic factors, causes and motivations – in addition to politico-strategic variables – of the Soviet arms trade with developing countries.

What about future trends? One of the problems of evaluating long-run trends is the presence of short-term fluctuations in weapons transfers. It is now thought that Soviet arms trade agreements declined during 1980–2 from their high levels of the late 1970s.[40] In 1979, there were about 110 transfer agreements of which more than 65 per cent were for new weapons. By 1982, the total had fallen to just over forty, with less than 50 per cent for new weapons. Yet very recent events suggest that things have begun to change again. The Soviet Union has started (albeit guardedly) to supply arms to Iraq, has made good Syrian losses in the Lebanon war, and has recently convinced India to import more Soviet arms after a few years of attempts by the Indian government to diversify sources of supply.

Looking at the future, then, on the supply side, if the need for hard-currency imports grows, as it is expected to do, then the potential for arms exports will rise. Energy exports in the form of oil and natural gas are also important exportables, but they have their own problems. Resource depletion has its own economic logic which may not mesh in with overall macroeconomic needs. Furthermore, the marginal cost of extraction is rising and is dependent on Western technology. In a sense it is much easier to export arms when the need arises. I therefore expect that, from the Soviet point of view, arms sales for hard currencies will be preferable, and the generous terms of military aid of the 1950s and 1960s may become less usual.

The crucial determinant is on the demand side. Can the LDCs sustain the massive annual volume of weapons purchased at almost commercial rates? There are signs that OPEC has become less extravagant than it was in the recent past. Poor LDCs, with their growth problems, may have to reduce the scale of their defence effort. Deger gives a comprehensive review of the critical development problems that LDCs are facing in their effort to increase their defence capacity.[41] But 'Third World wars' (wars fought in the Third World) continue, and arms races between neighbours still proliferate. In the field of the arms trade the Soviet Union will 'make hay while the sun shines': the question is whether developing countries will allow the 'sun' (or is it a nova?) of their defence expenditure to continue shining so brightly.

Notes

I am grateful to Professor Richard Portes, Somnath Sen, Ron Smith and to members of the study group for perceptive comments.

1. The data are taken from SIPRI, *World Armaments and Disarmament Yearbooks*, various years. Constant-price values of arms are effectively quantity indices, i.e. they reflect the volume of sales.

2. The most recent five years for which data were available is SIPRI, *World Armaments and Disarmament Yearbooks*.

3. See R. Portes, 'Deficits and Detente', background paper to the *Report of an International Conference on the Balance of Trade in the Comecon Countries* (New York: The Twentieth Century Fund, 1983), Table A-25.

4. U. Albrecht, 'Soviet Arms Exports', in SIPRI, *World Armaments and Disarmaments Yearbook 1983*, Ch. 12.

5. S. Deger, *The Economic Dimensions of Military Expenditure in Less Developed Countries* (London: Routledge and Kegan Paul, 1985, forthcoming).

6. See SIPRI, *World Armaments and Disarmament Yearbooks 1982* and *1983*; A.J. Pierre, *The Global Politics of Arms Sales* (Princeton, NJ: Princeton University Press, 1982); D. Holloway, *The Soviet Union and the Arms Race* (New Haven, Conn. and London: Yale University Press, 1983); R.E. Kanet, 'Soviet and East European Arms Transfers to the Third World: Strategic, Political and Economic Factors', in NATO Economic Directorate, *Colloquium 1983* (Brussels, 1983).

7. See A. Cardesman, 'US and Soviet Competition in Arms Exports and Military Assistance', *Armed Forces International Journal*, 1981.

8. Kanet, 'Soviet and East European Arms Transfers'.

9. See Pierre, *The Global Politics of Arms Sales*, for an excellent review with an unashamedly political emphasis.

10. The source of the US data is the *Handbook of Economic Statistics* (CIA/National Foreign Assessment Center, Washington, D.C., 1981) and that of the Soviet data is *Narodnoye Khozyaistvo v 1980 godv* (Moscow: Statistika, 1981), both reported in D. Fewtrell, 'The Soviet Economic Crisis: Prospects for the Military and the Consumer', *Adelphi Papers* No. 186, 1983.

11. Fewtrell, 'The Soviet Economic Crisis', reports that many of the 1985 targets in planned production of metallurgy and chemicals were originally set for 1980 and subsequently revised. Thus under an optimistic scenario of target fulfilment, Soviet industry will have taken ten years to attain output levels expected to have been reached in five.

12. F.D. Holzman, 'Soviet Central Planning and Its Impact on Foreign Trade and

Adjustment Mechanisms', pp. 280–305 in A. Brown and E. Neuberger (eds.), *International Trade and Central Planning* (Berkeley, California: University of California Press, 1968).

13. E. Malinvaud, *The Theory of Unemployment Reconsidered* (Oxford: Blackwell, 1977).

14. See R. Portes, 'Effect of the World Economic Crisis on the East European Economies', *The World Economy*, Vol. 3, No. 1, 1980, pp. 13–51.

15. *Ibid.*

16. The analysis here is brief. For a formal presentation of the relationship between the internal and external balance of open-economy CPEs, see R. Portes, 'Internal and External Balance in a Centrally Planned Economy', *Journal of Comparative Economics*, Vol. 3, No. 4, December 1979, pp. 325–45. A theoretical analysis of the relationship between domestic growth and investment on the one hand and trade deficits on the other can be found in S. Deger, 'The Economic Rationale of Soviet Arms Trade with LDCs' (Birkbeck College, mimeo, 1983), in which econometric evidence in support of the relevant hypotheses is also presented.

17. See R, Portes, 'The Impact of International Economic Disturbances on the Soviet Union and Eastern Europe: a Survey', in *East European Economic Assessment* (Joint Economic Committee of US Congress, Washington, D.C., 1981), Part 2.

18. Holloway, *The Soviet Union and the Arms Race*.

19. *Ibid*; italics added.

20. *Ibid.*

21. CIA, *Estimated Soviet Defense Spending: Trends and Prospects* (Washington, D.C., 1978).

22. Holloway, *The Soviet Union and the Arms Race*.

23. Pierre, *The Global Politics of Arms Sales*; italics added.

24. CIA, *Arms Flows to LDCs: US–Soviet Comparisons* (Washington, D.C., 1977).

25. Department of Defense, *Soviet Military Power* (Washington, D.C., 1981).

26. R. Portes, 'East, West and South: the Role of the Centrally Planned Economies in the International Economy', in Sven Grossman and Erik Lundberg (eds.), *The World Economic Order: Past and Prospects* (London: Macmillan, 1981), pp. 319–57.

27. See Albrecht, 'Soviet Arms Exports'.

28. See Fewtrell, 'The Soviet Economic Crisis'.

29. See M. Brzoska, 'Research Communications: The Military Related External Debt of Third World Countries', *Journal of Peace Research*, Vol. 20, No. 3, 1983, for a perceptive (and rare) discussion.

30. Afghanistan, Benin, Cape Verde, Bulgaria, Czechoslovakia, GDR, Hungary, Poland, Romania, Mongolia, Cuba, Vietnam, Finland, Angola, Algeria, Bangladesh, Botswana, Ethiopia, Guyana, India, Iraq, Jordan, Libya, Madagascar, Mozambique, Nicaragua, Peru, Seychelles, Syria, South Yemen and Zambia.

31. Albrecht, 'Soviet Arms Exports'.

32. S. Sen and R.P. Smith, 'The Economics of International Arms Transfers', Birkbeck College Discussion Paper No. 135 (London, 1983).

33. S. Deger and S. Sen, 'Military Expenditure, Spin-off and Economic Development', *Journal of Development Economics*, Vol. 13, 1983, pp. 67–83; and the same authors' 'Technology Transfer and Arms Production in LDCs', paper presented at the World Congress of the International Economic Association, Madrid, September 1983.

34. See Pierre, *The Global Politics of Arms Sales*.

35. R.E. Harkavy, 'The New Geopolitics: Arms Transfers and the Major Powers' Competition for Overseas Bases', in S.G. Neuman and R.E. Harkavy (eds.), *Arms Transfers in the Modern World* (New York: Praeger, 1979).

36. Kanet, 'Soviet and East European Arms Transfers'.

37. See P. Hanson, 'Economic Constraints·on Soviet Policies in the 1980s', *International Affairs*, 1981, pp. 21–42.

38. Albrecht, 'Soviet Arms Exports'.

39. This was reported by Tim McGirk, *Sunday Times*, 22 July 1984.

40. See SIPRI, *World Armaments and Disarmament Yearbook 1984*.

41. Deger, *The Economic Dimensions of Military Expenditure*.

10

The Soviet Union in North-South negotiations: revealing preferences

Colin W. Lawson

Introduction

At first glance, the idea of trying to deduce Soviet economic interests in LDCs from Soviet stances in North-South negotiations might seem overambitious: Soviet concessions to the South, after all, were meagre to the point of non-existence, and most of the sound and the fury of the negotiations occurred between the West and the South. Such a view would, however, be too pessimistic. It is true that the value of Soviet concessions was small, but the course of the negotiations did require the Soviet Union to articulate policy positions on almost all of the major and many of the minor issues in North-South relations. As the debate advanced, the position of the USSR became firmer and more coherent, and an analysis of its final position provides a clear and consistent picture of both short-run and long-run Soviet economic interests in the South.

In speaking of the economic interests of a major world power, particularly one where all trading decisions, however minor, are state decisions, it is very difficult to distinguish between economic and political motives. Although I will often distinguish between them, the distinctions may sometimes be rather artificial. A consequence of this problem is that it is possible to argue that there are no Soviet economic interests in the South which are not in large part determined by Soviet global political strategy. It follows therefore that the assumptions about such Soviet strategy should be stated, before an attempt is made to deduce Soviet economic interests in the South.

Assumptions

Soviet global strategy in relation to the South is assumed to be cautious and cost-conscious. It is certainly not provocative in the sense that substantial political, economic and military resources are consistently devoted to destabilizing pro-Western regimes. It might more accurately be described as restrained, in that only emerging anti-Western or perhaps more accurately anti-American regimes may be taken up as clients. Given the economic and military constraints facing the Soviet Union, and even allowing for the use of surrogate military and economic intervention, it seems unlikely that Soviet aims in the South extend much beyond weakening its ties with the West, and securing more consistent support for the Soviet position in the major East-West disputes which command the USSR's attention. The last thing the Soviet Union wants is any more poverty-stricken applicants for membership of the CMEA. Although the 'Law' of the levelling of development may not be quite the moral imperative to redistribution which the poorer members of the CMEA had hoped, the Cuban and Vietnamese cases illustrate that membership may still carry the benefits of considerable aid. The refusal to admit Mozambique – a state uniquely described in its Friendship Treaty as a 'natural ally' of the Soviet Union – presumably signals that the club has filled its quota of indigent members.

Given these global political objectives and economic constraints, my view is that the Soviet response to the South in North-South negotiations was directly determined by Soviet economic interests in the South. The Soviet Union's view of these interests is in turn a product of two distinct influences: its view of the role of foreign trade in the development of the domestic economy, and its view of the political and economic development of LDCs, both in terms of their socio-economic systems and in terms of their relations with advanced market economies.

This chapter is arranged as follows. I begin by discussing the development of Soviet perceptions of LDCs. Soviet responses to the North-South debates are then reviewed, and I conclude by discussing what these debates may reveal about Soviet economic interests in LDCs.

Soviet views of the Third World

The development of Soviet views of the Third World [1] is intimately linked to the evolution of the Soviet Union's views of the world economy, and of its desired position within that economy. Until after Stalin's death it would have been inaccurate to use the phrase 'the world economy', for the official ideology held that there were two world markets: a socialist one and a capitalist one, with LDCs inextricably linked with and subordinate to the latter. Although some intellectual effort was expended on developing theories which explained the operations of the two markets, little serious thought seems to have been given to the future course of Soviet economic relations with what were surely soon to become independent states.

In his haste to make up for time lost during Stalin's regime,

Khrushchev almost immediately launched into a series of Third World adventures which antagonized his domestic and foreign opponents, without producing any lasting clear-cut benefits. The explanatory theory of two world markets was not abandoned, but, through the opportunity afforded by the policy of peaceful coexistence, it was clearly hoped that emergent nations could be persuaded to attach themselves to the socialist world market.

During the early Brezhnev years the political and economic costs of Khrushchev's policies led to a cautious and more realistic assessment of the potential advantages of involvement in the South. Although severe setbacks such as the break with Egypt were still to come, it must already have been clear by the late 1960s that, owing to the volatility of political conditions in most developing countries, candidates for intensive long-term political and economic invest-ment would have to be chosen with extreme care if expensive mistakes were to be avoided. Although Soviet aims undoubtedly still involve the detachment of the South from the West and, ideally, its harnessing to the support of Soviet global ambitions, there has been a slow but steady growth in Soviet recognition of the heterogeneity of developing countries, and consequently a parallel growth in unwillingness to acquire new clients.

Soviet advice to LDCs has become fairly consistent and clearly stated. So has the analysis of the links between the East and the South. They have

> similar interests as far as actively countering the forces of colonialism and neo-colonialism ... are concerned ... [and] their interests also coincide, in the main, on issues relating to restructuring world-wide economic relations ... [But] the relations between socialist and developing countries do not rest on the principle of socialist solidarity, since the majority of the developing countries are developing along capitalist lines and only a few have taken a socialist orientation. There are no grounds, therefore, to claim the presence of class solidarity between them and the socialist countries[2]

Soviet advice to developing states
The advice which is offered to LDCs by the USSR generally has five components: nationalization, planning, redistribution, mobilization of domestic resources, and avoidance of enclave development.

Nationalization is necessary to provide scope for influencing the economy, and to reduce the influence of both domestic capital and transnational corporations. It can have an added attraction, as Fomin suggests, for it 'in some cases opens up additional opportuni-ties for the developing countries to organise economic cooperation with other states, particularly in the field of inter-state resource development'.[3]

But such an inducement to nationalize should be considered carefully. It is true that CMEA members seem to prefer to trade with states with large public sectors, and indeed with those state sectors.[4] It is also true that Soviet aid is directed into public enterprises.[5] But it is not true that Soviet authors have an uncritical attitude towards the public sectors of developing states. Nor is it true that the foreign trade organs of CMEA states will always trade with such a state sector, in preference to world markets. For example, Teodorovich argues that in itself the development of a state sector does not stimulate socialist relations of production; indeed the opposite may occur. In addition the Czech author Angelis, and the Polish authors Klerr and Zacher, note that sizeable proportions of Czech and Polish imports from the South come through Western intermediaries.[6] In both cases this is more efficient than trading direct with the producers, and the reason for this, according to Angelis, is the high prices demanded by Third World state traders.

Like a large public sector, planning is advocated because it enables the economy to be managed more precisely. But, like state ownership, it is not advocated uncritically. Although CMEA states clearly find it more congenial to deal with similar economic management systems, and indeed Klerr and Zacher argue that a lack of planning in the South is the main barrier to effective East-South technology transfer,[7] it is not uncommon to find advocates of the mixed economy among CMEA writers.

Planning can make easier redistribution and the mobilization of domestic resources. But in both cases CMEA writers stress that it is domestic and not foreign resources which are to be reshuffled. As Bogomolov puts it, 'The Soviet [Union] and many other Socialist countries resolutely oppose the diverse utopian projects for a world-wide redistribution of wealth which tend to distract the Third World peoples from the vital tasks of struggling for their national liberation and social emancipation and for the utmost use on that basis of their internal potential for socio-economic progress.'[8]

Soviet views of 'interdependence'

If Bogomolov's statement signals a Soviet willingness to accept the fact that most LDCs are not natural allies, and to acknowledge that some, especially the wealthier OPEC members, have effectively entered the capitalist camp, it does not signal acquiescence in their dependence on the West. For while talk of two world systems is less frequently heard than it was in the past, and a certain degree of East-West interdependence is accepted, for LDCs the 'bourgeois' concept of interdependence is vigorously opposed: opposed as a 'neo-colonialist' invention to legitimate continuing hegemony – as a doctrine of continuing exploitation. It is argued that in this sense interdependence involves one-way political influence, though perhaps two-way economic influence. Assessing the outcome of UNCTAD VI, Pankine reported, with some irony, that the Group of 77 had argued from the concept of interdependence to the conclusion that the world economy would not recover until the South was appropriately stimulated by loans and greater exports.[9]

Although opposing the thesis of interdependence between the West and the South, Soviet authors openly state that CMEA states' assistance will be limited in size and quite specific in destination. Bogomolov notes 'the socialist countries' cooperation with the developing world ... is mainly extended to those countries that are most active in the national liberation struggle and have embarked on progressive political development'.[10] In Bogomolov's favoured list are Angola, Afghanistan, Iraq, Mozambique, Syria and Ethiopia. In the list of socialist-orientated states, others include South Yemen, the Congo, Benin, Algeria, Libya, Guinea, and occasionally, Tanzania.

Inclusion in such a list does not mean that Soviet observers assume political development will ultimately result in vanguard parties of the East European type – though Soviet writers strongly advocate such a development for close LDC allies. For an LDC and for the Soviet Union, signing a treaty signals practically the closest form of relation. Imam argues that the minimum requirements a potential co-signatory must have fulfilled are to be actively involved in non-alignment; to be a major recipient of Soviet military and economic aid; to have neither belonged to, nor leased facilities to, a hostile power, and to have an active record of opposition to Western influence. Nevertheless, of the currently operative eleven treaties, all except those with Mozambique 'characterise their ideological orientations as nothing more than friendship and cooperation between states with different socio-economic systems'.[11] In some cases Imam may have over-estimated these ideological differences, but it is still true that there are distinct limits to Soviet involvement, as was shown by Mozambique's abortive application for membership of the CMEA.

Predictions from Soviet views of LDCs

Several aspects of Soviet views of LDCs have become clear only in the past decade: indeed I will argue below that the North-South negotiations often provided the impetus for their clarification. But it is worth putting a counterfactual question, and asking what might have been predicted about Soviet positions in the negotiations, had all these views on LDCs been known in advance.

Had the full panoply of Soviet views on development been known in advance, it is reasonable to suppose that opposition to any blanket concessions, in aid or trade, would have been predicted. As the Soviet Union is wary of acquiring Third World clients, one would have predicted that there would be no agreement to any proposals for long-run subsidies, whether through aid or terms-of-trade agreements. The experiences of the Soviet Union within the CMEA, including Vietnam and Cuba, may have been a salutory lesson on the economic cost of loyalty. The lack of any deep ideological affinity with most LDCs would have reinforced this effect. The self-help view of development strategy would have provided further support for this position, and LDC governments which were not willing to contemplate the necessary adjustments, including the development of the public sector, would have been foolish to think that the Soviet Union would adopt any other position. Indeed aid donors willing to offer long-term concrete economic concessions for only the most nebulous and probably short-lived political advantages have always been scarce.

Soviet responses to the North-South debate
The bundle of demands which the South presented to the North during the 1970s was multifarious and optimistic. Smyth claimed to have identified nine major issue areas and seventy-two sub-issues in what came to be called the demand for a New International Economic Order (NIEO).[12] The demands ranged across the whole gamut of international trade issues, and although in the beginning many were perhaps more statements of the ideal than serious negotiating positions, both the West and the East were sufficiently apprehensive to eschew the rhetoric of sympathy and concentrate on the diplomacy of rejection.

General position
In the case of the Soviet Union support for the South was precisely and inversely related to the specificity of the demands.[13] In the early 1970s the CMEA states generally supported the early, rather loosely formulated, NIEO resolutions. As the demands were elaborated during the mid-1970s the Soviet response became more tentative and qualified. Smyth noted that as early as 1975 the Soviet position at the Seventh Special Session of the United Nations was already less radical than it had been at the Sixth Special Session of the previous year.[14] But until the 1976 UNCTAD meeting in Nairobi there had never been a detailed response to the South's

position. When it came, the Joint Statement by all the full CMEA members (except Romania) was a disappointment to the South, for while reaffirming the justice of their demands it offered few concessions, and clearly stated that the demands were just only in relation to the West.[15] As a Soviet Government statement to the UN Secretary-General put it,

> There can be no ground whatsoever for presenting to the Soviet Union and other socialist countries the demands which the developing nations present to the developed capitalist states, including the demand for a compulsory transfer of a fixed share of the gross national product to the developing nations by way of economic assistance.[16]

To the chagrin of the Group 77, the basic outline of the Soviet position has remained fundamentally unchanged since the release of the 1976 Joint Statement. Consequently at UNCTAD's 1979 Manila conference and at the 1983 Belgrade meeting the CMEA states came under attack from the South for their parsimony and failure to provide unqualified support. As we shall see below, some of these attacks seem to have led to a change in the Soviets' rationale for their position, but not to any change in their general stand.

That stand has recently been reiterated in the Soviet assessment of the Belgrade conference. The Soviet government is willing to support proposals which, in Pankine's words, aim at 'the genuine restructuring of international economic relations on an equable, democratic basis, at promoting mutually advantageous, equal economic cooperation between all countries and ensuring the people's right to independent development'.[17] This is not a totally vacuous statement. It reflects the fact that a major reason for the USSR's cooling ardour for the South's position was a rapid realization that the NIEO proposals would not lead to a radical change in the political composition of the South. Consequently the USSR was understandably unwilling to provide subventions by granting concessions to states which its analysts were suggesting were unlikely to develop 'progressive tendencies'. As Bognar put, it, 'a genuine new international economic order can only be introduced when the revolution comes to power in the economically most powerful countries and makes it possible to introduce an international division of labour based on socialist principles'.[18]

The 'mutually advantageous ... cooperation' of Pankine's statement (quoted above) reflects two concerns. When concessions have been offered, the offer has been 'without reciprocity in respect of preferential measures but based on normal and equitable terms and without discrimination'.[19] The Soviet interpretation of conditions has meant actual or effective most-favoured-nation treatment. The second concern has been to try to ensure that any West-South concessions also apply to East-West trade. Returning from the 1979 UNCTAD meeting, the leader of the Soviet delegation complained that the conference resolution on protection was 'one-sided, protecting only the interests of the developing countries. The socialist countries believe that international measures against protectionist tendencies can be effective only if they are not confined to the interests of one group of countries'.[20]

This concern in turn reflects a major Soviet objective – to turn UNCTAD into a World Trade Organization dealing specifically with East-West trade. As Manzhulo has recently suggested, 'Any possible reorganisation of the UNCTAD should be aimed at raising its efficiency as a universal trade and economic forum'. He would be well pleased if 'UNCTAD's efforts could be concentrated on evaluating how the established principles and rules are being observed ... [and] on identifying the actual difficulties, processes and causes hindering the development of international trade with due regard for the interests of all nations'.[21] As the South does not want the focus of attention shifted from its own problems, and the West does not want to discuss East-West trade, there is no foreseeable possibility that these objectives will be attained.

Aid, finance and debt
Many of the most significant clashes between the East and the South have occurred over the question of aid. Aid to non-communist developing countries is tied, is rather small in volume and is geographically very concentrated. In the early 1970s Holzman estimated that Soviet net aid outflows (deliveries minus repayments) were as low as 0.05 per cent of GNP.[22] The narrow range of clients reflected Soviet economic and strategic interests. From 1954 to 1972 only five countries, Egypt, India, Iran, Iraq and Pakistan, were the recipients of more than half of Soviet commitments.

In the late 1970s there was a considerable rise in Soviet aid commitments – for example Cooper and Fogarty estimated 1978 commitments at $3.7bn*[23] This did not mean that the Soviet Union had become a major aid donor. A high proportion of the aid deliveries of the late 1970s in fact went into a $2bn investment in the Moroccan phosphate industry. In a not atypical arrangement, this investment is being repaid by the output of the additional facilities, which are being used as a much-needed input to the Soviet domestic fertilizer industry.

We have seen above that the Soviet Union has rejected LDC

---

* In this chapter the term 'billion' refers to the US thousand million (10^9).

demands for a fixed percentage of GNP to be transferred annually as aid. Indeed this is a position which the Soviet Union has consistently defended since the formative UNCTAD meetings of the early 1960s. Practically all Soviet and East European statements on the issue assert that they follow an approach which is different from that of the Western states. They argue that they have no historical responsibility for the problems, and that as current trading arrangements are not exploitative they have no duty to offer major concessions.

Unequivocal rejection has not silenced LDC voices, and criticism of Soviet attitudes is a common event at major UNCTAD gatherings. The criticism has had two results. First, Soviet rejection of the demands became more vigorous. There is an exasperated note in Manzhulo's report on UNCTAD V, where he writes that 'the Group of 77 again included in its draft several elements, being fully aware of the fact that they are unacceptable to the socialist countries, beginning with the demand that 0.7 per cent of their gross national product should be allotted annually as aid to the developing countries'.[24]

The second and later result was perhaps less predictable, for the claim is so implausible. Within the last three years or so the Soviet Union, Bulgaria and East Germany have all claimed to have met or exceeded the United Nations targets for resource transfers as a percentage of GNP. The boldness of the claim is matched only by its implausibility. A recent British Foreign and Commonwealth Office document, in a conclusion which is consistent with Development Assistance Committee findings, reported that in 1980 Soviet aid accounted for only 0.19 per cent of GNP. And, because of aid repayments, the flow of Soviet net aid to non-socialist developing countries in 1981 was estimated to be negative.[25]

The failure of the Soviet Union to turn UNCTAD into a World Trade Organization, coupled with its absence from the IMF, has meant that it has been unable to exert any pressure on behalf of LDCs on the issues of debt relief and finance for trade, which have so exercised the South in the past decade. Although the Soviet Union has had no special debt problems of its own, neither has it made any important initiatives to help LDCs who have. In part this reflects its recent aid to Poland, though in the main it reflects its cautious, a critic might say parsimonious, general aid policies.

Commodity agreements

It has already been noted that in North-South negotiations the Soviet Union has been a rather reluctant participant, and has been at pains to assert that East-South trading arrangements are qualitatively different from North-South ones. The response to the integrated programme for commodities is a further illustration of these characteristics.

The Joint Statement by the CMEA (except Romania) to UNCTAD IV begin its remarks on this question by stressing that consumer as well as producer interests must be protected, and that while improved terms of trade for LDCs are justified, they must devote more energy to the control of foreign capital. Priority should be given to the least developed countries and the CMEA was 'in principle favourably disposed' to a link between export and import prices for LDCs. But compensatory financing facilities 'cannot be seen as an effective means of perfecting the structure and organization of commodity markets'.[26] The CMEA countries were willing to agree that LDCs should enjoy better access to the markets for primary and processed commodities, but access should be limited to 'national undertakings'. In other words they were not willing to allow multinationals better access to the Soviet domestic market. Buffer stocks were viewed as alternatives to long-term bilateral agreements, and the Joint Statement urged that participating members should have the choice of which method they used.

One of the few achievements of the South at UNCTAD IV was to gain the agreement of the North to proceed to detailed negotiations on the creation of a Common Fund. The Fund's purpose was to finance a group of new commodity agreements, whose major objective was to increase and stabilize the incomes of primary commodity producers. The Soviet Union's attitude to the Common Fund was, and has continued to be, indistinguishable from that of leading Western states.

In the run-up to the signing of the preliminary agreement on the Fund in March 1979, the Soviet Union, like the United States, argued against providing a greater proportion of the necessary capital than their allocation of votes on the Fund's Council. More recently Polezhayev has suggested that, because of the stable long-term nature of intra-CMEA trade, it should not be included when interest in an agreement is being determined during the calculation of national contributions to agreements.[27]

Although the Soviet Union cannot be blamed for the failure of sufficient states to ratify the Common Fund, there is no evidence that it will view the idea's demise with more sorrow than do most Western states. In the negotiations on this, as on other issues, the Soviet Union has exhibited a careful and precise awareness of the costs of concessions. And in the future there is no reason to doubt Polezhayev's statement that 'the USSR's participation in international commodity agreements ... will, as before, be decided in every concrete case with due regard for a just balance of the rights and obligations of the participants in agreements'.[28]

Manufactures

The South's demands for an improved share of the world market for manufactures, by means of non-reciprocal trade concessions and tariff reductions, generally run counter to Soviet interests and past practices. The traditional structure of East-South trade is not dissimilar from that of West-South trade: raw materials and semi-finished goods are exchanged for manufactures, especially capital equipment.[29]

The 1976 UNCTAD IV statement offered only more long-term agreements 'without reciprocity in respect of preferential measures but based on normal and equitable terms and without discrimination'.[30] However, by the mid-1970s several centrally planned economies had introduced generalized system of preferences schemes. Unfortunately, as only in Hungary is there significant freedom of choice for the domestic user, a lower tariff has no impact on the volume of imports, and consequently such concessions are worthless. In the case of manufactured exports, LDCs have no choice but to seek concessions through explicit volume and price arrangements in new or renegotiated long-term agreements. As both the USSR and other Eastern European states feel increasingly threatened by LDC competition in the market for manufactures, such concessions will be hard to find.

Transfer of technology

The creation of a code of conduct to cover the transfer of technology showed the Soviet Union in a more flexible mood – but again the discussions on the details of the code led to some acrimonious exchanges. The flexibility may have been related to the possibility of making some gains at the expense of Western nations, for from the outset the Soviet Union made it clear that it did not wish concessions to be unilateral, and that the code should also apply to East-West trade.

As delay followed the initial progress on creating the code of conduct, differences between the East and the South began to emerge. As Leonidov noted, 'However fair and justified on the whole, [LDC] claims are sometimes a bit excessive, representing an attempt to turn the International Code of Conduct on the Transfer of Technology into a document serving solely their own interests'.[31]

The two chapters of the Code which caused particular problems were 'Institutional Machinery' and 'Applicable Law and Settlement of Disputes'. On the former, LDCs not unnaturally wanted control by an UNCTAD body; the advanced countries of East and West opposed this probable control by the LDCs of the administration of the Code. On the latter, the South wanted the settlement of disputes to take place under the acquiring countries' laws, and normally by a court of law. Clearly the acceptance of such a proposal would have created risks for Soviet exporters, and their negotiators put forward a suggestion for international arbitration as an attempt to reduce such risks. Having noted LDC-Soviet disagreements on this issue, it should be pointed out that the failure to issue a Code is not chiefly a consequence of East-South disagreements. In this area, and indeed in all the major areas of dispute on North-South issues, East-South arguments are no more than peripheral to the main arenas of contention. Presumably the Soviet Union is not wholly unhappy in this role of a virtual spectator.

Conclusions

In this chapter it has been argued that the North-South debates forced the Soviet Union to articulate its position on virtually the whole range of economic issues of interest to LDCs. It has also been argued that an examination of the roots of the response, in the Soviets' view of foreign trade and in their view of LDCs, enables us to discover much about their economic interest in the South.

It was noted that although the Soviets have recently shown little enthusiasm for rewarding political loyalty with substantial subsidies, at least outside of the CMEA, they would clearly like the economic ties between the South and the West to be weakened. Unfortunately they have very little power to achieve this goal. Nor, given their understanding of the heterogeneous nature of the South, would they expect any rapid progress in this direction. The same analysis which leads them to be not uncritical of the 'progressive' potential of public-sector growth in LDCs presumably also leads to scepticism about the lasting political advantage to be gained from such a weakening of West-South links.

Nevertheless, weaker West-South ties would allow an increase in East-South trade. As the wars of national liberation finally peter out, and as the South moves towards complete formal political independence from the North, the main levers of influence cease to be arms supply and become trade and aid. For this reason a weakening of West-South links, which might allow the Soviet Union to increase its commercial influence, would be an important goal. Nevertheless, the ability of the Soviet Union to exert a major economic influence on the South is very limited – certainly vastly more limited than its military influence might have been at an earlier stage of decolonization. Leaving aside only a few countries, trade with the CMEA is of marginal importance for the South. Only about 5 per cent of the LDCs' exports are sent to the CMEA; only about 7 per cent of their imports originate there.

For the moment Soviet economic interests in LDCs are quite limited. The LDCs are useful as an additional and perhaps growing source of raw materials. They are useful as sources of hard currency to offset deficits with the West. But as development occurs they are likely to be an increasingly difficult market for Soviet manufactures. In the 1960s the share of Soviet trade with LDCs rose rapidly, to stand at about 16 per cent by the end of the decade. It is still under 20 per cent, and is unlikely to rise above 25 per cent in the next decade. Thus the most clear-cut implication to arise from the Soviet Union's involvement in the North-South debates was that its primary interest and focus of attention was, and continues to be, East-West trade.

Notes

I should like to thank members of the study group, and particularly Robert Cassen, Alan Smith and Geoffrey Goodwin, for helpful comments on an earlier draft of this paper.

1. An extended survey of the development of Soviet views of LDCs can be found in Elizabeth K. Valkenier, *The Soviet Union and the Third World* (New York: Praeger, 1983).

2. O. Bogomolov, 'CMEA and the Developing World', *International Affairs* (Moscow), No. 7, 1979, pp. 23–24. It is worth noting that the author is Director of the Institute for the Socialist World Economic System. It was this Institute which was given the task of producing the draft CMEA response to the Group of 77 demands at the crucial Nairobi meeting of UNCTAD.

3. B.S. Fomin, 'The New International Economic Order as Viewed in the CMEA Countries', in E. Laszlo and J. Kurtzman (eds), *Eastern Europe and the New International Economic Order* (New York: Pergamon, 1980), p. 10.

4. See T. Teodorovich, 'The USSR's Role in Building Up the State Sector of the National Economy of Developing Countries', *Foreign Trade*, No. 2, 1979, pp. 37–41.

5. O. Bogomolov, 'CMEA and the Developing World', p. 3.

6. T. Teodorovich, 'The USSR's Role'; I. Angelis, 'Some Issues Concerning Economic Relations Between the CSSR and the Developing Countries', in E. Dobozi (ed.), *Economic Co-operation Between Socialist and Developing Countries* (Budapest, Hungarian Scientific Council for World Economy, 1978), pp. 173–89; J. Klerr and L. Zacher, 'Technology Transfer from CMEA Countries to the Third World', in Laszlo and J. Kurtzman (eds.), *Eastern Europe and the New International Economic Order*.

7. Klerr and Zacher, 'Technology Transfer'.

8. O. Bogomolov, 'The CMEA Countries in the Changing International Economic Climate', in Z. Fallenbuchl and C. McMillan (eds.), *Partners in East-West Economic Relations* (New York: Pergamon, 1980), p. 15.

9. M. Pankine, 'UNCTAD VI', *Foreign Trade*, No. 10, 1983.

10. O. Bogomolov, 'CMEA and the Developing World', p. 32.

11. Z. Imam, 'Soviet Treaties with Third World Countries', *Soviet Studies*, Vol. 35, 1983, p. 63.

12. D.C. Smyth, 'The Global Economy and the Third World', *World Politics*, Vol. 29, 1977, pp. 584–609.

13. For a more detailed description of the Soviet responses to the NIEO, see C.W. Lawson, 'Socialist Relations with the Third World: A Case Study of the New International Economic Order', *Economics of Planning*, Vol. 16, 1980, pp. 148–60.

14. D.C. Smyth, 'The Global Economy and the Third World'.

15. 'Joint Statement by the Socialist Countries at the Fourth Session of the United Nations Conference on Trade and Development', supplement to *Foreign Trade*, No. 9, 1976. For a discussion of the Romanian position, see Colin W. Lawson, 'National Independence and Reciprocal Advantages: The Political Economy of Romanian-South Relations', *Soviet Studies*, Vol. 35, 1983, pp. 362–75.

16. 'On the Restructuring of International Economic Relations', statement by the Soviet government to K. Waldheim, UN Secretary-General, 4 October 1976, *Foreign Trade*, No. 2, 1976, pp. 2–5.

17. M. Pankine, 'UNCTAD VI', p. 3.

18. J. Bognar, *The Fight for a New System of International Relations*, (Budapest, Hungarian Scientific Council for World Economy, 1977), p. 15.

19. 'Joint Statement by the Socialist Countries', p. 11.

20. A. Manzhulo and G. Krasnov, 'International Forum on Trade and Economic Problems: Results of the Fifth UNCTAD Session', *Foreign Trade*, No. 9, 1979, pp. 20–5.

21. A. Manzhulo, 'The 6th UNCTAD Session: Objectives and Tasks', *Foreign Trade*, No. 4, 1983, pp. 19–20. The creation of a World Trade Organization, which would subsume the functions of existing institutions such as the IMF and GATT, in which the Soviet Union is not represented, has been a Soviet objective since the immediate post-war period. For references to some early attempts to achieve this objective see Robert M. Cutler, 'East-South Relations at UNCTAD: Global Political Economy and the CMEA', *International Organisation*, Vol. 37, No. 1, 1983, p. 123.

22. F.D. Holzman, *International Trade under Communism: Politics and Economics* (London: Macmillan, 1976), p. 195.

23. O. Cooper and C. Fogarty, 'Soviet Economic and Military Aid to the Less Developed Countries, 1954–78', in US Congress, Joint Economic Commitee, *Soviet Economy in a Time of Change* (Washington, D.C.: Government Printing Office, 1979), Vol. 2, pp. 648–62.

24. A. Manzhulo and G. Krasnov, 'International Forum on Trade and Economic Problems: Results of the Fifth UNCTAD Session', *Foreign Trade*, September 1979, pp. 20–5, quoted pp. 21–2.

25. FCO, 'Soviet, East European and Western Development Aid 1976–82', Foreign Policy Document No. 85, London, 1983. It should be noted that Soviet and East European claims on aid are never accompanied by detailed evidence. Although the FCO document gives some details of its estimates, it does not include an extensive account of the calculations on which the refutation is based.

26. 'Joint Statement by the Socialist Countries', p. 8.

27. V. Polezhayev, 'UNCTAD VI: Some Problems in Commodity Trade', *Foreign Trade*, No. 4, 1983, pp. 21–4.

28. V. Polezhayev, 'UNCTAD VI', p. 22.

29. A more detailed discussion of the Soviet-South trade structure can be found in

C.W. Lawson, 'European Socialist States and the Third World in the Seventies: The Socialist View of the New Global Economy', in M. Stohl and H. Targ (eds.), *Global Political Economy in the 1980s* (Cambridge, Mass.: Schenkman, 1983).

30. 'Joint Statement by the Socialist Countries', p. 11.

31. V. Leonidov, 'International Code of Conduct on Technology Transfer', *Foreign Trade*, November 1980, pp. 27–32, quoted p. 29.

III
COUNTRY CASE STUDIES

11
Economic aspects of the Soviet-Vietnamese relationship

Adam Fforde

Modern revisionism distorts and discards the fundamental principles of the Moscow Declaration and Statement of 1957 and 1960; it advocates the policy of class conciliation and unprincipled cooperation with imperialism, blots out the demarcation line between ourselves, our friends and our foes, sabotages the revolutionary cause of the working class, divides the socialist camp and the international communist movement etc.

> *Communiqué of the 9th Session of the Central Committee of the Vietnam Worker's Party,* Hanoi, December 1967, p. 7.

All the actions taken by Peking rulers, from their betrayal of Vietnam at the 1954 Geneva Conference ... to their setting up of the Pol Pot-Ieng Sary genocidal regime, their armed invasion of Vietnam and their threats of invasion against Laos sprang from: one guiding thought: big-nation chauvinism; one policy: national selfishness; one strategic objective: big-nation expansionism and great power hegemonism.

> 'The Truth about Vietnam-China Relations over the last Thirty Years', in *The White Book* (Hanoi, 1979), pp. 83–4.

If 'politics in command' is a basic truism about the behaviour of communist states, then how should an analysis of economic interests proceed? Vietnam here provides a possibly useful example. In this chapter it will be argued that the economic aspects of the Soviet-Vietnamese relationship have, since 1979, been relatively free to reflect underlying economic interests. This assertion is of the nature of a plausible assumption rather than a strictly verifiable hypothesis, but should nevertheless be of value. A general conclusion of the chapter is that the interplay of Soviet and Vietnamese economic interests since 1979 has led to the adoption of relatively pragmatic aid, trade and structural policies not inconsistent with an attempt to maximize the long-term net joint economic benefit to both countries. This has taken place in a highly uncertain environment: after thirty years of responsibility for economic and social management the Vietnamese party is, at the time of writing, still far from clear either about the fine detail of optimal policies, or,

192

perhaps more important, the implementability of those that might be chosen. The important ideological shift at the 5th Congress (March 1982) to the view that the period of 'transition to socialism' had two distinct parts (see below) posed the important implicit question of how the transition between these two was to be effected, and in turn highlighted the extent to which the current 'demi-stage' remained uncharted waters.

The chapter is divided into six sections. The first two rapidly examine the general context of Soviet-Vietnamese relations up to 1979 and the economic conditions in Vietnam until then. The third looks at the events of 1978–9 and argues that the economic aspects of the relationship have been relatively free to reflect strictly economic interests since the Chinese invasion. The fourth and fifth deal with the evolving interaction between the socio-economic policies of the Socialist Republic of Vietnam (SRV) and its membership of the CMEA, and examine changes in the pattern of overseas trade. A final section re-examines the basic arguments of the chapter and draws some general conclusions.

Soviet-Vietnamese relations to 1979

It is impossible to separate fully the nationalist and socialist elements of the Vietnamese revolution and 'wars of national liberation'. Ho Chi Minh maintained that he turned to communism as a countryless (*mat nuoc*) Vietnamese because it offered a way to national independence,[1] whilst his relative eclipse in the Vietnamese communist movement in the 1930s probably resulted from his reported emphasis upon the nationalist struggle at the expense of 'proletarian internationalism'.[2] Yet, despite this, he survived in Moscow during the purges, when he was a teacher at the Lenin Institute.[3] His early work *The Party's Military Work amongst the Peasants* (1927) strongly stressed the need for the 'revolutionary proletariat' to be actively supported by the mass of the peasant population if the revolution were to be successful. At the time, the effects of the French presence upon the traditional rural society of North and Central Vietnam were already devastating.[4] Seminal work by other communist leaders also emphasized the need for fundamental change in peasant society.[5] This stress upon the role of the rural areas tended also to follow from the extremely low level of industrialization in French Indochina. It was likely that radical changes in social organization would be needed, or used, to generate support for the nationalist struggle.

From such considerations arise the tensions between nationalism and socialism that arguably underpin much of the development of Vietnamese communism.[6] The seizing of the 'moment of opportunity' (*thoi co*) in August 1945 and the subsequent Declaration of

Independence were marked by a pragmatic view of the immediate possibilities open to the communist leadership. Vietnamese attempts to manoeuvre between the Americans, French, British and Chinese necessarily concentrated upon the major local actors.[7] With its attention focused upon Europe the Soviet Union appears to have largely ignored Ho's activities in Vietnam: the Democratic Republic, established in 1946, was not recognized until 1950.[8] But after the Chinese communists' victory supplies of military material became available across the northern border, providing a basis for the set-piece battle of Dien Bien Phu in 1953–4. Another necessary condition for the battle, however, was the supply of willing porters, who, it has often been argued, were encouraged by the extension and 'radicalization' of land reform at that time. The avowedly classist nature of this stage of land reform marks the clear emergence of the formally socialist tendencies of the communist leadership. At Geneva in 1954 much evidence points to the role played by the superpowers (including China) in securing their own interests by a division of Vietnam at the 17th parallel.

From 1954–5 until the fall of the South in 1975 North Vietnam attempted, largely successfully, to maintain relations with both China and the Soviet Union in order to attain its own goals.[9] The basic apparatus of a 'proletarian state' was constructed in the 1950s: agricultural cooperativization in 1959–60, attempts at Soviet-style industrial organization based upon largely imported and aid-financed investment goods, the intellectual hegemony of the party established after the *Nhan Van* affair, etc. This parallelled developments in China. North Vietnam therefore appeared as a comparatively orthodox member of the 'bloc' and, as the Sino-Soviet dispute escalated, was able to reverse its allies' acceptance of the Geneva *status quo* and return to an armed struggle to complete the process of national liberation and reunify the country.[10] As a result, and before the high technological level of US military intervention necessitated a cultivation of the Soviet Union, frictions arose between Hanoi and Moscow as China pursued its policy of opposition to 'peaceful co-existence' with world capitalism.

The first quotation at the beginning of the chapter saw the North Vietnamese leadership forced to take sides in the Sino-Soviet dispute (but expressing the hope, later in the communiqué, that the two sides would come together again). Given the 'objective requirements' for economic development aid at the time, which could only really come from the Soviet Union, this tends to suggest the relative primacy of the principle of nationalist reunification at this stage.

There is some disagreement about the relative aid contributions of China and the Soviet Union to North Vietnam during 1955–64.[11] Whatever the truth of the matter, North Vietnam's position altered in 1965 when US bombing of the North and substantial direct involvement in the South marked a qualitative change in the requirements of the national liberation struggle. The technology needed for air defence and the matériel for the conventional forces used in 1975 could only have come from the Soviet Union. Theriot and Matheson reported that Soviet non-military aid to the Democratic Republic of Vietnam (DRV) in 1965–75 was around $1.8bn*, to compare with $1.5bn from China and $0.8bn from Eastern Europe. These estimates must be highly conjectural – a key difficulty is the absence of reliable data on Chinese food aid. The authors also maintain, without source, that Soviet military aid was approximately 8–14 times larger than that from China during 1955–75, at between $6bn and $10bn.[12] Given the importance attached to the struggle to reunify the country it is hardly surprising that such figures should have been widely taken to reveal a relative closeness between Vietnam and the Soviet Union during 1965–75. The Vietnamese *White Book* (from which the second chapter epigraph comes) points also to considerable tensions between Vietnam and China during the Cultural Revolution.

By 1975, the fundamental realignment of the great-power triangle demonstrated by the Sino-US rapprochement had emphasized, from the Vietnamese point of view, the divisions between the Soviet Union and China. Difficulties in post-war relations with the US created problems for the Vietnamese policy of 'openness' towards the West[13] that culminated in the remarkably liberal *Draft Code on Foreign Investment*[14] and included such interesting elements as membership of the IMF.

With Vietnam now finally reunited Vietnamese foreign policy might have been expected to shift towards an emphasis upon 'socialist construction' rather than remaining fixed on the nationalist cause. But, in hindsight, the period to 1978–9 appears as one of considerable unresolved regional tension, based, ultimately, upon Vietnam's continued attempt to maintain close relations with both China and the Soviet Union. Given the overt mutual hostility between China and the Soviet Union and China's closeness to the US, it is perhaps surprising that it took over three years for a regional realignment to occur. In the event, Chinese support for the Khmer Rouge exacerbated the situation, in particular because it increased Hanoi's concern over internal security problems in South Vietnam. The Vietnamese invasion of Kampuchea in December

---

* In this chapter the term 'billion' refers to the US thousand million (10^9).

1978 and the ensuing 'punitive' invasion by China of Vietnam's northern provinces marked a crystallization of the new position.

Vietnam, militarily antagonistic to China and supported by the Soviet Union both in that conflict and in Kampuchea, was no longer maintaining the previous balance. In return, the Soviet Union had acquired a firm supporter on China's southern frontier, the former US base at Cam Ranh for her navy and air force, and, in the 'Kampuchean question', a valuable *pièce de manoeuvre* in her geopolitical endeavours. Although the 1978 Treaty of Friendship and Cooperation and Vietnam's joining of the CMEA in June 1978 clearly mark the diplomatic turnaround, it is the military problems posed by the Chinese invasion that must surely have dominated Vietnamese strategic thinking.[15] The logic of defence requirements henceforth led to a continued military alliance with the Soviet Union – the priorities of national existence again largely determined international alignments.

TABLE 11.1
Aggregate data

	1975	1976	1977	1978	1979	1980	1981	1982	1983
Population (millions)	47.6	49.2	50.4	51.4	52.6	53.7	55.0	56.4	—
'GDP' at current prices (billion dong)	18.3	19.9	20.3	20.7	—	—	—	—	—
Real national income, Soviet basis	100	115	117	120	119	113	122	140	—
Gross output of industry (*constant* 1970 billion dong)	7.3	8.2	9.0	9.7	9.1	8.2	9.2	10.4	12.1
Gross output of agriculture (*constant* 1970 billion dong)	6.4	7.1	6.7	6.7	7.2	7.6	7.9	8.5	8.9
Food output (million tonnes paddy equivalent)	11.6	13.5	12.9	12.9	13.7	14.4	15.1	16.6	16.7
State procurement (million tonnes paddy equivalent)	—	2.0	—	—	1.4	1.9	2.5	2.9	3.7
Food imports	—	—	—	—	1.8	1.0	0.5	0.3	0.1

Source: SLTK, 'Statistics', various tables, and a variety of other official sources.

Vietnamese economic problems 1975–9

The years 1978–9 marked a major watershed in Vietnamese economic policy and the beginning of a 'new course'. Membership of the CMEA was a crucial part of this. The precise domestic political origins of these changes are not known, but the economic problems faced by Hanoi are far clearer. At root, the intense distributional struggle between the 'socialist' and the 'private' sectors stemmed from the poor output and productivity perform-ance of the former, of which state industry and the system of agricultural cooperatives were the dominant elements. Table 11.1 shows the low rates of gross output growth recorded: ignoring the isolated jump in 1975–6, 'national income' (on a Soviet statistical basis) reportedly grew by only 3–4 per cent p.a. during 1976–9. This was at a time when the population was rising at a rate of roughly 2.5 per cent p.a. Such virtual stagnation compared with trend rates of growth of roughly 10 per cent p.a. in 'total social product' in the DRV during the first Five-Year Plan (1961–5).[16] Furthermore, inflows of economic resources from abroad were not inconsiderable – Vietnam's total overseas debt reportedly rose by $1.7bn during 1976–9.[17] Admittedly, bad weather was a factor inhibiting agricul-tural output growth, but no real progress was made in reducing the chronic dependence upon food imports, which were around 12 per cent of crude domestic staples availability in 1979 (see Table 11.1). In a period of post-war reconstruction, and despite foreign assistance, Vietnam was unable to establish any sustainable long-term growth process: *domestic sources of accumulation were negligible*. This fact is of enormous importance in explaining the overall pattern of Soviet-Vietnamese economic relations after 1978–9.

There were a number of interrelated reasons for this failure. In principle, the socio-economic system established in the North during the late 1950s should have generated some form of more or less rapid economic growth. The combination of a collectivized agriculture, largely state-run industry, and (again, in principle) strict control over product distribution is not one that would ordinarily be expected to lead to economic stagnation. A rapid extension of the system to the South, while possibly resulting in short-term difficulties, should also have been 'progressive'. But in practice many problems arose, frequently bound up with issues left unresolved during the war. In the collectivized Northern agriculture material incentives did not, generally speaking, encourage active participation in collective production. For a number of reasons, little could be done to overcome this.[18] Until 1979 official policy had sought to amalgamate cooperatives into more and more compli-cated units. This tended to increase the relative attraction of 'outside' – non-collective – activity, and exacerbate the tensions between the socialist and private sectors. Peasants had always retained the right to 'free disposal' of the output from their private plots (the '5 per cent land', which in fact frequently exceeded the statutory limits). But in 1978–9 free market prices were roughly ten times state procurement prices, at which level 20 kg. of paddy was worth more than the monthly wages of a skilled state manual worker. It is possible that this in fact helped to protect rural incomes.[19]

Adverse material incentives interacted with differential sectoral output growth rates: a low real wage to state employees tended to reduce the output of state industry and give another twist to the spiral. Other factors were at work, however, and the basic poverty of much of the country should not be forgotten. Official policy in some ways seems to have betrayed what G. Boudarel describes as a 'leap' mentality: a belief that rapid rates of accumulation were possible and that relatively modern methods of production could be widely introduced in the short-term.[20] Investment policy tended to seek projects with an advanced level of technology which were in practice incapable of integration into the rest of the economy. Insufficient attention was paid either to basic infrastructure or to economic linkages.[21] This often resulted in sharp increases in the capital/output ratio and considerable short-run financing difficulties as domestic budgetary costs rose without adequate offsetting gains in budgetary receipts from the disposal of increased output. This again exacerbated inflationary processes and distributional problems.

The problems of economic inefficiency in state industry were made worse by the effects of wartime subsidies upon management methods. With wholesale prices largely unchanged since the late 1950s and enterprise economic accounting still based on 'full subsidy, full debit' (*thu du, chi du*) principles, the system of material-supply-based economic management was not even implementing contemporary Soviet 'best practice' methods.[22] Such a rigid set-up was almost incapable of responding to the high level of effective demand, which was instead reflected in the growth of an extensive 'outside' production sector selling onto the free market. In some areas of Hanoi, a third of the population were reportedly engaged fulltime in such activities, in which income flows reflected the high level of free market prices. Moonlighting by state employees and collective workers, coupled with the 'leaking' of non-labour resources, further reduced the production potential of the socialist sector. Continual attempts by the authorities to enforce legal norms were largely unsuccessful.

Two other areas should be mentioned: the weight of 'non-productive' state employment and the general official distaste for non-egalitarian distribution policies. A major feature of official policy was its emphasis upon such elements of social welfare spending as education and medical care.[23] In a poor country this placed considerable pressure upon the budget, and debates about this recall those surrounding IMF-supported deflationary packages elsewhere.[24] Much of the state bureaucracy was, however, grossly inefficient. The situation was exacerbated by the practice of guaranteeing job opportunities to demobilized officers. Such difficulties parallelled those in distribution: the pressure on the state not to abandon an egalitarian policy was considerable – the urban population was largely dependent on a food ration that, at roughly 12–13 kg of staples a month, barely guaranteed subsistence, and the collective distribution in many cooperatives[25] was only 5–6 kg per month – and in any case, it is highly debatable whether the short-term output gains resulting from a full-bodied shift to a non-egalitarian, incentive-based distribution policy would, in isolation, have been able to compensate those regions and sectors which could not respond to such a change. And, especially in agriculture, the South was far more capable of responding to such incentives than the North.

By 1975 South Vietnam was comparatively well integrated into the Western economic system. Substantial US aid inflows helped to support the urban population, and many Western companies had production facilities there. These frequently depended upon imported means of production and foreign technology. The rubber and rice exports that had so profited the colonial economy had, however, largely ceased. But the climatic and demographic conditions for them remained in the 'terres rouges' and the relatively low population density of the Mekong delta – at over 2m ha approximately twice the area of the northern deltas but with a similar population.

Apart from the short-term disruptions caused by the fall of the South in 1975, the economic effects of the change of government were considerable. Cut off from aid inflows and Western supplies to industry, the economy contracted. Distributional problems in the North were worsened by the need to divert supplies to the South, and by the appearance of highly desirable Western goods on Northern markets.[26] The early decision to proceed to rapid reunification of the country heralded an attempt to implement Northern methods of administration in the South. In the economic sphere, these took the form of state control of industry, coupled with a push for agricultural collectivization and control over distribution. Implementation of these policies was far more successful in south-central Vietnam than in the Mekong delta.

All three elements of this programme for the socialization of the southern economy faced considerably greater problems than they had during the comparable period in the North. These were: the far greater degree of development of Southern industry, and its dependence upon Western imports and technology; the substantial differences between the Mekong delta and the 'traditional' rural organization that had predominated in the North, coupled with the greatly increased role of a largely autonomous 'middle' peasant group; and the far more powerful and concentrated group of market and wholesale traders in the South, centred upon the substantial Chinese minority in Cholon. These and other issues inevitably interfered with the effective implementation of established methods of administration after 1975. Cadre corruption was a major difficulty, and the sharp move against the Cholon traders in early 1978 was a key step in the cumulative breakdown of relations with China.

It can be argued, therefore, that the Vietnamese economy was not operating anywhere near to expectations in 1979, when, as a result of the international realignment, the Soviet Union found itself as the dominant economic partner. It is then interesting, if it is accepted that economic interests were comparatively unconstrained by other considerations, to observe what happened in this partnership, and how Vietnamese domestic social and economic policies changed.

Soviet-Vietnamese relations since the Chinese invasion: the balance of interests

Analyses of the roots of the current close alliance between Vietnam and the Soviet Union search for causes: the Vietnamese desire to dominate Indochina ('dating from 1954');[27] the Soviet desire to put pressure on China ('now threatened with a two-front war');[28] or the Vietnamese and Chinese need for external 'threats' in order to overcome domestic political difficulties.[29]

In the end, the security implications of the Chinese invasion are probably sufficient to explain the strength of the Soviet-Vietnamese relationship after 1979. The Soviet Union clearly gained considerably from the non-economic aspects of its close relationship with Vietnam. Apart from the base at Cam Ranh and the ability to apply pressure on South China, the Soviet Union effectively proved that it both could, and would, provide support for 'anti-imperialist' movements when it saw fit. Vietnam's defeat of the US was seen by most left-wing activists in the Third World as *the* major 'anti-imperialist' victory in recent history. This was of incalculable value to the Soviet Union in its own activities elsewhere in the Third World, reinforcing its own ideological statements and enhancing its great-power status. Its self-image as the main supporter of liberation movements can only have been strengthened by its continuing close relationship with Vietnam.

The dominant element in calculating Vietnamese non-economic interests was the military support guaranteed by Article 6 of the 1978 Treaty.[30] To this was added the ideological value of continued membership of the 'socialist camp' which Vietnamese leaders have emphasized since well before 1978. The effects of this upon such areas as party discipline and ideology are probably very important, but cannot be discussed here.

It would appear to me that the non-economic interests of the two sides were extremely strong, and would be sufficient in themselves to ensure a firm and enduring relationship.[31] Crucial to this assessment is the fact of the Chinese invasion of 1979 and the inability of the Vietnamese either to provide adequate weaponry from their own resources or to obtain them from any source other than the Soviet Union, given the global geopolitical environment and the lack of the vast hard-currency earnings needed to purchase arms on the world market.

Economic interests, then, were relatively subordinate in explaining the overall strength of the Soviet-Vietnamese relationship. Yet they could be easily be identified. In the field of commodity trade, Vietnam was in a position to provide such raw materials as rubber and tin that the Soviet Union could only otherwise acquire on the world market. The Soviet Union could supply vital energy supplies and other commodities. Vietnam was a potential supplier of tropical food products, light industrial output and labour resources, while the Soviet Union could supply investment and consumer goods.

Vietnam was, above all, clearly interested in obtaining Soviet aid for her economic development plans. But such 'foreign investment', when considered in the context of Soviet-Vietnamese relations, cannot be divorced from the question of the *terms* upon which such relations (especially trade) are to be carried out, and the implied opportunity costs. Here it is argued that the entire picture must be considered, without viewing any one element in isolation: as the major supplier and coordinator of aid and exports to Vietnam the Soviet Union was in a position to influence Vietnamese structural policy and to encourage – if not to enforce – far-reaching changes in the pattern of production and trade. Supplies of consumer goods in one period may be seen as potential contributors to structural adjustments and increased 'returns' – in the form of exports – later on: in other words, as a form of 'long-term investment'.

In outline, it appears that economic interests led the Soviet Union to encourage the following major developments in Vietnam after 1979:[32]

1. The introduction of a system of 'household contracting' in agriculture, coupled with a shift towards greater reliance on material incentives in state procurement policy.[33] This was followed by a rapid growth in agricultural gross output, a sharp increase in staples procurement and a reduction to near zero of food imports (Table 11.1).
2. The introduction of a multi-level 'planning structure' in state industry, which permitted a somewhat more effective utilization of resources in response to demand, coupled with a greater emphasis upon light industry. This had not yet culminated, at the time of writing, in a formal 'reform' of the industrial management system.[34]
3. An overall and fundamental shift in general socio-economic policy based upon the theory of 'two stages' (*chang duong*) in the period of transition (*giai doan qua do*) to socialism.[35] In the first of these two 'demi-stages' Vietnam should concentrate upon creating and mobilizing domestic sources of accumulation. This demanded various prerequisites, including the ability to satisfy basic consumer demands (especially for food) and to guarantee increasing levels of exports. Part of this strategy, which (crucially) removed economic autarky as a mentionable goal in the near future, included a respect for the economic rationality behind trade specialization within the 'world socialist system'. The enhanced pragmatism that observers saw replacing the earlier tendencies to a 'leap' mentality was inseparable from the need for greater attention to be paid to resource allocation within the 'socialist international division of labour'.

From the point of view of the Soviet Union, these developments reflected its most fundamental economic interest: access to flows of economic resources, over time, at minimum net cost. These policy changes therefore directly affected two of the main problems faced by the Soviet Union as the dominant economic partner: the Vietnamese need for large imports of consumer goods, primarily of food, and the low response of output to deliveries of investment goods (a major element of the 'demi-stage' pragmatism was the decision to concentrate upon a strictly limited number of projects).

The question whether these changes reflected Vietnamese economic interests is not easily answered. Schnytzer implies that membership of the CMEA, by constraining policy options, would generate costs.[36] One might suggest that the constrained options were sub-optimal, and well worth abandoning. But not enough is known about the real Vietnamese policy options to make a reliable judgement on this.

Vietnam in the CMEA – Soviet and Vietnamese theories of underdevelopment

Vietnam was first an observer at the CMEA in 1961, although its subsequent participation was not continuous.[37] After the country became a full member in June 1978 there was a substantial discussion of related issues in the literature, which throws light both upon underlying trends and on the more theoretical issues discussed in the previous section.

P. Alampiev, whose work was officially and prominently translated into Vietnamese, discussed the 'structural problems' of underdeveloped countries during the initial stages of the period of the construction of socialism.[38] He presented an analysis of such countries, taken to include Mongolia, Cuba and Vietnam within the CMEA as well as Angola, Ethiopia, Mozambique and others. The categorization was based upon 'the importance they attach to Marxism-Leninism and the experience of fraternal countries'. The analysis emphasized the generally weak development of the forces of production in such countries, the possibly strong influence of finance capital and the need to create an 'advanced scientific-technical base from almost nothing'. He emphasized the basic contradiction between the need for very rapid rates of accumulation and the limitations of domestic sources of capital, and drew the logical conclusion that the conditions under which overseas resources were supplied was therefore very important.[39] From this followed a number of basic points. Because of capital shortages and constraints on supplies from donor countries structural policy should be aimed at those areas and at commodities producing clear economic results, and should allow traditional branches to play an important role in the early stages: 'they are the principal source of increases in the national income'.[40] Because results are ('inevitably') slow to appear structural plans needed to be long-term, but they should also pay attention to current problems: the potential contradiction between the two should be resolved 'intelligently'. He stressed the importance of not overvaluing the potential for rapid change, and suggested a tentative division of such countries into three groups:

1. Basically agricultural countries with 'semi-natural' agricultures. Here traditional systems were still widespread, and the domestic division of labour and degree of participation in world trade were both minimal.
2. 'Mono-culturalists', actively participating in world trade.
3. Countries 'averagely' developed by capitalism, with small factories, principally in the light or food-processing sectors. This group was characterized also as 'ex-dependent capitalist'.

In general, the initiation and continuation of development for countries in the third group was not seen as difficult, but the enormous variations within it made discussion problematic. The fundamental difference between the first two groups lay in the presence of a source of domestic accumulation in the second group, lacking from the first, members of which had usually to start 'from nothing'. The point is of direct and obvious relevance to Vietnamese development strategy.

A further simple differentiation was made on the basis of demography: for the biggest countries of over 100 million people, autarkic development was seen as both feasible and appropriate to the size of the internal market. The large and average-size countries of 10–100 million (i.e. including Vietnam) were ones where autarky was not accepted as a sensible policy goal. For the smallest countries of under 10 million dependence upon trade was essential. Here Alampiev was critical of policies of 'self-reliance' such as those adopted in Tanzania. Such an 'anti-imports' (*chong nhap khau*) ideology would only be justifiable in conditions of 'capitalist encirclement', but was inapplicable to trade with socialist countries.[41]

An important aspect of this presentation is the de-emphasis of political and ideological factors. Clearly the analysis is partial, but structural policies were seen as an adjunct to wider policies aimed at accelerated development of the forces of production in the most 'rational' way. This tendency is paralleled in the discussion of socialist international production relations by S. Niznujaja and V. Shatiko,[42] which specifically states that such relations derive from the 'most important aspects of the development of the forces of production' rather than from the 'external political activities of socialist countries'.[43]

It is not easy to fit Vietnam directly into Alampiev's schema. The export potential of the South was confirmed by the colonial experience, while in some ways the lack of sources of domestic accumulation in the North would put it into the first category.

M. Trigubenko, writing in the offical Soviet journal *Far Eastern Affairs*, presented a more sophisticated analysis that took explicit account of regional differences.[44] He was also extremely blunt about the mistakes of the late 1970s, consistent with Alampiev's position on the need to maximize the short-term effectiveness of decisions on the allocation of resources. He pointed out the differences between North Vietnam in 1954–5 and South Vietnam in 1975–6, asserting that South Vietnam was (unlike the North) not a 'backward agrarian area'. His characterization of the two regions is extremely interesting:

North Vietnam (1954–55)
I: Peasantry
Predominantly poor peasants, natural economy.

II: Private sector in industry and trade
Artisans and handicraftsmen predominated in industry. There was a considerable number of petty-traders. Capitalist factory industry and capitalist trade were almost undeveloped. There was practically no foreign capital.

South Vietnam (1975–76)
I: Peasantry
Predominantly strong middle peasants. There was a landlord class. The position of the rich peasants was strong. Existence of commodity production in agriculture.

II Private sector in industry and trade
Considerable influence was exerted on the economy (wholesale trade, transport, finance and credit business, industry, purchases of farm produce) by the big compradour bourgeoisie cooperating with foreign firms (Hong Kong, Singapore, Taiwan, the US, Japan, France etc.) which had many branches in South Vietnam. National capital figured prominently in industry and trade. There was a huge number of petty traders, including those of Chinese nationality.[45]

The different degree of development of the South had a number of policy implications. The need to preserve and utilize *existing* sources of accumulation, largely lacking in the North, suggested a slower and more pragmatic approach to the socialization of agriculture and industry, and an emphasis on the use of incentives to generate short-term output gains. The 3rd Congress (1960) had '… planned to develop heavy industry at a faster rate', and this line was reaffirmed at the 4th Congress (1976) where '… documents did not single out a pre-stage for industrialisation … preceding the beginning of mass construction of industrial enterprises'.[46] Thus Party General-Secretary Le Duan at the 5th Congress: 'We did not properly assess the complexity of the advance to socialism in the conditions of predominant small-scale production and the scope of the big economic and social changes which had occurred in the country after a long war.'[47]

Such statements suggest strong Soviet antagonism towards the pre-1979 policies (cf. the quotation of Le Duan's criticisms, from the same Congress, of a 'spongeing attitude' towards foreign assistance).[48] Indeed, Trigubenko flatly stated that 'what is new in the economic strategy of the Communist Party of Vietnam is that the 5th Congress defined the pre-stage pending industrialisation and determined branch priorities … it assigned a bigger role in economic development to the peasantry'.[49] This shift is confirmed, in 1974, by Truong Son's article in the Vietnamese party's theoretical journal, which definitively accepted the existence of a 'first stage' of the transition period. He maintained that there were three essential tasks of this stage: (1) A concentration of efforts on the strong development of agriculture; (2) encouragement for the production of consumer goods; (3) rational priority to be given to the development of heavy industry.[50]

In such a formulation there is not much trace of the 'leap' mentality criticized explicitly by Boudarel,[51] and implicitly by Trigubenko. Alampiev's opposition to over-hasty and over-optimistic accumulation strategies should already be obvious.

The abandonment of autarky as a general medium-term policy goal necessarily entailed concentrating upon foreign trade and forms of international specialization. During 1978–82 the role of the CMEA in this area was examined in Vietnamese articles: prior to 1978 the subject had received little attention in the major economic journal of the Economic Research Commission, Hanoi. These pieces revealed something about Vietnamese perceptions both of Vietnam's role within the CMEA and of the way in which a balance of interests arose between the two sides.

Vo Dai and Huy Khoat identified four forms of cooperation within the CMEA in the 'current stage', which was taken to date from 1969 and the beginnings of 'unification' of the (world) socialist economy with planning in a 15–20-year perspective.[52] These were:

1. In planning, dating from the 1971 25th Session. These plans were not 'super-national' (*sieu quoc gia*) and depended upon a harmony of interests:

   When participating in the harmonisation of plans, countries still have full rights to determine the proportions of development (*ty le phat trien*), the base of the national economy, the speed of development, the distribution of the national income ... when assessing the determination of these problems, (countries) cannot only pay attention to their own interests, but must also pay attention to the interests of other countries.[53]

2. Scientific-technical cooperation. This was primarily a combination of joint research and the exchange of information and experts.

3. International specialization and production cooperation. This was 'the most important form' for the realization of international 'unification'.

4. The exchange of commodities. Trade relations depended upon the states' monopolies of foreign trade. Attention was currently focused on the fixing of prices and the relationship between foreign trade and the branches of production.

But this article paid relatively little attention to another important issue within the CMEA – the wide differences between member countries. Later studies brought out this problem, and perhaps revealed a growing awareness of Vietnam's particular position within the CMEA.[54]

Especially interesting is the perception of the balance of interests. Uneven development between countries could lead at times 'to a lack of two-sidedness in relations'.[55] Experience of cooperation within the CMEA, based on only ten years' activities, was not great, and new difficulties had arisen. The use of world prices which were typically above domestic prices was of greater benefit to the producer than to the consumer. This contradicted the basic principle of mutual advantage. The return on invested captial (*lai suat khi co vay von*) was usually low, and therefore did not encourage lending. Increases in the cost of capital, however, could raise the cost price of raw materials because of the difficulties involved in increasing labour productivity in extractive industries. Finally, it was often necessary to stipulate the agreed-upon deliveries of capital in material terms, because the supplying country did not always supply the right goods – machinery was often out-of-date, and consumer goods were sometimes substituted. Additional criticisms of the 'price problem' were made in the context of agricultural cooperation in the CMEA. The main difficulty here stemmed from a wide variation in production costs compared with the world market, accentuated by the general rigidity of prices.[56]

Such formulations are consistent with a view of the world, and of the CMEA, that sought to maximize the perceived national interest while preserving the particular overall alliance relations and recognizing the existence of mutual interests. This shift away from autarky to a more trade-oriented approach is also revealed by Nguyen van Tho.[57] He argued that the 'current period' required deep changes in the international division of labour. He maintained that *all* countries, whether they liked it or not, had to have a strategy for participation in the international division of labour. It is of great interest that such an increase in the degree of trade orientation of economic policy should have followed on the effective abandonment of the policy of 'openness to the West' and closer economic alignment with the CMEA.

Soviet-Vietnamese aid and trade

The policy shifts described in the previous section influenced the *ex post* pattern of aid and trade. Direct resource flows between the two countries are reported in some detail in Soviet trade statistics. But, as is well known, all Soviet trade data should be treated with great caution.[58] Although some implicit rouble price data are given, little is known about the financial implications of the continuing recorded

TABLE 11.2
Total trade

	1975	1976	1977	1978	1979	1980	1981	1982
Vietnamese exports								
(1) SRV recorded total[a]								
(a) billion dong	0.54	0.84	1.17	1.24	1.10	1.15	1.21	1.41
(b) billion dollar[b]	0.30	0.46	0.67	0.60	0.54	0.55	0.13	0.14
(2) IMF hard-currency trade[c]								
billion dollar	0.11	0.13	0.13	0.18	0.16	0.15	0.15	0.19
(3) Soviet recorded imports[d]								
(a) billion rouble	0.05	0.07	0.13	0.15	0.15	0.16	0.17	0.21
(b) billion dollar[e]	0.07	0.09	0.18	0.22	0.23	0.25	0.24	0.29
Vietnamese imports								
(1) SRV recorded total[a]								
(a) billion dong	1.77	2.46	2.92	2.71	3.00	2.58	2.46	—
(b) billion dollar[b]	0.97	1.34	1.67	1.33	1.48	1.23	0.25	—
(2) IMF hard-currency trade[c]								
billion dollar	0.73	0.51	0.67	1.02	0.98	0.99	0.80	0.72
(3) Soviet recorded exports[d]								
(a) billion rouble	0.16	0.23	0.27	0.30	0.45	0.45	0.72	0.80
(b) billion dollar[e]	0.22	0.30	0.37	0.44	0.69	0.69	1.00	1.10

Sources: [a] SLTK, 'Statistics'.
[b] Exchange rate from *UN Monthly Bulletin of Statistics*, various issues.
[c] IMF, *Direction of Trade Yearbook*, based upon trading partners' returns.
[d] Soviet trade yearbooks, various years.
[e] Exchange rate derived from *Comecon Data*, 1981.

deficit (Table 11.2). It is likely that special conditions apply and that common CMEA prices are not always used.[59] It is not true, however, that the relative lack of sophistication of Vietnamese enterprise accounting means, with the general Soviet tendency eventually to write off development loans, that prices can be ignored entirely. Sharp changes in prices and exchange rates during 1978–82 suggest what is probably true: the relationship between recorded export unit values and producer prices was appreciable in some areas – most especially for collective and private producers.

Table 11.2 shows Soviet-Vietnamese trade in comparison with Vietnamese recorded hard-currency trade. Despite the considerable valuation problems, two tentative conclusions can be drawn. First, whereas the Soviet Union probably did not occupy a dominant position in recorded Vietnamese foreign trade during 1975–8, this had changed by the early 1980s, with the estimated dollar value of imports first exceeding the hard-currency total in 1981. Second, recorded trade flows remained relatively small. With an estimated 'total output' of over 20bn dong in 1978–9 (Table 11.1) the Vietnamese economy remained comparatively 'closed' with imports around 10 per cent of total 'output' and exports far lower. For the Soviet Union, Vietnam was a very insignificant trading partner: it took only 1.5 per cent of Soviet recorded exports and its imports represented only 0.5 per cent of total Soviet recorded imports in 1982.[60]

The wide reported deficits on both hard- and soft-currency trade are of particular interest. Table 11.3 gives the OECD's data on Vietnamese foreign debt. During 1979–82 the non-CMEA debt rose by $294m, most· of which was accounted for by $350m of concessional loans from OPEC countries, while the recorded net accrued hard-currency trade deficit over the same period was $2.84bn. Two possible explanations for this apparent discrepancy are the likely large remittances from overseas Vietnamese and the sales of gold associated with the refugee outflow. In addition, however, it is possible that the Soviet Union provided hard-currency assistance.

It is important to emphasize the degree to which the reported unit values were changing. Table 11.4 gives some information for this area, and compares the results with world dollar prices where appropriate. The data provide some perhaps surprising results. The degree of 'apparent subsidy' in Soviet exports was far from uniform and seems to have varied substantially over time. Indeed, for wheat flour the unit value averaged nearly 30 per cent above the world wheat price for the period 1975–82; in 1980–2 it averaged nearly 75 per cent above world prices. This suggests an attempt to use simple price incentives to discourage the continuing reliance upon imports. But the indications are that means of production such as fertilizers and wool were supplied at 'low' prices: during 1980–2 urea unit values were over 30 per cent below world prices, and wool unit values nearly 20 per cent below the world price (such conclusions are subject to strong caveats because of problems with the data). Sugar was apparently sold at a 'subsidy' based upon a difference of greater than 30 per cent between the unit value of refined sugar imports and the world raw sugar price in 1980–2. A tentative conclusion can therefore be reached that Soviet pricing policy attempted to reduce Vietnam's chronic dependency upon food imports while encouraging certain areas of domestic production through the supply of 'subsidized' means of production. In this context note the pattern of the volume of fertilizer supplies, which showed a large increase in 1979–80. This was the period of the shift to the 'contracting' system and a greater emphasis upon material incentives in agricultural procurement – such supplies could have been used to encourage the mobilization of surpluses as well as to

TABLE 11.3
Vietnamese overseas debt (million dollars)

Debt

	1975	1976	1977	1978	1979	1980	1981	1982
DACᵃ countries and capital markets	209	231	335	710	898	843	773	646
ODAᵇ	164	185	204	286	338	365	345	329
Total export credits	45	46	81	214	325	298	268	212
Total private	—	—	50	210	235	180	160	105
Bank loans	—	—	50	210	235	180	160	105
Bonds	—	—	—	—	—	—	—	—
Other	—	—	—	—	—	—	—	—
Multilateral	—	—	—	—	8	40	50	54
Concessional	—	—	—	—	8	40	50	54
CMEA countries	280	250	200	600	900	1,000	900	1,100
Concessional	280	250	200	600	900	1,000	900	1,100
OPEC countries	—	—	100	200	300	500	600	650
Concessional	—	—	100	200	300	500	600	650
Other LDCs	—	—	—	—	60	70	85	110
Concessional	—	—	—	—	60	70	85	110
Other and adjustments	50	60	80	110	100	150	188	200
Total debt	539	541	715	1,620	2,266	2,603	2,596	2,760
Concessional	444	435	504	1,086	1,606	1,975	1,980	2,243
Non-concessional	95	106	211	534	660	628	616	517

Debt service

	1975	1976	1977	1978	1979	1980	1981	1982
DACᵃ countries and capital markets	7	43	16	13	71	140	106	40
ODAᵇ	1	1	—	6	7	3	2	1
Total export credits	5	41	16	1	43	57	21	19
Total private	—	—	—	6	21	80	52	20
Bank loans	—	—	—	6	21	80	52	20
Bonds	—	—	—	—	—	—	—	—
Other	—	—	—	—	—	—	—	—
Multilateral	—	—	—	—	—	—	0	0
Concessional	—	—	—	—	—	—	0	0
CMEA countries	—	—	—	—	15	—	—	—
Concessional	—	—	—	—	15	—	—	—
OPEC countries	—	—	—	10	10	10	25	—
Concessional	—	—	—	10	10	10	25	—
Other LDCs	—	—	—	—	6	5	8	—
Concessional	—	—	—	—	6	5	8	—
Other and adjustments	—	—	4	6	10	5	5	35
Total debt service	7	43	20	29	112	160	144	75
Concessional	2	1	—	16	38	18	36	31
Non-concessional	5	41	20	13	74	142	108	44

ᵃ DAC = Development Assistance Committee.
ᵇ ODA = Overseas Development Assistance.
Source: OECD, *External Debt of Developing Countries.*

TABLE 11.4: Vietnamese-Soviet trade: recorded unit value data

	1975	1976	1977	1978	1979	1980	1981	1982
(a) Soviet exports to Vietnam								
Reinforced concrete (tonnes)	1,470	1,450	1,100	1,100	1,400	1,270	1,100	1,670
Potash fertilizer (tonnes)	19.1	19.3	19.3	19.3	25.5	25.5	57.2	59.4
Ammonia sulphate (tonnes)	36.3	36.7	36.5	36.6	36.5	36.2	45.6	54.4
Cement (tonnes)	7.6	9.3	3.7	2.6	7.2	13.5	28.2	36.7
Newsprint (tonnes)	118	130	136	—	126	117	215	284
Cotton fibre (tonnes)	782	765	710	721	715	726	1,168	1,182
Granulated urea (tonnes)	—	—	—	—	—	53.7	104.4	123.1
World urea price (roubles)	143	84.5	93.8	98.9	113.3	144.2	155.5	115.9
Wool (tonnes)	—	—	—	—	—	2,570	2,690	2,626
World wool price (roubles)	1,980	2,570	2,635	2,565	2,900	3,000	3,080	2,865
Wheat flour (tonnes)	81.2	81.3	90.9	80.0	101.7	188.1	207.2	156.0
World wheat price (roubles)	99.9	92.5	70.3	85.3	102.4	109.3	111.3	96.8
Refined sugar (tonnes)	90.8	90.8	95.3	94.4	94.8	87.4	232.0	238.4
World raw sugar price (roubles)	324	192	132	117	140	410	269	135
(b) Soviet imports from Vietnam								
Coffee (tonnes)	727	714	724	697	708	706	2,104	1,963
World coffee price (roubles)	1,301	2,624	3,967	2,772	2,669	2,717	2,539	2,322
Tea (tonnes)	898	918	988	974	956	1,025	1,243	1,341
World tea price (roubles)	999	1,159	1,979	1,495	1,412	1,449	1,452	1,410
Bananas (tonnes)	143	136	136	166	168	168	170	170
World banana price (roubles)	178	194	202	196	214	246	289	273
Natural rubber (tonnes)	—	—	—	—	—	539	661	759
World rubber price (roubles)	480	655	671	719	842	966	824	641
Vodka (litres)	1.39	1.39	1.39	1.41	1.50	1.42	1.44	1.45
Implied price (dollars per litre)	1.00	1.05	1.02	0.96	0.98	0.92	1.04	1.06
Rugs (square metres)	14.9	18.3	31.9	26.9	28.2	33.5	36.7	37.7
Note: dollar-rouble exchange rate	1.386	1.326	1.358	1.464	1.526	1.540	1.389	1.340

Sources: Trade data from Soviet trade yearbooks, various years; exchange rates from *Comecon Data*, 1981; world prices from World Bank, *Commodity Trade and Price Trends 1983–4* (Baltimore, Md.: Johns Hopkins University Press, 1984).

increase output directly. The combined potash, ammonia sulphate and urea tonnage rose from about 94,000 tonnes in 1978 to about 172,000 tonnes in 1979 and to over 275,000 tonnes in 1980.

This apparent pattern of an economic rationality, seeking both to encourage and facilitate desired structural changes, is also suggested by the Vietnamese export data. The picture is complicated by the likely relative 'stickiness' of recorded trade prices when compared with world market prices. In addition, there is some evidence that Soviet trade with Vietnam is carried out on a more *ad hoc* basis than trade with other CMEA members.[61] Four trading items (tea, coffee, rubber and tropical fruit) together occupied only around 16 per cent of reported total exports to the Soviet Union, but remained the focus of attempts to increase trade. Manufactured items (rugs, spirits, apparel and miscellaneous 'everyday goods') took up around another 40 per cent. The unrecorded items probably include minerals. But in both of the above areas pricing policy appears to have played a far more active role since 1979. Thus in Table 11.4, Section (b), it is clear that recorded coffee and rubber prices rose quite close to world prices (subject to the usual caveats), whereas in the earlier period there was a wide gap: in 1975–80 the unit value price of coffee was only just over a quarter of the world price but in 1981–2 the ratio was nearly 85 per cent; in 1981–2 the unit value price of rubber was over 95 per cent of the world price. The experience of tea is also generally consistent with this picture. Although the tea unit value was kept at around 90 per cent of world prices in the mid-1970s the rise in world prices in the late 1970s was not passed on until 1980–1. Thus while the 90 per cent ratio had been re-established by 1981–2, the average for the period 1975–82 was near 70 per cent. It was only bananas – taken as a proxy for tropical fruits – and vodka that did not reveal sharp price increases around 1980. The apparent use of price incentives in manufactures can also be seen in the case of rugs, where the recorded unit value per square metre in 1982 was 40 per cent up on 1978. This conclusion is necessarily weak, not least because so little is known about changes in the types of rugs exported.

The evidence from price data is therefore consistent with the view that Soviet policy aimed to use material incentives to encourage structural change. The same broad conclusion can be drawn from the behaviour of the dong-rouble exchange rate, which showed a rapid fall in the value of the dong. Here firm conclusions are made problematic by the lack of information on the level of domestic inflation in Vietnam, which is known to have been substantial. Reports mentioned rates of 5 per cent per month in 1983, when state savings accounts offered interest rates of over 20 per cent p.a. The Vietnamese dong was devalued twice during 1979–83 – by a

TABLE 11.5
Soviet exports to Vietnam (million roubles)

	1975	1976	1977	1978	1979	1980	1981	1982
Machines and equipment	68.0	102.9	120.3	129.1	224.2	215.0	244.1	255.7
Oil and oil products	11.3	14.2	27.8	28.0	31.8	38.2	213.8	263.3
Cotton fibre	5.5	16.8	18.9	20.3	31.0	23.5	34.2	55.2
Other	73.9	98.6	107.2	128.1	159.2	187.2	232.5	230.0
Total	158.7	232.5	274.2	305.5	446.2	454.9	724.6	804.2

Source: Soviet trade yearbooks.

factor of four in 1981 and by a factor of three at the CMEA meeting in 1983 – a cumulative fall of over 90 per cent in value. Even after making allowance for the relatively low price-responsiveness of many areas of the Vietnamese economy, this must have had some effect upon the more unplanned sectors. At the least, it again suggests an orientation of policy towards the use of material incentives.

The volume composition of Soviet-Vietnamese trade (Table 11.5) shows a sharp rise in machinery and equipment imports in 1979, which presumably reflects a combination of deliveries associated with military activity and an acceleration of supplies to compensate for the cessation of Chinese aid. The major change was the sharp rise in the value of imports of Soviet oil in 1980. This may have reflected price changes, or a change in the level of deliveries from other suppliers. The lack of any sharp rise in the Vietnamese current-price imports data (see Table 11.6) suggests that a shift in suppliers did indeed occur, leading to an increased import bill for Soviet oil. The most striking feature is the overall increase in the recorded level of Soviet-Vietnamese trade. The probable fall in the proportion of industrial investment goods ('machines and equipment' represented about 45 per cent of total exports in 1975–7, and around 32 per cent in 1981–2) is again consistent with the view that policy sought to shift resources into agriculture and light industry, but this conclusion is far from certain.

A second general source of information on Soviet-Vietnamese aid and trade is the reports on agreements and on the overall progress of those aspects of the relationship. A detailed summary is provided by M. Petrov who argues that the major elements of Soviet technical and economic project assistance in 1976–80 were in basic industrial inputs (electricity, oil-storage and cement), minerals extracting (coal and tin) and housing construction.[62] After 1980 the emphasis reportedly shifted to fertilizer plants (nitrogenous fertilizer and superphosphates) and metal-working (a forging-pressing

TABLE 11.6
Recorded Vietnamese trade (billion dong)

	1975	1976	1977	1978	1979	1980	1981
Exports[a]							
Industrial goods	0.40	0.58	0.90	0.90	0.78	0.80	0.84
Handicrafts	0.09	0.13	0.18	0.23	0.22	0.24	0.25
Non-transformed agricultural							
products	0.05	0.13	0.09	0.10	0.10	0.11	0.12
Total	0.54	0.84	1.17	1.24	1.10	1.15	1.21
Imports							
Means of production							
of which:	1.23	2.05	2.32	2.24	2.35	2.02	2.16
Machinery and equipment	0.32	0.35	0.50	0.63	0.77	0.91	0.90
Fuel and raw materials	0.63	1.32	1.41	1.21	1.00	0.78	1.03
Other means of production	0.28	0.37	0.41	0.40	0.58	0.33	0.24
Means of consumption	0.54	0.42	0.61	0.47	0.64	0.60	0.30
Total	1.77	2.46	2.93	2.71	3.00	2.58	2.46

[a] There is no separate entry in the source used to derive these figures that shows primary products from outside the agricultural sector; the Vietnamese definition of industry, however, includes mining.
Source: SLTK, 'Statistics'.

plant and a large planned metallurgical combine), and, on a smaller scale, to enterprises in the light and food industries, tea factories and agricultural projects. 'Easy credits' would be granted to cover the trade imbalance.[63] Trigubenko mentions a 'new approach' to project assistance since the early 1980s, with resources no longer 'scattered', but concentrated upon a limited number of projects, the Soviet Union providing resources for servicing and maintaining machinery and equipment supplied.[64] This echoes many problems encountered with 'turnkey' projects in the 'Western South'. Further details can be found in the 'Long-Term Programme' signed in late October 1983.[65] The developing pattern of Vietnamese integration with the Soviet economy was also revealed in the plans for specialized trade with the Soviet Far East.

Conclusions
In attempting to draw some general conclusions two points are of importance: first, that the level of Soviet exports to Vietnam was not, in fact, very high; second, that on balance the long-term economic benefits to the Soviet Union of the level of resources committed to assisting Vietnamese economic and social develop-ment were probably not very great. What seems to have occurred is

an attempt by the Soviet Union to minimize the net cost to itself of a definite, if rather limited, commitment to assisting Vietnamese economic development.[66] It is hard to imagine a more deserving case for Soviet development aid than Vietnam.

It is reasonably clear that the Soviet Union played an active role in encouraging shifts in economic policy, and took steps to ensure that the balance of economic incentives changed in such a way as to support these moves. This betrayed a pragmatic emphasis upon 'economic rationality'; it is striking that none of the Soviet sources used here had anything enthusiastic to say about the prospects for a collectivized agriculture in South Vietnam. And of course *the* major 'social transformation' confronting the Vietnamese party is precisely that of the Mekong delta.

It would appear, though, that the notion that the pattern of economic relations between the countries was largely independent of the non-economic aspects of the relationship is not really tenable. The latter are necessary to explain the willingness of the Soviet Union to incur current costs that were unlikely to be recovered. But it would not be true to say that economic interests have not been significant. On the contrary, they appear to have resulted in a push for far-reaching changes in Vietnamese economic and social policy.

It should be stressed that the notion of 'economic' used in this chapter is, in the final analysis, somewhat constraining. In the long term it is possible that the major effects of the relationship on Vietnamese society will be felt via the influence of Vietnamese migrant workers and students returning form the developed members of the CMEA; Vietnam's membership of the Soviet-led world is also likely to have other cultural effects. The influence of their Western patrons is easily observable in countries in the 'Western South', and there seems to be no reason to deny the existence of similar trends in those areas of the Third World that are within the Soviet orbit.

Finally, it is both striking and thought-provoking that the *de facto* opening up of the Vietnamese economy to foreign influence (at least on economic policy-making) post-dates the 1978–9 realignment of international relations and the effective abandonment of the pre-1978 policy of openness towards the West.

Notes

This chapter is based on research funded by the Economic and Social Research Council under its Post-doctoral Fellowship Scheme. Its contents are the responsibility of the author and do not necessarily reflect the views of the Economic and Social Research Council.

Apart from the stimulating comments of members of the study group, I have benefited from various points made by the following: Nguyen Huu Dong, John Kleinen, Suzanne H. Paine, Laura Summers and Christine White. I remain responsible for the content of this chapter. I should also like to thank Janice Giffen for assistance in obtaining access to Russian-language sources.

1. Ho Chi Minh, 'The Path which Led me to Leninism', 1960, in *Selected Writings* (Hanoi, 1977), pp. 250–2.

2. Huynh Kim Khanh, *Vietnamese Communism 1925–45* (Ithaca, N.Y.: Cornell University Press, 1982), Ch. 3.

3. Thai Quang Trung, 'Indochine: la faillité du communisme de guerre', *Politique internationale*, No. 8, 1980; *idem*, 'Hanoi-Pékin-Moscou: trente ans d'amitiés illusoires', *Défense nationale*, February 1980, p. 160.

4. A. J. Fforde, 'The Historical Background to Agricultural Collectivisation in North Vietnam', Birkbeck College Discussion Paper No. 148 (London, 1984), Section 2. The early work by Ho Chi Minh mentioned above is to be found in A. Neuberg (ed.), *Armed Insurrection* (London: New Left Books, 1970).

5. Vo Nguyen Giap and Truong Chinh, *Van de dan cay* (Hanoi, 1959), 2nd edn; trans. C.P. White, *The Peasant Question* (Ithaca, N.Y.: Cornell University Press, 1974).

6. Huynh Kim Khanh, *Vietnamese Communism*, pp. 20–1 and 341.

7. A. Patti, *Why Vietnam?* (Berkeley, Calif.: University of California Press, 1980), Part 3.

8. NNSK, *Vietnam: nhung ngay su kien 1945–75* ['Vietnamese Dates 1945–75'] (Hanoi, 1975).

9. G. Segal, *The Great Power Triangle* (London: Macmillan, 1982), pp. 79–120.

10. R.B. Smith, *An International History of the Vietnam War* (New York and London: St Martin's Press, 1983), Vol. 1: *Revolution versus Containment 1955–61, passim*, esp. pp. 161–81.

11. A. Schnytzer, 'The Socialist Republic of Vietnam', in P. Wiles (ed.), *The New Communist Third World*, (London: Croom Helm, 1982), p. 343.

12. L.H. Theriot and J. Matheson, 'Soviet Economic Relations with Non-European CMEA: Cuba, Vietnam and Mongolia', in *Soviet Economy in a Time of Change* (Joint Economic Committee of US Congress, Washington, D.C., 1979), p. 569.

13. A. Schnytzer, 'Vietnam', p. 356.

14. *Vietnam Courier*, July 1977.

15. In March 1979 the crucial battle for Lang Son was taking place less than 100 miles from Hanoi, but Jacobsen (C.J. Jacobsen, *Sino-Soviet Relations since Mao: the Chairman's Legacy* (New York: Praeger, 1981), p. 101) and Chen (King C. Chen, 'China's War with Vietnam, 1979: a Military Overview', *Journal of East Asian Affairs*, Spring/Summer 1983, p. 253) disagree over whether the town was captured or not. Chen suggests that China had been considering military action since 1977, and quotes a cadre briefing, at which Hua Guo-feng and Deng Xiao-ping gave 'punishment for arrogance' as the prime reason for the 1979 invasion.

16. *Tinh hinh phat trien Kinh te va van hoa mien bac xa hoi chu nghia Viet nam 1960–75 (KTVH)* [General Statistical Office, 'The Development of the Economy and Culture of the Socialist North of Vietnam 1960–75'] (Hanoi, 1978), Table 19.

17. OECD, *External Debt of Developing Countries* (Paris, 1984).

18. A.J. Fforde, 'Problems of Agricultural Development in North Vietnam', (Ph.D. thesis, University of Cambridge, 1982), *passim*, esp. Ch. 2. See also A.J. Fforde, 'Macro-economic Adjustment and Structural Change in a Low-income Socialist Developing Country – an Analytical Model', Birkbeck College Discussion Paper No. 163, (London, 1984).

19. For an interesting and unusually well-informed discussion of Northern peasants' attitudes to the regime, see P. Brocheux and D. Hémery, 'Le Vietnam exsangue', *Le Monde diplomatique*, March 1980.

20. G. Boudarel, *La bureaucratie au Vietnam* (Paris: L'Harmattan, 1983), p. 49.

21. A classic and well-known example of this is the large Swedish aid project at Bai Bang, where cost overruns and delays largely resulted from an underestimation of the difficulties involved in inserting modern production facilities into the Vietnamese context.

22. *Giao trinh kinh te cong nghiep* (*GTKNCN*) [Economic and Planning University, 'Industrial Economics'], (Hanoi, 1975), pp. 294ff.

23. In 1981–2 Vietnam had nearly 400,000 teachers in general education, supplemented by nearly 30,000 vocational and higher educational teachers and over 60,000 kindergarten teachers: *So lieu thong ke* (*SLTK*) [General Statistical Office, 'Statistics'] (Hanoi, 1982), Tables 62, 65 and 69.

24. Tony Killick *et al., The Quest for Economic Stabilization: the IMF and the Third World* (New York and London: St Martin's Press, 1984), pp. 48–9.

25. Le Trong, 'Ve thu nhap lao dong o hop tac xa nong nghiep' ['On labour income in agricultural cooperatives'], *Nghien cuu kinh te*, No. 115, 1980, p. 26.

26. The Northern currency was in use in the South well before the formal delegalization of the Southern currency.

27. Thai Quang Trung, 'Indochine'.

28. Jacobsen, *Sino-Soviet Relations*, p. 97.

29. J. Kleinen, 'The Sino-Vietnamese Conflict', *Monthly Review*, 1982.

30. *Vietnam Courier*, No. 79, 1978.

31. This is not to deny the strong counter-argument, with which the Vietnamese authorities had to deal, that Vietnam had not spent thirty years struggling for national independence only to find itself dependent upon the Soviet Union. Many sectors of the population probably viewed the relationship with considerable suspicion.

32. There has been considerable evidence of intense debate within the Vietnamese Communist Party – for example, the delaying of the 5th Congress. This area is somewhat under-researched.

33. Huu Hanh, 'Khoan lua' ['Rice Contracts'], *Tap chi cong san*, No. 12, 1980.

34. Mai Thu Van, *Vietnam, un peuple, des voix* (Paris: Pierre Horay, 1983), p. 44.

35. Truong Son, 'Cong nghiep hoa xa hoi chu nghia trong chang duong thoi ky qua do len chu nghia xa hoi' ['Industrialization in the First Part of the Period of Transition to Socialism'], *Tap chi cong san*, No. 1, 1974.

36. Schnytzer, 'Vietnam', p. 342.

37. Duy Hoang, 'Comecon and Vietnam', *Vietnam Courier*, No. 6, 1979.

38. P. Alampiev, 'Chinh sach co cau cua cac nuoc cong nghiep kem phat trien trong nhung giai doan dau xay dung chu nghia xa hoi' ['The Structural Policies of Underdeveloped Industrial Countries during the Initial Stages of Socialist Construction'], *Nghien cuu kinh te*, No. 4, 1981 (trans. from *Economicheskie Nauki*, No. 5, 1981).

39. *Ibid.*, p. 55.

40. *Ibid.*, pp. 55–6.

41. *Ibid.*, pp. 58–60.

42. S. Niznujaja and V. Shatiko, 'Quan he san xuat XHCN quoc te (mot vai khai niem va van de chung)' ['Socialist International Production Relations (Some Ideas and General Problems)'], Nghien cuu kinh te, No. 125, 1982 (trans. from *Social Sciences*, No. 4, 1980, in Russian).

43. *Ibid.*, p. 73.

44. M. Trigubenko, review of Y.P. Glazunov, *The Transformation of Private Industry and Trade in Vietnam* (Moscow: Publisher, 1981), in *Far Eastern Affairs*, No. 4, 1982; and his 'The CPV's Socio-economic Policy', *Far Eastern Affairs*, No. 1, 1983.

45. Trigubenko, 'The CPV's Socio-economic Policy', p.63.

46. *Ibid.*, p. 62.

47. *Ibid.*, p. 62.

48. M. Trigubenko, 'On the Participation of the Soviet Union's Far Eastern Areas in the USSR's Trade and Economic Cooperation with Vietnam', *Far Eastern Affairs*, No. 4, 1983, p. 45.

49. Trigubenko, 'The CPV's Socio-economic Policy', p. 66.

50. Truong Son, 'Industrialization', pp. 32–4. The overall statement cannot be fully understood outside of the ongoing debate on socio-economic strategy, which is not well understood and cannot be discussed in detail here. It should be noted that 'heavy' industry (Group A) includes such products as fertilizer, which is of major importance in encouraging peasants to supply agricultural output to the state; 'heavy' industry' does not, therefore, mean 'steel and iron'.

51. Boudarel, *La bureaucratie au Vietnam*, p. 49.

52. Vo Dai and Huy Khoat, 'Hoi dong tuong tro kinh te va nhung hinh thuc hop tac kinh te quoc te xa hoi chu nghia' ['The CMEA and Forms of Socialist International Cooperation'], *Nghien cuu kinh te*, No. 5, 1978.

53. *Ibid.*, p. 37.

54. R. Nyers, 'Tendencies of Tradition and Reform in CMEA Countries', *Acta Oeconomica*, No. 1, 1983, and Le Hang, 'Hop tac trong linh vuc nong nghiep cua cac nuoc HTK' ['Agricultural Cooperation among CMEA Countries'], *Nghien cuu kinh te*, No. 2, 1980; *idem*, 'Su hop tac cong nghiep trong HTK' ['Industrial Cooperation in the CMEA'], *Nghien cuu kinh te*, No. 3, 1979.

55. Le Hang, 'Industrial Cooperation', p. 49.

56. Le Hang, 'Agricultural Cooperation', p. 66.

57. Nguyen Van Tho, 'Nhung van de chu yeu trong chien luoc phat trien kinh te doi ngoai cua cac nuoc trong dieu kien phan cong lao dong quoc te hien nay' ['Principal Problems in External National Development Strategies in the Present State of the International Division of Labour'], *Nghien cuu kinh te*, No. 3, 1981.

58. A major difficulty with recorded trade data is the evidence suggesting that considerable smuggling was going on. Many Vietnamese exports were 'hard' goods that were readily saleable on world markets for hard currency (e.g. coffee, rubber, rice). Under certain conditions it is not inconceivable that the authorities might have been tempted to approve 'unrecorded' exports of goods, in return for hard currency, for which the CMEA countries nevertheless provided a ready market. For Vietnam, of course, labour is not subject to the same difficulties. The evidence for an 'active' price policy on the part of the Soviet Union is not inconsistent with such problems.

59. Wiles, *The New Communist Third World*, p. 25.

60. As in any analysis of international economic relations, the partial picture is inevitably somewhat misleading. Vietnamese-Soviet relations interact with many other areas – via other members of the CMEA, through 'intangibles' such as Soviet

training schemes for Vietnamese students, etc. The discussion presented here seeks only to highlight the possible role of recorded trade in interpreting various aspects of Soviet policies.

61. E.g. the statement in the article by Heikki Oksanen in *Euromoney*, September 1983, that the currency used in Soviet-Vietnamese trade was the domestic Soviet rouble, rather than the transferable rouble normally used for intra-CMEA transactions.

62. M. Petrov, 'Vietnam's Cooperation in the CMEA Framework', *Far Eastern Affairs*, No. 1, 1983.

63. *Ibid.*, pp. 169–71.

64. M. Trigubenko, 'On the Participation', p. 29. See also Petrov, 'Vietnam's Cooperation', p. 172, referring to '41 priority projects'.

65. *New Times*, No. 47, 1983.

66. Deputy Prime Minister Tran Phuong was quoted in the *Far Eastern Economic Review*, 24 May 1984, as saying that Soviet economic aid in 1976–80 was around $1.45bn. He stressed the valuation problems. Even if Soviet economic aid were to have doubled in the third Five-Year Plan (1981–85), this will still amount to only *ca.* $15 *per capita*, which is not a very large sum given the acute development problems faced by the country.

12

The political economy of Indo-Soviet relations

Santosh Mehrotra

This chapter attempts to disentangle the political and economic interests underlying the relationship between two Asian powers – India and the USSR. When Mrs Gandhi told Leonid Brezhnev at a civic reception in New Delhi in December 1980 that 'Indo-Soviet friendship ... is of equal importance to both India and the Soviet Union',[1] she was probably referring to the coincidence of interests of the two states on major issues of international and regional politics. In a similar vein, during Brezhnev's 1973 visit, she stated that Soviet leaders had never tried to influence an Indian decision,[2] and during his 1980 trip she emphasized that 'neither country' had 'ever sought to impose its perceptions on the other'.[3] As a matter of fact, there appears to be little need for the Soviet Union to attempt to influence India – precisely for the reason that there is such a broad mutuality of national interests between the two countries. There has long been a consensus that the Soviets have needed India as a counterweight to China, and that India has used its 'special relationship' with the Soviet Union to best advantage regionally in its relations with Pakistan (over Kashmir and the 1971 war) and China on the one hand and globally, with the US, on the other. Although there is an imbalance of power, India does retain sufficient flexibility to take a stand on international issues (e.g. the Indian Ocean, the Asian collective security system, the Non-Proliferation Treaty) in pursuance of its own national interests to the point of the exclusion of those of the Soviet Union.[4]

The mutuality of interests
In the 1950s the primary aim of Soviet policy in South Asia was to counter Western influence. In the 1960s and 1970s, with the increasing involvement of the US in South-East Asia and, later, in protecting its oil interests in the Middle East, US interest in South Asia diminished. Soviet policy thereafter became obsessed not so much with the US as with the containment of China. The decline of US interest in South Asia is reflected in Richard Nixon's foreign policy report to Congress in February 1972, which ruled out competing with the USSR for influence in South Asia. Moreover,

since the mid-1960s the USSR has seen itself as an Asian power. The Soviet goal of being perceived as an Asian power was in evidence in A.N. Kosygin's mediating role in Tashkent between Indian and Pakistani heads of government at the end of the Indo-Pakistani war of 1965. A final Soviet objective in South Asia has been to use India as an intermediary in such political forums as the non-aligned movement and economic ones as the Group of 77.

The stability of the Indian state is a crucial prerequisite for the successful execution of these Soviet objectives.[5] Soviet economic and military assistance has served to strengthen the Indian state both domestically as well as in the international arena, and the 1970s have seen the consolidation of India's dominant position in the region. Domestically, the close political and economic relationship with the USSR has enabled the essentially populist party in power to maintain a 'socialist' image. Of the three world powers, the USSR, the USA and China, the Indian elite sees only the Soviet Union as truly interested in the emergence of India as a major regional power.

The 1970s opened with two historic developments, one of which altered the balance of forces within the global triangle (China-USSR-USA), while the other did the same for the regional triangle (USSR-India-Pakistan). The first was the Sino-American détente which was heralded by Henry Kissinger's secret mission (from Islamabad) to Peking (arranged through the good offices of Pakistan) in mid-1971. The second was the Indo-Pakistan war of December 1971 which ended with the dismemberment of Pakistan. The Sino-American détente was identically perceived by India and the USSR as being directed against the USSR. Kissinger informed the Indian government on his return from Peking that his Chinese hosts had expressed to him an intent to intervene in the event of an Indo-Pakistani conflict, such as then loomed clearly on the horizon. And Kissinger warned that if China became involved on Pakistan's side during an Indo-Pakistan war, the US would be unable to help India.[6] The new power alignment led to a revaluation at the highest levels of the Indian government and played a major – though secret – role in India's decision to sign a twenty year friendship treaty with the USSR in August 1971.[7]

While India's isolation precipitated the signing of the treaty which had probably been discussed between the two signatories two years earlier, the motives of the USSR also need to be understood. The Soviet Union had tried to befriend Pakistan since the mid-1960s and had sold arms to Pakistan even at the risk of harming Indo-Soviet relations. But the Soviets had been successful neither in loosening the ties of Pakistan with China nor in persuading Pakistan to accept the regional economic grouping (of Iran, Afghanistan, Pakistan and

India, with Soviet participation) that Moscow wanted to create. The new Sino-US détente was probably the proverbial last straw, and although India's immediate need for the treaty was the greater, the Soviets were forced to respond to a Sino-US challenge.

Thus there existed a strong coincidence of Indian and Soviet interests at the beginning of the 1970s which resulted in the Indo-Soviet treaty. However, the hopes that the Soviet Union might have had of the treaty as a step towards an Asian collective security system (first proposed by Brezhnev in 1969) were not to be realized, since India did not quite subscribe to that view of the treaty. Perhaps the single most important factor explaining India's cautious attitude towards the collective security plan is its long-term goal of improving relations with China. Commenting on the security plan, in an interview with a Tass correspondent (reported in *Izvestia*, 19 February 1972), India's Foreign Minister said that the Indian government supported all initiatives directed towards strengthening peace and security. Brezhnev's proposal for an Asian collective security system, he added, came under this heading.[8] Similarly, the *Annual Report* of the Indian Ministry of External Affairs (1970–71) referred to the Soviet collective security proposal as a 'new development of some significance' and regarded it as 'a declaration of the fact that the Soviet Union is as much an Asian as a European power'. However, it should be noted that the report did not give full support to the proposal.[9] But since the proposal has not received much support from any non-socialist Asian country, Soviet authors grabbed upon any sympathetic statement by Indian leaders and made rather too much of it.

The Indian leaders had demonstrated that on the question of the collective security plan, they were prepared to cooperate up to a point and no further. On the question of naval power, while the Indians appreciated the importance of the presence of Soviet ships as a counterweight to the American presence, they did not wish the Soviets to become the dominant power in the Indian Ocean. A simultaneous reduction in the naval presence of both the USSR and the US is consistent with India's long-term interest in establishing its own dominance in the region. Thus Moscow has consistently abstained on the Indian Ocean resolution in the General Assembly of the United Nations, a resolution which India has consistently supported. The resolution, moved in 1971, called for the elimination of superpower rivalry from the Indian Ocean. The Soviets explained their abstention by pointing to 'the failure of the resolution to put the blame for the rising tension in the Indian Ocean where it truly belongs [on Western military bases] and the indirect attempt to put some of the blame for the continued arms race in this region on the Soviet Union ...'[10] Thus, again, while Soviet and Indian objectives are similar, they are certainly not the same.

It is this relative similarity of geopolitical interests that has prevented any public dispute arising over India's nuclear programme. Like the West, the Soviet Union has publicly opposed the expansion of the nuclear club and exhorted nations to sign the Non-Proliferation Treaty (which India has consistently refused to sign since 1968). But when India exploded its nuclear device in May 1974 the USSR, unlike the West, merely reported India's action, repeating India's claim that it was for peaceful purposes.[11] In contrast to the low-key Soviet response, Canada, which had provided most of the heavy water for the research reactor CIRUS from which the plutonium for the test was derived, immediately suspended nuclear and all other forms of aid to India. With revelations appearing in the US that some heavy water from the US had been used in the production of the plutonium for India's explosion, the US first delayed and then stopped shipments of low-enriched uranium. These shipments were being made under a thirty-year contract, signed in 1963, to India's Tarapur nuclear power station, and the US promised to resume supplies if full safeguards and inspection rights were granted. The Soviets stepped in and offered first heavy water in 1976 and then low-enriched uranium in 1978, under partial safeguards, rather than under the full safeguards to be supervised by the International Atomic Energy Agency. Early in 1979, India and the USSR also signed an agreement for Soviet assistance in developing fast-breeder reactor technology.

The military dimension: sale of equipment and transfer of technology
The Soviet Union has been India's single most important supplier of defence equipment since the mid-1960s. More important, the fact that it has been prepared to transfer defence technology is largely a reflection of the overridingly strong mutuality of geopolitical interests between the two nations. On the other hand, the differences between American and Indian perceptions of global issues have correspondingly been reflected in the very unstable – and from India's point of view, unreliable – military relationship with the US.

Up to 1959, India's armed forces depended exclusively on Western equipment, especially British. Considering that Soviet defence exports to India began only in the early 1960s, it is remarkable how quickly such exports gathered momentum. According to SIPRI, between 1965 and 1969 80 per cent of all

Indian defence equipment imports came from the USSR.[12] Having established itself as India's single most important supplier, in the period 1970–4, the USSR's share fell to 70 per cent of India's arms imports and in 1975–9 to 57 per cent.[13] In order to place this decline in trend in perspective, it is important to point out, firstly, that the USSR obviously still remains the most important supplier by far and, secondly, that in recent years India has been fairly successful in diversifying its sources of supply of weapons systems, which testifies to the bargaining capacity India has come to enjoy in its dealings with the Soviets.[14]

Perhaps an even more important point which places this decline in trend in perspective is the fact that India is one of the few countries outside the Warsaw Pact allowed to purchase Soviet military know-how, as opposed to weapons. As SIPRI points out in its *Yearbook 1983*, Western arms manufacturers are increasingly licensing their production to Third World countries, but the Soviet Union is not. According to SIPRI: 'It had been expected, when the Indian MiG-21 programme began, that this would start a new trend. This has not been the case: the Indian example remains one of a handful of exceptions to the rule.'[15]

The MiG-21 was chosen in 1961 in preference to Western alternatives because the Soviets were willing to make it available for licensed manufacture and also to extend credit for the manufacturing programme. While Lockheed was interested in selling aircraft to India, the US government, sensitive to Pakistan's worries, refused to allow the firm to transfer technology to India. The significance of the MiG deal lies in that the MiG-21 had been refused to the Chinese by the Soviets, but the USSR was willing to license production in India, with which China's relations were fast deteriorating.[16]

After the Sino-Indian war (1962) military aid was accepted by India from any country that was prepared to offer it. The US promised $50m of emergency assistance in 1962–3 and $60m in 1963–4. In May 1964, as much as $500m of military aid, half of it a grant and the rest a loan, was promised for the period 1964–9. But the Indo-Pakistani war (1965) resulted in the cancellation of military aid to both India and Pakistan, with the result that between October 1962 and September 1965 India was supplied about $80m against a promised commitment of $610m.

Facilities have been set up in India with Soviet help to meet the overhaul and servicing needs of its Soviet air and naval equipment. The Indian air force has chosen the Soviet AN-32 as a medium transport aircraft to replace ageing Dakotas, Packets and Avros and, given the significant role it plays in logistic operations to the forward areas, it was essential to establish the repair and overhaul facilities for the aircraft in India. Such a facility has been established in Chandigarh. Naval vessels purchased from the USSR can be serviced at the biggest naval dockyard in the country in Visakhapatnam. The dockyard was constructed with Soviet assistance, and includes an electrical and maintenance workshop.

In May 1980 a major arms agreement was signed, under the terms of which the Soviets would provide India with military and naval equipment, and in certain cases (e.g. the MiG-23 fighter, the T-72 main battletank) would grant licences for their manufacture by India on the basis of a loan of Rs13bn* at 2.5 per cent annual interest, to be repaid over fifteen years after a period of grace lasting two years. India bought 70 T-72 tanks outright; but 600 more were to be manufactured under license by the Avadi works in Madras. The MiG-21 was the first Mach-2 aircraft to be licensed for production in an LDC and non-socialist country, and now the MiG-23 will be the first variable-geometry aircraft to be manufactured in an LDC. (Production of the MiG-23 did not begin until January 1983; the current position is not known.) The new Godavari class frigate to be built in India will also incorporate some weapons and other sub-systems of Soviet origin.

Thus there is a strong new trend in evidence in defence planning – production of major weapons and equipment under licence as a step towards defence industrialization. And as a leading Indian defence analyst writes: 'Only the USSR has adequate mutuality of interest in India's development of defence technology and has necessary resources to support the effort with necessary credit. So India must approach the USSR for transfer of technology rather than weapon systems.'[17]

The Soviet view of Indian economic and political developments[18]
Although the Soviet Union claimed that India was neither 'socialist' nor of 'socialist orientation', it would be interesting to know if India was regarded as 'progressive' by the Soviets. Here, it is not enough to say that the emphasis was placed upon the state-to-state nature of Soviet aid to large-scale capital projects, modelled on the Soviet experience. According to Professor R.A. Ulianovsky (a senior expert on India and the deputy head of the Central Committee Secretariat's International Department) India has attained 'a middle level of capitalist development'. In this context, the Soviet leadership, like the pro-Moscow Communist Party of India (CPI) believes that the ruling Congress Party plays a progressive role in

---

* In this chapter the term 'billion' refers to the US thousand million (10^9).

Indian economic and political development in three particular respects: it is anti-monopoly, anti-feudal and anti-imperialist.[19]

By giving the label of 'national bourgeois regime' to the Indian state, Soviet commentators endorsed the Congress as 'progressive'. Like the CPI, the Soviets believe that the objective of the national bourgeoisie is to develop an independent economy on a capitalist basis. Industrial development by Indian capitalists is viewed as being contrary to the interests of imperialism, and also to the interests of landlords and princes. Hence the national bourgeoisie and its political representative, the Congress Party, are thought by the USSR to be both anti-imperialist and anti-feudal. The state is seen to play a progressive role because, by building public enterprises, it loosens the hold of monopolies, both foreign and Indian.

The economic relationship

A very important Indo-Soviet institutional arrangement is in the area of cooperation in planning. In a narrow sense, such cooperation involves assistance to planners in LDCs – this commenced in the mid-1950s, when some LDCs approached the USSR for assistance in preparing their national plans. India did not seek any such assistance. In 1973 a cooperation agreement of this narrow kind was signed between Gosplan (the Soviet State Planning Committee) and the Indian Planning Commission.

However, the more profound process of linking the national plans of partner countries in the fields of investment, production and trade conducive to the growth of complementarity is a rarer practice than the rather narrow exercise described above. This more profound process is largely confined to the less-developed members of the CMEA (Cuba, Vietnam) and to some extent Yugoslavia. In 1978 India and the USSR progressed to this second kind of cooperation at least on paper; they signed a protocol setting out guidelines for a long-term programme for economic, trade and scientific and technical cooperation up to 1990. It indicates areas for Soviet assistance in projects in India on a compensation basis. The agreement on the long-term programme was signed by the Janata government when Kosygin visited India in March 1979.

The following year, in December 1980, when Brezhnev visited India, an agreement was signed which identified projects to be constructed with Soviet assistance explicitly on a compensation basis. As is well known, joint production with LDCs of raw materials on a compensation basis has been pursued for a long time (phosphates with Morocco, gas with Iran and Afghanistan, oil with Iraq and Syria, bauxite with Guinea). Similar cooperation in the production of manufactures is relatively limited and mostly confined to the more developed of the LDCs. The 1980 agreement with India stipulates the construction of: (a) an alumina plant in Andhra Pradesh of the capacity of 600,000–800,000 tonnes of alumina p.a.; (b) enterprises for the production of canned fruits and vegetables in both finished and semi-finished form; and (c) a phyto-chemical plant (and other pharmaceutical plants) for the production of medicinal preparations.

The joint production of manufactures and finished items, as envisaged in the 1980 agreement, is not a new phenomenon. Already in April 1971 India and the USSR had signed an agreement providing for the supply of 20,000 tonnes of raw cotton annually from the USSR which would be converted into cotton textiles in India and re-exported to the USSR. Similarly, the Indian Council for the Promotion of Wool and Wool-product Exports and a Soviet foreign trade organization jointly organized the mass production of knitted wool items in Ludhiana with long-term Soviet commitments for the import of about 90 per cent of this production. Talks on a Soviet proposal to import 500 metres of cloth a year ended in agreement at the end of 1982. India would be creating new manufacturing capacity, so that there was no diversion to the USSR of existing exports; an original Soviet proposal to supply the machinery (to help reduce the Soviet import surplus) was dropped, and Indian machinery would be used. The Indians felt that Soviet textile equipment was obsolete and would be unsuitable for India's textile industry, which already faced a major problem of obsolescence.[20]

Soviet-assisted heavy industry plants constructed in the 1960s have also supplied equipment to the USSR and to third world countries where the USSR has building projects (Cuba, Bulgaria, Afghanistan). Thus it was agreed in November 1979, in a protocol on cooperation in machine-building, that the Heavy Engineering Corporation (HEC) would supply a total of 70,000 tonnes of equipment to the USSR, and that the Mining and Allied Machinery Corporation (MAMC) would supply 53,000 tonnes of equipment to the USSR and to third-country projects that were being set up with Soviet assistance between 1981 and 1985.[21] Of course, it must be admitted that in placing orders with HEC and MAMC, the Soviet Union was doing India a service, since these plants have suffered from very severe underutilization of capacity.

It is not at the institutional level alone that Soviet-Indian economic relations are more advanced than Soviet-LDC economic relations in general. The commodity composition of Soviet imports from India also demonstrates the rather different character of the relationship. According to UN data, the share of manufactures in Soviet imports from LDCs, far from rising, has tended to decline from its peak of between 15 and 20 per cent in the early 1970s to under 10 per cent in the case both of the USSR and of Eastern Europe; on the other hand, the share of manufactures in India's exports to the USSR has been rising.

In 1980 the share of manufactures and semi-manufactures in Soviet imports from India was around 50 per cent, while in overall exports from India the proportion of these goods was 59 per cent. The share of manufactures in CMEA imports from India has been rising steadily – from 15 per cent in the early 1960s to 40 per cent in the early 1970s.[22] So, the USSR is the biggest buyer of Indian cotton fabrics, garments, knitwear, detergents, cosmetics, medicines, handicraft products and carpets. More than 90 per cent of the output of India's knitwear industry goes to the USSR.

Especially interesting in these exports of manufactures to the USSR is the role of the two Special Export Zones (SEZs) or Free Trade Zones set up at Kandla (near Ahmedabad in west India) and Santa Cruz (near Bombay, exclusively for electronics). Several Western multinationals have set up plants in these SEZs in order to penetrate the Soviet market. Ciba-Geigy, Hoechst, Helene Curtis and American Home Products are among the companies whose local subsidiaries have set up factories in the Kandla SEZ to manufacture mainly for export to the USSR. A combination of multinational technology and cheap Indian labour will give the Russians access to Western-quality drugs, toothpaste, soap, shampoo, cosmetics and so on without having to spend hard currency. As a result of Indian policy changes in 1982, units devoted entirely to producing for export set up outside the SEZs will have the same benefits as those inside the SEZs. Rank Xerox has decided to invest in a plant with an Indian partner, Modi, to export photocopiers to the USSR.[23]

Agricultural commodities still constitute a substantial proportion of India's exports to the USSR. India's leading farm exports to the USSR, by value, are: tea, cashew kernels, tobacco, hides and skins, spices, peanuts, castor oil, wool, shellac, jute and horticultural products. Tea is by far India's largest agricultural export to the USSR. Russian consumers get about 90 per cent of their imported tea from India (the other suppliers being Sri Lanka, Bangladesh and China), and a substantial proportion of their coffee, cashew kernels and peanuts. When China phased out deliveries of tea, coffee and nuts to the USSR in the early 1960s the Soviet trade planners looked to India to fill the gap. Since then, the growth in Indian exports of these products, and of spices and hides, has provided Soviet consumers with more adequate supplies of these products, which in the 1950s were often scarce. Indian tobacco temporarily helped replace imported Chinese tobacco in Soviet cigarette factories following the cessation of Chinese deliveries in 1961. India's share in total Soviet imports of raw tobacco has been quite high – ranging between 20 and 25 per cent – during the past eight to ten years.[24]

Although India is the Soviet Union's biggest trade partner in the Third World, India's share in total Soviet foreign trade turnover declined during this period: its share in total Soviet imports declined from 2.34 per cent in 1965 to 1.35 per cent in 1979, but recovered to 1.8 per cent in 1980.[25]

Another important respect in which Soviet-Indian economic relations are quite different from Soviet-LDC relations in general is the mechanism of payment for trade. By early 1982 the clearing system remained in existence in Soviet trade relations with only six LDCs: India, Afghanistan, Egypt, Iran, Pakistan and Syria.[26] In 1976 these six countries accounted for roughly one-third of total Soviet-LDC trade.[27] With the remaining LDCs, trade is conducted in hard currency, and the overall Soviet trade surplus with these countries during the 1970s has enabled the USSR to cover a part of its trade deficit with the West. Soviet-Indian trade, obviously, cannot perform the same function since it is conducted under clearing agreements and since 1958 there has been no arrangement for settling balances at the expiry of the trade agreement or annually in convertible currency. Even Soviet arms exports to India are paid for by the export of goods.

As with Latin America, the Soviet Union has had a trade deficit with India almost throughout the 1970s. Table 12.1 demonstrates that between 1970–1 and 1980–1 the cumulative Indian trade balance with the USSR stood at Rs8,870m. (See Table 12.2 for some other trade statistics.) The total credit utilized over the same period was Rs2,779m. The aggregate repayment of development loans over the same period amounted to Rs6,746m. Thus, while a proportion of the Indian trade surplus can be explained by repayment (amortization plus interest) of developmental loans, the remainder (Rs8,870m plus Rs2,779m less Rs6,746m), Rs4,903m, must almost entirely consist of repayments of defence loans. It must be emphasized that the sum of Rs4,903m does not constitute the value of defence equipment imported from the USSR over the period 1970–1 to 1980–1. The value of defence equipment imported over this period must almost certainly be higher; Rs4,903m is only the figure for the repayment of defence loans extended in the 1960s which would have come up for repayment in the 1970s. Considering that Datar has come up with a figure of Rs750m for Indian defence

TABLE 12.1

Comparison of Indo-Soviet trade balance with net credits utilized by India
(million rupees)

Year	Indian exports	Indian imports	Balance	Credit repayment	Credit utilization
1970–1		1,061	1,037	602	367
1971–2	2,087	873	1,214	306	140
1972–3	3,048	1,144	1,904	488	85
1973–4	2,860	2,547	313	474	137
1974–5	4,213	4,089	124	477	140
1975–6	4,166	3,098	1,069	464	266
1976–7	4,540	3,160	1,380	818	258
1977–8	6,567	4,420	2,147	1,233	241
1978–9	4,106	4,690	−584	1,103	215
1979–80	6,382	8,242	−1,860	447	480
1980–1	12,263	10,137	2,126	334	450
1981–2	15,049	11,564	3,485		
Total			8,870[a]	6,746	2,779

Source: Trade balance figures are from Directorate General of Commercial Intelligence and Statistics, Calcutta. Repayment (inclusive of interest payments) and credit utilization data are drawn from *Explanatory Memorandum on the Budget of the Central Government* (Ministry of Finance, Government of India), various issues.

payments to the USSR over the period 1961–2 to 1965–6, a figure of Rs4,903m does not seem unreasonable at all for the later period.[28] For India, the possibility of paying for defence equipment without expending scarce foreign exchange is too attractive an arrangement to permit an early multilateralization of Indo-Soviet trade. No doubt the 1980 defence loan will have its repercussions on Indo-Soviet trade well into the 1980s, and India will find it inadvisable to multilateralize its payment arrangements with the USSR.

Apart from arms, the other crucial group of imports from the USSR is, of course, petroleum and petroleum products (kerosene, fertilizers, etc.). After several Indian requests, the USSR agreed to supply crude oil in 1976 (soon after India, it has been suggested, had made some friendly noises towards China). Since then crude oil supplies have continued uninterrupted. From the Soviet point of view the supply of crude oil, the opportunity cost of which should be measured in hard currency, is a considerable gesture.[29] For India, however, the petroleum products are perhaps more important; crude imports from the USSR constituted only 13 per cent of overall crude imports in 1981–2 and 15 per cent in 1982–3. For India, it is

TABLE 12.2
India's main trading partners (percentage of total exports and imports)

Year	Exports to		Imports from	
	USA	USSR	USA	USSR
1981–2	11.3	19.3	10.5	8.5
1980–1	12.7	17.3	12.2	9.6
1979–80	12.6	7.2	11.1	10.0
1978–9	13.4	10.0	7.3	8.3
1977–8	12.5	12.1	12.5	7.3
1976–7	11.0	8.9	21.0	6.1
1974–5	11.3	12.6	16.1	8.9
1973–4	13.8	11.4	16.9	8.6
1972–3	14.1	15.5	12.5	5.9
1971–2	16.8	13.3	23.1	4.5
1970–1	13.5	13.7	27.7	6.5
1965–6	18.3	11.5	38.0	5.9
1960–1	15.5	4.4	28.7	1.4
1951–2	18.1	0.9	30.4	0.1

Source: Monthly Statistics of the Foreign Trade of India (Directorate General of Commercial Intelligence and Statistics, Calcutta), various issues.

the advantage of being able to pay for crude in rupees which is invaluable; Soviet willingness to export crude in exchange for goods has certainly helped India's hard-currency balance of payments to weather the oil price storms of the 1970s.

The commodity composition of Soviet exports to India (Table 12.3) is also quite different when compared with Soviet exports to most other LDCs. While machinery and transport equipment (Standard International Trade Classification (SITC) 7) constitutes a sizeable proportion of Soviet exports to most LDCs, the share of these items has fallen considerably in Soviet exports to India. Other intermediate products, apart from petroleum and petroleum products (SITC 3), have also acquired importance in Soviet exports to India, for example non-ferrous metals and newsprint.

Most studies of Indo-Soviet trade have come to the conclusion that the terms of Indo-Soviet trade have been at least as good as, if not better than, India's terms of trade with the rest of the world.[30] A recent study has concluded that the argument that the USSR made substantial hard-currency earnings by re-exporting Indian goods to advanced capitalist countries is not valid. The USSR is a large producer of three commodities (tea, tobacco and cotton textiles) which are exported regularly and which are also imported from India. However, only a small proportion of these commodities is exported to hard-currency areas, most exports going to Eastern Europe. Besides, the unit values of exports in hard currency are far lower than the unit values of imports. Furthermore, the share of exports in domestic production for these three commodities is only 1 or 2 per cent. All this suggests that the hard-currency earnings from switch trade is minimal. Another interesting conclusion of the study is that there was an inverse relationship between the volume of imports and the unit value of imports of selected commodities from individual countries; thus, the USSR always managed to buy from the cheapest source of supply. For example, the USSR switched between India and Pakistan as sources of supply of cotton textiles and jute imports depending upon which of the two offered the lower price in any given year.[31]

TABLE 12.3
Commodity composition of Indo-Soviet trade (percentages)

SITC No.	Description	Exports to USSR		Imports from USSR	
		1980	1981	1980	1981
0	Food (and live animals)	32.2	39.5	—	—
1	Beverages and tobacco	4.4	5.4	—	—
2	Crude materials (inedible, except fuels)	2.4	2.7	0.7	0.4
3	Mineral fuels, lubricants and related materials	—	–	75.6	78.0
4	Animal and vegetable oils and fats	2.5	1.7	—	—
5	Chemicals	3.8	3.9	2.4	2.4
6	Manufactured goods classified by material	25.5	17.8	1.6	1.2
7	Machinery and transport equipment	4.7	—	13.6	11.3
8	Miscellaneous manufactured articles	7.2	7.6	0.2	0.2
9	Commodities and transactions not classified according to kind	17.1	14.9	0.4	5.1

Source: UNCTAD Secretariat, *Statistical Review of Trade among Countries having Different Economic and Social Systems* (Geneva, August 1983), TD/B/965/Add.1. These statistics are based on Soviet trade statistics.

Soviet transfer of technology to India

Several key sectors of the Indian economy have benefited enormously in the 1950s and 1960s from Soviet loans and transfer of technology: heavy engineering (a steel-making machinery plant at Ranchi and a mining machinery plant at Durgapur), heavy electricals (a power station equipment manufacturing plant at Hardwar), two steel plants (at Bhilai and Bokaro), basic bulk drugs and formulations (at Rishikesh and Hyderabad, with a plant at Madras producing surgical instruments), oil exploration and oil refining (three public-sector refineries at Barauni, Koyali and Mathura) and several power plants.[32] In addition, an aluminium smelter and fabrication unit (at Korba), an ophthalmic glass plant (at Durgapur), a precision instruments plant (at Kotah) and more than half-a-dozen state farms have been set up with Soviet assistance. In the late 1970s and early 1980s, the concentration has largely been on energy: coal-mining, onshore oil exploration, equipment for power stations, negotiations for a nuclear power plant; with the result that the entire Soviet (though not East European) economic and technical assistance programme has been to the public sector.

Shortage of power has placed a crucial constraint on Indian industrial growth during the 1970s. One of the four or five 'super' thermal power stations (1,000 MW capacity each) being constructed during the present plan is to receive technical and financial assistance from the USSR.

It is in coal-mining that the major Soviet contribution has been made over the past decade. After the 1979 oil price rise, the Indian government decided to step up its efforts both in the fields of oil exploration (especially offshore) and coal-mining. In the 1980 agreements signed by Brezhnev and Mrs Gandhi, Soviet assistance was sought for geological prospecting for coal in mutually agreed areas. As is well known, Soviet technology in open-cast mining is perhaps the best in the world, and it is precisely in this area that Soviet assistance is being sought.

A high proportion of Indian crude oil production comes from the offshore oilfields referred to as Bombay High, which were discovered with Soviet assistance. However, the Soviets do not possess the requisite offshore technology and hence the government has decided to seek the collaboration of Western oil companies in further offshore exploration and drilling work. Soviet assistance has concentrated on onshore areas since the 1950s. It is thought that a techno-economic plan for onshore oil and gas prospecting and extraction work in India for 1981–90 has been prepared by the public-sector Oil and Natural Gas Commission in collaboration with the USSR.

Another area of Soviet assistance mentioned in the 1980 agreement is the expansion of the Bhilai and Bokaro steel plants from 4m to 5m and 5.5m tonnes of steel p.a. respectively through the introduction of new technology and the modernization of equipment. Some of these projects in the 1980 agreement are to be financed by a 520m rouble loan. Other projects, including a new steel plant at Visakhapatnam, are to be financed from a 250m rouble loan granted in 1977 – the only loan given by the USSR in the 1970s.[33]

What is interesting about this new steel plant is that of the 30 per cent of total equipment requirements which are to come from abroad, only half will be from the USSR; the rest will come from the West. Such a contract testifies to the degree of manoeuvrability India has acquired in negotiations with the USSR; and it is comparable to its diversification of sources of defence imports in recent years. Similarly, the contract for the production under licence of MiGs is now explicitly framed to allow India to install non-Soviet equipment on the aircraft. For example, the electronics in the MiGs are entirely from the West – they will carry a French navigational system – and will be armed with French air to air missiles. Thus, in a sense, India will actually have more advanced MiGs than the Soviets themselves.

Earlier studies about Soviet and East European aid to India in the 1950s and 1960s rightly concluded that while the magnitude of that aid was not large, its 'main usefulness to India has lain in their [i.e. the socialist countries'] willingness to give aid for particular projects that are regarded as high-priority investment and to give aid for public sector development, at times when other major donors, such as the US, have shown an extreme reluctance to do so'.[34] A detailed examination of the projects has shown a Soviet willingness to allow Indian equipment and supplies to be used wherever possible. Table 12.4 compares the respective shares of imported and indigenous supplies for Bokaro with those of the three earlier steel plants in the public sector. There has been a progressive increase in the Indian supplies used and a corresponding reduction in imported equipment and materials. A similar process has been noticeable in the case of the three oil refineries, again in the public sector, set up with Soviet assistance.

Given that most of the Soviet technology transfer has been made on a near-turnkey basis, the question is whether it resulted in building an independent technological capacity in those sectors. Normally, where the manufacture of complex equipment is set up under turnkey projects, the technological impact is rather limited. Local learning hardly goes beyond absorbing the production

TABLE 12.4
Foreign and local supplies for steel plant construction

Steel plant	Capacity (million tonnes)	Equipment		Structurals		Refractories	
		Indian (%)	Imported (%)	Indian (%)	Imported (%)	Indian (%)	Imported (%)
1955–61							
Rourkela	1.0	—	100	4	96	22	78
Bhilai	1.0	13	87	22	78	6	94
Durgapur	1.0	13	87	28	72	50	50
1961–6 (expansion period)							
Rourkela	1.8	25	75	78	22	57	43
Bhilai	2.5	18	82	29	71	44	56
Durgapur	1.6	49	51	74	26	96	4
1964–							
Bokaro 1st stage (completed)	1.7	60	40	94	6	61	39
Bokaro (expansion) (in progress)	4.0	88	12	100	—	100	—

Sources: Report of the Capital Cost Sub-Committee of the Mahatab Committee on Steel Costs (Government of India, March 1966); *Bokaro – India's Largest Steel Complex* (Bokaro Steel Limited, Bokaro Steel City, October 1972).

technology. The question of transferring design capacity is not even posed. The USSR has excelled in training operatives in India (an activity not generally favoured by Western firms) and has successfully imparted machine-operating skills and manufacturing technology in steel-making, petroleum exploration and refining, drugs and capital goods (heavy machine-building and heavy electricals). But the other two inputs for building an independent technological capacity – product and process design capacity and R & D – seem to be lacking in LDCs, including India. While it is true that design capacity is a skill acquired over a certain period of time, and that the expansion of R & D facilities is in any case the responsibility of LDC governments, transfer of technology should nevertheless, involve the transfer of the methodology used for obtaining the product design if it is to build up the technological capacity of the recipients. If this is not the case, the recipient will simply receive a design for making the product in question but will not be able to understand how such a design was obtained. It is in this respect that the Soviet transfer of technology to India in some of the priority sectors was disappointing. Soviet transfer-of-technology agreements were primarily concerned with transfer of 'know-how', not 'know-why'. Thus while a fairly systematic transfer of the former took place, the latter was generally ignored.

However, some qualifications should be made here. First, 'know-why' cannot be transferred until know-how has been fully assimilated. Second, Western firms in the early stages of the industrialization of India were reluctant even to transfer know-how, let alone 'know-why' (the position has altered considerably in respect of know-how). Thus US Steel's proposal for Bokaro, prior to the Soviets' entry on the scene, required that Bokaro be managed by US Steel for ten years before being handed over to India. Third, perhaps the one exception to the rule (that the USSR transferred know-how, not 'know-why') is the large Indian public-sector metallurgical consultant firm, MECON.

India's experience as a recipient of Soviet technology cannot be appreciated without a more detailed disaggregated analysis; nor can it be appreciated without understanding the dynamics of the Indian development process. Limits on space preclude a more detailed discussion of the subject in this chapter.[35]

Conclusion

What are the long-term prospects for the Indo-Soviet relationship? The eventual resolution of the Sino-Soviet dispute, it has been suggested, is likely to have an adverse effect on the 'special relationship' known to exist between India and the USSR. This is indubitable; the more important question is, how adverse? I would argue that the effect would not be very damaging, since a Sino-Soviet rapprochement will simultaneously make possible an improvement in the Sino-Indian relationship.

More important, those who doubt the durability of the Indo-Soviet relationship underestimate the influence of the other Soviet political objectives mentioned at the beginning of this chapter. For example, even if the Sino-Soviet relationship improves, superpower competition for influence in the Third World in general, and in the Indian Ocean in particular, is unlikely to wane. And considering the geographical importance of India's position dominating the Indian Ocean, the Soviet Union will at least need friends, if not allies, in the region. Equally important is the role of India in the non-aligned world, particularly since India took over the chairmanship of the movement from Cuba in March 1983. The Soviet self-image of an Asian power, and not just a European one, would hardly be credible if relations with one of the two foremost countries of Asia were allowed to deteriorate beyond a certain point.

Besides, it has already been suggested, Soviet interest in the

import of Indian consumer goods, both agricultural and manufactured products, has tended to increase, not decrease, in recent
years. India is the one country in the Third World with a stable
enough government and an advanced enough manufacturing sector
for the USSR to consider as a reliable source of consumer goods in
the long term. And as long as the Indian elite is determined to strive
for the status of a medium, if not a great, power, Indian demand for
Soviet arms will continue, and hence the absorption of the Indian
trade surplus may not pose particularly serious problems for the
relationship. Moreover, the USSR Chamber of Commerce has been
emphasizing to the Federation of Indian Chambers of Commerce
(FICCI) in their annual meetings that the USSR may be willing to
collaborate with Indian private-sector firms in joint ventures
involving the export of Soviet machinery and the import of the
resulting product on a compensation basis.[36] Given the considerable
success of the Indian private sector in exporting consultancy services
and turnkey plants, in making direct investments and in licensing
production abroad, the Soviets have also shown interest in
collaborating with the private sector in setting up joint ventures in
South-East Asia and the Middle East.

Perhaps somewhat more surprising is the Soviet suggestion that
India can help in the construction and the running of enterprises in
the Soviet Union by supplying not only machinery, but also skilled
workers and technologists, because the USSR is short of such
personnel. All this tends to suggest that while the political aspect of
the relationship is still dominant for the USSR, its economic interest
in India is now much greater than it ever was before.

For India, on the other hand, the importance of the political and
diplomatic aspect of the relationship has changed in emphasis: in
the fifteen years since 1971 India has not fought a war; on the
contrary, there has been since then a slow but steady improvement
in Sino-Indian and Indo-Pakistani relations. The sense of insecurity
of the 1950s and 1960s, and the consequent need for Soviet
diplomatic assistance, has disappeared. But at the same time the
striving for medium-power status demands a steady supply of
Soviet, and for that matter Western, arms. As regards the economic
relationship, India's interest in the USSR certainly shifted ground in
the 1970s. In the earlier period Soviet transfer of technology to key
sectors of the Indian economy was of paramount importance.
Today, India's economic interest lies in (1) acquisition of arms
without the expenditure of hard currency; (2) intermediate products
like oil, fertilizers, newsprint and non-ferrous metals, against
payment in inconvertible rupees; and (3) the Soviet market, which
absorbed almost one-fifth of India's exports in 1981–2. The USSR

took 92.5 per cent of all India's ready-made leather exports, 96.8 per cent of its woollen knitwear, 69 per cent of its pepper, 45 per cent of its coffee, 42 per cent of its tobacco, 83 per cent of its cosmetics and detergents and 76 per cent of its mica in 1981–2. With such a convergence of economic and political interests, a dramatic deterioration in the Indo-Soviet relationship seems unlikely in the foreseeable future.

Notes

1. *Soviet Review*, No. 58, 15 December 1980.
2. *Pravda*, 28 November 1973.
3. *Soviet Review*, No. 58, 15 December 1980.
4. A recent study by an American scholar comes to precisely the same conclusion: that there is, in fact, a mutuality of 'influence'. See Robert C. Horn, *Soviet-Indian Relations* (New York: Praeger, 1983).
5. It is this stability which perhaps distinguishes, in Soviet eyes, India from other friends or allies in the Middle East (e.g. Egypt) and South-East Asia (e.g. Indonesia).
6. Seymour Hersh, *The Price of Power: Kissinger in the Nixon White House* (London/Boston: Faber and Faber, 1983).
7. In the aftermath of the war, Indo-American relations reached such a low point that the US, which had been extending economic assistance to India since 1951, did not do so from 1972 to 1977. (It was resumed in August 1978 and since then it has been made available each year.) See *External Assistance, 1980–81* (Ministry of Finance, Government of India, New Delhi, 1982), p. 33.
8. *USSR and Third World* (London: Central Asian Research Centre), Vol. II, p. 144.
9. India's non-aligned conscience probably constrained her from declaring full support for the Soviet collective security plan. Bhabani Sengupta, in *Soviet-Asian Relations, the 1970s and beyond, An Inter-Perceptional Study* (New York: Praeger, 1976), suggests that it was perhaps understood between the Soviet and Indian leaders that India should be one of the last, and not one of the first, countries formally to support the Soviet plan. He adds, on the authority of an Indian foreign service official, that India's support would be fatal for the concept as far as Pakistan and several smaller Asian countries were concerned, given India's dominant status in the region.
10. A. Alexeyev and A. Fialkovsky, 'Peace and Security for the Indian Ocean', *International Affairs* (Moscow), September 1979, p. 53.
11. Tass (18 May 1974) said: 'Striving to keep at the level of world technology in the peaceful uses of nuclear explosion, the Indian government had carried out a research programme. The results of these investigations could be used in mining and earth-moving. The Atomic Energy Commission stated that India has no intention of manufacturing nuclear weapons and reaffirmed its strong opposition to the use of nuclear explosions for military purposes.' *USSR and Third World*, Vol. 4, p. 199.
12. SIPRI, *Arms Trade with the Third World*, 1971.
13. SIPRI, *Yearbook 1982*.
14. The high share of the USSR in India's defence imports in the second half of the 1960s can be explained by the fact that after the 1965 Indo-Pakistani war the US

and Western countries imposed an embargo on arms exports to India. In the early 1970s, the Soviet share remained high for two complementary reasons: the USSR was replenishing Indian stocks during and after the 1971 war; at the same time, the US stopped all military assistance, along with economic assistance.

15. SIPRI, *Yearbook 1983*, p. 368.

16. K. Subramanyam, 'Soviet Help for Self-Reliance in Defence', in S.D. Sharma (ed.), *Studies in Indo-Soviet Cooperation* (New Delhi: 1981).

17. K. Subramanyam, 'Soviet Help'. Subramanyam has for many years been the Director of the Institute of Defence Studies and Analyses, New Delhi.

18. Bibliographical studies by scholars show that India has a central place in any discussion of Soviet development theory. India happens to be the Soviet Union's most analysed LDC. The India Department of the Institute of the Peoples of Asia has a long history going back to Tsarist times. By comparison, the writings on Africa and Latin America were superficial and dogmatic until the late 1950s. (See Stephen J. Clarkson, *The Soviet Theory of Development: India and the Third World in Marxist-Leninist Scholarship* (London: Macmillan, 1979), pp. 9–11.) India was one of the first post-colonial countries with which the USSR established diplomatic relations; besides, diplomatic relations have remained consistently friendly since Stalin's death. This makes for a stable, though not static, ideological line on India in Soviet orientology.

19. The Soviet view of the character of the Congress Party has evolved from the early 1950s (when Nehru was dubbed by Stalin a 'lackey of imperialism') to a much more positive view in the 1970s. See Robert H. Donaldson, *Soviet Policy towards India* (Cambridge, Mass.: Harvard University Press, 1974), pp. 61–266.

20. *Financial Times* (London), 29 September 1982.

21. *Foreign Affairs Record* (Government of India, New Delhi), Vol. 25, 1979, p. 210.

22. Deepak Nayyar, 'India's Trade with Socialist Countries', in D. Nayyar (ed.), *Economic Relations Between Socialist Countries and the Third World* (London: Macmillan, 1977), p. 116.

23. *The Economist* (London), 25 September–1 October 1982, p. 82.

24. R.G. Gidadhubli, 'India in the Soviet Union's Import Trade', *Economic and Political Weekly*, 18 December 1982, p. 2,057.

25. *Ibid.*, p. 2,055.

26. Hungary has clearing agreements with only five LDCs (Bangladesh, Brazil, Colombia, Iran and Pakistan), and Czechoslovakia has such agreements with only three (Bangladesh, India and Iran). Bulgaria makes the vast majority of payments (more than 95 per cent) in relations with LDCs in hard currencies. Where clearing agreements are still operational they have usually been concluded at the request of the LDC concerned. See UNCTAD Secretariat, *Trade Relations Among Countries having Different Economic and Social Systems and All Trade Flows Resulting Therefrom* (Geneva, June 1983), TD/280, p. 18.

27. The share of Soviet trade under clearing agreements in total trade turnover with LDCs has fallen from 78 per cent in 1965 to 73 per cent in 1970, 61 per cent in 1975, and about 33 per cent in 1982. See UNCTAD Secretariat, *Review of the State of Payments between the Socialist Countries of Eastern Europe and Developing Countries* (Geneva, 1977), TD/B/AC.22/2.

28. Asha Datar, *India's Economic Relations with the USSR and Eastern Europe, 1953–69* (Cambridge: Cambridge University Press, 1972), p. 95.

29. Another scarce commodity that the USSR had provided was 2m tonnes of wheat (in 1973–4) to be repaid over a period of five years.

30. The most recent published works on the subject appeared in the late 1970s: R. Banerji, *The Development Impact of Barter in Developing Countries. The Case of India* (OECD Development Centre, Paris, December 1977); O.P. Sharma, 'India's Exports to the East European Countries: Issues and Prospects', *Emerging Opportunities for India's Trade and Economic Cooperation with East Europe* (Proceedings of National Seminar, Indian Institute of Foreign Trade, New Delhi, 1977).

31. R.G. Gidadhubli, *Indo-Soviet Trade: A Study of Select Items of Export from India in the Soviet Market* (Bombay: Semaiya Publications, 1983).

32. These plants account for 80 per cent of India's output of metallurgical equipment; 60 per cent of its heavy electrical equipment; more than half of India's oil production; at least 30 per cent of its refined oil; over a third of its steel output and a fifth of the electricity generated.

33. All Soviet aid to India, as to most LDCs is project aid (as distinct from general-purpose programme aid). As the rate of utilization of project aid has fallen, since not so many Soviet-aided projects were coming up in the 1970s as had done in the 1950s and 1960s there was not much point in the USSR making further commitments of aid.

34. P. Chaudhuri, 'East European Aid to India', in Nayyar (ed.), *Economic Relations*, p. 160.

35. For a detailed discussion of Indo-Soviet trade and Soviet technology transfer to India, see Santosh Mehrotra, 'India's Economic Relations with the USSR' (Ph.D. thesis, University of Cambridge, 1984–5).

36. East European countries have been participating in joint ventures with Indian private-sector firms for a long time. 172 such firms already existed in 1967, with East Germany, Czechoslovakia, Poland and Hungary, in decreasing order of importance, accounting for 117 such agreements between 1964 and 1967. See the Moscow Institute's study for UNCTAD, *Innovations in the Practice of Trade and Economic Cooperation between the Socialist Countries of Eastern Europe and the Developing Countries* (Geneva, 1969), TD/B/238.

13

The Soviet Union and South Yemen: relations with a 'state of socialist orientation'

Fred Halliday

Introduction: no rush to socialism

Soviet relations with South Yemen have developed since it became independent from Britain in 1967, and have led to this Arab state, known since 1970 as the People's Democratic Republic of Yemen (PDRY), becoming perhaps the most consistent and closest ally of the USSR in the Middle East. On many criteria, USSR-PDRY relations are closer than are those of many other states in the region that are also allies of the USSR, such as Syria, Libya and Iraq, and South Yemen has come to occupy a clear and prominent position within the Soviet ranking of Third World countries. It is not one of the Third World states regarded as part of the core bloc: it is not ruled by what the Soviets consider to be a communist party, it is not an actual member of the CMEA, and it has not qualified for the level of Soviet economic aid accorded to core bloc members in the Third World. Only Mongolia, Vietnam, Kampuchea, Laos and Cuba fall into this category, as earlier did China and North Korea. But the PDRY is one of what the Soviets regard as 'states of socialist orientation', states that, while not yet characterized as socialist, are nonetheless seen as laying the groundwork for beginning a transition to socialism. And within this overall category, one that includes nearly two dozen states, South Yemen is part of the upper echelon, comprised of five such countries: Ethiopia, Nicaragua, Angola, Mozambique and the PDRY.[1]

The indices of this alignment are clear in the domestic field. The PDRY has organized its constitutional, legal, political, economic, press, educational and military systems on Soviet models. The 'scientific socialism' taught in the schools and cadre training institutes of the PDRY is based on Soviet textbooks. Recent party congresses have hailed the USSR as the leader of the 'socialist camp'.[2] The ruling Yemeni Socialist Party and the CPSU are linked by several agreements on 'party cooperation'. The USSR and its CMEA associates have provided substantial amounts of the foreign aid received by the PDRY – nearly 50 per cent of total aid disbursed to the PDRY by the end of 1982. In foreign policy, the general lines of alignment are equally evident. The PDRY has a twenty-year Treaty of Friendship and Cooperation with the USSR, and comparable agreements with most other Warsaw Pact states.[3] It has observer status with the CMEA. It has evolved close military ties to the USSR, receiving substantial aid from it, and providing the Soviet fleet and air force with facilities in the north-west Indian Ocean. The PDRY has supported many of the major Soviet foreign policy initiatives of recent years: for example, it is one of the few Third World states to vote consistently with the USSR on Afghanistan in the UN; it withdrew its team from the 1984 Los Angeles Olympic Games; and it has provided troops to an embattled Soviet ally, Ethiopia, across the Red Sea. Its political leaders and press are critical of Western governments on lines that mirror Soviet statements. It has had no diplomatic relations with the USA since it chose to break them in October 1969.

Yet this relationship also has clear limits, on both sides. On the PDRY side, the ruling party has evolved from what was in the 1960s a radical branch of Nasserism, the National Liberation Front (NLF) for Occupied South Yemen.[4] While, in 1975, it merged with a small local pro-Soviet communist party, the Popular Democratic Union, as well as a Ba'thist faction, power has remained very much in the hands of the former NLF leaders. There have been several post-independence disputes but these have revolved around these guerrilla veterans rather than between radical nationalists and communists. Neither in the civilian nor in the military apparatuses of state is power held by what can be seen as a cadre of orthodox pro-Soviet communists. In the constitutional and congress docu-ments of the PDRY, certain clear differences from the practices of the Soviet bloc can be noted: Islam is the official religion, and is taught in schools, in an 'anti-imperialist' version; non-party mem-bers make up around one-third of the membership of the Supreme People's Council, the legislature; and the PDRY's membership of the 'camp' is always matched by proclamations of adherence to the Arab national liberation movement. In economic matters, the divergences from Soviet bloc practice are perhaps more marked. The private sector plays a significant role in the PDRY, in trade and industry. The majority of its external economic transactions are conducted with states of the capitalist world, whether these be via the remittances sent by emigrant workers, which make up at least half of all the PDRY's foreign exchange receipts, or via trade with the developed capitalist countries, which supply the majority of the PDRY's imports.[5] In foreign policy too there are, despite the overall adherence of the PDRY to Soviet positions, a number of significant examples of a distinct stand. The PDRY has never openly criticized China, with whom it has also enjoyed good economic relations. In the Arabian peninsula, the PDRY has been far more consistent and outspoken than the USSR about supporting guerrilla movements in the neighbouring states of Oman and North Yemen. In 1971 there was a particularly marked divergence of Soviet and South Yemeni foreign policies when Aden waged an energetic campaign to prevent the admission of four Gulf states — Bahrain, Qatar, the Emirates and Oman — to the United Nations. When it came to the vote in the UN, the PDRY stood alone in opposing their entry: the USSR, and its associated delegations in the UN, not only voted for the admission of all four, but on each occasion made a speech of welcome to the representatives of states whom Aden considered to be still under British colonial domination. The most revered goal of PDRY foreign policy, unity with North Yemen (the Yemeni Arab Republic – YAR), is also one that Moscow has been careful not to endorse. In Arab affairs too there have been divergences on sensitive matters: the USSR has always, since 1948, favoured a two-state solution to the Israel-Palestine conflict, whereas the PDRY has endorsed the common position of the Arab left, which denies the legitimacy of a separate Israeli state. The two states have also disagreed on the issue of Western Sahara: the PDRY, like Cuba, has recognized the Saharan guerrillas' claims to be a legitimate state, the Saharan Arab Democratic Republic, a position that contrasts with the Soviet refusal to do so.

Some reserve can also be noted on the Soviet side, at both the policy and theoretical levels. When South Yemen became independent, the USSR was quick to proclaim good wishes, and to provide some economic and military aid. But the USSR was evidently quite sceptical about this new radical regime in the further corner of the Arabian peninsula. Soviet commentators stressed the dire nature of the economic problems facing the country, and warned against unwarrantedly radical attempts to move towards socialism. With a population of around 1.5 million, low and falling *per capita* income and no known natural resources, South Yemen was not an attractive economic option. A Soviet analysis of 1970 warned of the dangers of a rightist trend, and of a leftist one. The latter, it said 'is represented by leaders who are impatient to leap over all the stages of the revolution in one go, who wish to nationalise everything on co-operative lines in the hope of smashing the production relations formed through the centuries and the habits of people in one or two years. *They expect to build socialism with these largely illiterate people.* In reality following such a policy can only ruin the economy utterly and undermine the faith of the people in socialist principles.'[6] Soviet commentaries in 1975 talked of 'the need to take the real potential of the young republic into the fullest possible account and to prevent any arbitrary speeding up of objective social and economic processes'.[7] This same commentary went on to say that the PDRY was now going through a 'national democratic revolution', one in which the foundation for 'a future progressive developed modern state' was being laid: the implication was that the PDRY was definitely *not* in a transition to socialism itself.

There were several political reasons for Soviet caution. First, the Russians were from the late 1960s onwards sceptical about the claims of radical Arab nationalists: their experience in Syria, Iraq, Egypt and, later, Libya and Somalia all suggested that radical Arab regimes were dangerous allies, all too prone to veer from risky confrontations with the West to unprincipled accommodations with the foes of the USSR. Second, the Russians had had little direct contact with the NLF during the independence struggle. They had no clear idea of whom to work with in South Yemen and the factionalism that persisted after 1967 inside the National Front, later the Yemeni Socialist Party (YSP), made it the more difficult to assess the situation. The economic weakness of the PDRY and the prevalence of tribal factors made Soviet observers even more sceptical. Third, the Russians were concerned about what they saw as an 'ultra-left' trend in South Yemen, one that ran the risk of creating many problems: internally, by exacerbating an already weak economic situation, and externally by allying with China against the USSR, and, simultaneously, provoking Western intervention in the Arabian peninsula. Fourth, the USSR had other strategic and political interests in the region, not least in the YAR, which it had supported militarily during the civil war of the 1960s. While it evidently favoured the PDRY as against the North, it was not willing to sacrifice its position in the YAR entirely and back the PDRY in its attempts to change the government of the North by force.

These practical concerns were, however, compounded by the theoretical ones, about what kind of revolution had occurred in the PDRY and what policies the regime should pursue. For all its phrasing in what appear to be rigid and woodenly predictable terms, Soviet literature on Third World societies is usually marked by a strong dose of realism about what is not possible, as well as what is. Historically, this derives from the classic Marxist view of the socio-economic prerequisites for political processes. The Soviet experience in Central Asia has provided a set of practical lessons and models that also stress the need for caution in socio-economic transformation.[8] More recently Soviet relations with the Third World have, in addition, taught more than enough lessons to Soviet analysts about the limits, difficulties, ideological residues and possible reverses contained within the revolutionary processes of the Third World.[9] If to this cautious, at times bluntly pessimistic, view of what Third World radical states can achieve is added the limited Soviet ability to provide either military guarantees or substantial economic aid to all but core bloc members, then it becomes clearer why the theory of 'socialist orientation', evolved in the 1970s, serves such a dual role, both legitimizing and prudent. It is designed to justify the kind of commitment which the USSR has been prepared to make to these states and at the same time to restrain the policies and expectations of radical Third World states. Yuri Andropov's June 1983 warning on the need for the states of socialist orientation to rely on their own economic resources spelt out the Soviet view.

To review Soviet-South Yemen relations in this light may serve a number of analytic purposes. First, it can be of comparative interest, in showing how the PDRY, along with a number of other revolutionary Third World states, has been assisted and, to a considerable degree, transformed by the alliance with the USSR in recent years. Second, it can show from what general premisses Soviet actions in South Yemen itself have been derived. Soviet policy towards the PDRY is not just the product of local, south Arabian, considerations or of the strategic location of the PDRY. Third, it can help to explain what may otherwise appear to be the anomalies in military and economic ties, the Soviet reluctance to back the PDRY economically to the extent the Yemenis have desired, and the apparent Soviet acceptance, even encouragement, of greater ties between the PDRY and the capitalist economies, and of the 'normalization' of the PDRY's relations with the conservative states of the Arabian peninsula.

The development of an alliance

The history of Soviet-South Yemeni relations can be seen as falling into three broad periods – from independence to the Fifth Congress of the NF, in 1972; from 1972 until the resignation of President Abdul Fatah Ismail in April 1980; and the presidency of Ali Nasser Mohammad, from 1980 onwards. The first involved the establishment of the basic elements of the Soviet-PDRY alliance. In the second the alliance was greatly strengthened, but in a manner that was not sustainable. The third saw a continuation of the alliance, with certain significant modifications.

Diplomatic relations between Aden and Moscow were established in December 1967, soon after independence, and the first South Yemeni delegations visited the USSR in February 1968, led by Minister of Defence Ali al-Beedh.[10] A Soviet military delegation arrived in March 1968, and in August a Technical and Military Assistance Agreement was signed. During 1968 and 1969 significant quantities of Soviet military equipment were received in South Yemen, and the armed forces were largely re-equipped, with Soviet material replacing that of the British-trained army left behind at independence.

In February 1969 President Qahtan al-Sha'abi visited the USSR and signed an Economic and Technical Assistance Agreement. Under this the USSR agreed to help create a modern fishing industry, and to provide higher education for Yemenis in the USSR.[11] With the replacement of al-Sha'abi by the more militant Salem Robea Ali in June 1969, and the subsequent nationalization of virtually all foreign economic enterprises in the country, with the exception of the BP refinery, Soviet comment on developments in South Yemen was generally favourable. In 1970 an agreement on party cooperation between the CPSU and the NF was signed, and when South Yemen proclaimed a new constitution in 1970, enshrining the 'national democratic' character of the current phase of the revolution, this was also positively reported by the Soviet press.[12] In 1971 and 1972 further military and economic agreements were signed, culminating in a new Economic and Scientific-Technical Cooperation Agreement of November 1972, under which the USSR agreed to construct a thermal power station in Aden and a hospital, and to assist in geological surveys.[13] By February 1972 Tass reported that around thirty small-scale projects promised in the earlier, 1969, Agreement had been completed.[14]

The Fifth Congress of the NF in 1972 and the visit of President Salem Robea Ali to the USSR later in the year appeared to indicate that some of the initial worries of the Soviet leadership about the PDRY were unfounded. The influence of the 'leftist' and 'pro-Chinese' elements in the NF had been contained, the new regime had built up armed forces capable of guaranteeing the stability of the state, and the Front was gradually adopting appropriate 'national democratic' policies. The first, three-year, plan covered the period 1971–4, and a first Five-Year plan spanned 1974–8. Western influence in the internal affairs of the PDRY was minimal, and the PDRY had apparently gone further than Nasserism in Egypt or the Ba'thi regimes of Iraq and Syria in adopting 'scientific socialism'. In 1975 the ruling NF expanded to include two smaller parties, the pro-Soviet communist group, the Popular Democratic Union, and the left-wing Ba'thist Vanguard Party, and by the mid-1970s the Front's programme called for the 'creation of a party of a new type', a reference to the Leninist programme for creating a Bolshevik organization.

Yet this process of transformation of the PDRY was not carried out without its surprises and reverses. For within the Front itself there were divisions over how far this process should go, with one faction, led by President Salem Robea Ali, favouring a more spontaneous and independent path of change, while that around Secretary-General Abdul Fatah Ismail favoured fuller adoption of the Soviet line. Although not sympathetic to the West, Salem Robea Ali did hope to use Saudi money to maintain a margin of manoeuvre *vis-à-vis* the USSR. The crisis came to a head in June 1978. Outvoted by a majority of the Central Committee, Salem Robea Ali attempted to stage a coup, but was defeated and crushed after some hours of fighting in Aden.[15] In October the founding congress of the 'party of the new type', the Yemeni Socialist Party, was held, and later in the year Abdul Fatah Ismail became president. In 1979 the PDRY signed a twenty year Treaty of Friendship and Cooperation with the USSR, acquired observer status at the CMEA, and raised its level of military cooperation with the USSR.[16] Increased commitments of Soviet economic trade aid were also made in agreements of June 1979 and December 1980. Soviet commentators commented favourably on the outcome of the June 1978 crisis. Salem Robea Ali was accused of both 'left' and 'right' deviations, of an excessively voluntarist and accelerated approach to economic and social change, and of being in touch with right-wing governments abroad. After 1978 it also became possible for Soviet analysts to comment more explicitly on what they saw as the failings of the South Yemeni economy. They mentioned, in particular, the 'left-extremist' measures taken in agriculture and the antagonistic attitude adopted to small traders.[17]

The accession of Abdul Fatah Ismail to the presidency in November 1978 did not, however, produce a new, enduring, pattern of Soviet-PDRY relations, and in April 1980 he was forced to resign as president and secretary-general to give way to Ali Nasser Mohammad, prime minister since 1971. The official reason for Abdul Fatah's resignation was ill-health, and he went into exile in Moscow where he remained, as a guest of the Central Committee of the CPSU, until his return to an honorific party position in 1985. The real reasons for Abdul Fatah's fall were that he had proven himself to be an incompetent administrator, and had placed too great an emphasis upon the aid which the relationship with the USSR would bring. Economic problems, particularly in energy and consumer goods, worsened in Aden in the late 1970s, and Abdul Fatah was blamed for these. His successor adopted a more successful approach, and the Emergency Congress of the YSP in October 1980 stressed the need to raise popular living standards. In the early 1980s a number of economic restrictions were lifted:

emigration to the oil states, virtually frozen since 1974, was permitted again, and the number of migrants rose from around 125,000 to 210,000. A private construction industry was allowed to develop. More consumer goods were imported. Some emigrants were allowed convertible foreign exchange accounts in local banks, at preferential interest rates. And, in an attempt to boost agricultural output, farmers were allowed to sell up to 40 per cent of their output of ten products at 150 per cent of the official prices. The result was that supplies of goods in the cities greatly increased, and the overall discontent over economic conditions in the country apparently eased. In the period 1973–9 GDP grew at an average rate of 8 per cent p.a. GDP *per capita* in 1980 stood at $380.[18]

This loosening of controls on the economic front went together with improved relations with a number of Arab states. In North Yemen, a pro-Saudi state ruled by conservative coalitions with which the PDRY fought border wars in 1972 and 1979, anti-government guerrillas in the National Democratic Front were defeated in early 1982, and this led to some rapprochement between the two Yemeni states. After many years of conflict the PDRY and Oman established diplomatic relations in October 1982. Relations with Saudi Arabia also improved. But, although there were many reports in the West that the PDRY was in some way 'moving away from' the USSR, the evidence did not support this. Rather, Soviet commentators welcomed the relaxation of tensions in the PDRY's foreign relations, and the more prosperous economic situation in the country. Ali Nasser Mohammad maintained close contacts with the USSR and in no way questioned the links established by his predecessors. Almost complete military reliance on the USSR for supplies, a 'national democratic' orientation in domestic political and social policies, and a diversified economic orientation remained the hallmarks of the PDRY's policies. It appeared to be a more stable domestic combination than that of presidents Salem Robea Ali or Abdul Fatah Ismail, and one that was better suited to relations between the USSR and the PDRY as well.

Economic relations
Given the position of South Yemen as a distant, poor and still 'national democratic' state, it is inevitable that economic issues should have a limited place in the overall complex of Soviet-South Yemeni relations. Strategic-military and political ties were of prime importance for both parties. Yet a close and revealing economic relationship did develop, as can be seen by examining Soviet economic policies towards the PDRY in three areas: trade, aid and assessment.

Since 1967, South Yemeni trade has been continuously and massively in deficit. In the latter part of the 1970s and early 1980s imports were more than ten times exports, with workers' remittances and capital outflows from abroad covering the difference. South Yemen imports significant quantities of food – up to a third of the total value of goods imported – and exports cotton, fish, and animal hides. At independence, the Soviet Union was an insignificant trading partner, accounting for less than 1 per cent of total imports. After 1967 this rose somewhat, to around 4 per cent of the total in 1980, with the CMEA states as a whole comprising around 6 per cent of the PDRY's imports. Yet this total was small compared to that of the PDRY's major trading partners, who remained, as they had been before 1967, the larger industrialized capitalist states – Japan, Britain, France. As a whole these provided in 1980 over 60 per cent of the PDRY's imports, a high percentage roughly equal to that of pre-independence days.[19]

Soviet data do not give proportional evaluations of Soviet trade, but they do provide some gross figures that enable an assessment to be made. The trade total in 1968 was 1.3m roubles and, after the 1969 agreement, the annual total rose from 7m roubles in 1970 to 15m roubles in 1974.[20] By 1978 the total had reached 30m roubles. Following negotiations in 1978 and 1979; an important new agreement on long-run trade between the two countries was signed in June 1979 under which trade between them was to be substantially increased and in December 1980 an agreement for the five-year period to 1985 was signed. Trade then rose considerably. The total for 1982 was 73m roubles, doubling in 1983 to 141m roubles.[21] This trade was, however, very much a one-way process: thus of the 1983 total of 141m roubles, 136m roubles represented Soviet exports to the PDRY and only 5m roubles represented Yemeni exports to the USSR. A breakdown by commodity of Soviet exports indicates that over three-quarters consisted of machinery equipment and transport goods. Other components included cement, reinforced steel, petroleum products, timber, glass, furniture, clothing, sugar and other consumer goods. South Yemen's exports included fish meal, fish oil, frozen fish and cotton.[22] It is evident from these figures that Soviet exports were to a considerable extent directed at assisting the capital investment process of the PDRY, especially in construction and industry, but the supplies of oil to the Aden refinery, later despatched to Vietnam, helped to keep the Republic's largest industrial plant in operation.

Figures for aid are less available from the Soviet side. Soviet aid has covered three areas: agriculture, fishing and industry.[23] In the agricultural sector, Soviet aid has been concentrated on improving irrigation facilities, especially in the eastern, Hadramaut, province. Water surveys, irrigation pumps and canals have been the main elements of this aid. In fishing, the USSR has promised to provide fishing vessels, a fish canning plant at Mukalla, equipment and technical training. A joint Soviet-Yemeni fishing company has also been formed. In industry the USSR has provided a cement factory, the 125 MW thermal energy complex, and a water purification plant. The Soviet Union also constructed a hospital in Aden with 300 beds, for women and children. Building on the 1969 educational agreement, extensive links have also been established in the field of education, with several hundred PDRY students studying at any one time in the USSR.[24]

Soviet writing on aid, as is conventional in such reports, insists on the benefits which the USSR has brought to such a Third World ally. Perhaps to reassure Soviet readers sceptical of Arab constancy, stress is often laid on the 'gratitude' and 'appreciation' shown by the Yemenis.[25] Soviet writers also bring out a practical point of some importance in evaluating aid to the PDRY, namely the fact that it assists South Yemen in its hard-currency earnings. The agricultural aid is not, in the main, of this kind: this is an area of import substitution, designed to improve supplies to the domestic market. Aid to the fishing industry, by contrast, is located in the main export sector, since exports of shell-fish and other delicacies, mainly to Japan, have become the PDRY's main export earner since independence, overtaking cotton. Figures for 1980 give the PDRY's earnings from its own fishing as $6.2m, or about 60 per cent of total PDRY export earnings.[26]

As a total of aid received since independence, the Soviet figure is very significant, but not overwhelming. UN figures up to 31 December 1980 give a total figure of disbursed aid of $499m, of which $153m came from the USSR, and another $63m from four other CMEA countries – the GDR, Hungary, Czechoslovakia and Bulgaria. This yielded a CMEA total of $216m. China provided another $84m and the majority of the rest came from multilateral Arab sources or from the International Development Association and the IMF.[27] Figures for the end of 1982 gave total debt owed to the USSR and Eastern Europe as $389m, 48 per cent of the total of $817m.[28] Figures for 1984 suggested that Eastern bloc aid as a whole represented around 50 per cent of the total funds used in investment in the PDRY for the 1983–4 financial year: another 20 per cent came from international organizations, 17 per cent from Arab sources, and the remaining 13 per cent from local sources.[29]

Qualitative assessment of this Soviet aid is even more difficult than is its quantitative assessment. Soviet loans are generally agreed to be on favourable terms, with interest rates at 3–5 per cent p.a., and to run for a ten-year period, often with deferred repayment periods. This is more favourable than terms for most international loans or for loans from Arab sources. Some Soviet-PDRY agreements have involved rouble loans to be repaid in Yemeni dinars, which the USSR will then use to purchase Yemeni goods. Other agreements have involved the supply by the USSR of equipment and spare parts to be repaid by the PDRY in freely convertible currency.[30] While official Yemeni commentary upon such economic relations with the USSR is predictably favourable, informal assessments are less uniform. The training of PDRY specialists in the USSR appears to have been welcomed and contrasts well with an experience of British rule in which education was largely confined to the cities and almost no South Yemenis went to university. Soviet assistance in agriculture has, on occasion, been criticised as of a lower quality than that of the West, and there has been considerable friction over the fishing agreements, with Soviet trawler captains being accused of overstepping their rights. However, the greatest issue of disagreement has been over the al-Hizwa power plant: initially promised in 1972, it had not been started at the time of serious power cuts in 1979. Both sides have blamed the other for inefficiency in failing to implement the programme.[31] In overall terms, however, it would seem that Soviet-bloc aid, which represents up to half of the total received by the PDRY, has made an indispensable contribution to the Republic's economic development.

Soviet influence on the South Yemenis has gone beyond trade and aid. Soviet advisers are present in their hundreds in the PDRY, and the thousands of South Yemenis trained in the USSR and Eastern Europe have tended to reproduce Soviet patterns of planning and organization. Yet Soviet commentators have also maintained a cautious position in their assessment of the PDRY economy as a whole. They have time and again stressed the limited productive potential of the country, the shortage of specialized cadres and the small size of the population. Soviet writers also lay considerable stress on the social and ideological difficulties facing the PDRY – 'petty-bourgeois' tendencies among the working class, tribalism, absence of the requisite work ethic, the lack of a sufficient level of 'national-ethic consolidation' and so forth. Moreover, in warning of the dangers of 'leftist' policies, they also explicitly reject what they consider to be two 'leftist' criticisms of current PDRY policies – the role of the private sector and the ties to the capitalist world. In their view, neither the current level of development of the

PDRY, nor the aid capabilities of the Soviet Union itself, make any more accelerated moves towards socialism viable.[32] Yet awareness of these limits has not prevented the USSR and other CMEA states from increasing their commitment to the PDRY in recent years. The major increase in Soviet trade to the PDRY – which doubled between 1982 and 1983 alone – and the substantial increase in Soviet aid disbursed in the early 1980s suggest that the cautious economic policies pursued by the PDRY have reassured Soviet economic policy makers more than the loud professions of revolutionary commitment of the first post-independence years.

The limits of involvement

Relations between the Soviet Union and the PDRY in general, have illustrated the manner in which such ties, between the USSR and a non-communist Third World revolutionary state, can develop and the reasons why they remain limited. In the military sphere the PDRY is almost wholly reliant upon Soviet supplies and none of the last three PDRY presidents has sought to alter that. The volume and terms of this Soviet military aid are not known, but must be larger than the economic aid. The political integration, formally expressed in the rituals of the Soviet bloc – visits, delegations, anniversary and congratulatory telegrams, conferences, conveying of medals, and inter-party agreements – has also given the USSR a special position within the PDRY. The Yemeni Socialist Party, with a membership of 24,000, is a conventional Soviet-style organization.[33] In economic matters, the situation is rather different. The USSR and its allies have provided about half of all the aid received by the PDRY since independence, but this has been controversial in quality, less than the Yemenis have required, and, at around $400m over fifteen years, is small when measured against the overall scale of Soviet aid to Third World states. Soviet trade has helped in the economic development of some sectors of South Yemen, but it has represented a small part of the PDRY's total imports, and at least some of the Soviet trade surplus has been paid for in hard currency earned by the emigrant workers. The Soviet Unions's trade with the PDRY is far less than its trade with many other Arab states.[34] The most interesting feature of Soviet-PDRY economic relations is perhaps the manner in which these have expanded greatly in the early 1980s, just as the PDRY's relations with the Arab states have also grown. The USSR appears to feel confident that the changes introduced by President Ali Nasser Mohammad will not undermine its own position in the PDRY. As much as strategy and revolutionary solidarity, realism and commercially sound agreements have served to restrict, and then to develop, the USSR's relations with this 'state of socialist orientation' in south-west Arabia.

Notes

1. The status and distinct position of this group is evident from, for example, the listing of guests attending Leonid Brezhnev's funeral in November 1982 (*Soviet News*, 17 November 1982). Afghanistan is also included in this group, but this is not meant to indicate that Afghanistan is only a 'state of socialist orientation': it is ruled by an orthodox communist party, the People's Democratic Party of Afghanistan.

2. As, for example, in the resolutions of the 1980 Emergency Congress of the Yemeni Socialist Party (*al-Mo'tamar al-'Istithna'i lil-Hizb al-Ishtiraki al-Yamani*) (Beirut: Dar Ibn Khaldun, n.d), p. 452.

3. Text of the October 1979 Treaty in *Soviet News*, 13 November 1979. As with other such Soviet treaties, no commitment to military support in the event of an attack upon the other is included. But, since the late 1970s, Soviet commentators have stated that the PDRY is 'not alone' in its conflicts with 'imperialist' forces.

4. On the history of the NLF see my *Arabia without Sultans* (Harmondsworth: Penguin, 1974); Joseph Kostiner, *The Struggle for South Yemen* (London: Croom Helm, 1984); and Vitali Naumkin, *al-Jabha al-Qaumia fi Kifah min ajl-Istiqlal al-Yaman al-Junubia wa al-Dimoqratiya al-Watania* (Moscow: Progress Publishers, 1984). The National Liberation Front was known as the NLF between 1963 and 1967 and as the NF between 1967 and 1978.

5. On the South Yemeni economy see World Bank, *People's Democratic Republic of Yemen, A Review of Economic and Social Development* (Washington, D.C., March 1979), and World Bank, *PDRY-Economic Memorandum* (Washington, D.C., January 1982), 3 570 YDR.

6. A. Vasilyev, 'Visiting South Yemen', *New Times*, No. 3, 1970, p. 29.

7. I. Alexandrov, 'Democratic Yemen, Towards Unity of the National Forces', *New Times*, No. 42, 1985, p. 16.

8. For example, in an article that discusses the changing position of women, Soviet experience in Central Asia is invoked (Y. Gvozdev, 'Democratic Yemen Forges Ahead', *International Affairs*, No. 10, 1974, p. 126).

9. The theory of the 'states of socialist orientation' is elaborated in Veniamin Churkin, *A State of Socialist Orientation* (Moscow: Progress Publishers, 1979). Yuri Andropov's speech of June 1983 gave an authoritative summary of the official Soviet view: 'Most close to us in the former colonial world are countries which have chosen socialist orientation. We and those countries are brought together not only by anti-imperialist peaceful goals in foreign policy, but also by common ideals of social justice and progress. We see, of course, both the complexity of their position and the difficulties of their revolutionary development. It is one thing to proclaim socialism as one's goal and quite another thing to build it. A certain level of productive forces, culture and social consciousness are needed for that.' (*Soviet News*, 18 June 1983).

10. BBC, *Summary of World Broadcasts*, Soviet Union (hereafter SU)/2690/A4/1, SU/2694/A4/2.

11. *New Times*, Nos. 5 and 7, 1969.

12. O. Orestov, 'Dawn over the Desert', *Pravda*, 26 December 1970, translated in *Current Digest of the Soviet Press* (hereafter CDSP), Vol. 22, No. 52.

13. *Pravda*, 25 November 1972, in *CDSP*, Vol. 24, No. 47.

14. BBC, ME/W660/A1/6.

15. I have gone into this in greater detail in 'Yemen's Unfinished Revolution', *MERIP Reports*, No. 81 (Washington, D.C., October 1979).

16. *Pravda*, 25 October 1979, in *CDSP*, Vol. 31, No. 43.

17. For an example of Soviet criticism of 'left' policies in the PDRY, see Alexei Chistyakov, 'PDRY, Towards Consolidation of Economy', *Asia and Africa Today*, No. 1, 1980.

18. According to World Bank figures made available to me.

19. PDRY, Central Statistical Office, *Statistical Yearbook, 1980*, Table I/XI, pp. 157–60.

20. V.N. Burmistrov, *Narodnaya Demokraticheskaya Respublika Yemen, Ekono-mika i Torgovo-ekonomicheskia Otnosheniya* (Moscow: Nauka, 1981), pp. 135–6.

21. *Vneshnyaya Torgolya SSSR*, No. 12, 1983.

22. Burmistrov, *Narodnaya*, p. 137 and V. Kutuzov, 'SSSR-Idri, Novii Realnosti i Perspektivi', *Vneshnyaya Torgolya*, No. 5, 1980.

23. For a Soviet analysis of this aid programme see V.V. Naumkin, *Narodnaya Demokraticheskaya Respublika Yemen* (Moscow: Znanie, 1982), pp. 52–3.

24. World Bank, *People's Democratic Republic of Yemen*, Table 12.8 gives a figure of 822 students in higher education abroad for 1975–7: of these 286 were in the USSR, and 305 in other Eastern European countries and Cuba.

25. See, e.g., Orestov, 'Dawn over the Desert'.

26. World Bank, *Memorandum*, 1982.

27. *Ibid.*, p. 30.

28. *Middle East Economic Digest*, 20 April 1984.

29. *Ibid.*

30. Thus the protocol of 4 June 1978 on delivery of equipment and spare parts stipulated that repayment should be over a ten-year period and in dollars.

31. The USSR restated its commitment to implementing this project in 1980 and increased the projected capacity of the plant. Considerable comment was provoked in Aden to the effect that while it had apparently taken the Russians eight years to start this project a Japanese firm had completed the construction of a plant in eighteen months. Soviet officials put the blame on the incompetence of Yemeni officials appointed by Salem Robea Ali.

32. See, for example, Vassily Ozoling and Ruben Andreasyan, 'Some Problems Arising in the Process of the Non-Capitalist Development of the PDRY', paper presented to Conference on the Contemporary Yemens, Centre for Arab Gulf Studies, Exeter University, July 1983.

33. Alexander Guskov, in *New Times*, No. 49, 1982.

34. The figure for Soviet-PDRY trade of 141m roubles in 1983, double that of 1982, contrasts with figures of 169m roubles for trade with Saudi Arabia, 505m roubles for trade with Syria, 612m roubles for trade with Egypt and 760m roubles for trade with Iraq in 1983 (*Vneshnyaya Torgolya*, December 1983).

14
The Soviet Union in the Middle East: a case study of Syria

Kassem M. Ja'far

Aspects of Soviet Middle East policy: an overview
In order to understand Soviet policy towards the Middle East,* it is necessary first to determine Moscow's goals in the region. This poses, however, a major problem which has traditionally faced attempts at analysing Soviet attitudes and objectives not only in the Middle East, but in other parts of the Third World as well. There is no way of knowing what expectations Soviet leaders have for a particular policy, though guesses and estimates abound. Soviet leaders are not usually in the habit of telling us what they are after, and they are certainly less than candid about the considerations which might prompt specific policies. Given Moscow's far-ranging and increasingly clear pursuit of a number of simultaneous objectives in the Third World generally and the Middle East in particular – from strengthening anti-Western governments to acquiring military facilities, from exploiting US policy dilemmas and initiatives to aspiring to the former British role of arbiter of regional conflicts, from encouraging radical movements to undermining pro-Western governments and attempts by the United States to fashion its Pax Americana in the various regional conflicts (of which the Arab-Israeli dispute is but the most prominent) – the task of identifying Soviet policies and aims, and consequently the successes and failures of those policies, becomes extremely complex.

What, then, is the appropriate level of analysis at which to evaluate Soviet policy in the Middle East? Observers of Moscow's attitude in this oil-rich, strategically located and highly volatile region are generally divided into two schools of thought on the question. While both agree that the Soviet Union wants to be considered a major factor in Middle Eastern affairs, if only because

---

* For the purpose of this study, the 'Middle East' is defined in its broadest geographic and political sense: the Arab countries of south-west Asia and North Africa, Afghanistan, Iran, Turkey, Israel and, in the Horn of Africa, Ethiopia and Somalia. Not only does this area appear to possess geographic continuity, but, more important, in terms of the policies of world powers, it seems to be perceived by decision makers in the Soviet Union as well as in the United States as a single and integral strategic concern.

of its proximity to the area, they differ on the ultimate Soviet goal in the Middle East. One school of thought sees Moscow's Middle Eastern policy as being primarily defensive in nature: that is, directed towards preventing the region from being used as a base for military attack or political subversion against the USSR. The other tends to see it as primarily offensive: that is, aimed at limiting and ultimately excluding Western influence from the region. Both contain a certain, even equal, element of truth: it is my opinion that Soviet goals in the Middle East, at least since the mid-1970s, have been largely defensive and limited. In the Arab segment of the Middle East in particular, the Soviet Union appears to have been engaged in a fierce and to a great extent fruitless competition for influence with the United States.

Although the USSR has invested heavily in the Middle East, its policy has been basically a negative one, being directed mainly at limiting Western (particularly American) influence in the region. Soviet diplomatic initiatives have been limited at best. While the Soviet Union has been able to sell military hardware to some Arab states, it has been unable to induce the elite of the area to adjust their policies to meet Soviet foreign policy goals. Hence, the Middle East has become the scene of some rather important Soviet foreign policy setbacks.

The extent and gravity of the problems which have faced the USSR in the Middle East could be best described in a historical as well as a strategic context. In its efforts to weaken Western influence in the region and particularly in the Arab world while promoting Soviet influence, Moscow has employed a number of tactics. First and foremost has been the supply of military aid to its regional friends. Next in importance has been economic aid, with the Aswan dam in Egypt and the Euphrates dam in Syria providing prominent examples of Soviet economic assistance, although each project has had its own share of serious problems. In recent years Moscow has also sought to consolidate its influence through the conclusion of long-term Friendship and Cooperation Treaties such as the ones concluded with Egypt (1971), Iraq (1972), Somalia (1974), Ethiopia (1978), Afghanistan (1978), South Yemen (1979), and more recently with Syria (1980). However, the repudiation of the treaties by Egypt (1976) and Somalia (1977) and the practical non-existence of the treaty with Iraq, as has been shown in effect during the continuous conflict with Iran (1980–   ), indicate that this has not been too successful a tactic. In addition, the Soviets have offered the Arabs diplomatic support at such international forums as the United Nations and the now suspended Geneva Conference on an Arab-Israeli peace settlement. However, both its diplomatic and military aid to the Arabs against Israel have been limited in scope, and Moscow continues to support Israel's right to exist, both for fear of unduly alienating the United States and because Israel serves as a convenient rallying point for potentially anti-Western forces in the Arab World.[1]

The shortcomings of all these tactics were becoming increasingly obvious to the USSR. In the first place, the numerous inter-Arab and regional conflicts (Syria-Iraq, Iraq-Iran, Syria-Jordan, North Yemen-South Yemen, Ethiopia-Somalia, Algeria-Morocco, Egypt-Libya, Libya-Sudan, etc.) have usually meant that when the USSR has favoured one party, it has alienated the other, often driving it towards the West. Second, the existence of Arab communist parties has proven to be more of a liability than an asset for Moscow, as communist activities have, on many occasions, caused a sharp deterioration in relations between the USSR and the country in which the Arab communist party has operated.[2] This brings to attention the important question related to the nature and attitudes of those regimes with which the Soviets have had to deal ever since their introduction into regional Arab politics. Such regimes, though usually termed 'radical' or 'progressive', were constituted mostly of middle-class army officers sharing an intensely anti-communist feeling. Nasser in Egypt, Colonel Qaddafi in Libya, and the two Ba'thist regimes of presidents Hussain of Iraq and Assad of Syria are all clear examples of this phenomenon, the only notable exception perhaps being that of South Yemen, where local communists are actively involved in the government.[3] Third, the wealth which flowed to the Arab world (or at least to its major oil producers) since the early 1970s has enabled the Arabs to look to the West and Japan for technology, and this has helped weaken the economic bond between the USSR and a number of 'radical' Arab states such as Iraq, Syria, Algeria and Libya. Fourth, since 1967 and particularly since the 1973 Arab-Israeli war, Islam has been resurgent throughout the Arab world, and the USSR, identified in the Middle East with atheism, has as a result had its hands tied. Finally, the United States and to a lesser extent such West European countries as France have actively opposed Soviet efforts to achieve predominant influence in the region and this has frequently enabled Middle Eastern states to play the extra-regional powers off against each other, thereby preventing any one of them from securing predominant influence.

Given the problems that the USSR has faced, Moscow could only adopt one overall and rather 'flexible' strategy to maximize its influence while weakening that of the West. While eagerly seeking to expand its presence among the so-called 'progressive' Arab regimes, it continued to give a much higher priority to stable relations with the industrialized West than to destabilizing and quasi-revolutionary activities in the Middle East.[4] On the whole, it may be proper to characterize Soviet interests and constraints in the Middle East, particularly after 1973, as reflecting a long-range investment of resources, albeit with little prospect of immediate dividends – a policy of non-provocative and gradual penetration into societies which might be potentially receptive because of partial ideological congruence (at least as far as anti-Western feelings are concerned), dependence on Soviet arms and credits or sheer desperation resulting from looming defeat in the wars against Israel. Soviet policy was challenged to manoeuvre between the fear of superpower confrontation and the ideological, political, economic, and strategic lures of the volatility and stability inherent in the Middle East.[5]

Specifically, the policy of the Soviet Union was to support radical and 'progressive' regimes and movements in the region, link them under the Soviet aegis in anti-imperialist, anti-Western entities, make them dependent on the USSR, and finally try to shape and influence their domestic and foreign policies to conform with its own. Above all, the Soviet Union sought to avoid situations in which it would lose control over events while being forced to maintain or even increase its presence and commitments. *Faits accomplis* by its clients, blackmail, and catalytic developments were to be avoided at any cost; excessive Arab offensive strategic strength was thus to be avoided as well as excessive Arab vulnerability to Israeli offensive superiority. Either one of these contingencies could provoke violent confrontation ('wars of anni-hilation') between the local protagonists, with superpower involve-ment becoming inevitable. Since the Soviet Union clearly preferred a protracted stalemate in the area – either through a peace process in which it would be actively involved, or through a continuation of a state of 'no war, no peace' – it used its influence to shape the regional military and political balance and its friends' national capabilities and strategies to conform with this primary objective.

The Soviets were never short on scepticism or even criticism of their Arab friends. They found it difficult to accept such leaders as Sadat, Assad, or Qaddafi, who hardly fit the Leninist revolutionary mould. They were painfully aware of the drain on their resources in the seemingly boundless quagmire of Eygpt and Syria, and of the corrupt and inefficient Arab bureaucracies charged with managing Soviet aid. The Soviet military, while coveting Arab naval and air bases, were openly contemptuous of their Arab allies and found them poorly trained, poorly disciplined and utterly unreliable.

Soviet diplomats and leaders considered their Arab counterparts unpredictable and disloyal.[6]

Arab feelings towards their Soviet allies have not been very dissimilar. The Arabs viewed Soviet military aid as totally inadequate, with disastrous consequences on the battlefield against the Western-supplied Israelis. The Arab military never tried to hide their belief that Soviet weapons were much inferior to those being provided to Israel by the United States. They even questioned Soviet attitudes and practices being followed by the resident advisers working with the Arab armies. Not only Egyptian officers but also their Syrian counterparts frequently referred to these advisers as conceited, arrogant and virtually ignorant of the real needs of the Arabs facing Israel. Moreover, Soviet political and strategic aspirations in the region were becoming increasingly unpopular, even among some of their ostensibly staunch allies.[7] While remaining a source of military hardware, the Soviet Union exerted very little influence, if any, on the cultural, ideological, political, or economic inclinations of its Arab clients. Despite all the usual rhetoric, actual policies of Arab states towards the Soviet Union throughout the past twenty-five years have consistently reflected a belief that the whole of their military and political relationship with Moscow has been much more a matter of urgent needs dictated by the lack of suitable alternatives than one initiated through deliberate choice or design.[8]

The conflict with Israel was the single important issue upon which the otherwise feuding Arab countries could unite. No Arab ruler who aspired to a position of prominent power at home and in the Arab world could afford to compromise on his opposition to Israel. On the other hand, no Arab army could prove itself a match to its Israeli counterpart on the battlefield. The establishment of the state of Israel in 1948 provided the Arabs with the first example of their vulnerability, and this situation was aggravated by a series of clashes which took place during the early 1950s, all ending clearly in Israel's favour. When the Egyptian army suffered such a defeat in a clash which occurred in Gaza in February 1955, President Nasser came under mounting pressure from his officers to acquire weapons that would match Israeli equipment. His dependence on the support of the officer corps became an additional motivation for an intensified search for arms. Britain offered only token support; France refused support until Egypt stopped assisting Algerian nationalists. The United States made military aid conditional upon Egypt's agreement to join a mutual security pact, and was prepared to deliver only a limited supply in return for cash payments in dollars. Nasser, feeling that he could not accept any of these conditions, turned to the Soviet Union.[9]

Syria was perhaps the Arab state most adversely affected by the emergence of the Palestinian issue. Damascus has long been a centre for Arab nationalist extremism, and despite the generally pro-Western policy of its immediate post-independence governments, strong political forces within the country and its armed forces were continuously challenging this traditional attitude by the central authorities. The reasons why Syria was particularly affected by the Arab-Israeli conflict were twofold. First, an overwhelming majority of Syrian society held the belief that Palestine was a part of 'Greater Syria', a historical and ideological concept stressing that Syria, Lebanon, Jordan, and Palestine were virtually a single entity that must be reunited one day. From the Syrian standpoint, therefore, the loss of Palestine to the Jews was more than just the loss of 'an Arab land', but rather a calamity hitting Syria itself.

Second, the Syrians firmly believed (and this is also true of the traditionally conservative elements among the politicians and the military) in the leading role of Syria in Arab politics. For them, Syria was the focus of the Arab East, a sort of 'Arab Prussia', and the reunification of Greater Syria would be nothing but a first step towards achieving the long-sought unity of the Arab world.

The defeat of 1948 constituted a shattering blow to these pan-Arabist aspirations. While other Arabs shared in that defeat, some of them got at least something in return. Jordan got the West Bank and East Jerusalem, leading to the creation of the Hashemite Kingdom of Jordan; Egypt got the Gaza strip; Lebanon was not so much interested; Syria got nothing. Such a blow was not to be accepted lightly, and its first consequence was the virtual collapse of the credibility and legitimacy of the traditional political establishment. Two forces were to emerge in its place: the army, assuming a position of legitimate representation of the true aspirations of the Syrian nation; and a loosely-knit alliance of radical movements led by the Ba'th Arab Socialist Party. It was the amalgamation of forces and efforts by the army and the Ba'th in later years that was to lead to the complete transformation of Syria's political structure and future.[10]

The first military coup against the civilian government in Syria took place in 1949, less than six months after the 1948 defeat. Its political slogans were obvious: the dedication to fight Israel and to build up the armed forces. This was followed by four consecutive coups during the period 1949–54. However, all of those military governments remained quite interim in nature and had very little impact on Syrian foreign policy, which remained closely linked to the West.

By 1954, things were beginning to change. In that year, Syria witnessed its first free elections since 1947, and the results reflected the shift which had been taking place in the country's political and social structures. For the first time, Ba'thists, socialists and Arab nationalists started to have an obvious, if not totally dominant, voice in the Syrian parliament. Anti-Western policies were, for the first time, being voiced at an official or semi-official level rather than being confined to the popular press and party gatherings, as had been the case earlier. Damascus was clearly trying to regain its place as 'the heart of radical pan-Arabism'.

The arms deal between Egypt and the Soviet bloc was greeted with vociferous approval by militant Arab nationalists throughout the Middle East and particularly in Syria. The new breed of Syrian leadership was similarly embittered by the creation of Israel and the West's support for the Jewish state. Relatively weak, Syria was also becoming a target for the more powerful Arab countries, particularly Egypt and Iraq, which had traditionally competed for influence over Syria as a means of enhancing their own regional positions. By early 1955, Syria's more radical postures were being increasingly linked to those of Nasser's Egypt, much to the distaste of pro-Western Iraq. Shortly after, Iraq and Turkey tried to force Syria into joining the Baghdad Pact, while Egypt applied counter-pressures. Lacking the power to resist these moves, Syria approached the Soviet Union.[11] In early 1956 Syria accepted military aid from the Soviet bloc and became, thereby, the first Arab country to emulate Egypt's example. That move set the scene for a relationship of military and political cooperation between Damascus and Moscow that has become and has remained, to this very day, one of the most prominent features in Middle Eastern regional and superpower politics. Today, more than twenty-five years later, Syria remains Moscow's most trusted (or, more accurately, least distrusted) Arab ally in the Middle East. It is against this background that Syria looks, at present, to be Moscow's last and only real foothold in the region.[12]

Soviet-Syrian relations, 1974–84

The break with Egypt and the ascendancy of Syria
For nearly two decades the Soviet Union had looked upon Egypt as its most important ally in the Middle East. The reasons behind this particular emphasis on relations with Cairo were, from the Soviet point of view, justifiable as well as logical.

During the days of President Nasser, and even under his successor President Sadat, Egypt was the fulcrum of Arab nationalism and the cornerstone on which any semblance of Arab unity against Israel could be established. Moreover, with its large manpower resources, strategic geographical location and historically pivotal position in Arab politics, Egypt was a natural leader among Arab states.

It was therefore necessary for the Soviet Union, or, for that matter, any external power aspiring to extend its influence over the Middle East, to regard Egypt as the key to the whole region. While other Soviet allies in the Arab world, such as Syria, Iraq and Libya, kept their own important roles, they still had to settle for second position on Moscow's list of regional priorities, as long as Soviet-Egyptian relations maintained their close and special nature.

The situation was to change dramatically, however, with Egypt's drift to the West in the mid-1970s. This came as a traumatic shock from which Soviet policy planners found it very difficult to recover. Not only was the Soviet presence there of vital strategic value, but it was also perceived by Moscow as a model for cooperation between the USSR and other Arab states, as well as Third World countries in general. More important, perhaps, was the effect of the new Egyptian policy on the position of the Soviet Union *vis-à-vis* the Arab-Israeli conflict. Moscow was taken out of the picture when, after the October 1973 war, US Secretary of State Henry Kissinger negotiated the two Sinai disengagement agreements (1974–5) between Israel and Egypt. These were coupled with a similar American success which led to the signing of the first-ever disengagement agreement on the Golan Heights between Israel and Syria (1974).[13] There was a glimmer of hope for the Soviets when, in October 1977, President Jimmy Carter sought to bring the USSR back into the peace process through a joint declaration which essentially stated that the United States and the Soviet Union would push for the reconvening of the Geneva Conference on the Middle East to reach a general peaceful settlement of the Arab-Israeli dispute. The United States and the Soviet Union were co-chairmen of the conference, which had last met in 1973.[14]

However, no sooner had the Soviet Union regained a foothold in the Arab-Israeli peacemaking process than it was taken away. In November 1977, Moscow's one-time ally and now strongest critic, President Sadat, went to Jerusalem on his famous visit of reconciliation, which eventually led to the signing of the Egyptian-Israeli Peace Treaty in 1979.

Faced with these important setbacks, Moscow started to look for alternative policies aimed at safeguarding whatever influence it still had in the Middle East. It was, after all, an exercise in damage limitation the primary objective of which was to prevent the United

States and the West achieving any further gains in an area of vital strategic significance for the Soviet Union. Rather than embarking on some sort of 'counter-offensive' aimed at regaining whatever advantages it had already lost to the West, the USSR decided on a policy of caution, coupled with a growing distrust of Arab politics as a whole. It was natural that Moscow should give its support to those Arab countries opposed to Sadat's unilateral moves towards Israel, asserting that such moves would not lead to a lasting peace in the region.[15] However, Soviet support for the 'rejectionist' Arab front, which at the time comprised Syria, Libya, Algeria, South Yemen and the PLO, soon proved to be of an extremely limited as well as restrained nature, particularly as far as the Arab-Israeli dispute was concerned. In fact, Moscow was quite aware of the divergences and sometimes outright contradictions which were afflicting the priorities of its Arab allies. So while maintaining a generous influx of arms supplies to those countries, in exchange for valuable hard currency, little or nothing was achieved as far as broad strategic cooperation was concerned. Algeria was busy with her dispute with Morocco over the Western Sahara. Libya had obvious concerns in North and Central Africa. South Yemen was primarily interested in developments in the Horn of Africa and Southern Arabia. The PLO, while enjoying Moscow's support and recognition as the 'sole representative of the Palestinian people', had a lot to answer for, from a Soviet point of view, both in respect of its ultimate political objectives and its well-documented connections with Saudi Arabia and other conservative Arab states. It was the Syrian-Soviet relationship that had to become a kind of test case for Soviet policy in the Middle East as a whole, and as in respect of the Arab-Israeli conflict in particular.

The Egyptian-Israeli accords were of great significance for Soviet relations with Syria. While playing an important role in the Soviet Union's Middle East policy for several decades, Syria's significance had previously been second to that of Egypt. After the loss of Egypt in the mid-1970s, however, Soviet-Syrian relations were bound to take on much greater importance. The two sides started to view one another as indispensable partners in defending their national interests.

Nevertheless, the trend towards cementing Soviet-Syrian relations has not been as smooth, or as simple, as it might have seemed at first glance. It has been, rather, a slow and sometimes oscillating process which has passed through many ups and downs, and has reflected, to a very large extent, the overall posture of the USSR in the Middle East generally and in the Arab world in particular over the past decade.[16]

Perhaps uniquely among Moscow's Arab allies, Syria has been the one country in the Middle East which has maintained a relatively strong and steady working relationship with the Soviet Union continuously over the past quarter-century. While the Soviet presence in some of the other Arab states has been subjected to the most sudden and, at times, quite inexplicable shifts of fortune, Soviet-Syrian relations have remained remarkably stable despite the numerous internal power struggles and changes that were experienced in Damascus during that period.

Contrary to what might have been expected, Soviet-Syrian relations did not take a sudden turn for the better as a result of Egypt's unilateral peace initiatives. In fact, at a time when President Sadat was abrogating Egypt's treaty with Moscow, consolidating his links with the United States and contemplating his peaceful overtures to Israel, Soviet influence in Syria was possibly at its lowest ebb. During that period (1975–7), Soviet-Syrian relations were markedly cool for a number of reasons. The disengagement agreement over the Golan Heights had just been achieved, thanks largely to American mediation efforts. Syria was also tied at the time to a close alliance with Jordan's King Hussain, and was enjoying extremely strong financial and political backing from Saudi Arabia and other conservative Gulf states. Moreover, in 1976 the Syrian army went into Lebanon in an attempt to bring the civil war there to an end. The Syrian intervention was directed mainly against the forces of the PLO and their Lebanese left-wing allies, much to the benefit of their right-wing Phalangist opponents. It soon became clear that Moscow did not approve of the Syrian action in Lebanon. Although never reaching the point of openly criticizing Damascus for its Lebanese policies, the official Soviet line hinted strongly at Moscow's displeasure with events there, and urged instead the re-establishment of the lost alliance between Syria, the PLO, and the Lebanese National Movement (coalition of left-wing parties). In Moscow's view, such an alliance was 'the only means to counter the growing aggression by Israel and Imperialism in the region'.[17]

In line with the traditional feature of Syrian-Soviet relations, both sides did their best to play down the extent of their differences over the events in Lebanon during the period 1976–7. In fact, much as cooperation between Syria and the Soviet Union has been a 'controlled' process over the years, their differences as regards Lebanon and the PLO were kept equally under control. As a result, while clear contradictions of policy were in evidence, they were never allowed to reach crisis level, or to affect the overall framework of the relationship between the two states.

It took several months as well as the shockwaves left by Sadat's sudden visit to Jerusalem to overcome the effects on Syria's relations with the USSR of its intervention in Lebanon. The two sides evidently felt the need for closer cooperation in the face of the rapid deterioration in their respective regional positions. In February 1978, a few weeks after Sadat's visit to Jerusalem, President Assad of Syria paid a visit to Moscow in a bid to formulate a common strategy against 'the new American-Israeli-Egyptian alliance in the region'.[18] That visit was particularly significant, since it gave the first indication that Syria has finally begun to take Egypt's place at the top of the Soviet Union's list of priorities in the Middle East. The official organ of the ruling Syrian Ba'th Party expressed the feeling in Damascus regarding the urgent need to upgrade the alliance with Moscow in the wake of Sadat's move when it described the visit to Moscow by Assad in these terms: 'If the lapse of the Sadat regime has left a strategic gap between the Arabs and Israel, this does not imply acceptance of the situation ... The bulwark of steadfastness, Syria, must take over this strategic burden ... President Assad's fruitful visit to Moscow should be viewed within this context.'[19]

The ensuing developments in the Middle East since 1978 served to strengthen further Syria's position as the USSR's most important ally in the region. Moscow emphasized this importance mainly by increasing its military aid. During the period 1978–80, it supplied Damascus with substantial quantities of arms, including some of the most advanced equipment in the Soviet arsenal. Syria, for its part, was increasingly viewing its alliance with the Soviet Union as strategically essential to the safeguarding of Syrian security and interests in the region.

The growing strength of Syrian ties with Moscow was clearly reflected in 1980 when Syria refused to condemn the Soviet intervention in Afghanistan. Although the Syrian leadership was reportedly unhappy with the Soviet action, it abstained from voting alongside other Arab countries and the majority of the UN General Assembly in denouncing that action. It was probably not by coincidence that Soviet Foreign Minister Andrei Gromyko visited Damascus shrotly after the vote (27–29 January 1980) and reportedly offered to supply the Syrian armed forces with additional military aid and to cancel a $500m Syrian debt.[20]

The Syrian-Soviet treaty: a turning-point?

The movement towards a closer orientation to Moscow progressed appreciably during 1980. By June of that year reports from Damascus were indicating, quite openly, that the Syrians were planning to expand their relations and cooperative arrangements with the Soviet Union. A Syrian newspaper reported on 25 June that Syria 'is seriously preparing to take an advanced and qualitative step towards closer cooperation with the Soviet Union'.[21] Syria's Foreign Minister (later to become vice-president) Abdel Halim Khaddam was quoted in the Lebanese press as having stated in an interview that the Assad government would 'strengthen its ties with Moscow qualitatively in order to achieve military and strategic parity with Israel'.[22]

That 'qualitative' step was finally taken on 8 October 1980 when the Soviet Union and Syria signed a twenty-year Treaty of Friendship and Cooperation that binds them in a close political, military and economic relationship. According to the Soviet news agency TASS, the treaty called for 'continued cooperation in the military field',[23] language virtually identical with that used in similar treaties concluded by the USSR over the years with Egypt, Iraq and other Middle East countries. The treaty also called for mutual consultations on threats to each other's security, or 'violations of peace and security in the whole world', a provision never before seen in such a treaty. Both governments were to 'coordinate their positions and cooperate in order to remove the threat and restore peace'.[24]

As such, the Soviet-Syrian treaty should have come as an important turning-point in relations between the two sides, and indeed it was widely regarded as such. Above all, the treaty was expected to signal a new momentum in Soviet strategic policy in the Middle East, an achievement which should have been significant at the time in view of Moscow's earlier lack of success in galvanizing a stable Arab anti-American bloc, and in the face of Washington's steady progress in establishing new and stronger footholds in the region. On the other hand, the treaty had to be a welcome development for President Assad's government, first as a way for Syria to escape from a situation of growing isolation in the Arab world; and secondly, to strengthen its strategic position against any threats from Israel.

It is worth mentioning that for several years Syrian President Hafiz al-Assad had avoided signing a friendship and cooperation treaty with the Soviet Union, despite continued pressures from Moscow.[25] Such a move, he apparently felt, could have damaged Syria's image in the inter-Arab arena, hurt the generous flow of funds to Syria from the Arab oil countries, restricted political support from some of the 'Steadfastness Front' states (e.g. Algeria and Libya), and even set off unrest among religious and nationalist circles inside Syria.[26] In the early 1970s, Assad himself had denounced similar treaties between the USSR and Egypt and

Iraq.[27] At the same time he had called for an Arab policy of non-alignment regarding the East-West conflict. According to various reports, even as late as 1979, Assad, repeating his earlier objections, again rejected Soviet proposals for such a treaty.[28]

Shortly thereafter, however, several new domestic and regional considerations led the Syrian president to review his earlier objections. On the domestic level, the Syrian government was growing increasingly weary of the civil unrest, which by mid-1980 had spread and reached alarming levels. Organized subversion by the shadowy Muslim Brothers had begun to threaten the basic foundations of the Syrian regime, and in Damascus's view this subversion was instigated, to a large extent, by such hostile Arab neighbours as Jordan, Iraq and even Saudi Arabia.

In these circumstances, the Syrian leadership probably felt that a friendship and cooperation treaty would appear to be a logical way out. Such a pact would tie Moscow to the Assad government. Not only would it ensure Soviet acceptance of that government's continued existence, but would also provide the foundation for possible active Soviet assistance if matters were to deteriorate further.

On a broader regional level, a treaty with the Soviet Union was rapidly becoming something of a necessity. Since 1978, the Syrians were increasingly on the defensive on more than one front. In Lebanon, the situation was gradually getting out of Syria's control, with the Damascus-backed government of President Elias Sarkiss on the verge of total collapse. Syrian forces in Lebanon were getting bogged down in futile conflict against hostile Christian Maronite militias strongly allied to Israel. On the other hand, relations between Damascus and the PLO were again under considerable strain. Despite the indications that Syria and the PLO had already reconciled their earlier differences and supposedly joined forces in the 'Steadfastness Front' against Egypt's rapprochement with Israel, the actual fact remained that, by 1980, the two sides were increasingly viewing each other as rivals rather than allies. In Lebanon at least, Syria and the PLO were engaged in a bitter, though undeclared, power struggle over who should gain ultimate dominance there. The Syrians, moreover, were acutely aware of the possibility of PLO activities in Lebanon leading to a probable Israeli retaliation which would escalate the whole situation and involve them in a new all-out confrontation with the Israelis during circumstances which were, from Syria's point of view, unfavourable to say the least.

Aside from the Lebanese entanglement, the late 1970s witnessed a dramatic breakdown in Syrian-Jordanian relations after years of relative amity. That breakdown was to be coupled with a sudden resurgence in the historical animosity between the two Ba'thist regimes of Presidents Assad and Hussain in Syria and Iraq respectively. After a brief and eventually abortive attempt to reconcile the differences between Damascus and Baghdad in 1979, relations between the two sides slumped to their worst level ever. As if hostility with Baghdad alone were not enough, Damascus was faced at the time with a newly emerging alliance between Iraq and Jordan. Such an alliance was, in Syria's view, an immediate and most dangerous threat to its security. In fact, with Israel, with its problems with the PLO and in Lebanon, and with Jordan and Iraq joining forces for the first time since the 1950s, Syria regarded itself in 1980 a country under siege, perhaps with ample justification.

Amid all these strategic setbacks, the Israeli threat remained paramount as far as the Syrians were concerned. In the event, Damascus had indeed a cause for considerable concern. Ever since Egypt's exit from the military arena of the Arab-Israeli conflict, the Syrians had been developing a profound feeling of insecurity. That feeling was based on the Syrian realization that without Egypt the balance of forces with Israel has become hopelessly lopsided in the latter's favour. With its domestic problems, the situation in Lebanon, and growing hostility from the Jordanian-Iraqi sector, Syria's insecurity became compounded. The treaty with the Soviet Union was, for the Syrian leadership, the only viable alternative that would restore some of that sought-after security.

Taken at its face value the Treaty of Friendship and Cooperation was a major development in Soviet-Syrian relations; to what extent it actually affected the running of these relations is a different matter. During the first two years following the signing of the treaty, its effect on the level of mutual cooperation between Syria and the USSR was very small, to say the least. Until the outbreak of the June 1982 war in Lebanon, any detailed examination of developments in Soviet-Syrian political relations and military ties reveals that bilateral strategic coordination was, at best, very limited, and that each side carried out highly significant moves without even bothering to inform the other in advance. It also transpires that the Soviets did not build up a military intervention for the defence of Syria to any greater extent than previously. The supply of Soviet weapons to Syria also remained within the virtually same qualitative and quantitative parameters as had existed before the treaty.

The primary conclusion to be drawn from such an analysis is that the Syrian-Soviet treaty served to institutionalize already existing relations rather than to create new ones. The pattern of strategic relations between the two countries after the signing of the treaty still did not involve an absolute Syrian commitment to coordinate strategic moves with the USSR – just as there existed no firm Soviet undertaking to provide strategic support for Syrian initiatives. It was this conclusion that was strongly evident in the way both Moscow and Damascus conducted their relations during the period preceding Israel's invasion of Lebanon in summer 1982.

The first major test for the Soviet-Syrian treaty occurred merely weeks after its signing, when, in November 1980, Syrian military units were deployed along the borders with Jordan.[29] Thus began the military phase of the Syrian-Jordanian crisis, which was to last for nearly two weeks.

Throughout this entire period of tension the USSR's voice was not heard. Nor was its position on the crisis publicized in any other way. The Soviet silence was particularly noticeable in view of the visit to Damascus, on 2 December 1980, by the Soviet First Vice-President, Vasili Kuznetsov. The official purpose of the visit was to exchange ratification documents for the friendship and cooperation treaty, yet its high-level nature constituted a considerable breach of accepted protocol in such instances.[30] One possible explanation of the visit is that, rather than showing support for the Syrians, it was intended to convey Moscow's desire to restrain Damascus and avoid a conflagration in Jordan.[31]

It became apparent that Syria had not coordinated with its Soviet ally the decision to deploy its forces against Jordan in the first place. Just as they had had no foreknowledge of the Syrian intervention in Lebanon a few years earlier, so in the Jordan border crisis the Soviets were again presented with a Syrian *fait accompli*. This time, however, the situation threatened to involve the Soviets in an evolving inter-Arab crisis in which they had no direct strategic interest. Moreover, the crisis came at a particularly embarrassing time for Moscow: Jordan had just concluded its first-ever arms agreement with the USSR; an Arab summit conference was to begin in Amman, Soviet difficulties in Afghanistan were reaching their highest point and tension in Poland was increasing. Indeed, the last thing Moscow wanted at a time when it was attempting to dispel the stigma of the Afghanistan invasion was to abet or participate in a war involving two Arab countries.

The Soviet-Syrian treaty was again put to the test in April 1981, during what has become known as the Lebanese missile crisis. The Syrian army was involved at the time in heavy fighting against the Israeli-backed Phalangist militias. On 27 April 1981 Israeli fighters shot down two Syrian Mi-8 assault helicopters over the Sannine ridge, deep inside Lebanon. The Syrians responded angrily to the

Israeli move by deciding, for the first time since the entry of their forces into Lebanon in 1976, to deploy a number of surface-to-air missile (SAM) batteries in the Beka'a Valley.

The Syrian missiles were moved into Lebanon during the night of 29–30 April 1981. On 3 May, after Israel had discovered the missile deployment and tension in the area had reached a new high, the Soviet ambassador to Damascus was summoned urgently to Moscow for consultations. Two days later, a visit to Damascus by the Soviet deputy foreign minister was announced.[32] He arrived the next day and met with the Syrian leadership, including President Assad. No statement or communiqué concerning the meeting was released. Once again, it was becoming clear that there was no prior coordination between Syria and the Soviet Union regarding the introduction of the SAM batteries into Lebanon. There is no indication that the Soviets were asked about the matter, or were even informed in an orderly fashion.[33]

While tension kept rising steadily between Syria and Israel, Moscow was exercising extreme caution to avoid being dragged into the military sphere, even verbally. Despite Syrian efforts to create the impression that Damascus's firm stand derived, at least partly, from its friendship treaty with the USSR, Moscow avoided a single mention of that agreement throughout the Lebanese missile crisis. While Damascus was declaring that Soviet military aid to Syria would be forthcoming in the event of a conflagration, the Soviet media maintained absolute silence on the matter. Moreover, most of Moscow's official and semi-official statements during the crisis emphasized the Soviet Union's opposition to any escalation of the confrontation to the extent that, *de facto*, Moscow appeared to be making its political backing for Syria conditional on 'prevention of deterioration of the situation in Lebanon'.[34]

All this Soviet activity, or, rather, avoidance of activity, was taking place in the shadow of a tense military confrontation between Israel and Syria which included, according to various reports, reserve call-ups by both sides, mutual reinforcement of anticipated war sectors and a general 'eve-of-war' atmosphere. As for the Soviet-Syrian friendship and cooperation treaty, the two sides' behaviour during the Lebanese missile crisis appeared to indicate that even in the event of political-military crises in which Israel and, perhaps, the United States were involved there was still no guarantee either of full pre-coordination by the Syrians or of automatic Soviet aid and support.

It was against this background that the Israeli invasion of Lebanon and the ensuing confrontation between the Syrian and Israeli forces during the summer of 1982 took place.

The Israeli invasion of Lebanon, June 1982
If anything, it was the Lebanon war of 1982 and the emergence of the Andropov era that were to constitute what might be best regarded as the real turning-points in Soviet-Syrian relations. Regardless of the treaty and its effect on those relations during the first two years of its existence, it was only in the aftermath of Israel's invasion of Lebanon (and probably as a result of it) that the relationship between the USSR and Syria began to experience some of the most dramatic and far-reaching developments in its entire history.

Events in Lebanon during the summer of 1982 served to show the full extent of the inherent shortcomings of Arab-Soviet relations for decades, even when the two sides were bound by formal treaties of friendship and cooperation. The Soviet-Syrian treaty was of little practical effect when put to its ultimate test, namely a large-scale military conflict between Syria and Israel.

The reasons why the Soviet Union showed very little inclination to act in support of its Syrian ally in 1982 were varied and, perhaps, quite debatable. The fact remains, however, that for two sides bound by a treaty of friendship and cooperation to show such a lack of strategic consultation, let alone coordination, during a major crisis like the one which took place in Lebanon after the Israeli invasion is absolutely remarkable. An extensive Israeli military operation in Lebanon had been anticipated since early 1982. At first glance, one might have expected high-level consultations and coordination between Soviet and Syrian leaders and a joint plan of action for the military and political steps to be taken by each party if and when such an operation occurred. In fact, however, no summit meetings took place during the months preceding the Israeli invasion. No information was publicized or leaked concerning consultations or cooperation in this or any other sphere. Had such cooperation been in effect, there would have been an obvious deterrent value in making it public.

The confused Soviet reaction during the early days of the war likewise attests to a lack of prior coordination and planning. Up to 13 June 1982, approximately one week after the fighting had started and two days after the first ceasefire between Syria and Israel, there had been no high-level meetings or contacts between Damascus and Moscow. On that day, the deputy commander of Soviet air defence forces arrived in Damascus.[35] He conferred with Syrian Minister of Defence General Mustapha Tlas, and his entourage commenced an intensive investigation of the failure of the Soviet anti-aircraft system which the Syrian army had deployed in the Beka'a Valley. Neither the level nor the subject of these contacts were of a nature which ought to have characterized strategic coordination between partners in a friendship and cooperation treaty when one of them has been involved in a major war for a week.

The main conclusions that can be drawn from the behaviour of both the Soviet Union and Syria during the war in Lebanon reinforce the view that despite the signing of the treaty of friendship and cooperation two years earlier, the relationship between the two sides was still far short of the level at which it could be described as a true strategic alliance. These conclusions can be summarized as follows:

1. The Soviet Union and Syria did not prepare any coordinated plan of action regarding the predicted Israeli invasion of Lebanon. No significant consultations or contacts took place either before or in the course of the fighting itself.

2. The Soviets avoided taking any public stand which would create the impression of a commitment to Syria to intervene in the conflict actively. The Syrians, for their part, attempted to extract such a commitment from the Soviets, but were neither bitterly disappointed nor greatly surprised when it was not forthcoming.

3. Moves by the Soviets to create some sort of strategic deterrence in support of Syria were minimal, even by traditional Soviet standards (a limited naval presence in the eastern Mediterranean basin and a possible troop alert along the USSR's southern boundaries). Moreover, the timing of such moves deprived them of all significance. They were of very short duration and they actually took place after the bulk of the fighting between Syria and Israel was already over.

4. The Soviet supply of arms and military equipment to Syria during summer 1982 amounted to compensation for losses alone; its extent was quite minimal in comparison with aid generally granted in time of war to a country enjoying a supposedly close strategic relationship with the USSR.

There are many possible explanations for Moscow's decidedly inactive approach in dealing with the events in Lebanon during the summer of 1982. First of all, the Soviet Union apparently realized that it could not intervene militarily in the Lebanese crisis. Token involvement might have ended in a humiliating defeat at the hands of the Israelis. On the other hand, massive intervention was difficult to implement at such short notice, particularly in view of the lack of prior coordination or mutual preparation. Furthermore, such intervention was liable to escalate into a far from welcome potential conflict between the superpowers.

Second, the war in Lebanon was hardly a pretext, in Moscow's view, for Soviet military involvement. Lebanon, after all, had no formal agreements whatsoever with the USSR, nor does it border on the Soviet Union. The Palestinians were not a sovereign factor there, and even the Syrian presence was only the result of a limited inter-Arab mandate.

Third, and perhaps more important, the Israeli invasion of Lebanon caught the Soviet Union at a particularly unfortunate juncture, when there were clearly a number of more urgent issues to resolve before it would risk involvement in an unpredictable and potentially disastrous Middle Eastern venture. Soviet involvement in Afghanistan was already at its height, problems in Poland were still to be solved, and the process of preparing for disarmament and nuclear arms limitation talks with the United States demanded much caution. Moreover, within the Kremlin itself, 1982 was a time of considerable disarray, and an atmosphere of uncertainty was prevailing regarding the future of the Soviet leadership: the struggle for succession to Leonid Brezhnev had commenced.

In short, the Soviet reaction to the Lebanese crisis of summer 1982, at least during and immediately after the war, was typically cautious as well as somewhat perplexed. Moscow apparently decided to deal with the crisis by taking the least possible risks and, hence, by making the minimum of initiatives while trying at the same time not to get entirely out of the picture. On the one hand, the USSR decided to avoid, at all costs, any direct military involvement in support of either the Syrians or the Palestinians. On the other, it embarked on an immediate process of political damage limitation in an attempt to safeguard some of its prestige and presence in the region.

To follow such a cautious and, to some extent, negative approach in dealing with an event on the scale of the Israeli invasion of Lebanon was quite inadequate from both the Arab and the Soviet viewpoints. In fact, both Moscow and Damascus were soon to realize that the magnitude of the invasion and its outcome were to require a completely different level of cooperation if the results of the 1982 war were to be opposed, let alone reversed. It was, in effect, the reversal of these results that Syria and the Soviet Union apparently decided to achieve in the aftermath of the war.

Aftermath of the Lebanon war: the real breakthrough
The main, but by no means only, objective of the Israeli operation of June 1982 was obviously to expel the PLO from Lebanon, both militarily and politically. Israel's other objectives, however, were equally important, if not more so, when viewed from a broader strategic perspective. The invasion was indeed an attempt by Israel

to cancel out the influence of Syria over Lebanon as well as to break the backbone of Syrian forces there. Furthermore, Israel was clearly trying to establish a new Lebanese *status quo* whereby the civil war there would finally be brought to an end in favour of Israel's allies. As a consequence, any new government in Lebanon would fall directly under the influence and protection of Israel rather than of Syria. Such was the extent of Israeli ambitions in Lebanon that the then Israeli Prime Minister Menachem Begin was confidently predicting by late 1982 that Lebanon would be the second Arab state after Egypt to sign a peace treaty with Israel.[36]

Lebanon did indeed sign such an agreement with Israel on 17 May 1983. Far from signalling an end to the conflict in Lebanon (and to Israel's problems there), this agreement sparked off yet another round of violence. What the Israelis, as well as the Americans who had sponsored the agreement, obviously failed to see was that in Lebanon matters are not necessarily as clear-cut as they might appear. The Israelis were soon to find themselves bogged down in the Lebanese quagmire, and in an unfavourable military and political situation which they had never experienced in any other occupied Arab territory before.

In the early stages following the Israeli invasion, it had seemed possible that, with the infrastructure of the main PLO in Lebanon smashed, the Syrian army pushed back towards the areas immediately around its own frontiers, and a strong army of occupation in support of a new Lebanese central government determined to reassert its authority, there might be some chance of breaking the mould of recent Lebanese politics.[37] Indeed, these assumptions, shared by the United States, Israel and the Lebanese government under President Amin Gemayel, formed the basis of American policy towards what Washington clearly hoped would become a new order in Lebanon as well as a new strategic situation in the region as a whole. But the fragile hopes of autumn 1982 soon proved illusory. What everybody, not least the Israelis and the Americans, seemed to have miscalculated was the position of Syria and its willingness, as well as its capability, to defend what it had always believed to be its genuine interests in Lebanon.

The Syrians realized in the aftermath of the Israeli invasion that they were facing a new and extremely dangerous situation in the region which had to be resisted and 'corrected' at all costs. They also believed that what Israel was trying to achieve in Lebanon went much further than the elimination of the PLO presence there. If Damascus could tolerate that, it was never in a position to accept Israel's other objectives, namely to control Lebanon and turn it into a buffer zone dominated by forces hostile to Syria. In that, the

Syrians saw a potentially fatal blow not only to their vital interests in Lebanon, but also to the whole framework of their strategic security both domestically and regionally. They were also convinced that such a scheme was not merely an Israeli design, but formed part of an American plan to place the whole of the Middle East under the influence of the United States.[38] This plan, in Damascus's view, had come into being with the Israeli invasion of Lebanon, and with the subsequent deployment of American forces there under the pretext of the multinational peacekeeping force (which included French, British and Italian units). The next step, the Syrians believed, was 'to bring Damascus to its knees'.[39] While it was obvious that Syria was in no mood to accept that, the Syrian leadership was nevertheless faced with the reality that it would be practically impossible for Syria to resist such an eventuality on its own. Damascus, in effect, had no alternative but to seek a higher and more significant degree of cooperation with its superpower ally, the Soviet Union.

For its part, the USSR also came to realize the extent of the damage caused to its influence in the Middle East by the Israeli invasion of Lebanon and the developments that followed it. What the Soviet leadership became most anxious about in the aftermath of the 1982 war was the resurgence of US influence in the Middle East coupled with a sharp decline in its own image in the region. The developments of summer 1982, including such dramatic events as the Israeli seige of Beirut and subsequent entry into the city (the first time an Arab capital was overrun by Israeli forces), the massacres of the Sabra and Shatila Palestinian refugee camps, and the eventual expulsion of PLO forces from Lebanon, served to create an atmosphere of utter frustration among Arab governments and populations alike. One of the primary targets for that frustration was the Soviet Union, which as an ally of Syria and the Palestinians, would have been expected to act rather differently from the way in which it did. The Arabs, not least Syria and the Palestinians, were anticipating and hoping for a much more active role to be played by Moscow in their support. Such a role was not to materialize, however, and the result was a marked deterioration in Soviet prestige and credibility as a superpower capable of influencing events in the region.

Like Syria, the Soviet Union regarded the emerging strategic situation in the Middle East following the June 1982 war as posing a serious threat to its interests in the area both in the short and in the long terms. With their main remaining ally, Syria, seriously weakened, the PLO defeated, Lebanon falling under Israeli and American military and political influence and other Arab states increasingly turning towards the United States, the Soviets acquired a sharp awareness of the need to revitalize their Middle East policy. Such a revitalization demanded the adoption of a much more active, even aggressive, Soviet posture in the region. In effect, Moscow had no alternative but to join forces with Damascus and to extend what support the latter needed in its efforts to resist the outcome of the Israeli invasion of Lebanon, both politically and militarily. It was only then, and as a result of its strengthened links with the Soviet Union, that Syria became able by early 1983 to embark on her 'counter-offensive' in Lebanon and in the region generally.

The Syrian 'counter-offensive' was not military (at least not in the conventional sense). Throughout the events of the past two years, the Syrians have maintained that the whole framework of their policy was basically defensive. Moreover, they have always been fully aware of Israel's military supremacy to the extent that one can be reasonably safe in assuming that Syria entertains no illusions about its prospects for victory in a full-scale war in which it alone faces Israel.

What the Syrians opted for was to set in motion a process of active resistance to the prevailing political and military order in Lebanon in the wake of Israel's invasion. In so doing, they had three main objectives:

1. To prevent Israel from reaping any of the advantages that it had sought through its invasion of Lebanon. Particularly noteworthy was Syria's determination to oppose any peace agreement between Beirut and Jerusalem and, in the aftermath of the signing of the accord of 17 May, to bring about its cancellation. In addition, Damascus wanted to show the Israelis that their occupation of South and Central Lebanon would soon turn into a largely counter-productive venture unable to serve any of Jerusalem's stated purposes.

2. To reassert Syria's political influence over the Lebanese central government by making it clear to the latter that without Syrian support it would be practically impossible to govern the war-torn country. This meant, of course, that Beirut had to relinquish its dependence on the US and other Western powers for security and political support, and to turn back instead towards Syria.

3. To show the United States and its allies in the multinational peacekeeping force that their presence in Lebanon was a costly and to some extent futile affair which would pay no political or strategic dividends.

In effect, Syria was eager to prove to everyone concerned with the Arab-Israeli dispute that it was still a regional power to be reckoned with. Far from believing that it had been defeated in the June 1982 war, it regarded the war as an Israeli triumph over the PLO, and the Syrians were in no mood to foot the bills of that triumph themselves. Quite to the contrary, their aim was to show their ability to bounce back and to re-establish their position in the region. The result was that just a few months after the invasion, it was becoming increasingly clear that no semblance of stability in Lebanon, and – more important – no settlement for the Arab-Israeli conflict as a whole, could be achieved without the blessing and direct participation of Syria.

The Syrian objectives were quite in line with those of Moscow. Regardless of the intricacies of the various local and regional issues involved – such as the growing feud between Damascus and Yasser Arafat's PLO factions, and the internal political wheeling and dealing within Lebanon itself – the broad outline of this Syrian strategy following the summer 1982 war was very similar indeed to that envisaged by the Soviet Union. After all, the latter increasingly regarded that war as an Israeli-American plot to secure dominance in the region by weakening and, ultimately, excluding Moscow and its allies from any prospective settlement there. To get Israel and the United States out of Lebanon and to bring the latter back under the Syrian umbrella was, therefore, as much part of Moscow's strategy in the area as Syria's.

Hence came the qualitative change in Soviet-Syrian relations in the wake of the events of summer 1982. Such was the significance of that change, without which Damascus had practically no hope of bringing about the political and military achievements that it has sought during the past two years, that Syria's position as a major power-broker in the region stands now stronger than ever before.

What must be particularly emphasized, however, is that Syria has always been aware that it could not reach such a credible regional position, let alone maintain it for any length of time, without concurrently achieving a measure of military parity with Israel, if only to be able to meet any potential Israeli armed response and avoid actual defeat in the event of war.[40] If Syria, therefore, were to achieve defensive parity, it could then risk carrying out its 'controlled' political and military moves in the region – even directly confronting Israeli interests – secure in the knowledge that, should war result, it could rely on its army to put up an effective defence. Further, by building its own offensive capability, it should be able to secure at least a level of minimum credible deterrence that would be sufficient to neutralize Israel's own strategic offensive superiority and to deter the Israeli inclination to use it should war break out.[41]

More important, perhaps, were the reports which surfaced during

1984 about a secret visit that was allegedly paid to Moscow by President Assad himself shortly after President Andropov's coming to power.[42] Although there is still no confirmation of this visit, it is widely believed by Western and Arab sources to have resulted in what was described as 'an updating' of the terms of the Treaty of Friendship and Cooperation between Syria and the Soviet Union so as to include a specific pledge by Moscow to guarantee Syria's security and its military presence in Lebanon against any further Israeli incursions, as well as to help Damascus to attain its more than often stated goal of achieving 'strategic parity' with Israel.

Whether Assad's 1983 visit to Moscow did actually take place, let alone result in such an important Soviet pledge on Syria's presence in Lebanon after the Israeli invasion of 1982, remains highly conjectural. What is almost certain, however, is the fact that Syrian-Soviet military relations, as reflected by both the quantities and the quality of Moscow's arms supplied to Syria during the past two years, have witnessed developments which were unprecedented to say the least.

The military dimension in Syrian-Soviet relations after 1982

Expanding its military capability has always been the cornerstone of Syria's policy as well as the prerequisite for any Syrian strategic initiative in Lebanon and the region. This priority took on added urgency in the wake of the 1982 war and it was only through increased reliance on Moscow that Syria could accomplish its military build-up programmes.

It has become clear that after the Israeli invasion Soviet military aid to Syria has been more forthcoming than at any time before 1982. Various sources indicate that by the end of 1982 Syria was able, thanks to that aid, to compensate for all the losses in equipment its forces suffered in the war.[43] Since then the Syrians have undertaken a massive expansion of their armed forces, assisted by the USSR, which has shown itself more than willing to supply Damascus with substantial quantities of highly sophisticated arms. In the opinion of former Israeli Chief of Staff General Rafael Eitan, the war in Lebanon did not hamper the Syrian military build-up, but rather it has served to accelerate it considerably.[44]

Soviet arms supplies to Syria during the past two years were such that Damascus was able to increase the total of its armed forces by no less than 60 per cent as compared with the level at which they stood on the eve of the 1982 war.[45] Regular Syrian forces comprise at present some 360,000 troops compared with some 225,000 two years ago. Added to these are some 460,000 reservists who could be called upon in the event of general mobilization. Instead of five armoured and mechanized divisions, four independent armoured and mechanized brigades, six artillery brigades, ten special forces (Commando) airborne regiments and two surface-to-surface missile regiments, the Syrian army is believed now to possess eight armoured and mechanized divisions, seven independent armoured and mechanized brigades, at least twelve artillery brigades, fifteen special forces regiments and three surface-to-surface missile regiments.

What made it possible for the Syrians to increase the size of their military arsenal in such a sweeping way during a relatively short period of time was the willingness, on Moscow's part, to supply them with large and practically continuous arms shipments covering nearly every single military requirement. These shipments, which were intended both as replacements for war losses and as part of Syria's military expansion programme, have so far included:[46]

Some 1,200 main battle tanks, mostly modern T-72 and T-74 types, with the rest made up of T-62s

Some 800 BMP armoured fighting vehicles

Some 600–800 122 mm and 152 mm self-propelled guns

30 surface-to-surface missile launchers including 12 modern SS-21s and 9 long-range SCUDs

More than 50 SAM batteries, including such new types as the SA-5, SA-8 and possibly SA-11

Approximately 200 combat aircraft, including MiG-21s, MiG-23s, MiG-25s, MiG-27s and Sukhoi-20/22s.

The accelerating pace of Soviet-Syrian military relations was reflected not only by those quantitative increases; of much more significance were a number of trends which have characterized military cooperation between the two sides during the past two years and which could be easily described, when judged by traditional Soviet standards in dealing with the Third World nations, as fairly exceptional. It is noteworthy, for example, that Syria has become, for the first time, a recipient of some of Moscow's most up-to-date military equipment, including types which have never been previously issued to any of the Soviet Union's allies, even those belonging to the Warsaw Pact. Added to this, the Soviets have strengthened their direct military presence in Syria quite considerably, making a threefold increase in the number of Soviet military advisers operating within the Syrian armed forces. This number is estimated to be some 7,500–8,000 at present, compared with 2,500 two years ago.

In another indication of strengthened strategic ties, the USSR supplied Syria during 1983 with satellite communications equipment, in an effort to help Syria restore the credibility of its missile air defence system, tarnished by the results of the June 1982 war. The Soviet move was unprecedented, with American intelligence sources describing it as 'allowing the Soviet Command in Moscow to exercise direct control over Middle East air battles'.[47]

The Syrian efforts to redress the qualitative and numerical balance of forces with Israel started shortly after the 1982 war, and are still continuing. No one, not least the Syrians themselves, can claim, however, that these measures will be sufficient, on their own, to bring about the decisive change needed by the Syrians in order to achieve their strategic objective of 'parity' with Israel. Nevertheless, it remains true that the June 1982 war has marked a turning-point in the history of the Arab-Israeli conflict and the Soviet position in the region. For the first time ever, Israel has failed to achieve a sound strategic or political objective following a costly and drawn-out war, resulting in a costly and drawn-out occupation of an increasingly hostile Arab land, that of South Lebanon. The Syrians, on the other hand, have shown considerable skill in turning the tide in their favour. With their dominance over Lebanon restored, their posture in the region reasserted and their military capacity enhanced, they continue to reap the fruits of that Israeli failure, and to benefit from an equally important turning-point in their military and strategic relationship with the Soviet Union. It looks almost certain that, for the foreseeable future at least, the best interests of both Syria and the Soviet Union will lie in safeguarding and maintaining this close and evolving relationship.

Notes

1. For an analysis of the problems that have faced the Soviet Union in the Arab world, see Karen Dawisha, *Soviet Foreign Policy Towards Egypt* (London: Macmillan, 1979); Alvin Z. Rubinstein, *Red Star on the Nile: The Soviet-Egyptian Influence Relationship Since the June War* (Princeton, N.J.: Princeton University Press, 1977); Adeed Dawisha, 'The Soviet Union in the Arab World: The Limits to Superpower Influence', in Adeed Dawisha and Karen Dawisha (eds.), *The Soviet Union in the Middle East* (London: Heinemann, for the RIIA, 1982), pp. 8–23. For discussions of the Soviet positions on the issues of the Arab-Israeli conflict, see Paul Jabber and Roman Kalkowicz, 'The Arab-Israeli Wars of 1967 and 1973', in Stephen S. Kaplan *et al.*, *Diplomacy of Power: Soviet Armed Forces as a Political Instrument* (Washington, D.C.: Brookings Institution, 1981) pp. 412–67; Lawrence L. Whetton, 'The Arab-Israeli Dispute: Great Power Behaviour', *Adelphi Papers* No. 128 (London, IISS, 1977); Mohammed H. Heikal, *The Sphinx and the Commissar* (New York: Harper & Row, 1978); Mahmud Riyadh, *Al Bahth 'An as-Salam Wa'l Sira' fi'l as-Sharq al-Awsat* [The Search for Peace and the Conflict in the Middle East 1948–78] (Beirut: Al-Mu'assa al-'Arabiyya li'l Dirasat wa'l Nashr, 1981), in Arabic. For a view of the role of Israel in Soviet Middle East strategy, see Robert O. Freedman, *Soviet Policy Toward the Middle East Since 1970*, 2nd edn (New York: Praeger, 1978), Ch. 8. On the American factor influencing Soviet Middle East

strategy, an excellent discussion is to be found in William B. Quandt, *Decade of Decisions: American Policy Toward the Arab-Israeli Conflict 1967–1976* (Berkeley, Calif.: University of California Press, 1977). See also William B. Quandt, *Soviet Policy in the October 1973 War* (Santa Monica, Calif.: Rand Corporation, 1976).

2. For a study of Soviet policy toward the communist parties of the Arab world, see Robert O. Freedman, 'The Soviet Union and the Communist Parties of the Arab World: An Uncertain Relationship', in Roger E. Kanet and Donna Bahry (eds.), *Soviet Economic and Political Relations with the Developing World* (New York: Praeger, 1975), pp. 100–34; and John K. Cooley, 'The Shifting Sands of Arab Communism', *Problems of Communism*, Vol. 24, No. 2, 1975, pp. 22–42.

3. Although members of the communist parties were introduced, at one time or another, into the governments and popular assemblies (parliaments) of both Syria and Iraq during the past decade, such communist participation was always more of a formality than a real involvement in the decision-making processes in the two countries. Moreover, the whole network of communist activities remained subject to strict controls exercised by the two Ba'thist governments there. President Hussain of Iraq later moved against his communist 'partners', and by 1979 the Iraqi Communist Party was effectively banned from public life.

4. Jabber and Kalkowicz, 'The Arab-Israeli Wars', pp. 412.

5. *Ibid.*, pp. 414–18. See also Riyadh, *Al-Bahth 'An as-Salam*, pp. 102–5.

6. Jabber and Kalkowicz, 'The Arab-Israeli Wars', p. 418.

7. See, for example, Anwar as-Sadat, *In Search of Identity: An Autobiography* (New York: Harper & Row, 1977); and Heikal, *The Sphinx and the Commissar*.

8. Riyadh, *Al-Bahth 'An as-Salam*, p. 33.

9. *Ibid.*, pp. 18–27. See also Wynfred Joshua and Stephen P. Gibert, *Arms for the Third World: Soviet Military Aid Diplomacy* (Baltimore, Md.: Johns Hopkins University Press, 1969), p. 10.

10. For a good analysis of Syria's position *vis-à-vis* the Palestinian problem and the establishment of the state of Israel, see Patrick Seale, *The Struggle for Syria* (London: Oxford University Press, 1965).

11. Joshua and Gibert, *Arms for the Third World*, p. 11.

12. For a discussion of the present state of the relationship between Syria and the Soviet Union, see Amiram Nir, *The Soviet-Syrian Friendship and Cooperation Treaty: Unfulfilled Expectations*, Paper No. 19 (Tel Aviv: Jaffa Centre for Strategic Studies, Tel Aviv University, 1983). See also *Soviet Policy and the United States Response in the Third World*, prepared for the Committee on Foreign Affairs, US House of Representatives, 97 Cong., 1 sess. (Washington, D.C.: Government Printing Office, 1981), pp. 47–8.

13. See, for example, Freedman, *Soviet Policy Toward the Middle East*, pp. 334–6.

14. *Ibid.*, p. 305.

15. This was the line officially adopted by the USSR regarding the whole US-sponsored peace process leading to the Camp David accords. It was exemplified by Foreign Minister Andrei Gromyko in his speech of 25 September 1975 before the UN General Assembly as quoted by Tass and reported in Foreign Broadcasts Information Service, Daily Report, *Soviet Union*, 26 September 1979, p. C13.

16. For an excellent account of the nature of Soviet-Syrian relations after 1973, see Itamar Rabinovich and Galia Golan, 'The Soviet Union and Syria: The Limits of Cooperation', in Yaacov Ro'i (ed.), *The Limits of Power* (London: Croom Helm, 1979).

17. This, again, was the official policy line taken by Moscow as reflected on numerous occasions during the period June–October 1976 by such Soviet organs as *Pravda, Izvestia, Krasnaya Zvezda* and *Trud*; see also Rabinovich and Golan, 'The Soviet Union and Syria', p. 251.

18. Damascus Radio, quoted by *Al-Nahar*, 23 February 1978.

19. *Al-Ba'th*, as quoted in 'Soviet-Syrian Relations: Assad's Visit to Moscow', Radio Liberty Research, RL 46/78, p.3.

20. *Soviet Policy and the United States Response*, p. 47.

21. *Tishrin*, 25 June 1980.

22. *The New York Times*, 26 June 1980.

23. Tass, quoted in *Soviet Policy and the United States Response*, p. 48.

24. *Ibid.*

25. Rabinovich and Golan, 'The Soviet Union and Syria', pp. 213–31; see also Nir, *The Soviet-Syrian Friendship and Cooperation Treaty*, p. 5.

26. *Ibid.*

27. *Ibid.*

28. *Ibid.*

29. *An-Nahar*, 25 November 1980.

30. Nir, *The Soviet-Syrian Friendship and Cooperation Treaty*, p. 14.

31. *Ibid.*

32. Israel Broadcasting Service, 5 May 1981, quoted by Nir, *The Soviet-Syrian Friendship and Cooperation Treaty*, p. 16.

33. *Ibid.*, pp. 15–16.

34. A report on Amman Radio, 7 May 1981, quoting sources in the Soviet Foreign Ministry in Moscow who claimed that the USSR was to persuade Syria not to do anything which could lead to a direct confrontation with Israel; quoted by Nir, *The Soviet-Syrian Friendship and Cooperation Treaty*, p. 17.

35. *An-Nahar*, 14 June 1982.

36. *Ibid.*, 12 December 1982.

37. For an analysis of the political situation in Lebanon after the Israeli invasion see Geoffrey Bowder, 'Lebanon's Struggle for Survival', *The World Today*, Vol. 39, No. 11, November 1983, pp. 443–9.

38. See, for example, Zeev Schiff, 'The Green Light', *Foreign Policy*, No. 50, Spring 1983, p. 73.

39. *Tishrin*, 22 November 1982.

40. Interview with Syrian Defence Minister General Mustapha Tlas, *Al-Majalla*, No. 151, 1–7 January 1983, p. 18.

41. *Ibid.*

42. *The Times*, 17 October 1984.

43. Hirsh Goodman, 'Syrian Rebuilding Forces', *The Jerusalem Post* (international edition), 2 January 1983; see also *The Times*, 3 March 1983 and *The International Herald Tribune*, 22 March 1983.

44. General Rafael Eitan quoted by *Al-Hamishmar*, 10 January 1983.

45. Primary sources on figures relating to the development of Syrian military power during the period 1982–4 include the yearbooks of the London-based International Institute for Strategic Studies, namely *Strategic Survey* and *The Military Balance*, and publications of the Stockholm-based Institute for Peace Research (SIPRI), particularly the annual *World Armaments and Disarmament*. Other sources used include Mark Heller (ed.), *The Middle East Military Balance 1983* (Tel Aviv: Jaffa Centre for Strategic Studies, Tel Aviv University, 1983); and Kassem M. Ja'far,

The Balance of Forces in the Middle East 1984 (Beirut: The Arab Institute for Research and Publishing, 1984). Use was also made of regular news despatches in the daily press (*The Times, The Financial Times, International Herald Tribune*) and other periodicals (such as *Flight International, Aviation Week and Space Technology, International Defence Review, Jane's Defence Weekly, Strategy Week* and *DMS International Defence Intelligence*).

46. See preceding note.
47. *International Herald Tribune*, 23 February 1983.

15

Soviet relations with Angola and Mozambique

Jonathan Steele

The People's Republics of Angola and Mozambique are the Soviet Union's longest surviving friends in Africa.[1] Twenty-year treaties of friendship and cooperation were signed by Angola and Mozambique as long ago as October 1976 and March 1977 respectively. Both countries are not only listed as 'socialist-oriented' states (a category which includes other African countries such as Tanzania, Ethiopia, Guinea, Madagascar and the Seychelles); they are two of only four African countries (the others are Benin and the People's Republic of the Congo) which are described by Soviet analysts as states 'where scientific socialism is the official ideology and the basis of their development programmes'.[2]

In Angola's case, there is an even closer bond with the Soviet Union. With the exception of Ethiopia, no other country in Africa has received so great a commitment of Soviet military aid and personnel for its defence.

Yet in spite of these political, ideological and, for Angola at least, military links with Moscow, the Soviet relationship is far from being all-embracing, particularly on the economic side. Both countries conduct the overwhelming proportion of their foreign trade with non-socialist countries, a practice which contrasts with that of the Soviet Union's Eastern European allies or Cuba. When Mozambique asked the Soviet Union if it could join the Council for Mutual Economic Assistance (CMEA), it was told to wait.

On the military side, although Angola and Mozambique occupy geographic positions of potential strategic value in the South Atlantic and the Indian Ocean respectively, neither has provided the Soviet Union with the kinds of port and storage facilities which it has in South Yemen, Cuba or Vietnam. In spite of massive incursions by South African regular forces in Angola since the late 1970s and by South African-organized insurgents in Mozambique, the Soviet Union has not provided sufficient help to defeat the intruders. In Afghanistan the Soviet Union has tried and failed to crush a national uprising, aided by external forces. In Angola and Mozambique, where local rebels have much less popular backing

284

but where the outside enemy is clear, the Soviet Union has made much less effort. In Angola it has confined itself to supplying arms and some logistical help, and has approved a Cuban strategy of avoiding front-line combat. In Mozambique it has only given arms.

These contradictory aspects of the Soviet relationship with Angola and Mozambique make it clear that there is little accuracy in the conventional picture of both states as Soviet 'clients', and even less in the concept of a 'total onslaught' by the Soviet Union on southern Africa, using them as springboards. The picture is complex and has varied over time. In the sections which follow I shall look at the overall context for the Soviet Union's interest in southern Africa, the history of Soviet links with Angola and Mozambique before independence, its subsequent stake in their political and economic development, its military relationship and its reaction to the current strategy of South Africa and the Reagan administration in that part of the African continent.

The Soviet Union and southern Africa

Until the mid-1970s southern Africa was an area of low or minimal interest for Moscow. Traditionally, the Soviet Union has defined its security needs in terms of countries' proximity to the Soviet border and the historic routes taken by the many armies which have invaded the Russian land mass. In this context Eastern Europe was always, and still remains, the region of maximum Soviet concern. China and the Far East are areas of secondary concern, and in recent years the Middle East has been added to the list.

Only in rare cases has the Soviet Union chosen to invade countries on or close to its borders in order to try to preserve its security, Eastern Europe and Afghanistan being the obvious examples. More frequently, the Soviet Union has chosen a strategy of denial. By forging political, economic and, to a lesser extent, military links with countries, Moscow has sought to prevent them from joining Western- or US-dominated security groupings.

The development of nuclear-powered submarines and intercontinental ballistic missiles led to a radical change in the Soviet Union's military strategy. No longer could Moscow expect to rely on its land armies or on short-range coastal defence for its security. In October 1961 it revealed a shift in naval strategy from coastal defence to forward deployment. The world's oceans became increasingly significant for the Soviet Union, partly because they were being plied by the expanding Soviet merchant marine, which Moscow wished to be able to protect, but also because they were used by the United States' nuclear submarines. As Professor Michael MccGwire has written, 'Most specialists in the field now accept that the initial shift to forward deployment by the Soviet Navy was a response to the threat to Russia from sea-based nuclear delivery systems ... triggered by President Kennedy.'[3] Initially, the Soviet Union embarked on the new strategy of forward deployment in the Mediterranean, but as US sea-launched missiles extended their potential range, Moscow's concern for the north-west corner of the Indian Ocean increased: from here the United States had target coverage of both Russia and China with 2,500-mile-range Poseidon missiles. In 1966 the British and American plan to make a military stronghold out of the island of Diego Garcia in the middle of the Indian Ocean caused new alarm in Moscow. In subsequent years the Soviet Union looked for shore facilities for its own navy in Somalia and South Yemen.

Southern Africa, however, was too remote to be of concern to the Soviet Union. It clearly posed no military threat to Moscow, either in itself or as a base for Western military operations. The North Atlantic and the northern part of the Indian Ocean from the mouth of the Persian Gulf to the Red Sea were Moscow's main areas of interest and the fact that they were linked by the naval route around South Africa's Cape of Good Hope was of little relevance. The Soviet Navy is not large enough to patrol everywhere.

Southern Africa was also of little economic interest to the Soviet Union. Although the area is richly endowed with mineral resources, the Soviet Union is virtually self-sufficient in all of the raw materials found in the region, and has little need to trade with it.

Until the mid-1970s southern Africa's only value to Moscow was as a political symbol. The Soviet Union was able to capitalize at the United Nations and in its bilateral contacts with newly independent African nations on the West's close identification with the region. While Western leaders argued that they abhorred apartheid and were trying to end Ian Smith's rebellion in Rhodesia, the Soviet Union continually pointed to the West's large economic investment in the region and to the war being waged against national liberation movements in Angola and Mozambique by Portugal, a member of NATO. For Moscow southern Africa was a cost-free political asset, perhaps the best one it had anywhere in the world. The Soviet Union could side with the international majority at the United Nations in vote after vote without any fear of contradiction. But beyond its propaganda value, southern Africa was of little concern to the Kremlin. In his report from the Central Committee to the 24th Congress of the Communist Party of the Soviet Union, – the Politburo's five-yearly analysis of the state of the world – in 1971 Leonid Brezhnev did not mention the region.[4] Whereas the former French and British colonies north of the Zambezi were now independent and, at least during the Khruschev era, seemed to offer Moscow a chance of gaining political and diplomatic influence, white rule seemed reasonably secure further south.

The Soviet Union give diplomatic support, and provided some arms, to five of the liberation movements operating in the region, the African National Congress, the South West Africa People's Organization, the Zimbabwe African People's Union, the Frente para a Libertação de Moçambique and the Movimento para a Libertação de Angola. All five movements were officially recognized by the OAU, and Moscow's help was designed more to show that it was putting some money where its propaganda mouth was than to bring about early military victories for the movements. The aid was small-scale and sometimes inconsistent, as the next section points out.

Soviet links with Angola and Mozambique up to independence

The collapse of the Caetano dictatorship in Portugal on 25 April 1974 took Moscow as much by surprise as it did the West. In 1972 the Soviet Union had scaled down its military support for the MPLA, and in early 1974 it halted it altogether. But suddenly, in April 1974, the whole picture in southern Africa changed. With the coup by Portugal's Armed Forces Movement, independence for Portugal's African colonies became not merely a long-range possibility, but an imminent probability.

In Mozambique Frelimo was the undisputed heir to power, but in Angola the situation was confused. Besides the MPLA there were two other movements, the Frente Nacional para a Libertação de Angola (FNLA) and the União Nacional para a Independência Total de Angola (UNITA). UNITA had relations with the US Central Intelligence Agency while the FNLA had relations both with the CIA and China. China was the first outside power to send military advisers to Angola. At the end of May 1974 China sent 112 men, led by a major-general, to train the FNLA. Two months later the CIA increased its funding to the FNLA. In October 1974 the Soviet Union resumed military supplies to the MPLA.

As the danger of civil war between the three factions mounted, the OAU managed to persuade them to seek a trilateral accord with the Portuguese government. In January 1975 they reached an agreement on a provisional government. The accord did not last long. Only days after its signature, the US National Security Council authorized a grant of $300,000 to the FNLA, which already had the largest army. Wayne Smith, who was director of the US State Department's Office of Cuban Affairs from 1977 to 1979, has commented: 'The fact is that the United States had done more to provoke the fighting in Angola than the Cubans. Washington encouraged Holden Roberto [the FNLA leader] to ignore the agreement to share power with the MPLA and UNITA.'[5]

Two months later the Soviet Union made a major increase in its arms supplies to the MPLA, flying weapons to Congo-Brazzaville which were then transferred to small craft for unloading along the coast.[6] From then on it was probably inevitable that the final outcome of the struggle between the three factions would be decided by force of arms. Nevertheless it was again a decision in another foreign capital which prompted the Soviet Union to make its next major move. In June 1975 South Africa sent forces across the Namibian border into Angola. In August they occupied the site of the South-African-financed hydroelectric project on the Cunene river and in early September South African troops advanced thirty-five miles into Angola.

The MPLA responded to the incursions with some alarm but no panic. A delegation went to Havana to request Cuban military instructors but not combat troops to train new MPLA recruits. The Cubans made a leisurely sea crossing, arriving in Angola on 4 October. Ten days later the South Africans launched a major ground attack, sending an armoured column north with the aim of capturing Luanda. Wayne Smith wrote of this action: 'In August and October South African troops invaded Angola with full US knowledge. No Cuban troops were in Angola prior to this intervention.'[7]

It was at this point that the Soviet Union and Cuba took the major decision to send several thousand Cuban troops backed by heavy Soviet equipment to Luanda in a move which was soon to give the MPLA the chance to defeat both UNITA and the FNLA and to force the South Africans to retreat. The operation was unprecedented. For the first time Moscow and its allies had not only been able to project power decisively thousands of miles from their own shores, but they had done it in circumstances which most African states considered legitimate.

The motives for the Kremlin's boldness have been the subject of much debate. Conservative analysts in the United States have seen Moscow's move as a sign of a new Soviet expansionism, prompted by Washington's post-Vietnam weakness. In fact there is some doubt whether the most dramatic part of the operation, the despatch of Cuban combat troops, was the result of a Soviet intitiative. Evidence suggests that Fidel Castro may have been the prime mover. As early as November 1974 he had declared that Cuba's armed forces would be 'on the side of the peoples who face up to imperialism in all parts of the world'.[8] Nevertheless Moscow's approval was clearly vital, even though the Soviets had traditionally been more concerned than Castro not to jeopardize détente with the United States.

But by then they had been shut out of Egypt, thanks to the United States, and had watched one of their friends, President Salvador Allende of Chile, being removed by a military coup, of which Washington approved. The United States was also beginning to forge a partnership with China which was perceived in Moscow as an anti-Soviet move. Finally at the end of 1974 the US Congress rejected an attempt by the administration to give the Soviet Union 'most-favoured-nation' treatment in trade. In the face of these developments, the Kremlin may well have felt it had little need to show 'restraint'. Asked by the North Vietnamese in late December 1974 for a massive infusion of military aid which was to support Hanoi's capture of the South in April 1975, the Russians complied. Faced with a similar chance to turn the tide in Angola, they also complied.

Soviet relations since independence

Angola: political and economic links

The MPLA's military triumph at the end of 1975 did not end its political problems, and for almost a year and a half there were severe internal debates and dissension culminating in an abortive coup by Nito Alves, one of its political officers on the Northern Front. Exactly what role, if any, the Soviet Union played in the turmoil is unclear. In early October 1976 Agostinho Neto, the President, flew to Moscow to sign a Treaty of Friendship and Cooperation with the Soviet Union.

A cooperation agreement was also signed between the MPLA and the CPSU, and it can safely by assumed that the Soviet Union urged Neto to transform the MPLA from being a liberation movement into a Marxist-Leninist party as soon as possible. Two weeks after his return from Moscow Neto presided over a plenary meeting of the MPLA's Central Committee, the first since independence, which launched the 'transition to socialism' and announced preparations for turning the MPLA into a vanguard party towards the end of 1977. There was no mention of 'African socialism', a formula which Moscow distrusted as unscientific.

After its disappointments in Ghana, the Soviet Union was convinced that only a vanguard party could guarantee the success of any Third World nation's post-revolutionary reconstruction, and prevent them being subverted by internal divisions and neo-colonial Western pressures. This was advice that Moscow had consistently given to Castro in the 1960s with eventual success and was to give the Ethiopians, without success, in the late 1970s. Neto's agreement with the CPSU, and his warm welcome in Moscow in October 1976, suggest that Moscow had fully endorsed his plans.

Nevertheless a number of factors have prompted doubts. Nito Alves, the leader of the coup of May 1977, had been the MPLA's delegate to the CPSU's Twenty-Fifth Congress in Moscow in March 1976 and subsequently kept close contact with Soviet diplomats in Luanda, apparently presenting himself as a more reliable ally than Neto, who talked of non-alignment. It was also noticed that when President Podgorny became the first Soviet head of state to visit East and Central Africa in March 1977, he went only to Tanzania, Zambia, Mozambique and Somalia. He missed out Angola, even though Castro on a similar tour of Africa at about the same time was warmly received in Luanda.

However, two of the best-informed analysts of the Angolan revolution, Michael Wolfers and Jane Bergerol, do not believe that the Soviet Union encouraged Alves.[9] Alves's political line, though never fully clarified, appeared to be less in favour of a vanguard party than of retaining the MPLA as a mass movement.

Too much should probably not be made of the question marks over the Soviet role in the Alves affair. Soviet interest in Angola after independence remained broad rather than deep. Moscow encouraged the MPLA to become a Maxist-Leninist party, and underwrote its survival as the sole government of Angola, supporting the MPLA's refusal to contemplate a coalition with UNITA. But it does not have Soviet advisers in key Angolan government departments, and probably does not seek to influence most decisions.[10] Moscow has not tried to reorient the Angolan economy away from its traditional links with the West, nor did it encourage Angola to join the CMEA. Having had to subsidize Cuba, there was little stomach in the Soviet Union for other similar burdens. It is noticeable that the only three countries outside Eastern Europe which belong to the CMEA are Mongolia and Vietnam, which are under continual pressure from China, and Cuba, which is under continual pressure from the United States. Angola has been under continual pressure from South Africa but the apartheid regime is not seen in Moscow as an ideological and political rival like China and the United States. This is one reason why Moscow's commitment to Angola is so small.

Soviet economic relations with Angola have not progressed far. The most important single project was the fishing agreement signed in April 1977 under which the Soviet Union acquired rights to fish in Angolan waters in exchange for providing ships and technical assistance and landing a proportion of the catch in Angola. After complaints that this proportion was too low and because some of the catch has ended up on the black market, President José Eduardo dos Santos has announced that Angola must develop its own fishing industry. This is now being done through cooperation agreements with Sweden and Cuba. A national fishing fleet and cold storage system are also being built.

Soviet non-military exports to Angola consist almost exclusively of machinery and transport equipment (aircraft, lorries and cars). Moscow imports mainly coffee. Angola's trade deficit with Moscow is striking. In the first nine months of 1983 the Soviet Union exported goods to the value of 170.3m roubles (about £150m), and imported goods worth 2.8m roubles (£2.4m).[11] Angola's exports to all the CMEA countries still represent less than 10 per cent of its total exports.

On the aid front the Soviet Union's contribution to Angola is modest. Neither country publishes figures and the amounts can only be estimated roughly. The British Foreign and Commonwealth Office calculates that it has averaged little more than US $4m a year since 1977, about a tenth of what Moscow gave to Turkey, a member of NATO.[12] Table 15.1 gives the FCO's figures for Soviet aid to Angola and Mozambique; figures for Turkey, Syria, Cuba and Afghanistan are given for comparison.

Soviet loans to Angola according to OECD sources, are provided at an interest rate of 3 per cent and must be paid back over ten years. These terms are slightly less generous than normal Soviet loans to Third World countries which are at 2.5 per cent interest, repayable over twelve years. However, the Soviet Union has

TABLE 15.1
Soviet gross aid disbursements (US $ millions)

	1978	1979	1980	1981	1982
Angola	3.5	3.5	4.0	5.0	5.0
Mozambique	1.8	1.5	1.5	14.5	5.0
Turkey	38.5	39.6	38.2	42.0	8.7
Syria	25.8	24.8	30.5	30.0	23.5
Cuba	400.0	400.0	450.0	500.0	500.0
Afghanistan	37.0	34.0	276.0	235.0	286.0

Source: FCO, 'Soviet, East European and Western Development Aid 1976–82', Foreign Policy Document No. 85, London, 1983.

granted Angola longer than average periods of grace before which the loans have to start being repaid.

Angola: military links

One of the articles of the twenty-year Friendship Treaty between the Soviet Union and Angola promised that both sides would develop cooperation in the military sphere 'in the interests of strengthening their defence capacity'. In practice this meant the provision of arms supplies and some military advisers and instructors, roughly 500 according to US estimates. Weapons included jet fighters, tanks and guided anti-aircraft missiles. However the number of Cuban troops declined during 1976 from a peak of 16,000 at the end of the war to 10,000.

Neither the Soviets nor the Cubans apparently saw their victory in Angola as an immediate springboard for advances elsewhere in southern Africa. Although the MPLA's triumph gave a new sanctuary to SWAPO, the Namibian independence movement, there was no dramatic increase in Soviet aid or logistical support received by SWAPO after 1975. Similarly, although the Soviet Union was interested in the outcome of the war in Rhodesia, it did not seek to have Cuban troops used on the side of the liberation movements, as had been done so successfully in Angola. Indeed, Moscow continued to misread the situation in Rhodesia and did not predict that Joshua Nkomo's ZAPU would fail to emerge as the main ruling party. (In this error Moscow was in good company. No Western government predicted it either.)

With the onset of South African military incursions into southern Angola in 1977, and the revival of UNITA, supported by South Africa, the MPLA turned to the Cubans for renewed assistance. The number of Cuban troops rose again. No official figures are available, and outside analysts can only go by Western intelligence sources, whose methodology is not open to scrutiny. According to these, the Cuban contingent rose to roughly 19,000 by the end of 1977 and 25,000 by 1984. The same sources say that Angola paid for the upkeep of these troops with hard currency earned from oil.

The Soviet Union has continued to keep the MPLA periodically supplied with arms, the most recent occasion being an announcement on 12 January 1984 by the official Soviet news agency Tass that defence aid was being increased. In line with standard Soviet practice the type and quantity of arms deliveries were not revealed. In spite of these reported increases, Soviet weaponry has not been sufficient to turn the tide of war. Up to the beginning of 1984 the South Africans and their UNITA clients seemed to be continuing to gain ground. Soviet and Cuban aid provided a shield of last resort against the capture of Luanda and the major towns in the Central Highlands but was not enough to clear the MPLA's enemies out of the country permanently.

To set against these military costs, the Soviet Union has acquired airfield facilities in Angola for military reconnaissance flights over the South Atlantic to monitor Western shipping. It does not have a naval or a submarine base.

Mozambique: political and economic links
Soviet involvement in Mozambique has not been as great as in Angola. Indeed, because it is so much less, it provides a useful illustration of the degree to which Soviet relations with Third World nations arise from historical circumstances, and are limited by the specific geopolitical environment. Superficially, Angola and Mozambique are similar. Both were Portuguese colonies which came to independence via an armed struggle, in part supported by Moscow. At independence the successful liberation movement in each country felt alienated from the Western world. According to right-wing theory, the Soviet Union had an opportunity in both countries to 'fill the vacuum' and exploit its position to further the aim of challenging the West's *de facto* regional partner, South Africa.

In practice – as the first section of this chapter argued – there is little evidence that the Soviet Union is actively interested in changing the apartheid regime in the near future. Second, the 'vacuum' was not the same in Angola as it was in Mozambique, and it is not even clear that the Soviet Union wanted to fill it. Unlike the MPLA, Frelimo held an unchallenged position as Mozambique's only liberation movement against the Portuguese. It received military aid from China as well as from the Soviet Union. At independence it did not seem to require massive assistance from either the Soviet Union or Cuba to consolidate itself against internal or external opposition.

But Moscow must have been pleased when Frelimo turned itself into a Marxist-Leninist vanguard party in early March 1977. Later that month Mozambique signed a twenty-year Treaty of Friendship and Cooperation with the Soviet Union. Mozambique also turned to the Soviet Union for aid in setting up a huge state farm development covering 300,000 ha in the Limpopo valley. As it had done in Angola, the Soviet Union signed a fishing accord, giving it the right to fish from Beira and Maputo in return for providing equipment and a proportion of the catch.

But problems between the two countries began to emerge in 1979. President Samora Machel's endorsement of the Lancaster

House conference on Rhodesian independence appears not to have been approved of in Moscow. The conference was criticized throughout by the Soviet Union as a Western-sponsored exercise which the liberation movements ought to be wary of. A year later Machel led a delegation to Moscow with the aim of joining the CMEA, but was turned down on the grounds that his country's economy was too far below the level of that of the other members.

Mozambique's economy was always shakier than Angola's. It possesses neither oil nor diamonds, Angola's two principal foreign-exchange earners. Yet the Soviet Union was hardly more generous to Mozambique than it had been to Angola, as Table 15.1 makes clear.

The Soviet Union has helped Mozambique to prospect for iron ore, coal, bauxite and oil, and provides pilots to operate the harbour of Maputo, but trade between the two countries remains at a low level. Between January and September 1983 the Soviet Union exported goods to the value of 77m roubles (£70m) but its imports from Mozambique were worth only 0.8m roubles (£0.7m). Mozambican exports to all the centrally planned economies in 1982 represented only 13 per cent of its total exports.[13] The Soviet Union has supplied about 400 non-military technicians, mainly doctors and teachers.

Moscow's refusal to accept Mozambique as a member of the CMEA reflected an unwillingness to provide the country with the massive economic assistance which Machel wanted. It was this lack of Soviet generosity and the tenuous basis for trade between Mozambique and the Soviet Union which ultimately led Machel to review his country's links with Moscow and in part encouraged him to contemplate restoring relations with Mozambique's neighbour South Africa – as the final section of this chapter explains.

Mozambique: military links

Within two years of Mozambique's independence cross-border raids by the white-minority regime of Ian Smith in Rhodesia – ostensibly against Zimbabwean guerrilla bases – as well as sabotage by the Mozambique National Resistance (MNR) which was organized by the Smith regime were causing problems for Frelimo. The Friendship Treaty with the Soviet Union in March 1977 led to Soviet deliveries of tanks, anti-aircraft guns and rocket launchers as Machel turned his former guerrilla force into a conventional army.

According to Western intelligence sources, some 200 Soviet instructors and advisers were working with Frelimo's army. After Zimbabwe's independence in 1980 South Africa began to take a more aggressive stance towards Mozambique in order to prevent the increased movement through Mozambique of ANC guerrillas. In January 1981, a South African army tank force raided ANC houses at Matola on the outskirts of Maputo. Moscow's response a month later was to send two Soviet warships to Maputo in a show of force. The Soviet ambassador to Mozambique, Valentin Vdovin, issued a warning that the Soviet Union would help Mozambique in case of further attacks.

In mid-1982 General Alexei Yepishev, the head of the political department of the Soviet Army, spent a week in Mozambique assessing the deteriorating security situation. Whether or not he was asked to recommend a dramatic increase in Soviet military aid is not clear, although subsequent comments by Mozambique officials suggest Frelimo had hoped for more economic and other forms of Soviet help. At all events, no Soviet military aid followed. Action by the South-African-supported MNR increased.

The Soviet reaction to 'constructive engagement'
Soon after coming to power, the Reagan administration announced a new strategy of 'constructive engagement' with South Africa. It was presented publicly as a deliberate contrast to what was said to be the Carter administration's policy of giving Pretoria a cold shoulder (even though under Carter US investment and trade with South Africa continued to grow). Reagan administration officials argued that the Carter policy had failed to modify South African actions, and that it was better to engage South Africa in dialogue. The policy was initially said to be intended to achieve change inside South Africa, but as time went by it became increasingly clear that the strategy was mainly geared to South Africa's foreign policy, more particularly to South Africa's efforts to destabilize its neighbours and force them to put limits on the ANC and make deals with South Africa. It was the revival of the old South African dream of creating a 'constellation of states' which would be tied economically and even politically to Pretoria. The aim was to weaken the armed struggle inside South Africa.

The Reagan administration announced its policy of 'constructive engagement' when South African forces were occupying parts of southern Angola and arming and supplying the MNR in Mozambique. On the surface the new US policy looked at best like tacit acceptance of South Africa's destabilization strategy, at worst like convergence with it. In the months that followed the United States pursued intensive diplomacy in the region, presenting itself as a mediator and the only major power with influence in Pretoria who could call off the war. The strategy was not unlike that adopted by

Henry Kissinger in the Middle East in the early 1970s, when the United States acted simultaneously as a partner with Israel and as a mediator, constantly telling the Arab states that the Soviet Union was an unreliable ally and a paper tiger which had no power to make peace since it had no links with Israel.

South Africa's strategy of making war and calling for peace caused major debates in the leadership of the MPLA and Frelimo. Moscow was wary of this strategy, suspecting rightly that one of its aims was to prevent the Soviet Union exerting any influence in the region. On a visit to Moscow in January 1982 Lucio Lara, the Secretary-General of the MPLA, was reportedly told by Soviet Prime Minister Nikolai Tikhonov that the United States was plotting to return Angola to the American sphere of influence.[14] Later Moscow was to warn the Angolans that the aim was to topple the MPLA either outright or by forcing it into coalition with UNITA, and to end Angola's support for SWAPO. 'The strategic goal of the rulers of Pretoria and Washington is the undermining and toppling of the progressive regime in Angola, while their tactical objective is to get Luanda to renounce its support of the Namibian patriots', as one Soviet commentator put it.[15]

However, short of enormously increasing its own military commitment in both Angola and Mozambique, there was little, apart from argument and propaganda, which Moscow could do to influence developments. Faced with the local superiority of South African arms the Soviet leadership was not willing to increase its stake. At best it was prepared to mount a holding operation. In Angola this enabled the MPLA, at least at the time of writing, to confine the disengagement pact it signed with South Africa in February 1984 to a limited ceasefire in the border regions. In Mozambique, where Soviet influence was smaller and there were no Cuban combat troops, the balance of power was overwhelmingly on South Africa's side. Frelimo signed a wide-ranging non-aggression pact with Pretoria in March 1984 (the Nkomati accord) which was intended to pave the way for 'peaceful co-existence' between the two countries and an increase in South African trade and investment in Mozambique, as well as ending the transit of ANC guerrillas through Mozambique.

The Soviet Union criticized the South African-Mozambique accord – albeit in an indirect way, since it still hoped to retain some access to Frelimo. 'Strong-arm methods hardly make for durable understandings, especially when the groundwork for them is shaky', said a Soviet commentator.[16] In a communiqué in April 1984 after talks in Moscow between President Chernenko and the Ethiopian leader Mengistu Haile Mariam, Tass said 'both sides believe that the political and diplomatic pressure exerted by Washington and Pretoria is aimed at changing the strategic situation in the south of Africa in their favour and subordinating the whole of that region to their influence'.[17]

Conclusion

The Soviet commitment to Angola and Mozambique has been strictly limited. Both countries came to independence at a time when the Soviet Union had started to take a more pessimistic view of the opportunity for promoting socialism in the Third World. The earlier concept of 'two world economies' had been revised and Soviet theoreticians increasingly wrote of a single world economy dominated by the capitalist system. Yevgeni Tarabrin, the deputy director of Moscow's Africa Institute, writing in 1977 conceded that 'in spite of their different socio-political orientations, African countries have much in common. So far all of them are part of the capitalist world economic system.'[18] Or, as another Soviet analyst has stated, 'It is extremely hard to develop economic ties and run government-owned enterprises in countries where private capitalist, small-commodity, and semi-natural economies predominate. Individual enterprises built in African countries often do not maintain close economic ties with other enterprises, receive financial support from private credit banks, lack the necessary economic and technical leadership, and are left to themselves in a hopeless fight against overseas companies engaged in a similar line of business.'[19]

If this analysis makes Africa's socialist potential sound bleak for countries at peace how much worse it must be for Angola and Mozambique, which are countries at war and under constant pressure from South Africa. With hindsight, Moscow's dramatic involvement alongside Cuba in the Angolan civil war which turned the tide of battle at the end of 1975 can be seen as an aberration. Faced with a second, more sustained onslaught by South Africa against the front-line African states, the Soviet Union studiously tried to avoid direct contact with South Africa's forces and showed itself unwilling to provide the economic, political and military assistance necessary to thwart South Africa's aims.

Whether or not particular front-line governments asked for more Soviet assistance is not the issue. Like the South Africans, they perceived that Moscow was not ready for full-scale involvement. The Soviet Union calculated that South Africa enjoyed tacit backing from the United States. It was not willing to face the risk of an open-ended engagement in a situation of geographical disadvantage. As Chernenkò put it on 29 March 1984: 'We are strongly against turning that continent [Africa] into a scene of global political, let alone military confrontation.'[20] Repeated Soviet statements make it clear that the Soviet Union is concerned about recent changes in Southern Africa. But the degree of its commitment to prevent them, and particularly its willingness to use force, is minimal. Ten years after Angolan and Mozambican independence, southern Africa remains a region of low priority for Moscow.

Notes

1. The United Arab Republic (Egypt) signed a friendship treaty in May 1971 but abrogated it in March 1976; Somalia signed one in July 1974 but abrogated it in November 1977.

2. Y.A. Tarabrin, *USSR and Countries of Africa* (Moscow: Progress Publishers, 1977), p. 122.

3. Michael MccGwire and John McDonnell, *Soviet Naval Influence: Domestic and Foreign Dimensions* (New York: Praeger, 1977), p. 653.

4. 'Report of the Central Committee of the CPSU to the Twenty-Fourth Congress' (Moscow: Novosti Press Agency Publishing House, 1971).

5. Wayne Smith, 'Dateline Havana: Myopic Diplomacy', in *Foreign Policy*, Fall 1982, p. 164.

6. For more detail, see Jonathan Steele, *World Power* (London: Michael Joseph, 1983), pp. 228–31.

7. Smith, 'Dateline Havana', p. 170.

8. Steele, *World Power*, p. 232.

9. Michael Wolfers and Jane Bergerol, *Angola in the Front Line* (London: Zed Press, 1983), p. 78.

10. *Ibid.*, p. 156.

11. *Vneshnaya Torgovlya SSSR za 1983* (Moscow, 1983).

12. FCO, 'Soviet, East European and Western Development Aid 1976–82', Foreign Policy Document No. 85, London, 1983.

13. Mozambique National Planning Commission, quoted in *Quarterly Economic Review of Mozambique, Annual Supplement, 1984* (London: Economist Intelligence Unit, 1984).

14. *Keesing's Contemporary Archives* (Bristol, 1982), 9 April 1982.

15. *New Times* (Moscow), No. 2, 1984, p. 7.

16. *New Times* (Moscow), No. 12, 1984, p. 12.

17. Tass, 2 April 1984, in *Soviet News* (London, Soviet Embassy Press Department), 4 April 1984.

18. Tarabrin, *USSR and Countries of Africa*, p. 314.

19. *Ibid.*, p. 222.

20. Tass, 29 March 1984, in *Soviet News*, 4 April 1984.

16
Soviet development policy in Central Asia

Alastair McAuley

Introduction

This volume is concerned with the question of relations between the Third World and the socialist countries of Eastern Europe. Attention has been focused primarily on Soviet relations with independent states in South and South-East Asia, Africa and Latin America. But the Soviet Union contains within its own borders regions whose history and cultural affiliations suggest that they too should be thought of as part of the Third World. So this chapter extends the meaning of East-South relations to include aspects of Soviet regional policy. It is concerned with two issues: the extent to which Soviet policy towards the less-developed regions of the USSR can be seen as a model of socialist relations between the First and Third Worlds and, second, the degree to which Soviet development effort in these regions should be considered to be part of the socialist bloc's contribution to world economic development. Unfortunately, limitations of data mean that the second issue is barely touched upon.

Soviet territory covers much of the northern part of the Eurasian land mass; it includes areas settled by primitive hunter-gatherer tribes along the Arctic seaboard, regions of traditional pastoral nomadism and ancient irrigated agriculture and, finally, the complex patchwork of settlement in the Caucasus Mountains. Each of these areas has some claim to be regarded as part of the Third World, and, since Soviet policy towards each has been different, it is not possible to deal with all of them in this chapter. Consequently, I will restrict myself to a discussion of Soviet policy towards Central Asia.

The four republics of Soviet Central Asia, perhaps together with the Transcaucasian republic of Azerbaijan, form a cultural unit. They cover an area of traditional irrigated agriculture in middle Asia with a fringe of transhumant or nomadic pastoralism. The languages spoken by the native populations belong to the Turkic or Persian groups. And, since their conquest by the Arabs in the eighth century, they have formed part of the Islamic culture area. Geographically and culturally, they have much in common with the

299

independent states of the Middle East. Central Asia is one of the two largest developing regions in the USSR (the other is Kazakhstan); it is also the most densely populated. The pattern of Soviet policy towards it will therefore dominate any more general assessment of the contribution of Soviet regional policy towards East-South relations.

As the terms are commonly used, the difference between a developed and an underdeveloped economy involves both the structure of output and the level of productivity. A far higher share of output is generated in the manufacturing sector of a developed economy than in that of an underdeveloped one; and it is usually assumed that output per worker (and hence the standard of living) is higher in the former as well. Furthermore, a modern economy is identified not only by what is produced but also by the uses to which its production is put. Consequently, the analysis of Soviet policy towards Central Asia should consider each of these three topics. Ideally, we should like to be able to say how the economic structure of the region has changed over the past fifty years or so, what has happened to labour productivity and how the pattern of resource use has evolved; we should also like to know whether there has been a net flow of resources into or out of the region. Unfortunately, the nature of the available material makes precision on this last question impossible at least for the present.

Published Soviet statistics and the studies of Soviet and Western economists allow us to chart the changes that have taken place in the economies of the republics of Central Asia; but they do not permit us to do much more than determine the direction of net resource flows. This is partly a consequence of distortions introduced by the Soviet price system; it is much more a consequence of the absence of quantitative information about the redistributive impact of the state budget and estimates of interregional balances of payments. This chapter is therefore largely confined to an account of the changes that have taken place in Central Asia and a discussion of some of their implications for Soviet relations with countries in the Third World. More precisely, in the next section I provide a description of the economy of Central Asia on the eve of rapid industrialization. This is intended to provide a benchmark against which the Soviet achievement can be measured. The following section looks at the present state of the Central Asian economy in an attempt to measure the success of Soviet policy. The last section addresses the wider issues of the applicability of Soviet development policy to other parts of the Third World.

Central Asia on the eve of industrialization

This section contains a description of the Central Asian economy on the eve of rapid industrialization (which in practical terms means 1926–7 or as near to that date as I have been able to find appropriate information). In line with what was said about the nature of economic development in the introduction, attention will focus upon the structure of the economy, levels of productivity (or, rather, the standard of living that they entail) and, lastly, the pattern of final demand. Soviet economic historians[1] who have written about Central Asia emphasize how much more backward the region was than Russia proper in the 1920s. So a subsidiary aim of this section will be to determine the ways in which the economies of the two regions differed.

Before describing the structure of the Central Asian economy, however, I should like to provide a few words of demographic introduction. At the 1926 census, the population of Central Asia amounted to 7.6m persons; the region thus contained some 5 per cent of the country's population. Within the region, Uzbekistan was by far the largest republic: it contained some three-fifths of the region's total population. The other three republics, Tadjikistan, Kirgizia and Turkmenistan, were of approximately equal size.

At this time, indigenous groups made up some 87 per cent of the population while Russians and other Slavs accounted for 7.5 per cent. The region was predominantly rural. As urbanization is measured in the census (that is, in terms of the proportion of the population living in localities designated as urban) there was no difference between Central Asia and the rest of the USSR: in each case 82 per cent of the population was listed as living in rural areas. But it is almost certainly the case that a larger proportion of Russians than of Uzbeks or other Central Asians lived in large industrial centres. Finally, although Russians generally were country-dwellers in 1926, those who had migrated to Central Asia were concentrated in towns; in the census, two-thirds are listed as urban residents. Nevertheless, the towns of Central Asia, like the countryside, were still predominantly native in character since Slavs made up little more than a quarter of the urban population.

There are two ways of describing the industrial structure of a country or region: either one can determine the shares of output (national income or net material product) originating in particular sectors or one can examine the sectoral composition of factor use. The first of these procedures probably gives a more accurate picture of what is meant by the level of industrialization in a region; but it is more susceptible to the sorts of distortions that Soviet national income statistics are known to suffer from (i.e. double counting, inadequate price deflation and so on). Also, it is difficult to obtain national income and product data on a republic or regional basis – particularly for the 1920s. For this reason, the second method is used here. In particular, the industrial structure of Central Asia is defined in terms of the occupational structure of the economically active population given in the 1926 census. (This approach has the added advantage of avoiding the distinction commonly made in current Soviet labour-force statistics between state, cooperative and private activity.) The structure of employment in Central Asia as recorded by the 1926 census is given in Table 16.1. In terms of the categories given, the employment structure in Central Asia in 1926 was remarkably similar to that in the rest of the USSR. In both cases more than nine-tenths of all those employed were to be found in agriculture, about 5 per cent were in industry and the remainder were split between construction and transport on the one hand and all non-manual occupations on the other. As one might expect, engineering and metal-working were more common in the rest of the USSR than in Central Asia, as were also such activities as education and health care. But the differences were not large. In fact, this comparison in terms of census employment categories is too favourable to Central Asia. A higher proportion of workers in Central Asian industry than in that of the rest of the USSR was engaged in handicraft and artisanal activities and a correspondingly lower proportion was employed in large-scale (factory) industry. And, of course, output per man is higher in the latter. (Available figures also suggest that labour productivity was significantly higher in Russian than in Central Asian factories.) But even allowing for these factors, differences in economic structure hardly seem sufficient to warrant the assertion that Central Asia was significantly less developed than the rest of the country.

The same can be said about differences in the standard of living between the two regions. I have discovered two contemporary

TABLE 16.1
Structure of employment in Central Asia in 1926
(percentage of total employment)

Manual employment	
Agriculture	91.6
Engineering and metal-working	0.6
Light and food industries	3.5
Other sectors[a]	1.5
Non-manual employment	2.7

[a] In the categorization used here, other manual employment consists largely of jobs in construction and transport.

Source: Tsentralnoe Statisticheskoe Upravlenie, *Itogi vsesoiuznoi perepisi naseleniia Sovetskogo Soiuza v 1959* (Gosstatizdat, 1962), Vol. SSSR.

sources which cast light on the level of income in Central Asia and
they both indicate that it differed little from average incomes in the
Slav areas. Both of these contemporary sources emanate from the
People's Commissariat of Finance: first there are estimates of
peasant incomes based on the agricultural tax returns; then there
are also more complete estimates of personal income in different
regions produced by the Commissariat's Research Department.

The agricultural tax was paid by individual peasant households,
by cooperatives and, apparently, by state farms (but not by those
employed on *sovkhozy* (state farms)). Tax was levied on agricultural incomes and on household earnings from non-agricultural
activities. Agricultural earnings were determined on the basis of the
assets owned or leased by the household; non-agricultural earnings
were recorded directly. For a number of years *Narkomfin* (the
People's Commissariat of Finance) used the material it amassed in
the course of collecting the tax as the basis for a publication about
the state of the peasant economy in the USSR. These tax-based data
surely contain inaccuracies but there is no reason to suppose that
there are systematic biases between the regions; and the figures they
give are much more detailed than any other available source for the
period.

Unfortunately, only the last of the *Narkomfin* surveys contains
estimates of peasant incomes in Central Asia so the following
figures relate to 1928–9. For that year I have attempted to calculate
the *per capita* income of all those engaged in agriculture in Central
Asia and in other regions of the USSR (Table 16.2). Income is
defined as consisting of the net proceeds of agricultural activity,
earnings from artisanal activity, from wage-work and so on; the
agricultural population consists of members of peasant households

TABLE 16.2
Per capita income of agricultural population in 1928–9
(USSR average = 100)

RSFSR[a]	103
Russian regions only	107
Uzbekistan	81
Kirgizia	90
Tadjikistan	49
Turkmenistan	79
Central Asia	78

[a] RSFSR = Russian Soviet Federated Socialist Republic.
Source: Selskoe khozyaistvo Soyuza SSR v 1928/29 godu (Moscow: Gos. Finansovoe
Izdatelstvo, 1931).

(including those recorded as having too little income to pay the agricultural tax) and those in households whose breadwinner was a member of a cooperative. I have had to exclude the families of those who worked on state farms since no information about these was contained in the relevant publication. But this should not lead to substantial bias since in the late 1920s there were very few people in this category.

For ease of comparison, *per capita* income in each of the regions in which we are interested has been expressed as a percentage of *per capita* income in the USSR as a whole. The figures given in Table 16.2 suggest that peasant living standards in most of Central Asia were about three-quarters or four-fifths of those in the rest of the USSR. It was only in Tadjikistan that the rural population was distinctly worse off than the Russian peasantry. But even the ratio of 2:1 was modest when compared with prevailing urban-rural disparities elsewhere in the country.

The other set of income estimates produced by economists at *Narkomfin* relate to 1925–6 (Table 16.3). They refer to the population as a whole rather than just the peasantry. Income was defined to include the net proceeds from agriculture, wages and salaries paid to state employees and income liable to tax received by artisans, traders and the bourgeoisie. The estimates in Table 16.3 are in nominal roubles; that is, they make no allowance for differences in prices between regions. In 1929, the price level was higher in Central Asia than in European Russia and presumably the same was true in 1925–6; but I doubt that price level differences were sufficiently large to modify the relativities of Table 16.3 substantially. That is, we may infer that average living standards in Central Asia were approximately the same as those in the Russian

TABLE 16.3
Comparative income estimates in 1925–6

	Roubles p.a.	Percentage of USSR average
RSFSR	152.36	99.5
Russian regions only	164.17	107.2
Uzbek SSR (inc. Tadjikistan)	183.04	119.6
Kirgizia	67.19	43.9
Turkmenistan	182.71	119.3
Central Asia	167.15	109.2

Source: *Finansovye problemy planovogo khozyaistva*, 1930, No. 5.

regions of the RSFSR – although annual *per capita* income in Uzbekistan was clearly less than the 231 roubles recorded for the Central Industrial Region and less than half the income of 396 roubles given for Moscow Gubernia.

One final point should be noted: according to the *Narkomfin* tax data referred to above, the *per capita* income of the rural (peasant) population of the Leningrad-Karelian region in 1928–9 was 72 roubles per year. If we assume it was approximately the same in 1925–6 then the figures for *per capita* income in the region as a whole together with data on the relative size of the urban and rural populations imply an urban *per capita* income of 600–650 roubles per year. That is, in the best-off parts of the Russian Republic urban incomes were eight or nine times as large as those of the peasantry. For the country as a whole in 1928, another source gives a ratio of about 4:1.[2]

It is difficult to specify indicators which can characterize a modern style of life adequately; and, of course, it is not always possible to find information on the variables that seem relevant. Nevertheless, it seems to me that modern societies are characterized by a secular literate culture that emphasizes 'the desirability of acquiring technical skills. And, from the statistics that are easily available in the USSR, these features are reflected by the availability of further and specialist education, of public libraries and, perhaps, of health care. They will also be reflected in the literacy statistics.

In 1922, the availability of hospital beds, of further education and culture in Central Asia and in the rest of the USSR was as is given in Table 16.4. In each case Central Asia is substantially worse off than the rest of the USSR. And, of course, the crude indicators used here take no account of differences in quality. Also, insofar as one is

TABLE 16.4
Social indicators in 1922 (provision per 10,000 population)

	Central Asia	Rest of USSR
Hospital beds	3.9	14.7
Students in VUZy[a]	4.0	16.6
Student in secondary specialist establishments	3.0	9.3
Public libraries	0.2	1.3

[a] VUZy = Higher Educational Establishments.
Source: Tsentralnoe Statisticheskoe Upravlenie, *Narodnoe khoziaystvo SSSR za 50 let* (Moscow: Statistika, 1972).

interested in making comparisons between the Russians and the indigenous populations of the region, one should remember that services like further education are more readily available in urban areas – which, in Central Asia, was where the immigrant population was concentrated.

The cultural differences between Russia proper and Central Asia are further stressed by figures on literacy. At the 1926 census, some 43 per cent of the population of the RSFSR was recorded as literate (although it is not clear what criterion of literacy was used). In Central Asia, literacy was put at 8 per cent, presumably on the same criterion. Since this latter figure includes immigrant Slavs, most of whom could read, it is clear that literacy was rare among the indigenous population.

But simple literacy is not enough to be able to provide a modern industrial culture. Various sorts of specialist training are also required. And the 1926 census revealed just how few of the indigenous population of Central Asia possessed these skills. In Uzbekistan, for example, only 319 out of 4,911 medical personnel were Uzbek or from other local ethnic groups. Among technical peronnel in state and 'commercial' institutions the dominance of immigrants was even greater: less than 5 per cent were drawn from the indigenous population. The position in the other Central Asian republics was no better. Although they accounted for no more than 11–12 per cent of the total population, Russians and other immigrants made up between two-thirds and three-quarters of the leading cadres. In engineering and medicine, their dominance was almost complete.

The material presented here suggests that on the eve of rapid industrialization there was considerable similarity between the industrial structures of Central Asia and those of the rest of the USSR. Also, there were only moderate differences in living standards as measured by personal incomes. If this were all that mattered, it is difficult to see how one could claim that Central Asia was very much less developed than Russia proper. But, as I have tried to argue, the structure of output and the level of productivity are only part of the story. Russia may have been backward in these respects in the 1920s when compared with Western Europe or North America, but it still shared with these two areas many features of a common secular culture and history. There was far greater similarity in attitudes to science and technology, to medicine, law and the individual between Russia and the West than between Russia and the Central Asian provinces. And in this respect at least, the Ukraine and Byelorussia were similiar to Russia itself. If we are to accept the claim made by Soviet economic historians[3] that Russia was more developed than Central Asia, we must also accept that development and underdevelopment, progress and backwardness, imply, in addition to differences in productivity, closeness to a West European cultural tradition.

Economic development in Central Asia, 1928–79

The adoption of the first Five-Year Plan in 1928 and the mass collectivization of agriculture in 1929–30 mark the beginning of rapid industrialization in the Soviet Union. For the country as a whole, the Stalin years constitute a decisive break with the past. They witness an enormous expansion in the size and sophistication of Soviet industry. By 1953 the USSR had emerged as a military-industrial surperpower capable of exploding the hydrogen bomb and about to launch the world's first artificial satellite. But this achievement had been bought dear; quite apart from the brutality and political repression that will forever be associated with the name of Stalin, rapid industrialization in the USSR was associated with a precipitous decline in living standards. Recent estimates[4] suggest that real wages in 1932 were only half of what they had been in 1928. Even in 1952, they had barely regained their pre-industrialization level. But this concerted attack on personal consumption was accompanied by a substantial expansion of expenditure on social consumption. Facilities for a modern industrial culture were made more widely available: an attack on illiteracy was mounted, a universal health service was established, a start was made in bringing the benefits of twentieth-century urban society to the timeless backwardness of the Russian village. And progress has continued under Khrushchev and his successors. The rate of growth of output has been declining in the last quarter-century, but the 1950s and 1960s saw a rapid increase in personal consumption. It was at this time that the Soviet population began to enjoy the fruits of development.

In this section I attempt to describe the impact that the policies which brought about such changes to Soviet society had on the economy of Central Asia. Speaking generally, although Stalinist development also led to the expansion of industrial capacity in the region, its primary impact was to transform Central Asia into a specialist supplier of raw materials and in the first instance into a supplier of raw cotton. Soviet policies have not secured the all-round development of productive forces in the region; rather, it has been converted into a specialized (agricultural) component and incorporated into a wider interregional division of labour. Before examining these processes more closely, however, I propose to summarize their impact on the demographic evolution of the area.

Economic development in the Soviet Union has had the expected effects on population and population growth. In 1926, the crude birth rate was 44 per thousand; in 1979 this had declined to 18 per thousand. In spite of a substantial decline in the death rate, the net reproduction rate (the number of girls to which a woman gives birth during the course of her life who survive to adulthood – which approximates to the long-run growth rate of the population) is little more than unity. In Central Asia, by way of contrast, demographic response to modernization has been radically different or at least has been delayed. For the region as a whole, the crude birth rate in 1979 was 34 per thousand. Even allowing for the fact that age-specific death rates are higher here than elsewhere in the country, they are sufficiently low for the region to have experienced a net population growth rate of 2.8 per cent per annum during the 1970s.

As a result of rapid population growth throughout the period 1926–79, aided by substantial immigration during the Stalin period, the population of Central Asia rose to 25.5m in 1979. At that date it accounted for almost 10 per cent of the Soviet population; thus, in a little over fifty years the share of the region in the total has virtually doubled Over the same period, the number of Russians and other Slavs in Central Asia has increased sevenfold. By 1979, these immigrants and their descendants accounted for almost a fifth of the region's population.

For the USSR as a whole, development has been accompanied by a process of urbanization. By 1959 almost half the Soviet population lived in towns; in 1979 it was more than three-fifths. The process of urbanization has occurred more slowly in Central Asia, however, and even in 1979 three-fifths of the population still lived in the countryside. As one might expect, the experience of immigrant and indigenous groups differed in this respect. In 1970 (the latest year for which relevant data are available) three-quarters of the indigenous population lived in rural areas while more than four-fifths of Russians and other Slavs were to be found in the towns. At this date, for every five urban natives there were four urban Slavs. The town had become distinctively more Russian than the countryside.

The population trends reviewed here have certain implications for the process of development. First, the high rates of natural increase mean that Central Asian society is still a very young society; in 1970 (again, the latest year for which data are available) 45 per cent of the population were under the age of fifteen. This places a significant strain on the state's welfare services – and upon the economically active population. And, of course, high birth rates lead to lower rates of female participation in the economy. Second, high rates of natural increase imply a need to ensure a similarly rapid increase in job opportunities. Work must be found for large numbers of new entrants to the labour force each year. Finally, the substantial in-migration of Russians and other Slavs has probably been associated with their continued predominance in leading cadre positions. Insofar as Soviet policies have been successful in raising the educational standards of the indigenous population there is probably now some rivalry for elite positions.

Let me turn now to a more detailed study of the impact of Soviet development policies on the economies of Central Asia and the rest of the USSR. As in the previous section, I start with an examination of the structure of employment. The figures given in Table 16.5 relate to average annual employment in 1975 – the most recent year for which a breakdown of capital stock by sector and region is available. In calculating agricultural (and total) employment those working on collective farms have been added to those who work on *sovkhozy* but no allowance has been made for private-sector activities. Finally, by way of introductory explanation, what I call the Industrial Centre consists of the RSFSR, the Ukraine and Byelorussia. This is too large a grouping: the Far East and the largely rural *oblasti* (provinces) in the north and west ought to have been excluded. But appropriate date at the sub-republican level is not available.

TABLE 16.5
Average annual employment in 1975 (percentage share)

	Central Asia	Industrial Centre[a]
Industry	16.1	31.1
Agriculture	36.1	19.7
Transport	7.7	9.2
Construction	8.8	9.0
Trade etc.	8.1	8.6
Other	23.2	22.4

[a] RSFSR, the Ukraine and Byelorussia.
Source: Tsentralnoe Statisticheskoe Upravlenie, *Narodnoe khoziaystvo SSSR za 1975* (Moscow: Statistika, 1976), pp. 441, 536.

Two features about the statistics given in Table 16.5 merit comment. First, in Central Asia as in the rest of the USSR economic development has led to the disappearance of the unspecialized peasant economy. No longer is the peasant involved in construction, transport and trade – or rather, he is no longer involved in these activities to the extent that he was before the 1920s. Second, the direction in which specialization has proceeded in Central Asia is different from that of the Industrial Centre: in the former, more than a third of the economically active population was employed in agriculture and less than a fifth were in industry; in the Slav republics the proportions were reversed.

It is important to realize that the continuing importance of agriculture in the Central Asian economy does not reflect a simple lag in industrialization. It is not the case that this region is following in the path of the Slav areas but with a few years' delay. Rather, it reflects the value attached to a particular resource in the inter-regional division of labour. This is brought out by the pattern of capital investment that has been undertaken since 1928 and the capital/labour ratios that now exist. In 1960 (the earliest year for which complete figures are available) some 39 per cent of the non-residential capital stock of the Industrial Centre was to be found in industry; at the same date only 17 per cent of the capital stock was in agriculture. In 1975, the relevant figures were 42 and 15 per cent. In Central Asia, on the other hand, only 28 per cent of the capital stock in 1960 was in industry and 32 per cent in agriculture; in 1975 the analogous figures were 30 and 29 per cent. Thus, in terms of the structure of capital, Central Asia experienced virtually no change in the relative importance of agriculture and industry in this fifteen-year period and there was no tendency for the region to become more like the Slav areas.

The analysis of occupational structure shows the continuing importance of agriculture to the Central Asian economy. And, in fact, the agriculture of the region is now dominated by cotton. Between 1928 and 1979 the output of this crop increased elevenfold; by contrast, the output of grain has increased only two and a half times – and under Stalin it actually fell. Increases in agricultural output have been achieved by increases in areas sown and by an intensification of production. In the last fifty years the area sown to cotton in Central Asia has doubled and this increase has necessitated a substantial investment in irrigation facilities. This has been complemented by the switch to high-yielding varieties and by increasing applications of chemical fertilizer, etc.

Thus, there was substantial structural change after 1928 in both Central Asia and the Industrial Centre. However, the experience of the two regions has diverged. The effect of Soviet policies in the 1930s, 1940s and 1950s was to make the Central Asian economy more specialized, to integrate it with that of the rest of the country but at the same time make it more dependent. It comes as no surprise that in 1940, in spite of producing 90 per cent of the country's raw cotton and containing more than 5 per cent of its population, Central Asia produced less than 3 per cent of its cotton cloth. Perhaps one can say that during this period the region became more backward than the rest of the USSR; but at the same time I am sure that the rate of growth of both industrial and total output has been higher than it would have been under most conceivable policy alternatives. Central Asian success has, however, been heavily dependent upon expansion of a labour-intensive cotton-based agriculture. This has provided work for a rapidly growing population and 'exports' with which to purchase food and the products of Soviet industry. This strategy in turn had been dependent on increases in sown areas – and hence increases in water supply. At a time when the population (and hence the supply of labour) is still growing very rapidly, available supplies of water are being exhausted. Either additional supplies must be found (for example by diverting Siberian rivers) or previous policies must be supplemented by more intensive industrial development.

Rapid industrialization resulted in a sharp fall in real wages and, it appears, a similar fall in the real income of the peasantry. The income levels of the late 1920s were not regained until the end of the Stalin period. Since that date, however, there has been continuing (and relatively rapid) growth in living standards and a marked reduction in urban-rural disparities. In their book on Central Asia, A. Nove and J. Newth argue that the peasants of the region suffered less than those of Russia under Stalin.[5] And some more recent analysts implicitly agree.[6] But this assertion is based on an interpretation of the intersectoral flow of resources in the 1930s that has recently come under attack.[7] And I have not yet discovered any additional material that might resolve the question.

For the 1960s, however, rather more information is available. For 1961, Yu. Vorobyev provides estimates of national income *per capita* in the RSFSR and in the various republics of Central Asia, reproduced in Table 16.6.[8] (National income in this context means net material product – i.e. it excludes services; this will reduce the measured differential since the services sector was larger in Russia than in Central Asia.)

TABLE 16.6
National *per capita* income in 1961 (USSR average = 100)

RSFSR	110
Uzbekistan	65
Kirgizia	67
Tadjikistan	57
Turkmenistan	69
Central Asia	64

If *per capita* national income is accepted as an appropriate indicator of material welfare, the figures given in Table 16.6 indicate that at the beginning of the 1960s living standards in Uzbekistan, Kirgizia and Turkmenistan were much the same. Those in Tadjikistan were distinctly lower. Living standards in Central Asia as a whole were between a half and three-fifths of those in the RSFSR. It will be remembered that this was the relationship between income *per capita* in Central Asia and the two best-off regions of the RSFSR in 1925–6. Insofar as the two different indicators are measuring the same thing, this would suggest that disparities in living standards widened in the first thirty years or so of rapid industrialization.

Another set of national income estimates, for 1968, are provided by L. Telepko and cast light on relative living standards at the end of the decade. Unfortunately, he does not provide figures for individual republics, but for Central Asia as a whole; his figures imply a *per capita* income of 624 roubles.[9] This is less than three-fifths of the figure for the rest of the USSR of 1,085 roubles. These figures imply that disparities were increasing during the 1960s and although I do not have comparable figures for the last fifteen years or so I have no reason to believe that the trend has been reversed.

TABLE 16.7

Social indicators in 1979 (provision per 10,000 population)

	Central Asia	Rest of USSR
Hospital beds	110	125
Students in VUZy[a]	160	200
Students in secondary specialist establishments	134	180
Public libraries	4	5

[a]VUZy = Higher Educational Establishments
Source: Calculated from *NK SSSR*, 1979, various pages.

At the beginning of this chapter I suggested that the level of development in an economy or society was not only a function of the structure of output and the level of productivity. Equally important was the extent to which it created a secular and technical culture. I suggested that backwardness was associated with the absence of a European lifestyle; hence development must connote its acquisition. In terms of the indicators that I proposed in Table 16.4, at any rate, Soviet development policy has been remarkably successful in equipping Central Asia with the material facilities for such a secular culture (see Table 16.7). In every category, the increase in provision since 1922 is enormous. And, at the same time, differences between Central Asia and the rest of the USSR have been much reduced. (In fact, disparities were smaller proportionately and absolutely in 1960 than at the end of the 1970s. This suggests that the Soviet welfare system is having difficulty in maintaining adequate level of provision in the face of rapid population growth.) The narrowing of the gap in the provision of these services has been an important aim of Soviet policy. It has been achieved by the specification of uniform standards on a European scale and their attainment through central control. It is this transformation in the provision of services that forms the basis of Soviet claims to have been successful in developing Central Asia.

The Soviet strategy of development

Development, as the concept has been used in this paper, involves three interrelated processes. It involves a growing specialization of employment, an increasingly refined division of labour. Normally, this implies the growth of sectors like manufacturing but, on occasion, it may result in concentration on the production of a single crop or commodity and greater participation in interregional or international trade. Specialization will also be accompanied by changes in technology: one would expect the capital/labour ratio to rise but, perhaps more important, one would also expect to observe a more consciously 'scientific' approach to production, more positive attitudes towards experimentation and the more rapid diffusion of new technology. This growth in occupational specialization is associated with (and is partly the cause of) the second feature of development: increases in productivity. This in turn implies that the living standards of the bulk of the population will rise. Finally, development results in (and is itself the result of) cultural modernization. That is, it involves the creation of the material underpinnings of what I have called a European civilization: primary and secondary schools, technological colleges and universities, hospitals, public libraries, museums and so on.

In 1926, the territories that had previously formed the Tsarist provinces of Turkestan and Transcaspia, although more specialized in the production and 'export' of cotton than before their incorporation into the Russian Empire, were still overwhelmingly agricultural in character. Their economies, like that of Russia itself, were dominated by peasant households, that is by production units that were responsible for crop-growing and livestock-farming, for construction and transport and for the manufacture of many of the tools and implements used in everyday life. In degree of urbaniza- tion, in occupational structure, in levels of income, all characteris- tics that correlate closely with development as I have defined it, there were only moderate differences between Central Asia and the rest of the Soviet Union. But in Central Asia the indigenous population was almost completely illiterate. Higher administrative and technical occupations were dominated if not monopolized by Slav immigrants. In part this reflected the fact that the Russians were heirs to imperial power; but it was also a consequence of differences in cultural tradition. Russia was immeasurably closer to the secular mainstream of Western Europe. And, despite the relative backwardness of the Russian economy and Russian society in the 1920s, the Slavs were able to dominate Central Asia, impose their policies on the region, because it was so small: Central Asia contained only 5 per cent of the population of the Soviet Union.

There can be no doubt that, in terms of the definitions used here, Soviet policy has been successful in securing the substantial development of Central Asia after 1928. In Russia itself, the predominance of the peasant economy was challenged and replaced by a differentiated system of specialized production structures. And the Central Asian economy has been incorporated into this framework. (This incorporation of Central Asia into a wider Soviet economy appears to be a successful continuation and intensification of policies first adopted in the third quarter of the nineteenth century.) But Soviet policy has done more than incorporate Central Asia into the Russian economy. It has resulted in the transforma- tion of production structures and relationships within the region itself. There too, the dominance of the unspecialized peasant economy has been successfully challenged. Soviet planners have built up a separate planning system, a network of construction organizations; they have installed manufacturing capacity. In this respect, the evolution of the Central Asian economy has paralleled developments elsewhere in the country.

After twenty-five or thirty years of penury under Stalin, the fruits of modernization and development have been translated into rising living standards for the Soviet population under Khrushchev and his successors. The population of Central Asia has shared in this improvement. But the belief that disparities in income between the region and European Russia have narrowed appears to be mis- taken. In 1960 as in 1926 *per capita* incomes in Central Asia were between a half and three-fifths of those in the RSFSR. And the gap may have widened somewhat in the last twenty or twenty-five years. Finally, although Central Asians are well-off when compared to Turks or Iranians, from the standpoint of Moscow or Riga the region is poor: in the late 1970s, the average *per capita* income of collective farmers – and probably those of the rural and indigenous populations more generally – was below the officially defined poverty level of 50 roubles per month.

There is a difference, however, between the standard of living and the style of life – what Soviet specialists now refer to as *obraz zhizni*. In this latter respect, the transformation that has occurred in Central Asia (as in Russia itself) in the last fifty years is astounding. Central Asia now has a network of paved roads; in urban areas the houses are, for the most part, connected to main drainage, to the main electricity or gas supply; there is a dense network of rural and urban schools; there is a complete rural health-care system; there are universities and technical colleges, museums and public libraries. For want of a better word, one must say that the material environment of Central Asian culture has been substantially Europeanized. Those who live in neighbouring countries must envy Central Asians their access to all these facilities.

What was it about Central Asia, or about Central Asia's relationship with Moscow, that has made these policies successful? Nove and Newth have argues that Central Asian development was 'paid for' by the Russian (and Ukrainian) peasantry.[10] But the analysis of Soviet industrialization on which this assessment was based has been challenged in the past decade[11] and I have not been able to discover alternative or additional information that would resolve the question of how Central Asian development was financed. But, in the last analysis, I think that the question of finance, of subsidization or exploitation, is secondary.

The RSFSR benefited from the fact that Central Asia enjoyed production possibilities not open to European Russia, and Central Asia too gained from this complementarity. The existence of a unitary framework of law, currency and fiscal policy made it easier to reap these benefits. But it is not only in the sphere of product specialization that Central Asia benefited from the closeness of the Russian connection: it was also responsible for the rate and direction of evolution of the region's cultural institutions. In the 1920s it was only the immigrants who had the knowledge and training to staff the region's hospitals or the scientific and technical faculties of its universities and the various administrative organizations. And Slavs have continued to play these roles although they have been joined in increasing numbers by members of a new indigenous elite. It is doubtful whether the transfer of personnel involved in these processes would have occurred if Central Asia had been an independent country.

Further, in both the economic and the cultural spheres, the integration of Central Asia into the Soviet Union will have allowed the region to benefit from the commitment and drive of the modernizing elite in Moscow. It is their authority that was instrumental in the largely successful attack on the peasant economy (i.e. mass collectivization). And levels of provision of such services as health-care or primary education are the result of decisions taken in Moscow (and applicable throughout the USSR). In this context Central Asia probably also benefited because it was small – both in terms of population and political weight. As a result, no special arrangements were made for the application of different policies in the region; the policies chosen in Moscow were designed to achieve 'European' standards and Central Asia has been dragged up by Russia's coat-tails.

There is one further benefit that Central Asia may have derived from the Russian connection to which I should like to draw attention. Economic development as defined here may be desirable, it may be desired by a majority of the population, but it is not necessarily a Pareto-superior process. That is, it is not necessarily the case that everyone is made better off and no one made worse off as a result of development. Indeed, in many countries, it is the tenacity with which those who are threatened defend their vested interests that constitutes the major obstacle to development.

If development involves the adoption of a secular, literate and 'European' culture, it must threaten the indigenous cultures of less-developed countries and, consequently, the social and political status of groups whose position depends on that culture. In the case of Central Asia, those threatened by development included the official institutions of Islam – the religious courts, the religious monopoly over education, the religious administration of *wakf*,* property and so on. Under Soviet power these Islamic institutions were deprived of their coercive powers and many of those who staffed them were physically liquidated. Although this view is controversial, some scholars have argued that as a consequence of the Sovietization of Central Asia the northern frontier of the Islamic culture-zone now coincides with the southern frontier of the USSR.[12] Within the Soviet Union, Islam has been reduced to a

---

* *Wakf* is a tax-free grant given by an individual to be held in trust by a Muslim state or institution, the income from which is to be devoted to charitable or pious purposes.

collection of 'folk' practices, a dressing of local colour on an essentially atheistic civilization. This is probably an excessive claim; but at the very least, incorporation has made it impossible for obscurantist imams or mullahs to impose their prejudices on the rest of the population. And there are probably other significant differences in *Weltanschauung* and social organization between Central Asia and Islamic countries of the Middle East. Perhaps one could go so far as to suggest that the existence of an atheist state has played a fundamental role in the success of Soviet development policy in Central Asia

In conception, the Soviet strategy for development as manifested in Soviet policy towards Central Asia differs little from approaches advocated in the West. It involves regional specialization and participation in interregional (international) exchange; within Central Asia itself it involves the adoption of an increasingly refined division of labour. These processes have resulted in increases in productivity and thus in rising living standards. Structural change in the economy has been accompanied by, indeed has been predicated on, cultural modernization. An illiterate peasantry dominated if not cowed by an obscurantist religious elite has been replaced by a literate and increasingly educated labour force which has been taught to approach the world from the standpoint of 'European' science. Such a strategy is certainly applicable elsewhere in the Third World. But it involves risks (as the example of Iran suggests) and these risks may be lessened if the developing region is constitutionally incorporated into a larger 'European' political unit. Perhaps it is only this final feature that can be seen as the distinctively socialist component of Soviet development policy.

Notes

1. V.A. Vinogradov et al. (eds), *Istoriia sotsialisticheskoi ekonomiki SSSR* (Moscow: Nauka, 1976), especially Vol.II, Chs 12, 16. O.B. Dzhamalov, *Istoriia narodnogo khoziaystva Uzbekistana*, Iz-vo AN. (Tashkent: UzSSR, 1962). F.Kh. Kasymov, *Perekhod narodov srednei Azii k sotsializmu minuia kapitalizm* (Tashkent: Fan, 1979) and additional sources cited in this work. P.I. Liashchenko, *Istoriia narodnogo khoziaystva SSSR*, Vol.II (Moscow: Ekonomika, 1948).

2. J. Pavlevski, *Le Niveau de vie en URSS de la révolution d'octobre à 1980* (Paris: Economica, 1975), p.66.

3. See note 1.

4. M. Ellman, 'Did the Agricultural Surplus Provide the Resources for the Increase in Investment in the USSR during the First Five-Year Plan?' *Economic Journal*, Vol. 85, No. 4 (December 1975), pp. 844–63; especially pp. 857, 860. See also A. Vyas, 'Real Wages in the Soviet Economy, 1928–1937', Ph.D. thesis, Birmingham University.

5. A. Nove and J. Newth, *The Soviet Middle East: A Communist Model for Development* (London: Allen and Unwin, 1967), pp. 99–103.

6. A. Khan and D. Ghai, *Collective Agriculture and Rural Development in Soviet Central Asia* (London: Macmillan, 1979), Ch. 4, *passim*.

7. See, for example, J. Millar, 'Soviet Rapid Development and the Agricultural Surplus Hypothesis', *Soviet Studies*, Vol, 22, No. 1 (July 1970); and M. Ellman, 'Did the Agricultural Surplus Provide the Resources for the Increase in Investment in the USSR during the First Five-Year Plan?', *Economic Journal*, Vol, 85, No. 4 (December 1975).

8. Yu. F. Vorobyev, *Vyravnivanie urovnei ekonomicheskogo rezvitia soyuznikh respublik* (Moscow: Nauka, 1965), p. 193.

9. L.N. Telepko, *Urovni ekonomicheskogo razvitia raionov SSSR* (Moscow: Ekonomika, 1971).

10. Nove and Newth, *The Soviet Middle East*.

11. M. Ellman, *op.cit.;* J. Millar, 'Soviet Rapid Development and the Agricultural Surplus Hypothesis', *Soviet Studies*, Vol, 22, No. 1 (July 1970), pp. 77–93; and J. Millar, 'Mass Collectivization and the Contribution of Agriculture to the First Five-Year Plan', *Slavic Review*, Vol, 33, No. 4 (December 1974), pp. 750–66.

12. M. Rywkin, *Moscow's Muslim Challenge: Soviet Central Asia* (Armonk, NY.: M.E. Sharpe, 1982), pp. 150–1 and further sources cited there.

Name index

Aczel, Gyorgy, 53
Agursky, Mikhail, and Adomeit, Hannes, 112n
Alampiev, P. 203, 204, 206, 217n
Al-Beedh, Ali, 246
Albrecht, U. 160, 172, 174n, 175n, 176n
Albright, David, 65n, 86n
Alexandrov, I. 253n
Alexeyev, A., and Fialkovsky, A., 238n
Aliev, G. 24, 30n
Allende, Pres. Salvador, of Chile 10, 121–4, *passim*, 125, 129, 130, 138, 289
Al-Sha'abi, Pres. Qahtan, of S. Yemen, 246
Alves, Nito, 290
Amin, Idi, 8, 70, 79, 110
Andrei, Stefan, 47
Andropov, Yuri, 30n, 74, 75, 106, 126, 132, 245, 253n, 278
Angelis, I. 180
Arafat, Yasser, 277
Aspaturian, Vernon A., 112n
Assad, Pres. Hafiz al-, of Syria, 257, 258, 265–8 *passim*, 270, 278
Astor, David, and Yorke, Valerie, 65n

Badrus, Gheorghe, 55, 66n
Banerji, R. 240n
Barnds, William, 28n, 29n
Barré, Pres. Siad, of Somalia, 70
Begin, Menachem, 274
Bergson, Abram, 65n
Berliner, Joseph, 34
Bethkenhagen, Jochen, 67n
Bhargava, B.S., 44n
Blasier, Cole, 120, 138n
  and Mesa-Lago, C., 138n
Bodansky, Yossef, 45n
Bognar, J., 183, 190n
Bogolomov, O., 180, 181, 189n, 190n
Bokassa, Gen. 65, 99
Bonsal, Philip W., 117, 118, 137n, 138n

Booth, Ken, and Dowdy, Lee, 112n
Borge, Tomás, 131, 132
Borisov, O., 30n
Boudarel, G., 198, 217n, 218n
Bowder, Geoffrey, 282n
Bowman, Larry W., and Clark, Ian, 45n
Bradsher, Henry S., 29n, 45n
Braeckman, Colette, 87n
Braun, Dieter, 45n
Brezhnev, Leonid, 22, 39, 106, 122, 164, 179, 220, 222, 226, 233, 273, 286
Brocheux, P., and Hemery, D., 217n
Brzezinski, Zbigniew, 65n, 85
Brzoska, Michael, 112n, 175n
Bulganin, Marshal, 32, 43n
Burmistrov, V.N., 254n

Caetano, Dr, 287
Campbell, Horace, 113n
Cardesman, A., 174n
Carrère d'Encausse, Hélène, 112n
Carter, Pres. James, 65n, 126, 262, 295
Cassen, Robert, 1, 189n; and Jolly, A.R., Sewell, J. and Wood, R.N., 12n
Castro, Fidel, 102, 116, 119, 121, 123, 129, 133, 138n, 288, 289, 290
Ceausescu, Pres., of Romania, 49
Chadzynski, Henryk, 52
Chaudhuri, P. 240n
Chekhonin, B., 44n
Chen, King, C., 216n
Chernenko, Konstantin, 27, 106, 296, 297
Chicharov, A., 45n
Chistyakov, Alexei, 254n
Chou Enlai, 17
Churkin, Veniamin, 253n
Clarkson, J., 239n
Clissold, Stephen, 137n
Coker, Christopher, 6, 46
Cooley, John K., 281n
Cooper, O., and Fogarty, C., 184, 190n

319

Csaba, Laszlo, 66n
Cutler, Robert M., 190n

Dasgupta, Biplab, 44n
Datar, Asha L., 34, 43n, 239n
Dawisha, Adeed, 280n; and Dawisha, Karen, 28n, 65n, 280n
Deger, Saadet, 4, 113n, 159, 160, 174, 174n, 175n, 176n; and Sen, S., 169, 175n
Deng Xiao-ping, 216n
Desai, Morarji, 39
Dietz, R., 67n
Dobozi, I., 67n, 189n
Donaldson, Robert H., 29n, 44n, 137n, 239n
Dunn, Keith A., 112n
Dupree, Louis, 45n
Duy Hoang, 217n
Dzhamalov, O.B., 317n

Edquist, Charles, 119, 138n
Efrat, Mosche, 111n, 113n
Eisenhower, Pres. Dwight D., 47, 137n
Eitan, Gen. Rafael, 278, 282n
Ellison, Herbert, 29n
Ellman, M., 317n, 318n
Ericson, P.G. and Miller, R.S., 151, 152, 153, 157n

Fahmi, Ismail, 48
Fallenbuchl, Z., and McMillan, C., 189n
Fatah Ismail, Pres. Abdul, of S. Yemen, 245, 247, 248
Feinberg, Richard, E., 138n
Fewtrell, D., 174n, 175n
Fforde, Adam J., 5, 192, 216n, 217n
Finley, David D., 112n
Fischer, Oskar, 47
Fomin, B.S., 189n
Freedman, Robert O., 29n, 280, 281n

Gandhi, Mrs Indira, 39, 220, 233
Gelbard, José, 125, 138n
Gelman, Harry, 28n
Gemayel, Pres. Amin, of Lebanon, 274
Gidadhubli, R.G., 239n, 240n
Giffen, Janice, 216n
Gittings, John, 28n

Glazunov, Y.P., 218n
Goodman, Hirsh, 282n
Goodwin, Geoffrey, 189n
Gorshkov, Adm., 101
Grechko, Marshal, 113n
Griffith, William, 28n
Gromyko, Anatoly A., 113n
Gromyko, Andrei, 48, 106, 113n, 173, 265, 281n
Guardia, Alexis, 138n
Guskov, Alexander, 254n
Gvozdev, Y., 253n

Haberstroh, John, R., 66n
Haile Selassie, Emperor, 79
Halim Khaddam, Abdel, 266
Halliday, Fred, 7, 45n, 241; and Molyneux, M., 87n
Halperin, Maurice, 138n
Hamrin, Carol Lee, 29n
Hanson, P., 176n
Harkavy, R.E., 171, 176n
Harris, Lillian Craig, 29n
Heikal, M.H., 280n
Heimsath, Charles, 43n
Heller, Mark, 282n
Henderson, P.D., 44n
Hersh, Seymour, 238n
Ho Chi Minh, 193, 216n
Holliday, David, 150, 164, 175n
Holloway, Davud, 112n, 113n, 157n
Holzman, F.D., 162, 174n, 184, 190n
Horelick, Arnold, 28n
Horn, Robert C., 238n
Hosmer, Stephen T. and Wolfe, Thomas W., 112n
Hu Yaobang, 23, 30n
Hua Guo-feng, 216n
Huan Xiang, 30n
Huang Hua, 29n
Hudson, Cam, 65n, 66n, 67n
Hussain, King, of Jordan, 264
Hussain, Pres., of Iraq, 257, 268, 281n
Huu Hanh, 217n
Huynh Kim Khanh, 216n

Imam, Z., 181, 190n
Iran, Shah of, 19, 53, 59

Jabber, Paul, and Kalkowicz, Roman, 280n, 281n

Jacobsen, C.J., 216n, 217n
Ja'far, Kassem M., 7, 255, 282n
Jahn, Egbert, 112n
Jain, R.K., 43n
Jaruzelski, Gen., 52
Jencks, Harlan, 28n
Ji Pengfei, 29n
Jones, David R., 112n
Joshua, Wynfred, and Gilbert,
    Stephen P., 281n

Kanet, R.E., 28n, 88n, 161, 174n, 176n;
    and Bahry, Donna, 281n
Kapitsa, M., 24, 25, 26, 30n
Kaplan, Stephen, S., 112n, 280n
Kapur, Ashok, 44n
Karol, K.S., 138n
Kasymov, F. Kh, 317n
Katz, Mark, N., 107, 113n
Keeble, C., 12n
Kennedy, Pres. John F., 286
Khalilzad, Zalmay, 45n
Khan, A., and Ghai, D., 318n
Khrushchev, Nikita, 32, 106, 116–19
    passim, 121, 129, 138n, 144, 145, 156,
    179, 287, 307, 314
Killick, Tony *et al.*, 217n
Kissinger, Henry, 19, 221, 262, 296
Kleinen, John, 216n, 217n
Klerr, J., and Zacher, L., 180, 189n
Klinghoffer, Arthur, 28n
Kohli, S.N., 45n
Kolodziej, E.A., 111n
Kostiner, Joseph, 253n
Kosygin, A.N., 221, 226
Kova, A. Cvet, 66n
Kuzmin, Anatoli, 139n
Kuznetsov, Vasili, 269

Ladozhsky, A., 44n
Lamm, H.S., and Kupper, S., 67n
Lara, Lucio, 296
Laszlo, E., and Kurtman, J., 189n
Lavigne, M., 13n, 66n, 87n
Lawson, Colin W., 4, 5, 13n, 65n, 177,
    190n, 191n
Lawson, Eugene, 29n
Le Duan, 205
Le Hang, 218n
Le Trong, 217n

Legum, Colin, 29n, 30n
Leifer, Michael, 28n
Leiken, Robert S., 137n, 139n
Leonidov, V., 187, 191n
Li, Pres., of China, 29n
Li Xianian, 28n
Liashchenko, P.I., 317n
Lieberthal, Kenneth, 28n
Lowenthal, Abe, 138n
Luckham, Robin, 8, 89, 112n
Lumumba, Patrice, 90
Luttwak, E.N., 12n
Lyon, Peter, 5, 32, 44n

McAuley, Alastair, 11, 299
MccGwire, Prof. Michael, 285; and
    McDonnell, John, 298n
McGirk, Tim, 176n
Machel, Pres. Samora, of Mozambi-
    que, 293–4
Mai Thu Van, 217n
Malinvaud, E., 163, 175n
Mandi, Peter, 67n
Manzhulo, A., 184, 185, 190n; and
    Krasnov, G., 190n
Mao Zedong, 17
Mehrotra, Santosh, 6, 220, 240n
Mengistu Haile Mariam, 296
Menon, M. Rajan, 44n
Mesa-Lago, C. and Belkin, June S.,
    113n
Mikoyan, Anastas, 117, 118
Mikoyan, S., 138n, 139n
Millar, J., 318n
Miller, Nikki, and Whitehead, Laurence,
    10, 114, 148, 156
Misra, K.P., 45n
Mitchell, R. Judson, 113n
Moreton, Edwina, 65n
Mugabe, Robert, 18, 19

Nasser Mohammad, Pres. Ali, of S.
    Yemen, 245, 247, 248, 252`
Nasser, Pres. Abdul, of Egypt, 15, 117,
    257, 259, 261
Nation, Craig, 65n
Naumkin, Vitali V., 253n, 254n
Nayyar, Deepak, 239n
Nehru, Jawaharlal, 32, 43n, 239n
Neto, Pres. Agostinho, of Angola, 289,
    290

Neuberg, A., 216n
Neumann, S.G. and Harkavy, R.E., 176n
Nguema, Pres. Macais, of Equatorial Guinea, 110
Nguyen Huu Dong, 216n
Nguyen Van Tho, 218n
Nikitin, Afanasy, 43n
Nikolayev, D., 45n
Nir, Amiram, 281, 282n
Nitze, P.H., 12n
Nixon, Pres. Richard M., 122, 123, 220
Niznujaja, S. and Shatiko, V., 218n
Nkomo, Joshua, 19, 292
Nkrumah, Kwame, 8, 90, 96
Nolutshungu, Sam C., 8, 68, 87n
Nove, A., and Newth, J., 311, 315, 318n
Numeiry, Pres., of Sudan, 69
Nyers, Rezso, 67n, 218n

Obote, Milton, 79
Oksanen, Heikki, 219n
Onganía, Gen., 126
Orestov, O., 253n, 254n
Ortega, Daniel, 131, 132
Ovchinnikov, V., 30n
Ozoling, Vassily, and Andreasyan, Ruben, 254n

Paine, Suzanne H., 216n
Pankine, M., 181, 183, 189n, 190n
Pao-min Chang, 30n
Parrott, Bruce, 157n
Patolichev, N., 113n
Patti, A., 216n
Pavelevski, J., 317n
Payton, Gary D., 112n
Perón, Juan, 124
Petrov, M., 213, 219n
Philip, George, 137n
Pierre, A.J., 174n, 175n, 176n
Pike, Douglas, 28n
Pineye, D., 13n
Pinochet, Gen. 124
Podgorny, Pres., of Soviet Union, 290
Polezhayev, V., 186, 190n
Portes, Richard, 163, 165, 174n, 175n
Prasad, Bimal, 43n
Pryblyla, Jan, 28n
Psule, I. Horvath, 66n

Qaddafi, Col., 52, 257, 258
Quandt, William B., 281n
Qian Qichen, 23

Rabinovich, Itamar, and Golan, Galia, 281n, 282n
Radu, M., 88n
Ramanna, Dr Raja, 39
Rawlings, Flt-Lt Jerry, 76
Reagan, Pres. Ronald, 10, 47, 120, 126, 127, 131, 149, 295
Remnek, R.B., 87n
Riyadh, Mahmud, 280n, 281n
Robea Ali, Pres. Salem, of S. Yemen, 246, 247, 248, 254n
Roberto, Holden, 288
Robinson, Peter, 44n
Ro'i, Yaacov, 281n
Rosen, Steven, 112n
Rosenberger, Leif, 30n
Rosfielde, S., 67n
Rothenberg, M., 86, 139n
Rubinstein, Alvin Z., 28n, 29n, 280n
Rywkin, M., 318n

Sabolcik, Michael, 49
Sadat, Pres. Anwar el, of Egypt, 19, 46, 171, 258, 261-5 *passim*, 281n
Salamat Ali, 44n
Sandbrook, Richard, 113n
Sankara, Pres., of Upper Volta, 76
Santos, Pres. José dos, of Angola, 291
Sarkiss, Pres. Elias, of Lebanon, 267
Schichor, Yitzhak, 28n, 29n, 30n
Schiff, Zeev, 282n
Schnytzer, A., 202, 216n, 217n
Schulz, S., and Machowski, H., 13n
Seale, Patrick, 281n
Segal, Gerald, 5, 14, 28n, 29n, 30n, 31n, 216n; and Tow, William, 29n
Sekou Touré, Pres., of Guinea, 68, 87n, 91, 96
Sela, Amnon, 29n
Sen, S., 174n; and Smith, R.P., 169, 175n
Sengupta, Bhabani, 238n
Sharma, O.P., 240
Sharpe, M.E., 318n
Shmelyev, N. 153, 158n
Smirnova, N. Yu., 139n

Smith, Alan H., 3, 5, 13n, 113n, 140, 189n; and Schnytzer, A., 158n
Smith, Ian, 286, 294
Smith, R.B., 174n, 216n
Smith, Wayne, 287, 288, 298n
Smyth, D.C., 190n
Stalin, Joseph, 144, 178, 239n, 307, 308, 310, 311, 314
Steele, Jonathan, 9, 13n, 284, 298n
Stevens, Christopher, 112n, 157n
Stohl, M., and Targ, H., 191n
Stuart, Douglas, and Tow, William, 29
Subrahmanyam, K., 44n, 45n, 239n
Sumners, Laura, 216n

Tajima, Takashi, 28n
Tarabrin, Yevgeny A., 297, 298n
Telepko, L.N., 312, 318n
Teodorovich, T., 180, 189n
Thai Quang Trung, 216n, 217n
Theriot, L.H., and Matheson, J., 195, 216n
Thomas, Raju G.C., 28n, 44n
Thompson, E.P., and Smith, Dan, 113n
Tikhonov, Nikolai A., 142, 296
Tiraspolsky, A., 66n
Tlas, Gen. Mustapha, 271, 282n
Tran Phuong, 219n
Tretiak, Daniel, 28n
Trigubenko, M., 204, 205, 206, 214, 218n, 219n
Truong Chinh, 24
Truong Son, 205, 217n, 218n

Ulianovsky, Prof. R.A., 225

Valkenier, Elizabeth K., 113n, 142, 144, 145, 157, 157n, 189n
Vanous, Jan, 67n
Vasilyev, A., 253n
Vdovin, Valentin, 295
Vertzberger, Yaacov, 29n
Videla, Gen. Jorge, 126
Vinogradov, V.A. *et al.*, 317n
Vivo, Raúl Valdes, 113n
Vo Dai and Huy Khoat, 206, 218n
Vo Nguyen Giap and Truong Chinh, 216n
Vorobyev, Yu. F., 311, 318n
Vyas, A., 317n

Waldheim, K., 190n

Weinstein, Warren, and Henriksen, Thomas, 28n, 29n
Whetton, Lawrence L., 280n
White, C.P., 216n
Wilcox, Wayne, 44n
Wiles, P.J.D., 218n
Wolf, C. *et al.*, 12n
Wolf, T., and Hewett, E., 157n
Wolfers, Michael, and Bergerol, Jane, 290, 298n

Xinhua, 24, 29n, 30n

Yahuda, Michael, 28n
Yepishev, Gen. Alexei, 295
Yu, George, 28n, 29n

Zagoria, Donald, 28n
Zamostny, T.J., 87n
Zhao Ziyang, 29n, 30n
Zhivkov, Todor, 46
Zoeter, Joan Parpart, 151, 152, 153, 157n
Zubkov, I. 66n

General index

Afghanistan, 3, 6, 32, 41–2, 105, 106, 181, 229, 269; natural gas exports to Soviet Union, 150; Sino-Soviet conflict and, 19–20, 23–7 *passim*; Soviet aid, 42, 144, 155; Soviet invasion, 2, 6, 12, 20, 40, 41, 77; Treaty of Friendship with Soviet Union, 256

Africa, Afro-Soviet trade, 78–85, 148; foreign military presence, 1981, 97; indebtedness to CMEA, 1975 and 1982, 83; main arms suppliers, 1964–82, 92, 93, 94, 98; major weapons supplied, 1978–82, 94; non-alignment of states, 85; post-independence turbulence, 89; refugees, 89; Soviet arms sales, 9, 70, 89 *et seq.*, 154; Soviet and Cuban troops in, 8, 9, 91–2, 97, 100, 284, 288, 292, 293; Soviet policy and relations with countries of, 8–9, 20, 68 *et seq.*, 72, 285–7, 298; Soviet shortage of military facilities, 75, 76, 102, 103; Soviet strategic and economic interests, 100–2; Soviet training assistance, 84; weakness of socialism in, 68–9, 73, 110; Western hegemony, 76, 90, 100

African National Congress, 287

Algeria, 181, 263; joint ventures with Soviet Union, 81; natural gas competition with Soviet Union, 154; Polish-FRG metallurgical project in, 81; Soviet arms sales to, 96, 105, 154, 161; trade with Soviet Union, 80, 81

Angola, 3, 69, 73, 77, 102, 106, 107, 110, 111, 181; confusion following independence, 287–8; emergence of Marxist-Leninist regime, 60, 72, 109, 289, 290; possible oil supplier to GDR, 54; Soviet aid, 155, 291–2; Soviet and Cuban military assistance, 91, 96, 98, 100, 172, 284, 288, 292–3; Soviet relations with, 8, 9, 18, 71, 73–4, 82, 284, 285, 289–93, 296–7; Soviet support for MPLA, 17, 287, 288; trade with Soviet Union, 290–1; Treaty of Friendship with Soviet Union, 284; UNITA, 73, 100, 288, 296

Argentina, 4; grain supplies to Soviet Union, 126, 127, 128, 149; relations with Soviet Union, 10, 124–9; Soviet credits, 1974, 122; Soviet oil exports to, 116; trade with Soviet Union, 124–6, 128–9

Bangladesh, relations with Soviet Union, 40, 41; tea sales to Soviet Union, 228

Benin, 70, 76, 107, 181; socialist vanguard party, 108; Soviet arms supplies, 98

Bourkina Fasso, 76, 77

Brazil, Soviet oil exports to, 116

Bulgaria, aid to PDRY, 250; condemns Camp David settlement, 46; search for oil supplies, 54

Burundi, 75

Central African Republic, 99

Chad, 99

Chile, Allende's Popular Unity Party victory, 1970, 121; competes with Cuba for Soviet assistance, 123–4; fall of Allende regime, 124, 289; obstacles to Soviet economic assistance, 122–3; Soviet credits, 121–2; Soviet relations with, 10, 116, 121–4

China, aid to PDRY, 250; conflict with Soviet Union, 5, 15, 236; Cultural

Revolution, 16; develops new Third World strategy, 1980s, 20–1, 25–6; enters UN, 17; failure of African interventions, 18; invasion of Vietnam, 1979, 18, 196, 200; Sino-American détente, 221, 222; support for Khmer Rouge, 195; supports FNLA in Angola, 17; tea sales to Soviet Union, 228; *see also* Sino-Soviet competition in Third World

CMEA, 3, 50, 51, 58, 134; Cuban sugar exports to countries of, 119; International Bank for Economic Cooperation (IBEC), 81; preference for state-sector trade, 180; problem of supply shortages, 60; similar relations with Africa as EEC, 61; stance on commodity agreements, 187; stance on N–S negotiations, 183; unwillingness to accept indigent members, 178

Congo, 69, 75, 82, 99, 103, 107, 111, 181; socialist vanguard party, 108; Soviet arms sales, 90, 98, 144, 171; Soviet landing rights, 171

Contadora states, 134n

Cuba, 3, 12, 73, 105, 182; membership of CMEA, 119, 136; military presence in Africa, 8, 9, 91–2, 100, 284, 288, 292, 293; pact with Soviet Union, 1960, 116, 117, 121; Soviet assistance, 118, 121, 155; Soviet oil exports to, 117, 118; sugar exports to Soviet Union, 118–19, 155; trade with Soviet Union, 4, 10, 117–21, 135, 156; training assistance in Africa, 84

Czechoslovakia, aid to PDRY, 250; condemns Camp David agreement, 46; effect of oil price rises, 1973–9, 48–9; energy crisis, 56–7; problem with oil supplies, 53

Eastern Europe, energy crisis, 1970s, 49–51, 56–9; failure in African development, 60–1; forecast of energy imports from Third World, 64; impact of oil price rises, 1973–9, 48–9; importance of Middle East to, 6, 46–8, 51, 58; military training of

Africans, 92; price of Soviet oil in, 1975–82, 63, 64

Egypt, 107, 229; abrogates Soviet-Egyptian Treaty, 171, 179, 256, 262; acquires Gaza strip, 260; arms supplies from US, 100; Aswan Dam, 256; failure to repay Soviet arms credits, 154, 170; relations with Soviet Union, 71, 79, 144, 261–2; trade with Soviet Union, 79; turns to Soviet Union for arms supplies, 1950s, 259–60, 261

Egyptian-Israeli Peace Treaty, 1979, 262

Equatorial Guinea, Soviet arms supplies, 110

Eritrea, 100, 102, 111

Ethiopia, 3, 75, 106, 107, 110, 181; Derg, 74, 102, 105, 108, 111; emergence of revolutionary regime, 72, 109; FRG-GDR cotton-spinning project, 81; joint ventures with Soviet Union, 81; reasons for Soviet intervention, 102; Soviet aid, 155; Soviet and Cuban military presence, 91, 96, 100, 108; Soviet arms supplies, 105, 161, 172; Soviet military and naval bases, 171; Soviet relations with, 8, 9, 12, 18, 74, 79, 82; trade with Soviet Union, 79; Treaty of Friendship with Soviet Union, 256; Workers Party, 108

European Economic Community (EEC), Lomé Convention, 82; similar relations with Africa as CMEA, 61

Falklands-Malvinas War, 1982, 127

France, arms sales, 168; military presence in Africa, 99

German Democratic Republic (GDR), aid to PDRY, 250; attempts at developing African reserves, 60–1; military assistance to Ghana, 90; oil shortages, 1979, 59; oil supplies to, 54

Ghana, 76, 107; military assistance from Soviet Union and GDR, 90, 96; trade with Soviet Union, 79, 80, 144, 148

Group of, 77, 183
Guinea, 68, 102, 107, 181; bauxite
    exports, 82; joint ventures with
    Soviet Union, 81; relations with
    Soviet Union, 79, 102; Soviet military
    assistance, 91, 96, 171; Soviet naval
    facilities, 171; trade with Soviet
    Union, 79, 144
Guinea Bissau, 110; Soviet arms
    supplies, 98

Hungary, 187; aid to PDRY, 250;
    condemns 'imperialism' in Middle
    East, 47; problem with oil supplies,
    52–3

India, energy production, 233; Free
    Trade Zones, 228; Indo-Soviet
    economic planning, 226–7; Indo-
    Soviet nuclear collaboration, 38–40,
    223; Indo-Soviet Treaty, 1971, 34–5,
    222; main trading partners, 231;
    mutuality of Indo-Soviet interests,
    220–3; payment for Soviet supplies,
    229–30, 231; relations with Soviet
    Union, 12, 32–3, 43, 144, 236–8;
    Soviet arms supplies, 38, 145, 147,
    170–3 *passim*, 223–5, 229; Soviet
    transfer of technology, 233–6; Soviet
    view of development in, 225–6; steel
    production, 233, 234, 235; trade with
    Soviet Union, 6, 33–8, 147, 227–9,
    230, 231–2; 'understanding' of Soviet
    invasion of Afghanistan, 6
Indo-Pakistan wars, of 1965, 294; of
    1971, 221
Indonesia, 107; failure to repay Soviet
    arms credits, 154, 170; relations with
    Soviet Union, 144
International Atomic Energy Agency,
    223
International Development
    Association, 250
International Monetary Fund, 250
Iran, 229; fall of Shah, 19; natural gas
    supplies to Soviet Union, 150; oil
    supplies to Czechoslovakia, 53; oil
    supplies to Romania, 55; post-
    revolutionary oil crisis, 47
Iraq, 181; breakdown of relations with
    Syria, 1970s, 268; oil supplies to

GDR and Bulgaria, 54; oil supplies
    to Hungary, 52; oil supplies to
    Romania, 55; oil supplies to Soviet
    Union, 149, 150; Soviet arms sales,
    154, 161, 170, 173; Soviet strategic
    facilities in, 171; Treaty of Friendship
    with Soviet Union, 256
Israel, 26; deals with Lebanon missile
    crisis, 1981, 270; invasion of
    Lebanon, 1982, 7, 270–6 *passim*;
    Lebanon campaign's failure, 280;
    military dominance in Middle East,
    259; rapprochement with Egypt,
    1979, 262, 267
Ivory Coast, trade with Soviet Union,
    79, 80, 148

Jordan, arms deal with Soviet Union,
    269; breakdown of relations with
    Syria, 1970s, 267; Hashemite
    Kingdom created, 260

Kampuchea, 3, 105, 106; Sino-Soviet
    conflict and, 17, 18, 22–3, 24, 26, 27
Kuwait, arms deal with Soviet Union,
    173

Laos, 3, 23, 105; Soviet aid, 155
Latin America, Soviet relations with,
    10–11, 114 *et seq.*; Soviet trade with,
    114–17, 148–9
Lebanon, 7, 26, 70, 260; Israeli
    invasion, 1982, 7, 268, 270–6 *passim*;
    missile crisis of 1981, 269–70
Libya, 59, 109, 181, 263; joint ventures
    with Soviet Union, 81; limited oil
    supplies to Poland, 52; oil supplies to
    Bulgaria, 54; oil supplies to
    Romania, 55; Soviet arms sales, 96,
    105, 154, 161; Soviet relations with,
    70; Soviet strategic facilities in, 171;
    trade with Soviet Union, 80, 149

Madagascar, Soviet arms supplies, 98
Malaysia, rubber exports to Soviet
    Union, 144, 148
Mali, Soviet landing rights, 171; Soviet
    military assistance, 91, 96, 171; trade
    with Soviet Union, 79
Mexico, oil supplies to Nicaragua, 133;
    PEMEX, 116

Middle East, Arab inability to cope with Israel, 259; defined, 255n; importance to E. European countries, 6, 46 *et seq.*; main arms suppliers, 1964–82, 98, 100; mutual Soviet-Arab criticism, 258–9; nature of regimes in, 257; resurgence of Islam, 257; Soviet arms supplies, 16, 256, 263; Soviet economic aid, 256; Soviet exclusion from, since 1977, 48, 262; Soviet friendship treaties, 256; Soviet policy towards, 7, 255–61; Soviet setbacks in, 19, 256, 257; Soviet strategy in, 257–8; trade with Soviet Union, 145, 149–50

Mongolia, 3; Soviet aid, 155; trade with Soviet Union, 156

Morocco, 70, 72; joint venture companies, 81; phosphate exports, 81–2; trade with Soviet Union, 79–80, 81, 93

Mozambique, 3, 69, 73, 75, 90, 107, 110 181; emergence of Marxist-Leninist regime, 60, 72, 109, 293; Frelimo, 287, 293; Nkomati accords, 10, 83, 100, 296; relations with Soviet Union 8, 9, 18, 82, 285, 293–4, 297; refused permission to join CMEA, 82, 178, 181, 294; Soviet aid, 155; Soviet arms supplies, 285; Soviet military assistance, 98, 172, 294–5; trade with Soviet Union, 294; Treaty of Friendship with Soviet Union, 84, 284, 293

Namibia, 18, 111; SWAPO, 287, 296

New International Economic Order (NIEO), 182, 183

Nicaragua, revolution of 1979, 129–30, 133; Sandinistas, 10, 11, 129; Soviet credits and aid, 131, 132, 155; Soviet relations with, 10–11, 12, 93, 129–34; Soviet reluctance to support, 130–4 *passim*; trade with Soviet Union, 132–3; US attitude to Sandinistas, 131

Nigeria, 90; joint venture companies, 81; Soviet arms sales, 105; Soviet military assistance, 96; trade with Soviet Union, 79, 80, 81; UK-Soviet pipeline project, 81

North Korea, 3, 105; effect of Sino-Soviet conflict on, 15, 172

Pakistan, 229, 232; anti-Soviet stance, 221–2; dismembered after Indo-Pakistan War, 1971, 221; opposition to Soviet invasion of Afghanistan, 6, 40

Palestine Liberation Organization (PLO), 70, 263, 267; expelled from Lebanon, 275; Israeli attempt to destroy, 1982, 273, 274

Philippines, sugar exports to Soviet Union, 148, 155

Poland, crisis of late 1970s, 51–2; reaction to oil price rises, 1970s, 49; search for extra oil supplier, 52

Romania, 59; and oil supplies, 1979–80, 49, 55–6; policy concerning Middle East, 47–8

Saudi Arabia, oil supplies to Soviet Union, 149, 150

Sino-Indian War, 1962, 224

Sino-Soviet competition in Third World, 14, 26–7, 96; in 1960s, 14–16; in 1970s, 16–20; in 1980s, 20–6; reduction in tension, 1980s, 25–6

Somalia, 102; abrogates Treaty of Friendship with Soviet Union, 170, 171, 256; Somalia Revolutionary Socialist Party (SRSP), 108; Soviet military assistance, 91; Soviet-Somali relations, 8, 70, 71

South Africa, 10, armed forces, 99; pressure on African neighbours, 73, 99, 100, 111, 288, 296, 297; support for rebels in Mozambique, 100, 111

South Asia, effect of great-power rivalry on states of, 43; relations with Soviet Union, 5–6, 32–3; Soviet policy in, 220–1; *see also* countries concerned

Soviet arms exports to Third World, 5, 6, 89 *et seq.*, 150–4, 159–62, 172–4; balance of trade in 165–7; developing country recipients, 168–70; political and strategic factors, 170–2; sale of surplus equipment, 164, 165; Soviet defence industry,

164; supply side, 162–8; value, 1970–81, 160

Soviet Central Asia, agricultural income, 1928–9, 303; cotton-based agriculture, 311; development policy, 11, 299 *et seq.*; economic development, 1928–79, 307–13; employment, 1975, 309–10; Europeanization of material environment, 315; eve of industrialization in, 301–7; incomes compared with RSFSR, 1925–6 and 1961, 304–5, 311–12, 314–15; integrated into Soviet economy, 314, 316; population growth by 1979, 308, 309; reduction of Islamic influence, 316–17; republics of, 299, 301; social indicators, 1922 and 1979, 305, 306, 312, 313; strategy of development, 313–17; structure of employment, 1926, 302; urbanization, 308, 315

Soviet stance in North-South negotiations, 177, 188–9; advice to developing states, 179–80; general position, 182–4; Soviet global strategy, 177–8; stance on aid, finance and debt, 184–5; stance on commodity agreements, 185–7; stance on transfer of technology, 187–8; views on increase in Southern manufacturing, 187; views on 'interdependence' 180–1; views on Third World, 178, 181–2

Soviet trade with Third World, 3–4, 5, 140 *et seq.*; categorization of trade partners, 147–50; changes in policy towards non-socialist countries, 144–5; exports by commodity, 1974–83, 146; imports by commodity, 1972–83, 146; partner structure, 142–3; post-Khrushchev, 145–7; profitability of arms sales, 150–4; trade with socialist countries, 154–7

Soviet Union, aid to Third World, 5; arms economy, 103–6; arms exports, *see* Soviet arms exports to Third World; beleaguered state of, 2–3; conflict with China, 5, 15, 236; countries supported by, 3; declining growth rates, 1966–80, 162; energy export earnings, 166, 167; increase in

intra-CMEA oil prices, 50–1, 64; Indian Ocean naval capabilities, 6, 101, 102, 222, 286; military training for Africans, 92; naval build-up, 101, 170–1; oil subsidies for E. Europe, 49–50, 58; policy in own Central Asian area, *see* Soviet Central Asia; problem of profitability in mining investments, 60; projected oil development, 1973–90, 63; theory of expansionist Soviet foreign policy, 1–2; theory of military aid and socialist transformation, 109–11; theory of military force and defence of socialism, 106–9; trade with Third World, *see* Soviet trade with Third World; *see also* Sino-Soviet competition in Third World, and references to Soviet Union under other countries

Sri Lanka, relations with Soviet Union, 40

Stockholm Peace Research Institute, 93

Sudan, 69; arms supplies from US, 100; trade relations with Soviet Union, 79

Syria, 70, 181, 229; becomes Soviet Union's Middle East ally, 265; bogged down in Lebanon, late 1970s, 267, 269, 270; breakdown in relations with Jordan and Iraq, 267–8, 269; effect of Palestinian issue on, 260; Euphrates Dam, 256; military aid from Soviet Union, 1956, 261; military coups, 1949–54, 260; Muslim Brothers in, 267; Soviet arms supplies, 170, 173, 278–80; Soviet relations with, 7, 263–70, 275–8; Syrian-Soviet reaction to Israeli invasion of Lebanon, 271–3, 274, 275; takes anti-Western stance after 1954, 261; takes 'counter-offensive' after Israeli invasion of Lebanon, 276–7; Treaty of Friendship with Soviet Union, 1980, 256, 266–9 *passim*

Tanzania, 18, 75, 90, 107, 110, 181; Soviet military assistance, 96, 172

Thailand, sugar exports to Soviet Union, 148, 155

Tunisia, trade with Soviet Union, 79, 80, 93

Uganda, 70; relations with Soviet Union, 79; Soviet military assistance, 96, 110

UNCTAD, 80, 81, 183–5 *passim*, 188; IV, 186, 187; V, 185; VI, 181

United States of America, arms sales, 168; 'constructive engagement' with S. Africa, 295–6; détente with China, 221, 222; grain supplies to Soviet Union, 126–7; Monroe Doctrine, 134; Rapid Deployment Forces, 100, 102

Uruguay, trade with Soviet Union, 116

USSR Academy of Sciences' African Institute, *Society and State in Tropical Africa*, 107

Vietnam, 3, 182; alliance with Soviet Union, 5, 16, 17, 18; Chinese invasion, 1979, 18, 196, 200; comparison of Chinese and Soviet aid, 1955–64, 194–5; comparison of North and South, 204–5; economic data, 1975–83, 196; economic problems, 1975–9, 196–200; fall of Dien Bien Phu, 1954, 194; foreign debt, 1975–82, 209, 210; invasion of Kampuchea, 18, 19, 195–6; membership of CMEA, 193, 196, 202, 203–7, 215; relations with Soviet Union, 193–6, 200–7; Sino-Soviet conflict and, 15, 16, 24, 194, 195; Soviet military aid, 289; Soviet-Vietnamese aid and trade, 19, 20, 155, 194, 207–14; Soviet-Vietnamese economic relations, 192–3, 214–15; triumph of North Vietnam, 1975, 17, 199

Western Sahara, 69

Yemen (PDRY), 3, 102, 181, 263; development of alliance with Soviet Union, 240, 242, 245–8; differences in policy with Soviet Union, 242–3, 244; foreign aid, to 1980, 250; National Liberation Front, 242, 244, 246, 247; rapprochement with N. Yemen, 1982, 248; relations with Soviet Union, 7–8, 12, 241–5; 'scientific socialism' in, 241; Soviet Aden base, 171; Soviet advisers in, 251; Soviet aid, 7, 155, 241, 249–51, 252; Soviet arms supplies, 252; trade with Soviet Union, 248–9, 252; Treaty of Friendship with Soviet Union, 256; Yemeni Socialist Party, 252

Zaire, 99; *see also* Congo

Zambia, 18; Soviet arms sales, 161; Soviet military assistance, 96; trade with Soviet Union, 79

Zimbabwe, 19, 69, 76; relations with Soviet Union, 18; revolutionary regime, 109; Soviet military assistance, 96; ZAPU, 287